An **ITC** publication in

QUANTITATIVE METHODS

Quantitative Methods
for Business and
Economic Analysis

Quantitative Methods for Business and Economic Analysis

KONG CHU

College of Industrial Management

Georgia Institute of Technology

INTERNATIONAL TEXTBOOK COMPANY

Scranton, Pennsylvania

70-5571

Standard Book Number 7002 2247 2

To Adam, Roy, and Michele

Foreword

Courses in "Quantitative Analysis" or "Quantitative Methods" are a commonplace in Economics and Business School curricula today. This is a reflection of the considerable usage being made in industry, commerce, government, and academia of the quantitative tools of analysis.

Professor Chu's book does not purport to push forward the frontiers of knowledge of quantitative methods. His goal is to introduce the business, economics, or management major to the current "state of the art" with a concise, well-written presentation of the three major areas of quantitative methods.

Not only will undergraduate students find this book useful, but master's and doctoral candidates entering business or economics programs with backgrounds in other disciplines will find this book helpful and it will be for some the first step toward careers in the use of quantitative tools for decision-making.

Sherman Dallas
Dean,
College of Industrial Management
Georgia Institute of Technology

Preface

Quantitative Methods for Business and Economic Analysis is grouped around three major areas. In the first area, deterministic or mathematical programming models are defined. In these models we assume all relevant information concerning the problem is completely and surely known. The analysis is to search among all feasible alternatives and find the one which will optimize the objective function. The second area is concerned with probabilistic or statistical models in which information concerning the problem is not completely known, but can be specified by probabilities. The analysis is to search for the decision strategy which will optimize the expected value of the outcomes. The modern digital computer is the subject of the third area. Its electronic computing speed and vast memory open doors to methods for quantitative analysis which were not feasible prior to its existence. The simulation method is just one of the important ways economic and business analysis can utilize the computer. It enables us to study the causes and effects of different events which we cannot observe in real systems.

Since this text is for introductory purposes only, it does not go to the frontiers of these areas, but lists the more important elements in each area. After having been exposed to these elements, students may do further study or research by reading texts and journal articles on specific topics.

I wish to acknowledge the encouragement of Dean Sherman F. Dallas and Dr. Robert E. Green of the College of Industrial Management, Georgia Institute of Technology, and the assistance of Mrs. Sarah Born in typing the original manuscript. The responsibility for any errors, of course, is entirely mine.

KONG CHU

Decatur, Georgia
June, 1969

Contents

Contents

Quantitative Methods for Business and Economic Analysis

Introduction

Most of the classical economists assume that for a customer, the main objective is to maximize utility; for a firm, to maximize profit, and for a community, to maximize welfare or benefit. Differential calculus is generally used as the major analytical tool in searching for an optimum solution. Thus to a consumer, the economist's advice will be something like the following.

Suppose a consumer has an income of Y_0 in a given period of time, and he wants to spend the income among two goods, the price of the first good is p_1 and the price of the second good is p_2. Let the quantity that the consumer will obtain of the first good be q_1 and the second good be q_2. Then

$$Y_0 = p_1 q_1 + p_2 q_2$$

or

$$q_2 = \frac{Y_0 - p_1 q_1}{p_2}$$

Also, let the preference of the consumer for the two goods be expressed by a continuous utility function, which normally will indicate diminishing marginal utility of the consumer with respect to both the first good and the second good:

$$U = f(q_1, q_2)$$
$$= f\left(q_1, \frac{Y_0 - p_1 q_1}{p_2}\right)$$

1

Assuming that the consumer's behavior is to maximize the utility function with the constraint of the given income, we may use calculus methods:

$$\frac{dU}{dq_1} = f_1 \frac{dq_1}{dq_1} + f_2 \frac{d\left(\dfrac{Y_0 - p_1 q_1}{p_2}\right)}{dq_1}$$

$$= f_1 - f_2\left(\frac{p_1}{p_2}\right)$$

where f_1 is the partial derivative of the utility function with respect to q_1 and f_2 is the partial derivative of the utility function with respect to q_2. They may be interpreted as the marginal utility of the goods to the consumer.

Set the first derivative equal to zero to obtain the optimum solution:

$$f_1 - f_2\left(\frac{p_1}{p_2}\right) = 0 \qquad \text{(The second derivatives can be shown to satisfy the maximum condition)}$$

or

$$\frac{f_1}{f_2} = \frac{p_1}{p_2}$$

The result is what an economist would advise the consumer to do—spend the income on the two goods until the ratio of the marginal utility of the two goods to the consumer equals the ratio of the prices of the two goods. Thereby the consumer will be maximizing the total utility (the utility of q_1 plus the utility of q_2 to the consumer) within his income constraint.

The economist's advice to the management of a firm in perfectly competitive markets both of factors of production and products will be something like the following.

Suppose the firm's product is made of two factors of production, and that the two factors are perfectly substitutable for each other, which means a continuous production function:

$$q = f(x_1, x_2)$$

where q is the quantity of the product, x_1 is the quantity of the first factor of production, and x_2 is the quantity of the second factor of production.

Further, we assume that the price of the product is p, the price of the first factor of production is r_1 and the price of the second factor of production is r_2. The cost function may be written as

$$C = r_1 x_1 + r_2 x_2$$ (Fixed cost is not included here because it will not affect the decision rule)

and the profit function may be written as

$$F = pq - C$$

$$= p(f(x_1, x_2)) - r_1 x_1 - r_2 x_2$$

Using differential calculus method to maximize profit, we take partial derivatives of F both with respect to x_1 and x_2:

$$\frac{\partial F}{\partial x_1} = pf_1 - r_1$$

$$\frac{\partial F}{\partial x_2} = pf_2 - r_2$$

where f_1 is the marginal product of the first factor of production and f_2 is the marginal product of the second factor of production. Setting the partial derivatives equal to zero to obtain the optimum solution,

$$pf_1 - r_1 = 0$$ (The second derivatives can be shown
$$pf_2 - r_2 = 0$$ to satisfy the maximum condition)

Thus

$$p = \frac{r_1}{f_1} = \frac{r_2}{f_2}$$

or

$$\frac{f_1}{f_2} = \frac{r_1}{r_2}$$

The result is what an economist would advise the management to do—employ factors of production for producing the product to the point where the ratio of the marginal product of the two factors of production equals the ratio of their prices, or the ratio of the price of each factor of production and its marginal product equals the price of the product.

In the situation where the markets are not competitive —that is, the firm buys factors of production under monopsonistic conditions and sells products under monopolistic conditions—then neither factors prices nor products prices are constants. Suppose a firm employs two factors of production (1 and 2) and produces and sells two products (a and b), and that the production function is represented by a single-valued continuous function:

$$Q(q_a, q_b, x_1, x_2) = 0$$

where $q_a, q_b, x_1, x_2 > 0$, which indicates that given amounts of factors 1 and 2 (x_1, x_2) will produce given amounts of products a and $b(q_a, q_b)$.

The firm's profit function is

$$F = R_a + R_b - C_1 - C_2$$

where F is total net profit, R_a is the revenue received from selling q_a, R_b is the revenue received from selling q_b, C_1 is the cost of purchasing X_1, and C_2 is the cost of purchasing X_2. Using a Lagrangian multiplier, we may write the firm's objective function as

$$F' = R_a + R_b - C_1 - C_2 + \lambda Q$$

where $R_a = p_a q_a$, $R_b = p_b q_b$, $C_1 = r_1 x_1$, $C_2 = r_2 x_2$, p_a is a function of q_a, p_b is a function of q_b, r_1 is a function of x_1, and r_2 is a function of x_2, since we assume that the prices are not constants but vary with quantities sold or purchased.

The objective of the firm is still assumed to be maximizing profit. Thus we let all the partial derivatives of F' equal to zero.

$$\frac{\partial F'}{\partial q_a} = \frac{\partial R_a}{\partial q_a} + \lambda \frac{\partial Q}{\partial q_a} = MR_a + \lambda \frac{\partial Q}{\partial q_a} = 0$$

$$\frac{\partial F'}{\partial q_b} = \frac{\partial R}{\partial q_b} + \lambda \frac{\partial Q}{\partial q_b} = MR_b + \lambda \frac{\partial Q}{\partial q_b} = 0$$

$$\frac{\partial F'}{\partial x_1} = -\frac{\partial C_1}{\partial x_1} + \lambda \frac{\partial Q}{\partial x_1} = MC_1 + \lambda \frac{\partial Q}{\partial x_1} = 0$$

$$\frac{\partial F'}{\partial x_2} = -\frac{\partial C_2}{\partial x_2} + \lambda\frac{\partial Q}{\partial x_2} = MC_2 + \lambda\frac{\partial Q}{\partial x_2} = 0$$

$$\frac{\partial F'}{\partial \lambda} = Q(q_a, q_b, x_1, x_2) = 0$$

where MR_a and MR_b are the marginal revenues for products a and b, and MC_1 and MC_2 are the marginal costs for factors 1 and 2.

From the equations, we obtain the optimality condition:

$$\lambda = -\frac{MR_a}{\partial Q/\partial q_a} = -\frac{MR_b}{\partial Q/\partial q_b} = -\frac{MC_1}{\partial Q/\partial x_1} = -\frac{MC_2}{\partial Q/\partial x_2}$$

or

$$MC_1 = MR_a\frac{\partial q_a}{\partial x_1}$$

$$MC_2 = MR_b\frac{\partial q_b}{\partial x_2}$$

Thus the advice that an economist would give the manager of the firm would be to employ a factor for the production of a product until the cost of the last unit of the factor (marginal cost) equals the revenue yielded by the amount of product that this last unit of the factor can produce (marginal revenue product of the factor with respect to the product).

The same method of analysis may be applied to a consumer's decision among many commodities (including leisure), a firm facing a mixture of competitive and noncompetitive markets, or a community trying to find the optimum situation of product transformation and commodity substitution which will maximize the welfare of all the people in that community. This kind of analysis is known as *marginal analysis*.

However, in the empirical world we sometimes find that this kind of advice is not realistic, especially for the decision maker of a complex system. For example, the objectives of a firm may not be limited to profit maximization, and the manager of the firm may not know the marginal cost or the marginal product of each unit of the factors of production—at least not until the information system is more efficiently developed and strengthened. Also in many instances the products and the factors of production may not be adequately considered as infinitely divisible; or among different products and among different factors of production they may not be perfectly substitutable. This means that the manager has only a limited number of choices and the factors of production can only be mixed in a finite number of ways to produce the product.

Because of these reasons, calculus methods alone seem not sufficient to provide tools for business and economic analysis. Thus in this text calculus methods, mathematical programming methods, statistical methods, computer-simulation methods, and other tools dealing with both deterministic and probabilistic models are introduced. And the usefulness of these quantitative methods may be applied to business firms and public administration as well.

PROBLEMS

1. Using marginal analysis, derive the optimal condition that the manager of a firm, which buys factors in competitive market and sells products in noncompetitive market, should follow as guidance for decision making.

2. Using marginal analysis, derive the optimal condition that the manager of a firm, which buys factors in noncompetitive market and sells products in competitive market, should follow as guidance for decision making.

3. Discuss situations where marginal analysis will apply and situations where marginal analysis will fail to apply.

4. Discuss the compatibilities and conflicts among the objectives of an individual consumer, a firm and a community. Also discuss the limitations or constraints each faces in obtaining the objectives.

SELECTED REFERENCES

Allen, R. G. D., *Mathematical Analysis for Economists.* London: Macmillan and Company, Ltd., 1938.

Allen, R. G. D., *Mathematical Economics.* London: Macmillan and Company, Ltd., 1956.

Baumol, William J., *Economic Theory and Operations Analysis.* 2d ed. Englewood Cliffs, N.J.: Prentice-Hall, Inc., 1965.

Dean, B. V., M. W. Sasieni, and S. K. Gupta, *Mathematics for Modern Management.* New York: John Wiley & Sons, Inc., 1963.

Henderson, James M., and Richard E. Quandt, *Microeconomic Theory.* New York: McGraw-Hill Book Company, 1958.

chapter 1

Linear Programming

When the available quantities of resources or factors of production are limited and when there are only a finite number of production processes to choose from, there is a mathematical optimizing technique available to help the decision maker make rational decisions, given the objectives. The technique is called *linear programming.* The term "programming" indicates the procedure we must follow to put the decision-making scheme into a proper framework, while the term "linear" indicates that the objectives and the constraints of the problem must be expressed by linear functions. In the latter section, we will also discuss the techniques of solving problems with nonlinear objective functions. Since linear programming provides the necessary theoretical framework for the organization and analysis of data, some special terms should be introduced first to describe the common characteristics of the framework.

A Linear Objective Function

The objective of a linear programming problem is to optimize a given linear function, which consists of several variables and parameters, the general form is as follows:

$$f(X) = c_1 x_1 + c_2 x_2 + \cdots + c_n x_n$$

where $x_1, x_2, \ldots, x_n$ are the variables and $c_1, c_2, \ldots, c_n$ are the parameters.

Many business operations can be expressed with this type of goal seeking. For example, in the operation of a manufacturing firm, $x_1, x_2, \ldots, x_n$ may represent quantities of different products to be produced and $c_1, c_2, \ldots, c_n$, the unit profits that each of the different products can bring to the firm. Then the objective of the firm is to maximize the total profit, which is the sum of the profits obtained by producing the different products.

Number of Linear Constraints

A business firm or an economic unit always operates with limited resources, such as skilled labor, capital or a special kind of raw material. In a linear programming problem, each of these limitations or constraints is represented by a linear inequality. Thus a set of linear inequalities may be included in a linear programming problem together with the objective function. The inequalities may be in the following forms:

$$a_{11}x_1 + a_{12}x_2 + \cdots + a_{1n}x_n \leq b_1$$
$$a_{21}x_1 + a_{22}x_2 + \cdots + a_{2n}x_n \leq b_2$$
$$\vdots$$
$$a_{m1}x_1 + a_{m2}x_2 + \cdots + a_{mn}x_n \leq b_m$$

There are m constraints, with constants $b_1, b_2, \ldots, b_m$ indicating the availabilities of different required resources, and constant coefficients $a_{11}, a_{21}, \ldots, a_{m1}$ indicating the necessary units of input of the m scarce resources to produce one unit of product 1, etc.

In the problems of minimizing the objective function such as minimizing total cost, some of the linear constraints have to be greater or equal instead of smaller and equal, otherwise we will have unbounded solutions—which are discussed in the later sections.

Nonnegativity Constraints

The application of linear programming techniques in business and industry indicates that the solution can only consist of nonnegative values. For example, we can only decide to produce zero or some positive number of units of a given product. Thus in a linear programming problem we also add the nonnegativity constraints:

$$x_1, x_2, \ldots, x_n \geq 0$$

Putting the three parts together, the general form of a linear programming problem is formed.

$$\text{Maximize}\{f(x_1, \ldots, x_n) = c_1 x_1 + c_2 x_2 + \cdots + c_n x_n\}$$

subject to

$$a_{11} x_1 + a_{12} x_2 + \cdots + a_{1n} x_n \leq b_1$$
$$a_{21} x_1 + a_{22} x_2 + \cdots + a_{2n} x_n \leq b_2$$
$$\vdots$$
$$a_{m1} x_1 + a_{m2} x_x + \cdots + a_{mn} x_n \leq b_m$$
$$x_1, x_2, \ldots, x_n \geq 0$$

When the problem requires to find the minimum of $f(x_1, \ldots, x_n)$, we may write the objective function as

$$\text{Maximize}\{-f(x_1, \ldots, x_n) = -c_1 x_2 - \ldots - c_n x_n\}$$

In the following section, methods for solving linear programming problems are introduced.

TWO-VARIABLE MODEL—GRAPHICAL METHOD

When there are only two variables in the model, geometry may be used to illustrate the solution of the problem. The steps are:
1. Define the feasible region by the given constraints.
   (a) A convex set*—optimum solution exists.
   (b) Nonconvex set:
       i. Unbounded—infinite number of feasible solutions (no optimum solution)
       ii. Inconsistent—no feasible solution
2. Find all the extreme points in the convex set.

---

*A *convex set* is defined as a set of points which has the property that the line segment joining any two points in the set is also entirely in the set.

3. With the reference of the objective function (slope), determine which extreme point is the optimum solution. (If the slope of the objective function coincides with one of the boundary lines of the convex set, more than one equally optimum solution may exist.)

Example 1

$$\text{Max } \{f(x_1, x_2) = 3x_1 + 4x_2\}$$

subject to

$$x_1 + x_2 \leq 6$$
$$2x_1 + 4x_2 \leq 20$$
$$x_1 \geq 0, x_2 \geq 0$$

1. Since $x_1 \geq 0$ and $x_2 \geq 0$, the feasible region has to be in the first quadrant.
2. The first constraint $x_1 + x_2 \leq 6$ limits the feasible region on the southwest side of the line $x_1 + x_2 = 6$ and the line itself.
3. The second constraint $2x_1 + 4x_2 \leq 20$ limits the feasible region on the southwest side of the line $2x_1 + 4x_2 = 20$ and the line itself.
4. Thus the feasible region is the convex set $OABC$, which includes the boundaries OA, AB, BC, and CO.
5. The extreme points of the convex set are

$$O\,(0,0),\ A\,(0,5),\ B\,(2,4) \text{ and } C\,(6,0)$$

6. The objective function can be written as

$$3x_1 + 4x_2 = K$$

or

$$x_2 = \frac{K}{4} - \frac{3}{4}x_1$$

The slope is $(-\sqrt[3]{4})$. In Fig. 1-1, when the line with

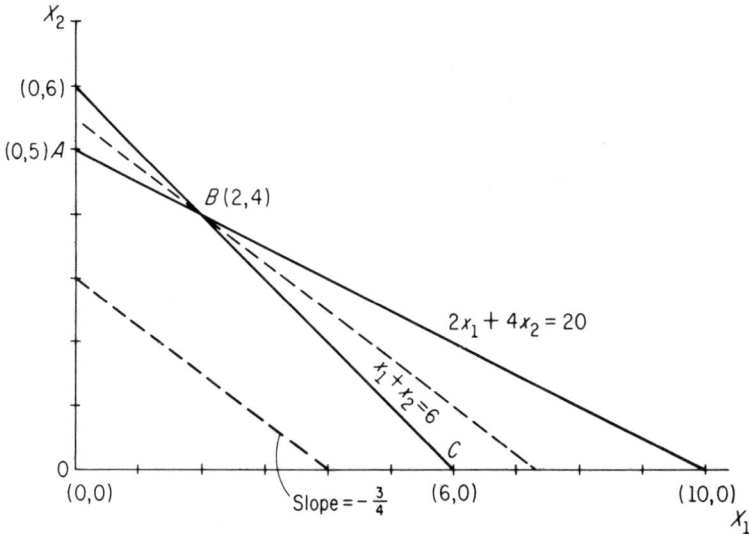

Fig. 1-1

slope $-{}^3/_4$ moves to the upper right direction the value of the objective function K will increase, and K will be the greatest when the line last touches the feasible region $OABC$ at B, which indicates the extreme point B is the optimum solution.

7. The value of the objective function at B is

$$f(2,4) = 3 \times 2 + 4 \times 4 = 22$$

which is greater than

$$f(0,0) = 0, f(0,5) = 20, f(6,0) = 18$$

Example 2

Unbounded case—the following constraints define a feasible region which is unbounded:

$$-x_1 + x_2 \leq 5$$
$$-2x_1 + x_2 \leq 4$$
$$x_1 \geq 0, x_2 \geq 0$$

The shaded area in Fig. 1-2 is the feasible region which extends to infinity.

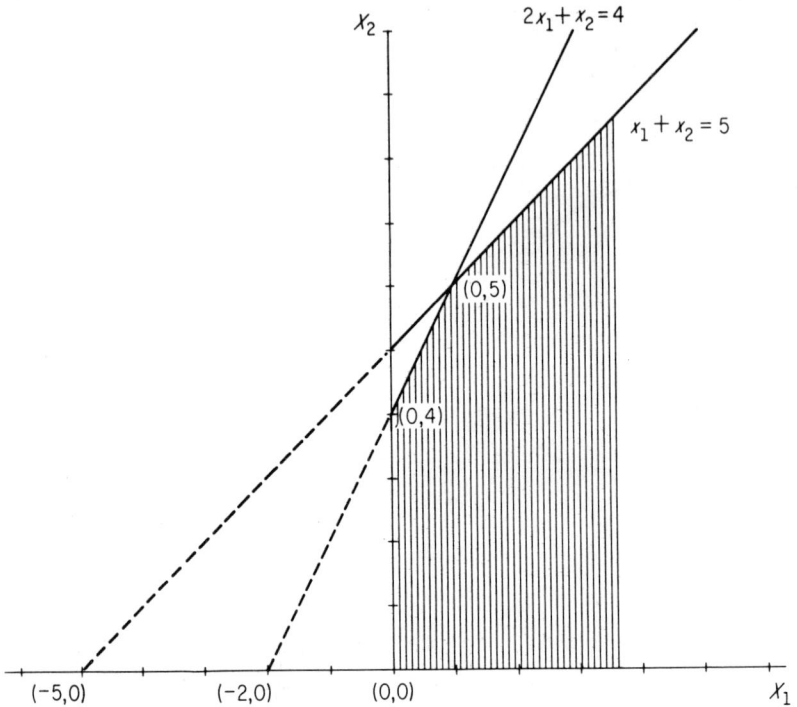

Fig. 1-2

Example 3

Inconsistent case—the following constraints do not define a feasible region:

$$2x_1 + x_2 \leq 10$$
$$-x_1 \leq 8$$
$$x_1 \geq 0, x_2 \geq 0$$

The first constraint specifies the feasible region as on the southwest side of $2x_1 + x_2 = 10$ in the first quadrant (see Fig. 1-3), but the second constraint specifies the feasible region as on the east side of $x_1 = 8$. Since no point can satisfy both constraints, there is no solution to the problem.

MULTIVARIABLE MODEL—SIMPLEX METHOD

When the model includes more than two variables,

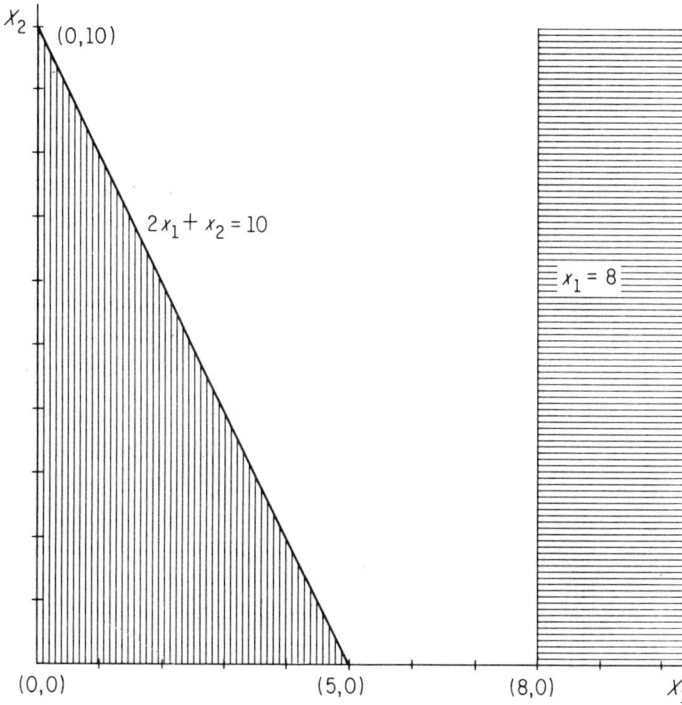

Fig. 1-3

algebra is used to obtain solutions of the problems.   The steps are:

1. Set up the problem in linear programming form:

Max $\{f(x_1, x_2, \ldots, x_n) = c_1 x_1 + c_2 x_2 + \cdots + c_n x_n\}$

subject to

$$a_{11} x_1 + a_{12} x_2 + \cdots + a_{1n} x_n \leq b_1$$
$$a_{21} x_1 + a_{22} x_2 + \cdots + a_{2n} x_n \leq b_2$$
$$\vdots$$
$$a_{m1} x_1 + a_{m2} x_2 + \cdots + a_{mn} x_n \leq b_m$$
$$x_1, x_2, \ldots, x_n \geq 0$$

2. Change the linear inequality constraints to linear equalities by adding one slack variable (with coefficient equal to one) to each constraint:

$$a_{11}x_1 + a_{12}x_2 + \cdots + a_{1n}x_n + x_{n+1} = b_1$$
$$a_{21}x_1 + a_{22}x_2 + \cdots + a_{1n}x_n + x_{n+2} = b_2$$
$$\vdots$$
$$a_{m1}x_1 + a_{m2}x_2 + \cdots + a_{mn}x_n + x_{n+m} = b_m$$

The linear programming model if expressed in matrix form will be as follows:

$$\text{Max}\{f(X) = C'X\}$$

subject to $AX = P_0$ and $X \geq 0$.

3. Define basic solutions. If the linear programming model has n variables and m constraints the augmented form will contain m additional slack variables. The basic solution will then contain at most m elements. If the solution contains less than m elements, it has a degenerate solution.

Let B be a square matrix of m rows and m columns, X_B be a basic solution, we may derive the following:

$$AX \equiv BX_B + CX_c = P_0$$

where C contains the other vectors of A not contained in B and X_c are those variables not included in the basic solution. Thus $X_c = 0$ and $BX_B = P_0$.

When we find the inverse of B, we can obtain the basic solution by

$$B^{-1}BX_B = B^{-1}P_0$$
$$X_B = B^{-1}P_0$$

4. Define basic feasible solutions. Since all the x_i in a feasible solution have to be nonnegative the basic solution is a feasible one when $X_B \geq 0$.

5. Transform from one basic feasible solution to another. Suppose we have a basic feasible solution:

$$a_{11}\bar{x}_1 + a_{12}\bar{x}_2 + \cdots + a_{1m}\bar{x}_m = b_1$$
$$a_{21}\bar{x}_1 + a_{22}\bar{x}_2 + \cdots + a_{2m}\bar{x}_m = b_2$$
$$\vdots$$
$$a_{m1}\bar{x}_1 + a_{m2}\bar{x}_2 + \cdots + a_{mn}\bar{x}_m = b_m$$

where $(\bar{x}_1, \bar{x}_2, \ldots, \bar{x}_m)$ is the solution. The equations may be expressed as

$$P_1\bar{x}_1 + P_2\bar{x}_2 + \cdots + P_m\bar{x}_m = P_0 \qquad (1\text{-}1)$$

We want to bring in another variable x_k which is not in the solution, we express the transformation ratios among the coefficients as

$$\begin{bmatrix} a_{11} \\ a_{21} \\ \vdots \\ a_{m1} \end{bmatrix} r_{1k} + \begin{bmatrix} a_{12} \\ a_{22} \\ \vdots \\ a_{m2} \end{bmatrix} r_{2k} + \begin{bmatrix} a_{1m} \\ a_{2m} \\ \vdots \\ a_{mm} \end{bmatrix} r_{mk} = \begin{bmatrix} a_{1k} \\ a_{2k} \\ \vdots \\ a_{mk} \end{bmatrix}$$

where $r_{1k}, r_{2k}, \ldots, r_{mk}$ are the ratios.

In abbreviation, the equation can be written as

$$P_1 r_{1k} + P_2 r_{2k} + \cdots + P_m r_{mk} = P_k \qquad (1\text{-}2)$$

Multiplying Eq. 1-2 by x_k,

$$x_k P_1 r_{1k} + x_k P_2 r_{2k} + \cdots + x_k P_m r_{mk} = x_k P_k \qquad (1\text{-}3)$$

Subtracting Eq. 1-3 from Eq. 1-1,

$$P_1(\bar{x}_1 - x_k r_{1k}) + P_2(\bar{x}_2 - x_k r_{2k}) + \cdots \\ + P_m(\bar{x}_m - x_k r_{mk}) + x_k P_k = P_0$$

Since a basic feasible solution should only contain m elements or variables, one of the $\bar{x}_i - x_k r_{ik}$ $(i = 1,2,\ldots,m)$ has to be zero (if more than one, we will have a degenerate solution), since P_i is not zero. Also since a basic feasible solution cannot have negative elements, the maximum value we can assign to x_k is

$$\text{Max } x_k = \min \left\{ \frac{\bar{x}_i}{r_{ik}} \right\} \ (i = 1,2,\ldots,m)$$

Example 4
Constraints

$$x_1 + x_2 + x_3 = 6$$
$$2x_1 + 4x_2 + x_4 = 20$$
$$x_1, x_2, x_3, x_4 \geq 0$$

where x_3 and x_4 are slack variables.

(a) One of the basic solutions:

$$x_1 = 0, x_2 = 0 \qquad (X_c = 0)$$
$$1x_3 + 0x_4 = 6$$
$$0x_3 + 1x_4 = 20$$

$$B = \begin{bmatrix} 1 & 0 \\ 0 & 1 \end{bmatrix} \qquad B^{-1} = \begin{bmatrix} 1 & 0 \\ 0 & 1 \end{bmatrix} \qquad X_B = \begin{bmatrix} x_3 \\ x_4 \end{bmatrix}$$

$$\begin{bmatrix} 1 & 0 \\ 0 & 1 \end{bmatrix} \cdot \begin{bmatrix} x_3 \\ x_4 \end{bmatrix} = \begin{bmatrix} 6 \\ 20 \end{bmatrix}$$

$$\begin{bmatrix} x_3 \\ x_4 \end{bmatrix} = \begin{bmatrix} 1 & 0 \\ 0 & 1 \end{bmatrix} \cdot \begin{bmatrix} 6 \\ 20 \end{bmatrix} = \begin{bmatrix} 6 \\ 20 \end{bmatrix}$$

$$\bar{x}_3 = 6, \bar{x}_4 = 20$$

(b) Bring x_2 into the solution $x_k = x_2, P_k = P_2 = \begin{bmatrix} 1 \\ 4 \end{bmatrix}$

$$P_3 r_{32} + P_4 r_{42} = P_2$$

$$\begin{bmatrix} 1 \\ 0 \end{bmatrix} r_{32} + \begin{bmatrix} 0 \\ 1 \end{bmatrix} r_{42} = \begin{bmatrix} 1 \\ 4 \end{bmatrix} \qquad r_{32} = 1, r_{42} = 4$$

$$P_3(\bar{x}_3 - x_2 r_{32}) + P_4(\bar{x}_4 - x_2 r_{42}) + x_2 P_2 = P_0$$

$$\begin{bmatrix} 1 \\ 0 \end{bmatrix}(6 - x_2) + \begin{bmatrix} 0 \\ 1 \end{bmatrix}(20 - 4x_2) + \begin{bmatrix} 1 \\ 4 \end{bmatrix} x_2 = \begin{bmatrix} 6 \\ 20 \end{bmatrix}$$

When $x_2 = 5$,

$$20 - 4x_2 = 0$$

.which will let x_4 out of the solution, and

$$6 - x_2 = 1$$

which is nonnegative and makes the new solution still feasible. Thus

$$\text{Max } x_2 = \min \left[\frac{6}{1}, \frac{20}{4} \right] = 5$$

and the new feasible solution is

$$\bar{x}_2 = 5, \bar{x}_3 = 1$$

6. Efficient moves toward the optimum solution. To check whether the entry of x_k into the solution will increase

the value of the objective function, we need to compare the unit gain of x_k with the sum of the product of the unit loss of all the $x_i (i = 1, 2, \ldots, m)$ originally in the solution and the transformation ration (r_{ik}).

Return to the previous example,

$$\text{Max } \{f(x_1, x_2, x_3, x_4) = 3x_1 + 4x_2 + 0x_3 + 0x_4\}$$

subject to

$$x_1 + x_2 + x_3 + 0x_4 = 6$$
$$2x_1 + 4x_2 + 0x_3 + x_4 = 20$$
$$x_1, x_2, x_3, x_4 \geq 0$$

(a) First solution:

$$\bar{x}_1 = 0, \bar{x}_2 = 0, \bar{x}_3 = 6, \bar{x}_4 = 20$$

(b) Transform to second solution:

Bring in x_2.

The transformation ratios: $P_3 r_{32} + P_4 r_{42} = P_2$

$$\begin{bmatrix} 1 \\ 0 \end{bmatrix} r_{32} + \begin{bmatrix} 0 \\ 1 \end{bmatrix} r_{42} = \begin{bmatrix} 1 \\ 4 \end{bmatrix}$$

$$r_{32} = 1, r_{42} = 4$$

The unit gain: $c_2 = 4$

The unit loss: $c_3 = 0, c_4 = 0$

Net gain: $c_2 - c_3 r_{32} - c_4 r_{42} = 4$

Compare to bringing in x_1:

The transformation ratios: $P_3 r_{31} + P_4 r_{41} = P_1$

$$\begin{bmatrix} 1 \\ 0 \end{bmatrix} r_{31} + \begin{bmatrix} 0 \\ 1 \end{bmatrix} r_{41} = \begin{bmatrix} 1 \\ 2 \end{bmatrix}$$

$$r_{31} = 1, r_{41} = 2$$

The unit gain: $c_1 = 3$

The unit loss: $c_3 = 0, c_4 = 0$

Net gain: $c_1 - c_3 r_{31} - c_4 r_{41} = 3$

Thus it is more efficient to bring in x_2, and in the process drop x_4.

The second solution is

$$\bar{x}_1 = 0, \qquad \bar{x}_2 = 5, \qquad \bar{x}_3 = 1, \qquad \bar{x}_4 = 0$$

(c) Transform to third solution.

To bring in x_1, the transformation ratios will be

$$P_2 r_{21} + P_3 r_{31} = P_1$$

$$\begin{bmatrix} 1 \\ 4 \end{bmatrix} r_{21} + \begin{bmatrix} 1 \\ 0 \end{bmatrix} r_{31} = \begin{bmatrix} 1 \\ 2 \end{bmatrix}$$

$$r_{21} + r_{31} = 1$$

$$4 r_{21} = 2$$

$$r_{21} = \frac{1}{2}, r_{31} = \frac{1}{2}$$

The unit gain: $c_1 = 3$

The unit loss: $c_2 = 4$, $c_3 = 0$

Net gain: $c_1 - c_2 r_{21} - c_3 r_{31} = 3 - \dfrac{4}{2} = 1$

Thus it will gain if x_1 is brought into the solution, and

$$\text{Max} \quad x_1 = \min \left[\frac{5}{1/2}, \frac{1}{1/2} \right] = 2$$

$$P_2(\bar{x}_2 - x_1 r_{21}) + P_3(\bar{x}_3 - x_1 r_{31}) + P_1 x_1 = P_0$$

$$\bar{x}_2 - x_1 r_{21} = 5 - 2 \times \frac{1}{2} = 4$$

$$x_3 - x_1 r_{31} = 1 - 2 \times \frac{1}{2} = 0$$

x_3 is dropped from the solution and the optimum solution is

$$\bar{x}_1 = 2, \qquad \bar{x}_2 = 4, \qquad \bar{x}_3 = 0, \qquad \bar{x}_4 = 0$$

It is optimum, because bringing in either x_3 or x_4 to the last solution will only decrease the value of the objective function.

The algebraic method illustrated above is known as the *simplex method*. The procedure from an initial basic feasible solution toward the final optimum solution can be seen clearer in tableau form. We use the following example to illustrate this.

$$\text{Max} \{ f(x_1, x_2, x_3) = x_1 + x_2 + 2x_3 \}$$
$$2x_1 + x_2 + 4x_3 \leq 20$$

$$x_1 + 2x_2 + x_3 \leq 10$$
$$x_1, \quad x_2, \quad x_3 \geq 0$$

The augmented form is

$$\text{Max}\,\{f(x_1, x_2, x_3, x_4, x_5) = x_1 + x_2 + 2x_3 + 0x_4 + 0x_5\}$$
$$2x_1 + x_2 + 4x_3 + x_4 + 0x_5 = 20$$
$$x_1 + 2x_2 + x_3 + 0x_4 + x_5 = 10$$
$$x_1, \quad x_2, \quad x_3, \quad x_4, \quad x_5 \geq 0$$

The first tableau is

c_j		1	1	2	0	0		
	P_i	P_1	P_2	P_3	P_4	P_5	P_0	$\dfrac{\bar{x}_i}{r_{ij}}$
0	P_4	2	1	4	1	0	20	$^{20}/_4 = 5\left(\min \dfrac{\bar{x}_i}{r_{ij}}\ x_4 \text{ to exit}\right)$
0	P_5	1	2	1	0	1	10	$^{10}/_1 = 10$
$z_j = \sum\limits_j c_j r_{ij}$		0	0	0	0	0	0	(value of the objective function)
c_j	$-z_j$	1	1	2	0	0		

Choose x_3 to enter

In the tableau, c_j is the unit gain of the variable not in the solution, z_j is the loss that results from bringing in one unit of variable j into the solution. The net gain is expressed by $c_j - z_j$. We thus choose to bring in the variable with the largest positive $c_j - z_j$ value.

The second tableau is

c_j		1	1	2	0	0		
	P_i	P_1	P_2	P_3	P_4	P_5	P_0	$\dfrac{\bar{x}_i}{r_{ij}}$
2	P_3	$^1/_2$	$^1/_4$	1	$^1/_4$	0	5	$\dfrac{5}{^1/_4} = 20$
0	P_5	$^1/_2$	$-^7/_4$	0	$-^1/_4$	1	5	$\dfrac{5}{^7/_4} = \dfrac{20}{7}\left(\min \dfrac{\bar{x}_i}{r_{ij}}\ x_5 \text{ to exit}\right)$
	z_j	1	$^1/_2$	2	$^1/_2$	0	10	
	$c_j - z_j$	0	$^1/_2$	0	$-^1/_2$	0		

x_2 to enter

The third tableau is

c_j		1	1	2	0	0	
P_i		P_1	P_2	P_3	P_4	P_5	P_0
2	P_3	$3/_7$	0	1	$2/_7$	$-1/_7$	$30/_7$
1	P_2	$2/_7$	1	0	$-1/_7$	$4/_7$	$20/_7$
	z_j	$8/_7$	1	2	$3/_7$	$2/_7$	$80/_7$
	$c_j - z_j$	$-1/_7$	0	0	$-3/_7$	$-2/_7$	

Since all c_j is smaller than z_j there will not be any net gain to bring in variables which are not in the solution, namely x_1, x_4, x_5. We have reached the optimum solution

$$x_2 = \frac{20}{7}, x_3 = \frac{30}{7}$$

The objective function then has the maximum value of

$$f\left(0, \frac{20}{7}, \frac{30}{7}\right) = 0 + \frac{20}{7} + 2 \times \frac{30}{7} = 11\frac{3}{7}$$

As a check,

$$2x_1 + x_2 + 4x_3 = \frac{140}{7} = 20$$

$$x_1 + 2x_2 + x_3 = \frac{70}{7} = 10$$

which are consistent with the constraints.

THE DUAL SIMPLEX METHOD

The linear programming problem introduced above may be viewed as a problem of allocating scarce resources (the elements $b_1, b_2, \ldots, b_m$) to different uses (the activities $P_1, P_2, \ldots, P_n$) with the objective of maximizing profit (Max $f(x_1, \ldots, x_n) = c_1 x_1 + c_2 x_2 + \cdots + c_1 x_n$). This set-up we now call the *primal* of a linear programming problem. The dual of an initial linear programming problem is the image of the primal. The objective of the dual may be interpreted as to minimize forgone profits and the solutions represent the marginal values of the scarce resources. The primal and dual in matrix notation would be like the following.

Primal

$$\text{Max}\, \{f(x_1, x_2, \ldots, x_n) = c_1 x_1 + c_2 x_2 + \cdots + c_n x_n\}$$

subject to

$$a_{11} x_1 + a_{12} x_2 + \cdots + a_{1n} x_n \leq b_1$$
$$a_{21} x_1 + a_{22} x_2 + \cdots + a_{2n} x_n \leq b_2$$
$$\vdots$$
$$a_{m1} x_1 + a_{m2} x_2 + \cdots + a_{mn} x_n \leq b_m$$
$$x_1, x_2, x_3, \ldots, x_n \geq 0$$

Dual

$$\text{Min}\, \{f(u_1, u_2, \ldots, u_m) = b_1 u_1 + b_2 u_2 + \cdots + b_m u_m\}$$

subject to

$$a_{11} u_1 + a_{21} u_2 + \cdots + a_{m1} u_m \geq c_1$$
$$a_{12} u_1 + a_{22} u_2 + \cdots + a_{m2} u_m \geq c_2$$
$$\vdots$$
$$a_{1n} u_1 + a_{2n} u_2 + \cdots + a_{mn} u_m \geq c_n$$
$$u_1, u_2, \ldots, u_m \geq 0$$

where u is the value placed on one unit of the ith resource and represents the amount by which the total profit could be increased by increasing the availability of this resource one unit and using this added unit optimally. In economic terms, u is the *opportunity cost* of the resource. It is also called the *shadow price* of the resource.

Example 5
Primal

$$\text{Max}\, \{f(x_1, x_2, x_3) = x_1 + x_2 + 2x_3\}$$

subject to

$$2x_1 + x_2 + 4x_3 \leq 20$$
$$x_1 + 2x_2 + x_3 \leq 10$$
$$x_1, x_2, x_3 \geq 0$$

Dual

$$\text{Min}\,\{f(u_1, u_2) = 20u_1 + 10u_2\}$$

subject to

$$2u_1 + u_2 \geq 1$$
$$u_1 + 2u_2 \geq 1$$
$$4u_1 + u_2 \geq 2$$
$$u_1, u_2 \geq 0$$

Solution:

$$\text{Min}\,\{f(u_1, u_2) = 20u_1 + 10u_2 + 0u_3 + 0u_4 + 0u_5\}$$
$$2u_1 + u_2 - u_3 = 1$$
$$u_1 + 2u_2 - u_4 = 1$$
$$4u_1 + u_2 - u_5 = 2$$
$$u_1, u_2, u_3, u_4, u_5 \geq 0$$

P_1	P_2	P_3	P_4	P_5	P_0
2	1	−1	0	0	1
1	2	0	−1	0	1
4	1	0	0	−1	2

In this tableau we cannot find an initial basic solution, so we change the signs of every element.

c_j		20	10	0	0	0	
	Basis	P_1	P_2	P_3	P_4	P_5	P_0
0	P_3	−2	−1	1	0	0	−1
0	P_4	−1	−2	0	1	0	−1
0	P_5	−4	−1	0	0	1	−2 →
z_j		0	0	0	0	0	0
$z_j - c_j$		−20	−10	0	0	0	

Now we have a basic solution ($u_3 = -1$, $u_4 = -1$, $u_5 = -2$) with all ($z_j - c_j$) values nonpositive. In a minimizing problem, this evaluation indicates that the optimum condition exists. However, it is not a feasible solution because u_3, u_4, u_5 are not nonnegative. The corresponding value of the objective function (zero) is below the minimum for the feasible solutions. What we want to do next is to remove the non-feasible variables from the basis while at the same time increasing the value of the objective function. Our choice of which variable to bring into the basis is guided by the following rule:

For all $r_{ij} < 0$, choose min $\left[\dfrac{z_j - c_j}{r_{ij}}\right]$.

If any variable other than the one with the minimum ratio is selected then the new $(z_j - c_j)$ will no longer be all non-positive. In our problem, the procedure of solving the problem is as follows:

1. Since u_5 has the largest negative value, we choose u_5 to exit from the basis.

2. $r_{13} = -4$, $r_{23} = -1$

3. Min $\left\{\dfrac{z_1 - c_1}{r_{13}}, \dfrac{z_2 - c_2}{r_{23}}\right\} = $ min $\left\{\dfrac{-20}{-4}, \dfrac{-10}{-1}\right\}$
$= $ min $\{5, 10\} = 5$

4. The variable we select to enter is u_1.

Thus the tableau becomes

c_j		20	10	0	0	0	
	Basis	P_1	P_2	P_3	P_4	P_5	P_0
0	P_3	0	$-\frac{1}{2}$	1	0	$-\frac{1}{2}$	0
0	P_4	0	$-\frac{7}{4}$	0	1	$-\frac{1}{4}$	$-\frac{1}{2}$ →
20	P_1	1	$\frac{1}{4}$	0	0	$-\frac{1}{4}$	$\frac{1}{2}$
z_j		20	5	0	0	-5	$f(u_1, u_2) = 10$
$z_j - c_j$		0	-5	0	0	-5	

$$\dfrac{-5}{-\frac{7}{4}} = {}^{20}\!/_7 \qquad \dfrac{-5}{-\frac{1}{4}} = 20$$

The solution becomes $u_1 = \frac{1}{2}$, $u_3 = 0$, $u_4 = -\frac{1}{2}$. Since u_4 is negative, the solution is still nonfeasible.

The next iteration then will be

1. Since u_4 is negative, u_4 will be taken out of the basis.

2. $r_{22} = -\frac{7}{4}$, $r_{25} = -\frac{1}{4}$

3. Min $\left[\dfrac{z_2 - c_2}{r_{22}}, \dfrac{z_5 - c_5}{r_{25}}\right] = $ min $\left[\dfrac{20}{7}, 20\right] = \dfrac{20}{7}$

4. u_2 is selected to enter the basis:

c_j		20	10	0	0	0	
	Basis	P_1	P_2	P_3	P_4	P_5	P_0
0	P_3	0	0	1	$-2/7$	$-3/7$	$1/7$
10	P_2	0	1	0	$-4/7$	$1/7$	$2/7$
20	P_1	1	0	0	$1/7$	$-2/7$	$3/7$
z_j		20	10	0	$-20/7$	$-30/7$	$f(u_1,u_2) = 80/7$
$z_j - c_j$		0	0	0	$-20/7$	$-30/7$	

The new solution is $u_1 = 3/7$, $u_2 = 2/7$, $u_3 = 1/7$, $u_4 = 0$, $u_5 = 0$. Since all the $(z_j - c_j)$'s are nonpositive, the minimum condition is fulfilled. The minimum value of the objective function is $80/7$.

$$f(u_1, u_2) = 20u_1 + 10u_2 = 20 \times 3/7 + 10 \times 2/7 = 11\,3/7$$

Note that the value of the objective function is the same as in the primal case. The $z_j - c_j$ values of the primal equal to the solution of the dual,

$$\begin{aligned}
z_1 - c_1 &= u_3 = 1/7 \\
z_2 - c_2 &= u_4 = 0 \\
z_3 - c_3 &= u_5 = 0 \\
z_4 - c_4 &= u_1 = 3/7 \\
z_5 - c_5 &= u_2 = 2/7
\end{aligned}$$

and the $c_j - z_j$ values of the dual equal to the solution of the primal,

$$\begin{aligned}
c_1 - z_1 &= x_4 = 0 \\
c_2 - z_2 &= x_5 = 0 \\
c_3 - z_3 &= x_1 = 0 \\
c_4 - z_4 &= x_2 = 20/7 \\
c_5 - z_5 &= x_3 = 30/7
\end{aligned}$$

The linear programming method has been adopted by governments and industries for solving practical problems in business and public administration. Some of the development is illustrated in the following.

The Assignment Problem

The problem confronting a business manager may be the efficient assignment of men or equipment to various jobs. For example, we may have three persons of different skill and qualifications and two different jobs to be filled. Each person can do either of these jobs, but with different speed and dexterity. Also, because the wage rates of these three persons are different, the cost of assigning any two of these persons to do the two jobs will be different from other alternatives. The problem then is to find the best assignment (leaving one man for other jobs) which will involve the least cost.

Suppose the cost matrix associating man to job is as follows:

Man \ Job	1	2
A	3	6
B	5	4
C	2	8

We may first find the relative cost of the man doing the job by setting the most efficient one to zero, and changing the elements in each column to the differences between the less efficient one and the most efficient one. Also, since one of three persons are different, the cost of assigning any two of the three persons to do the two jobs will be different from relative cost matrix becomes as follows:

Man \ Job	1	2	3
A	1	2	(0)
B	3	(0)	0
C	(0)	4	0

By selecting the minimum relative cost in each row we can easily determine that the most efficient assignment should be to (1) save A for other jobs, (2) assign B to job 2,

and (3) assign *C* to job 1. The minimum total cost will be
4 + 2 = 6.

The Traveling-Salesman Problem

A similar kind of problem is to decide the route of a traveling salesman who has to cover all the cities or territories assigned to him continuously with the least traveling cost. For example, if a traveling salesman has to cover five cities, the cost of traveling from one city to another is indicated in the following cost matrix. Since he cannot stay in one city all the time, the entry on the diagonal of the cost matrix is infinity, indicating the assignment of staying put in one city is not allowed.

City	1	2	3	4	5	
1	∞	2	5	5	1	(−1)
2	2	∞	7	8	2	(−2)
3	5	7	∞	4	1	(−1)
4	5	8	4	∞	5	(−4)
5	1	2	1	5	∞	(−1)

Transforming the cost matrix into relative terms will result in the following:

City	1	2	3	4	5
1	∞	1	4	4	0
2	0	∞	5	6	0
3	4	6	∞	3	0
4	1	4	0	∞	1
5	0	1	0	4	∞
	(−1)		(−3)		

City	1	2	3	4	5
1	∞	(0)	4	1	0
2	0	∞	5	3	(0)
3	4	5	∞	(0)	0
4	(1)	3	0	∞	1
5	0	0	(0)	1	∞

Since the traveling salesman has to cover all five cities in each route, the optimum route will be

$$1 \rightarrow 2 \rightarrow 5 \rightarrow 3 \rightarrow 4 \rightarrow 1$$

and the total cost will be

$$2 + 2 + 1 + 4 + 5 = 14$$

The Transportation Problem

Another practical example is to assign available transporting equipment to carry cargo from several initial points to destinations in such a way that the total cost will be minimized. For example, suppose we have five ships to transport cargoes from five ports to one destination, three of the ships being of a newer type and the other two of an older type. The cost of having the ships to carry the cargoes from each port to the destination is as follows:

Port Ship	1	2	3	4	5	
A	8	8	6	6	4	(-4)
B	8	8	6	6	4	(-4)
C	8	8	6	6	4	(-4)
D	11	11	7	7	6	(-6)
E	11	11	7	7	6	(-6)

Transforming cost matrix into relative terms will be as follows:

Port Ship	1	2	3	4	5
A	4	4	2	2	0
B	4	4	2	2	0
C	4	4	2	2	0
D	5	5	1	1	0
E	5	5	1	1	0
	(-4)	(-4)	(-1)	(-1)	

Port Ship	1	2	3	4	5
A	(0)	0	1	1	0
B	0	(0)	1	1	0
C	0	0	1	1	(0)
D	1	1	(0)	0	0
E	1	1	0	(0)	0

The decision then should be sending the three newer-model ships to ports 1, 2, and 5 and the two older-model ships to ports 3 and 4. The total cost will be

$$8 + 8 + 4 + 7 + 7 = 34$$

However, since some of the ships are of the same model and the cost of carrying cargoes from some ports to the destination are identical, we may collapse the cost matrix into the following:

Demand Supply	I	II	III
I	8	6	4
II	11	7	6

and the associated matrix of available number of ships and required number of shipping assignments is as follows:

Demand Supply	I	II	III	Available Total
I	2		1	3 ships
II		2		2 ships
Required assignments	2 ports	2 ports	1 port	

The entries in the matrix are the optimum assignments obtained previously.

Putting this problem in general notation, the cost matrix is

$$\begin{bmatrix} c_{11} & c_{12} & c_{13} \\ c_{21} & c_{22} & c_{23} \end{bmatrix}$$

and the requirement matrix is

$$\begin{matrix} \begin{bmatrix} x_{11} & x_{12} & x_{13} \\ x_{21} & x_{22} & x_{23} \end{bmatrix} & \begin{matrix} s_1 \\ s_2 \end{matrix} \\ \begin{matrix} d_1 & d_2 & d_3 \end{matrix} \end{matrix}$$

The objective function is

Minimize $\{[f(x) = c_{11}x_{11} + c_{12}x_{12} + c_{13}x_{13}$
$$+ c_{21}x_{21} + c_{22}x_{22} + c_{23}x_{23}\}$$

and the constraints are

$$\begin{aligned} x_{11} + x_{12} + x_{13} &= s_1 \\ x_{21} + x_{22} + x_{23} &= s_2 \\ x_{11} + x_{21} &= d_1 \\ x_{12} + x_{22} &= d_2 \\ x_{13} + x_{23} &= d_3 \\ x_{11}, x_{12}, x_{13}, x_{21}, x_{22}, x_{23} &\geq 0 \end{aligned}$$

This then becomes a linear programming problem with the technical coefficients all equal to one.

Using the numbers in the numerical example,

$$\text{Min}\{f(x) = 8x_{11} + 6x_{12} + 4x_{13} + 11x_{21} + 7x_{22} + 6x_{23}\}$$

subject to

$$\begin{aligned} x_{11} + x_{12} + x_{13} \quad\quad\quad\quad\quad &= 3 \\ x_{21} + x_{22} + x_{23} &= 2 \\ x_{11} \quad\quad\quad\quad + x_{21} \quad\quad\quad\quad &= 2 \\ + x_{12} \quad\quad\quad\quad + x_{22} \quad\quad &= 2 \\ + x_{13} \quad\quad\quad\quad + x_{23} &= 1 \\ x_{11}, x_{12}, x_{13}, x_{21}, x_{22}, x_{23} \geq 0 \end{aligned}$$

which may be solved by simplex method to yield an optimum solution of

$$\bar{x}_{11} = 2, \bar{x}_{12} = 0, \bar{x}_{13} = 1, \bar{x}_{21} = 0, \bar{x}_{22} = 2, \bar{x}_{23} = 0$$

Input-Output Analysis

Input-output analysis is a method for describing the structure of an economy and the interrelationship between its industries and the final users of their products. Each industry is considered as the sole producer of a particular output, whether it is a commodity or a service. The production process of an industry j is described as the quantities of inputs it purchases from each of the other industries (including firms in the same industry) and the quantities of primary inputs—such as labor, land, and capital—it employs for the production. The ratio between the input from another industry i and the total output of industry j is called the *input-output coefficient*, a_{ij}. And the ratios of the primary inputs and the total output of industry j are the labor-output ratio a_{lj}, the capital-output ratio a_{cj} and the land (or natural resources)-output ratio a_{rj}. The distribution of the output is divided among the intermediate users, which are the other industries (including firms in the same industry) and the final users, which are the consumers, governments, exports, etc. Thus the distribution of industry i may be represented by the equation

$$y_i = x_i - \sum_j a_{ij} x_j \qquad (j = 1, 2, \ldots, n \text{ industries})$$

(Final use = total output – intermediate use)

In a linear programming setting, we may consider the problem as to maximize total income with the constraints of total available primary inputs as the following.

Objective Function

$$\text{Max} \left\{ I = \sum_i p_i y_i \right\} \qquad (i = 1, 2, \ldots, n)$$

where I is the income, y_i is the quantity of output for final use of each industry, and p_i is the price of the output of each industry.

Constraints:

(1) $\sum_j a_{lj}x_j + x_l = L$

(2) $\sum_j a_{cj}x_j + x_c = C$

(3) $\sum_j a_{rj}x_j + x_r = R$

where L, C, and R are total labor, capital, and natural resources available, and x_1, x_c, and x_r are unused labor, capital, and natural resources.

Example 6

Assume that only two industrial sectors 1 and 2 are in the economy, outputs are represented by x_1 and x_2, and final uses are represented by y_1 and y_2. Price of output 1 is $1.5 and of output 2 is $1. Input-output coefficients are $a_{11} = 0$, $a_{12} = .4$, $a_{21} = .6$, and $a_{22} = 0$.

For industrial sector 1, labor-output ratio is 6, capital-output ratio is 1, and natural resources-output ratio is 2. For industrial sector 2, labor-output ratio is 2, capital-output ratio is 4, and natural resources-output ratio is 2. Total available labor is 1,000 units, capital 500 units, and natural resources 400 units.

$$\text{Max } \{I = 1.5y_1 + 1.0y_2\}$$

where

$$y_1 = x_1 - .4x_2$$
$$y_2 = x_2 - .6x_1$$

Thus the objective function is

$$\text{Maximize } \{I = 1.5(x_1 - .4x_2) + (x_2 - .6x_1)$$
$$= .9x_1 + .4x_2\}$$

The constraints are

(1) $6x_1 + 2x_2 \leq 1,000$ (labor)

(2) $x_1 + 4x_2 \leq 500$ (capital)

(3) $2x_1 + 2x_2 \leq 400$ (natural resources)

Graphical analysis:

(1)   (2)   (3)

x_1	x_2	x_1	x_2	x_1	x_2
0	500	0	125	0	200
167	0	500	0	200	0

Slope of the objective function: $x_2 = \dfrac{I}{.4} - 2.25x_1$

The objective function tangents the feasible region at the intersection of (1) and (3) (see Fig. 1-4).

$$6x_1 + 2x_2 = 1{,}000$$
$$-)\ \ 2x_1 + 2x_2 = \ \ \ 400$$
$$\overline{4x_1 \ \ \ \ \ \ \ \ = \ \ \ 600}$$
$$x_1 = 150$$
$$x_2 = \ \ 50$$

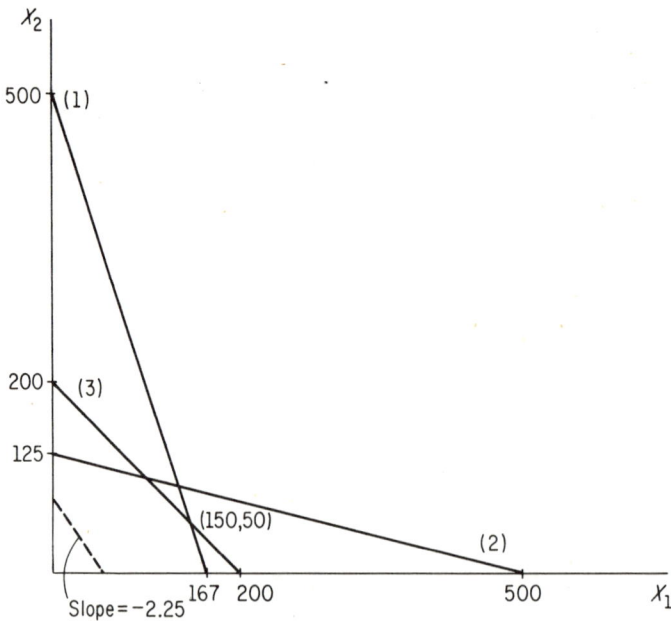

Fig. 1-4

Substituting in (2),

$$x_c = 500 - 150 - 4 \times 50 = 150 \quad \text{(unused capital)}$$

The maximum income is

$$I = .9 \times 150 + -4 \times 50 = 155$$

Simplex method:

c_j		.9	.4	0	0	0		
	Basis	P_1	P_2	P_L	P_C	P_R	P_0	
0	P_L	6	2	1	0	0	1000	$\dfrac{1000}{6} = 167 \rightarrow$
0	P_C	1	4	0	1	0	500	$\dfrac{500}{1} = 500$
0	P_R	2	2	0	0	1	400	$\dfrac{400}{2} = 200$

$\uparrow$

c_j		.9	.4	0	0	0		
	Basis	P_1	P_2	P_L	P_C	P_R	P_0	
.9	P_1	1	$\dfrac{1}{3}$	$\dfrac{1}{6}$	0	0	$\dfrac{1,000}{6}$	$\dfrac{1}{3} = 500$
0	P_C	0	$\dfrac{11}{3}$	$-\dfrac{1}{6}$	1	0	$\dfrac{1,000}{3}$	$\dfrac{11}{3} = \dfrac{1,000}{11}$
0	P_R	0	$\dfrac{4}{3}$	$-\dfrac{1}{3}$	0	1	$\dfrac{200}{3}$	$\dfrac{4}{3} = 50 \rightarrow$
z_j		.9	.3	$\dfrac{3}{20}$	0	0	150 (value of the objective function)	
$c_j - z_j$		0	.1	$-\dfrac{3}{20}$	0	0		

$\uparrow$

c_j		.9	.4	0	0	0		
	Basis	P_1	P_2	P_L	P_C	P_R	P_0	
.9	P_1	1	0	$1/4$	0	$-1/4$	150	(Product 1)
0	P_C	0	0	$3/4$	1	$-11/4$	150	(Unused capital)
.4	P_2	0	1	$1/4$	0	$-3/4$	50	(Product 2)
z_j		.9	.4	$1/8$	0	$3/40$	155	(Maximum income)
$c_j - z_j$		0	0	$-1/8$	0	$-3/40$	(optimum)	

INTEGER PROGRAMMING

In some businesses each unit product is very expensive and is useful only as an integer unit—for example, airplanes and computers. The decision which calls for the production of some fraction of a unit is impracticable. Accordingly, the integer programming method has been developed—using a linear programming model with the additional requirement that all variables appearing in the optimal solution be integers. One method for solving the integer programming model is the Gomory method. The method proposes that we first treat the model as a typical linear programming model and solve it by the simplex method. Then, if the variables appearing in the solution are not all integers, for each noninteger variable, we use the respective row in the optimal tableau to construct an equation which expresses the basic variable as a function of the nonbasic variables. When this new equation is added to the tableau, the new solution of the variable obtained by simplex method will not only be integer but also will reduce the value of the objective function the least. The method can be best understood through a numerical example.

Example 7

$$\text{Max} \quad \{f(x_1, x_2, x_3) = x_1 + x_2 + 2x_3\}$$

subject to

$$2x_1 + x_2 + 4x_3 \leq 20$$
$$x_1 + 2x_2 + x_3 \leq 10$$

where x_1, x_2, and x_3 have to be positive integers. Applying the simplex method, we obtain the following optimal tableau:

c_j		1	1	2	0	0	
	Basis	P_1	P_2	P_3	P_4	P_5	P_0
2	P_3	$3/7$	0	1	$2/7$	$-1/7$	$30/7$
1	P_2	$2/7$	1	0	$-1/7$	$4/7$	$20/7$
$c_j - z_j$		$-1/7$	0	0	$-3/7$	$-2/7$	

The solution is $x_2 = 2\tfrac{6}{7}$, $x_3 = 4\tfrac{2}{7}$, which are not integers. Following the Gomory method,

1. We choose the one with the largest fraction. In this case, x_2 has the largest fraction, $\tfrac{6}{7}$.

2. From the optimal tableau we find the relationship of x_2 with the nonbasic variables as follows:

$$\tfrac{2}{7}x_1 + x_2 - \tfrac{1}{7}x_4 + \tfrac{4}{7}x_5 = (2 + \tfrac{6}{7})$$

3. Since we have stipulated that all the variables (x_1, x_2, x_4, x_5) in the solution have to be positive integers, all the fractions have to be combined as integers. Thus

$$\tfrac{2}{7}x_1 - \tfrac{1}{7}x_4 + \tfrac{4}{7}x_5 = \tfrac{6}{7} + \text{an integer}$$

Further, we note that x_1, x_4, and x_5 all have to be positive integers. Thus,

$$\tfrac{2}{7}x_1 - \tfrac{1}{7}x_4 + \tfrac{4}{7}x_5 \geq \tfrac{6}{7}$$

4. Let x_6 be a positive slack variable.

$$\tfrac{2}{7}x_1 - \tfrac{1}{7}x_4 + \tfrac{4}{7}x_5 - x_6 = \tfrac{6}{7}$$

5. Include the equation in the original optimal tableau, we have the following tableau:

c_j	1	1	2	0	0		
	P_1	P_2	P_3	P_4	P_5	P_6	P_0
	$\tfrac{3}{7}$	0	1	$\tfrac{2}{7}$	$-\tfrac{1}{7}$	0	$\tfrac{30}{7}$
	$\tfrac{2}{7}$	1	0	$-\tfrac{1}{7}$	$\tfrac{4}{7}$	0	$\tfrac{20}{7}$
	$\tfrac{2}{7}$	0	0	$-\tfrac{1}{7}$	$\tfrac{4}{7}$	-1	$\tfrac{6}{7}$ →
$c_j - z_j$	$-\tfrac{1}{7}$	0	0	$-\tfrac{3}{7}$	$-\tfrac{2}{7}$		
	↑						

6. In order not to reduce the value of the object function more than necessary, we choose the vector whose absolute ($c_j - z_j$) value is the smallest. In this case, $\tfrac{1}{7}$ is the smallest, thus we bring x_1 into the basis. P_6 then has served its purpose and can be omitted from the tableau.

c_j		1	1	2	0	0	
	Basis	P_1	P_2	P_3	P_4	P_5	P_0
2	P_3	0	0	1	$\frac{1}{2}$	-1	3
1	P_2	0	1	0	0	0	2
1	P_1	1	0	0	$-\frac{1}{2}$	2	3
z_j		1	1	2	$\frac{1}{2}$	0	11
$c_j - z_j$		0	0	0	$-\frac{1}{2}$	0	

In this case, all the variables in the solution are integers already. However, in other cases, some of the variables may still not be integers, then steps from (1) to (6) have to be repeated until every variable becomes an integer.

7. Since all the $(c_j - z_j)$'s are now nonpositives, the optimum solution has been obtained. In this case, it is $x_1 = 3$, $x_2 = 2$, $x_3 = 3$. The value of the objective solution is $f(3,2,3) = 3 + 2 + 2 \times 3 = 11$, which is smaller than the optimal solution where the variables do not have to be integers.

BOUNDED-VARIABLE PROBLEMS

Sometimes in a linear programming model the solution is further restricted by the constraints that the values of some variables cannot be greater (or smaller) than some given constants. For example, in planning menus for a military organization the objective may be to minimize the total cost. However, at the same time the nutrients supplied by the menu have to exceed certain given minimums; thus they are lower-bounded variables. These kinds of problems are called *bounded-variable linear programming problems*.

For example,

$$\text{Max} \quad \{f(x) = c_1x_1 + \cdots + c_nx_n\}$$

subject to

$$a_1,x_1 + \cdots + a_{1n}x_x = b_1$$

$$\vdots$$

$$a_{1m}x_m + \cdots + a_{mn}x_n = b_m$$

$$0 \leq x_i \leq k_i \qquad (i = 1, \ldots, n)$$

where x_i are upper-bounded by k_i.

Of course, these kinds of problems can be solved by straightforward simplex method if we set them in the following form:

$$\text{Max} \quad \{g(x) = c_1 x_1 + \cdots + c_n x_n\}$$

subject to

$$a_1, x_1 + \cdots + a_{1n} x_n \qquad\qquad = b_1$$
$$\vdots \qquad\qquad\qquad\qquad\qquad \vdots$$
$$a_{m1} x_m + \cdots + a_{mn} x_n \qquad\qquad = b_m$$
$$x_1 \qquad\qquad + u_1 \qquad\quad = k_1$$
$$\vdots \qquad\qquad\qquad \vdots$$
$$x_n \qquad\qquad + u_n = k_n$$

where $u_1, \ldots, u_n$ have zero coefficients in the objective function. (For lower-bounded problem, $x_i - u_i = k_i$).

In putting the problem into simplex tableau, the matrix notation of the tableau may be written as follows:

$P_1 \cdots P_m$	$P_{m+1} \cdots P_{m+s}$	$P_{m+s+1} \cdots P_n$	$Q_1 \cdots Q_m$	$Q_{m+1} \cdots Q_{m+s}$	$Q_{m+s+1} \cdots Q_n$	
$a_{11} \cdots a_{1m}$ $a_{1,m+1} \cdots a_{1,m+s}$ $a_{1,m+s+1} \cdots a_{1n}$						b_1
$\vdots$						$\vdots$
$a_{m1} \quad a_{mn}$ $a_{m,m+1} \quad a_{m,m+s}$ $a_{m,m+s+1} \quad a_{mn}$						b_m
$1 \cdots 0$ $\vdots$ $0 \quad 1$			$1 \cdots 0$ $0 \quad 1$			k_1 $\vdots$ k_m
	$1 \cdots 0$ $\vdots$ $0 \quad 1$			$1 \cdots 0$ $0 \quad 1$		k_{m+1} $\vdots$ k_{m+s}
		$1 \cdots 0$ $\vdots$ $0 \quad 1$			$1 \cdots 0$ $0 \quad 1$	k_{m+s+1} $\vdots$ k_n

$$= \begin{bmatrix} B & A_2 & A_3 & 0 & 0 & 0 & P_0 \\ I & 0 & 0 & I & 0 & 0 & K_1 \\ 0 & I & 0 & 0 & I & 0 & K_2 \\ 0 & 0 & I & 0 & 0 & I & K_3 \end{bmatrix}$$

The detailed breakdown of the matrix notations is for the convenience of introducing the method of Charnes and Lemke,* which is as follows:

1. There are three possible situations that x_i and u_i will be included in the solution basis.

(a) When $0 < x_i < k_i$; $u_i > 0$. (There are m pairs of vectors, $P_1, \ldots, P_m$, $Q_1, \ldots, Q_m$, included in the basis.)

(b) When $x_i = k_i$; $u_i = 0$ (there are s vectors, $P_{m+1}, \ldots, P_{m+s}$, included in the basis, the counterparts, $Q_{m+1}, \ldots, Q_{m+s}$, are not included.)

(c) When $x_i = 0$; $u_i = k_i$ (there are $(n - m - s)$ vectors; $Q_{m+s+1}, \ldots, Q_n$, included in the basis, the counterparts, $P_{m+s+1}, \ldots, P_n$ are not included.)

In other words, according to the notations in the simplex tableau, we assume that $P_1, \ldots, P_m$ are in the basis and the values of the respective $x_1, \ldots, x_m$ do not exceed their upper bounds (which means that $Q_1, \ldots, Q_m$ are also in the basis), $P_{m+1}, \ldots, P_{m+s}$ are in the basis and $x_{m+1}, \ldots, x_{m+s}$ equal to their upperbounds (which means that $Q_{m+1}, \ldots, Q_{m+s}$ are not in the basis) and $P_{m+s+1}, \ldots, P_n$ are not in the basis (which means that $Q_{m+s+1}, \ldots, Q_n$ are in the basis and $u_{m+s+1}, \ldots, u_n$ equal to the respective upper bounds).

2. The matrix which includes all basis vectors then can be written as follows.

$$
C = \left[
\begin{array}{cccccccc}
a_{11} \cdots a_{1m} & a_{1,m+1} \cdots a_{1,m+s} & 0 \cdots 0 & 0 \cdots 0 \\
\vdots & & & \\
a_{m1} \quad a_{mm} & a_{m,m+1} \quad a_{m,m+s} & 0 \quad 0 & 0 \quad 0 \\
\hline
1 \cdots 0 & 0 \cdots 0 & 1 \cdots 0 & 0 \cdots 0 \\
\vdots \quad \vdots & \vdots & & \\
0 \quad 1 & 0 \quad 0 & 0 \quad 1 & 0 \quad 0
\end{array}
\right] \Bigg\} 0 < x_i < k_i
$$

*A. Charnes and C. E. Lemke, "The Bounded Variable Problems," ONR Research Memorandum No. 10, Carnegie Institute of Technology, Pittsburgh, 1954.

$$C = \begin{array}{l} \left| \begin{array}{cccccccc} 0 & 0 & 1 & 0 & 0 & 0 & 0 & 0 \\ \vdots & \vdots & \vdots & & & & & \\ 0 & 0 & 0 & 1 & 0 & 0 & 0 & 0 \\ \hline 0 & 0 & 0 & 0 & 0 & 0 & 1 & 0 \\ \vdots & \vdots & & & & & & \\ 0 & 0 & 0 & 0 & 0 & 0 & 0 & 1 \end{array} \right| \begin{array}{l} \left. \begin{array}{l} \\ \\ \\ \end{array} \right\} x_i = k_i \\ \\ \left. \begin{array}{l} \\ \\ \\ \end{array} \right\} x_i = 0 \end{array} \end{array}$$

$$= \begin{bmatrix} B & A_2 & 0 & 0 \\ I & 0 & I & 0 \\ 0 & I & 0 & 0 \\ 0 & 0 & 0 & I \end{bmatrix}$$

3. The inverse of C is as follows:

$$C^{-1} = \begin{bmatrix} B^{-1} & 0 & -B^{-1}A_2 & 0 \\ 0 & 0 & I & 0 \\ -B^{-1} & I & B^{-1}A_2 & 0 \\ 0 & 0 & 0 & I \end{bmatrix}$$

4. Following simplex algorithm, multiply the original matrix by C^{-1}:

$$\begin{bmatrix} B^{-1} & 0 & -B^{-1}A_2 & 0 \\ 0 & 0 & I & 0 \\ -B^{-1} & I & B^{-1}A_2 & 0 \\ 0 & 0 & 0 & I \end{bmatrix} \begin{bmatrix} B & A_2 & A_3 & 0 & 0 & 0 & P_0 \\ I & 0 & 0 & I & 0 & 0 & K_1 \\ 0 & I & 0 & 0 & I & 0 & K_2 \\ 0 & 0 & I & 0 & 0 & I & K_3 \end{bmatrix}$$

$$= \begin{bmatrix} I & 0 & B^{-1}A_3 & 0 & -B^{-1}A_2 & 0 & B^{-1}P_0 - Y_2K_2 \\ 0 & I & 0 & 0 & I & 0 & K_2 \\ 0 & 0 & -B^{-1}A_3 & I & B^{-1}A_2 & 0 & K_1 - (B^{-1}P_0 - Y_2K_2) \\ 0 & 0 & I & 0 & 0 & I & K_3 \end{bmatrix}$$

Let $\overline{X}$ represent the vector $(B^{-1}P_0 - Y_2K_2)$, then the last column can be written as

$$\begin{bmatrix} \overline{X} \\ K_2 \\ K_1 - \overline{X} \\ K_3 \end{bmatrix}$$

5. The basis P vectors are represented by the third column of the matrix.

$$
\begin{bmatrix} B^{-1}A_3 \\ 0 \\ -B^{-1}A_3 \\ I \end{bmatrix} =
\begin{bmatrix} r_{1j} \\ \vdots \\ r_{mj} \\ 0 \\ \vdots \\ 0 \\ -r_{1j} \\ \vdots \\ -r_{mj} \\ 0 \\ \vdots \\ 1 \\ \vdots \\ 0 \end{bmatrix}
$$

where $m + s + 1 \leq j \leq n$, r_{ij} is the transformation ratios, and 1 is for u_j. The optimum evaluation formula for nonbasis vectors P_j is then

$$
c_j - \left[\sum_{i=1}^{m} c_i r_{ij} + \sum_{i=m+1}^{m+s} c_i(0) \right.
$$
$$
\left. + \sum_{i=1}^{m} 0(-r_{ij}) + 0(1) \right]
$$
$$
= c_j - \sum_{i=1}^{m} c_i r_{ij} = c_j - z_j
$$

(for maximizing problems, the optimum condition is that all $c_j - z_j \leq 0$, and for minimizing problems $c_j - z_j \geq 0$).

6. The nonbasis Q vectors are represented by the fifth column of the matrix:

$$
\begin{bmatrix} -B^{-1}A_2 \\ I \\ B^{-1}A_2 \\ 0 \end{bmatrix} = \begin{bmatrix} -r_{1j} \\ \vdots \\ -r_{mj} \\ 0 \\ \vdots \\ 1 \\ 0 \\ \vdots \\ r_{1j} \\ \vdots \\ r_{mj} \\ 0 \\ \vdots \end{bmatrix}
$$

where $m + 1 \leq j \leq m + s$, r_{ij} are the transformation ratios, and 1 is for x_j. The optimum evaluation formula for nonbasis vectors Q_j is then

$$
0 - \left[\sum_{i=1}^{m} c_i(-r_{ij}) + c_j(1) + \sum_{1=1}^{m} 0(r_{ij}) + 0(0) \right]
$$

$$
= 0 - \left(-\sum_{i=1}^{m} c_i r_{ij} + c_j \right) = -(c_j - z_j)
$$

7. Since the evaluation of the nonbasis Q vectors is simply the negative of that of the nonbasis P vectors, the criteria become the following.

(a) If the entering vector is a P vector, say P_e,

$$
x_e = \min \left\{ k_e, \frac{\overline{x}_i}{r_{ie}} \text{ for } r_{ie} > 0; \frac{k_i - \overline{x}_i}{-r_{ie}} \text{ for } r_{ie} = 0 \right\}
$$

(b) If the entering vector is a Q vector, say Q_e,

$$
u_e = \min \left\{ k_e, \frac{\overline{x}_i}{r_{ie}} \text{ for } r_{ie} < 0; \frac{k_i - \overline{x}_i}{r_{ie}} \text{ for } r_{ie} = 0 \right\}
$$

Example 8

$$\text{Max } f(x_1, x_2, x_3) = x_1 + x_2 + 2x_3$$

subject to

$$2x_1 + x_2 + 4x_3 \leq 20$$
$$x_1 + 2x_2 + x_3 \leq 10$$
$$x_1 \geq 0, \quad 0 \leq x_2 \leq 2, \quad 0 \leq x_3 \leq 6$$

First tableau:

k_j	∞	2	6	∞	∞		
c_j	1	1	2	0	0		
P_i	P_1	P_2	P_3	P_4	P_5	P_0	
						$\overline{x_i}$	u_i
0 P_4	2	1	4	1	0	20	$\infty - 20$
0 P_5	1	2	1	0	1	10	$\infty - 10$
Vectors in the basis	Q_1	Q_2	Q_3	P_4, Q_4	P_5, Q_5		
z_j	0	0	0	0	0	$f(X) = 0$	
$c_j - z_j$	1	1	2 $\uparrow$	0	0		

Apparently we have not reached the optimum position if we choose to bring P_3 into the basis. The selecting of outgoing vector is based on the formula

$$\text{Min} \left\{ k_3, \frac{\overline{x_i}}{r_{i3}} \text{ for } r_{i3} > 0; \frac{k_i - \overline{x_i}}{-r_{i3}} \text{ for } r_{i3} < 0 \right\}$$

In this case, all r_{i3} are greater than zero.

$$\text{Min } \{6, {}^{20}\!/_4, {}^{10}\!/_1\} = 5$$

So vector P_4 will exit from the basis. (Note: Q_3 will still be in the basis, since $x_3 = 5$ does not exceed the upper bound of 6.)

Second tableau:

k_j		∞	2	6	∞	∞		
c_j		1	1	2	0	0		
P_i	P_i	P_1	P_2	P_3	P_4	P_5	P_0	
							$\bar{x}_i$	$\bar{u}_i$
2	P_3	$\frac{1}{2}$ $\frac{1}{4}$		1	$\frac{1}{4}$	0	5	$6 - 5 = 1$
0	P_5	$\frac{1}{2}$ $\frac{7}{4}$		0	$-\frac{1}{4}$	1	5	$\infty - 5$
Vectors in the basis		Q_1	Q_2	P_3, Q_3	Q_4	P_5, Q_5		
z_j		1	$\frac{1}{2}$	2	$\frac{1}{2}$	0	$f(X) = 10$	
$c_j - z_j$		0	$\frac{1}{2}$ ↑	0	$-\frac{1}{2}$	0		

P_2 should enter the basis. The selecting of outgoing vector is based on the formula

$$\text{Min}\left\{2, \frac{5}{\frac{1}{4}}, \frac{5}{\frac{7}{4}}\right\} = 2$$

(Note: Q_2 will not be in the basis, since $x_2 = 2$ is equal to its upper bound.)

k_j		∞	2	6	∞	∞		
c_j		1	1	2	0	0		
P_i	P_i	P_1	P_2	P_3	P_4	P_5	P_0	
							$\bar{x}_i$	$\bar{u}_i$
2	P_3	$\frac{1}{2}$ $\frac{1}{4}$		1	$\frac{1}{4}$	0	$5 - 2(\frac{1}{4}) = \frac{9}{2}$	$6 - \frac{9}{2} = \frac{3}{2}$
0	P_5	$\frac{1}{2}$ $\frac{7}{4}$		0	$-\frac{1}{4}$	1	$5 - 2(\frac{7}{4}) = \frac{3}{2}$	$\infty - \frac{3}{2}$
Vectors in the basis		Q_1	P_2	P_3, Q_3	Q_4	P_5, Q_5		

Since all the other $c_j - z_y \leq 0$, the optimum condition has been reached:

$$\bar{x}_1 = 0, \qquad \bar{x}_2 = 2, \qquad \bar{x}_3 = \frac{9}{2}, \qquad \bar{x}_4 = 0, \qquad \bar{x}_5 = \frac{3}{2}$$
$$f(\bar{x}_1, \bar{x}_2, \bar{x}_3) = 0 + 2 + 2(\frac{9}{2}) = 11$$

Check the constraints:

$$2\bar{x}_1 + \bar{x}_2 + 4\bar{x}_3 + \bar{x}_4 = 2(0) + 2 + 4(^9/_2) + 0 = 20$$
$$\bar{x}_1 + 2\bar{x}_2 + \bar{x}_3 + \bar{x}_5 = 0 + 2(2) + ^9/_2 + ^3/_2 = 10$$
$$\bar{x}_1 = 0; \quad \bar{x}_2 = 2, \bar{u}_2 = 0; \quad \bar{x}_3 = ^9/_2, \bar{u}_3 = 6 - ^9/_2 = ^3/_2$$

OPTIMALITY ANALYSIS

When we have solved a linear programming problem, it means that with a given linear objective function and a finite number of linear constraints we can use the methods introduced above to find a set of values for the level of activities that will optimize the objective function within the feasible region specified by the linear constraints. However, in a changing economic world the objectives and the constraints may change quite often. Each time when the values of the parameters—either in the objective function or in the constraints—have been changed, we need to check whether the optimality condition has also been violated. If it is violated, the solution has to be altered. This section is devoted in the discussion of those changes with respect to the original optimality condition, and introduces methods that can avoid recomputing the entire problem. We assume that the linear programming problem is as follows.

$$\text{Max } f(X) = C^T X$$

subject to

$$AX \leq P_0$$
$$X \geq 0$$

(The optimality analysis for minimizing problems may be analysed in the same light.)

1. When c_j (unit profit of the variable not in the basis) is changed. Since the optimality condition is all $c_j = z_j \leq 0$, then if c_j changes to $c_{j'}$, any $c_{j'} - z_j > 0$ will destroy the original optimality condition. Using the previous example, the solution tableau for

c_j		1	1	2	0	0	
	P_i	P_1	P_2	P_3	P_4	P_5	P_0
0	P_4	2	1	4	1	0	20
0	P	1	2	1	0	1	10

is

c_j		1	1	2	0	0	
	P_i	P_1	P_2	P_3	P_4	P_5	P_0
2	P_3	$3/7$	0	1	$2/7$	$-1/7$	$30/7$
1	P_2	$2/7$	1	0	$-1/7$	$4/7$	$20/7$
z_j		$8/7$	1	2	$3/7$	$12/7$	$f(X) = 11\,3/7$
$c_j - z_j$		$-1/7$	0	0	$-3/7$	$-2/7$	

Variable x_1 is not in the basis. If c_1 changes from 1 to 2, $c_1 - z_1 = 2 - 8/7 = 6/7$, which is greater than zero (thus violating the optimum condition), the simplex method should be carried on until a new optimum solution is reached.

2. When c_i (unit profit of the variable in the basis) is changed: since the optimality condition is all $c_j - z_j \le 0$ and

$$z_j = c_1 r_{1j} + c_2 r_{2j} + \cdots + c_i r_{ij} + \cdots + c_m r_{mj}$$

(r_{ij} is the transformation ratio, m indicates the number of variables in the basis). If c_i changes to $c_{i'}$,

$$z_{j'} = c_1 r_{1j} + c_2 r_{2j} + \cdots + c_{i'} r_{ij} + \cdots + c_m r_{mj}$$

The original optimality condition will be destroyed if any $c_j - z_{j'} > 0$, which is the same as $c_j - (z_j - c_i r_{ij} + c_{i'} r_{ij}) > 0$. Now,

(a) If $r_{ij} > 0$,

$$c_{i'} r_{ij} < c_i r_{ij} - z_j + c_j$$

$$c_{i'} < c_i - \frac{z_j - c_j}{r_{ij}}$$

The lower bound for $c_{i'}$ not violating the optimality condition is therefore,

$$c_{i'} = \max\left\{c_i - \frac{z_j - c_j}{r_{ij}}\right\} \text{ or } \max\left\{c_i + \frac{c_j - z_j}{r_{ij}}\right\}$$

(b) If $r_{ij} < 0$,

$$c_{i'} > c_i - \frac{z_j - c_j}{r_{ij}}$$

since both sides of an inequality divided by a negative constant will reverse the inequality sign. The upper bound for $c_{i'}$ not violating the optimality condition is therefore

$$c_{i'} = \min\left\{c_i - \frac{z_j - c_j}{r_{ij}}\right\} \text{ or } \min\left\{c_i + \frac{c_j - z_j}{r_{ij}}\right\}$$

In the previous example, x_2 is in the basis and $c_2 = 1$.

$$\frac{c_1 - z_1}{r_{21}} = \frac{-\frac{1}{7}}{\frac{2}{7}} = \frac{-1}{2}, \quad c_2 + \frac{c_1 - z_1}{r_{21}} = \frac{1}{2}$$

$$\frac{c_5 - z_5}{r_{25}} = \frac{-\frac{2}{7}}{\frac{4}{7}} = -\frac{1}{2}, \quad c_2 + \frac{c_5 - z_5}{r_{25}} = \frac{1}{2}$$

Lower bound $c_{2'} = \max\left\{\frac{1}{2}, \frac{1}{2}\right\} = \frac{1}{2}$

$$\frac{c_4 - z_4}{r_{24}} = \frac{-\frac{3}{7}}{-\frac{1}{7}} = 3, \quad c_2 + \frac{c_4 - z_4}{r_{24}} = 4$$

Upper bound $c_{2'} = \min\{4\} = 4$

x_3 is also in the basis, and $c_3 = 2$.

$$\frac{c_1 - z_1}{r_{31}} = \frac{-\frac{1}{7}}{\frac{3}{7}} = -\frac{1}{3}, \quad c_3 + \frac{c_1 - z_1}{r_{31}} = 1\frac{2}{3}$$

$$\frac{c_4 - z_4}{r_{34}} = \frac{-\frac{3}{7}}{\frac{2}{7}} = -\frac{3}{2}, \quad c_3 + \frac{c_4 - z_4}{r_{34}} = \frac{1}{2}$$

Lower bound $c_{3'} = \max\left\{1\frac{2}{3}, \frac{1}{2}\right\} = 1\frac{2}{3}$

$$\frac{c_5 - z_5}{r_{35}} = \frac{-\frac{2}{7}}{-\frac{1}{7}} = 2, \quad c_3 + \frac{c_5 - z_5}{r_{35}} = 4$$

Upper bound $c_{3'} = \max\{4\} = 4$

3. When b_k ($k = 1, 2, \ldots, m$ constraints, elements of P_0) is changed, let B be the basis matrix:

$$X_B = B^{-1} P_0$$
$$f(X_B) = C^T X_B$$
$$= C^T B^{-1} P_0$$

The same basis will remain optimal until some x_i (variables in the basis) become negative because of change in P_0. Thus the optimality analysis becomes an examination of the feasibility of the solution. To find the upper bound and lower bound of b_k, the formula is similar to that for c_i:

$$\text{Upper bound } b_{k'} = \min\left\{b_k - \frac{x_i}{r_{ik}}\right\}, \quad \text{when } r_{ij} < 0$$

$$\text{Lower bound } b_{k'} = \max\left\{b_k - \frac{x_i}{r_{ik}}\right\}, \quad \text{when } r_{ij} > 0$$

In the previous example,

$$P_0 = \begin{bmatrix} b_1 \\ b_2 \end{bmatrix} \begin{bmatrix} 20 \\ 10 \end{bmatrix}$$

and in the solution matrix,

$$B^{-1} = \begin{bmatrix} 2/7 & -1/7 \\ -1/7 & 4/7 \end{bmatrix} \qquad \bar{X}_B = \begin{bmatrix} x_3 \\ x_2 \end{bmatrix} = \begin{bmatrix} 30/7 \\ 20/7 \end{bmatrix}$$

Thus

$$\text{Upper bound } b_{1'} = \min \quad 20 + \frac{30/7}{1/7} = 50$$

$$\text{Lower bound } b_{1'} = \max \quad 20 - \frac{30/7}{2/7} = 5$$

$$\text{Upper bound } b_{2'} = \min \quad 10 + \frac{20/7}{1/7} = 30$$

$$\text{Lower bound } b_{2'} = \max \quad 10 - \frac{20/7}{4/7} = 5$$

When b_1 is smaller than 5, say 4, the first tableau becomes

c_j		1	1	2	0	0		
	P_i	P_1	P_2	P_3	P_4	P_5	P_0	
0	P_4	2	1	4	1	0	4	$4/4 = 1, x_4$ to exit
0	P_5	1	2	1	0	1	10	$10/1 = 10$
	z_j	0	0	0	0	0	$f(X) = 0$	
$c_j - z_j$		1	1	2	0	0		

↑ Choose x_3 to enter

The second tableau becomes

c_j		1	1	2	0	0	
	P_i	P_1	P_2	P_3	P_4	P_5	P_0
2	P_3	$1/2$	$1/4$	1	$1/4$	0	$\cdot$ 1
0	P_5	$1/2$	$7/4$	0	$-1/4$	1	9
z_j		1	$1/2$	2	$1/2$	0	$f(X) = z$
$c_j - z_j$		0	$1/2$	0	$-1/2$	0	

$\frac{1}{1/4} = 4$, x_3 to exit

$\frac{9}{7/4} = {}^{36}/_7$ (note the difference from the previous example)

↑ x_2 to enter

The third tableau is

c_j		1	1	2	0	0	
	P_i	P_1	P_2	P_3	P_4	P_5	P_0
1	P_2	2	1	4	1	0	4
0	P_5	-3	0	-7	-2	1	2
z_j		2	1	4	1	0	$f(X) = 4$
$c_j - z_j$		-1	0	-2	-1	0	Optimum

The solution includes different variables (x_2, x_5) in the basis.

4. When a_{ij} (the coefficients of the matrix) is changed; there are two different cases. In one of these the respective P_j is not in the basis, but only when

$$c_j - z_j < 0 \quad \text{or} \quad c_j - C^T B^{-1} P_j < 0,$$

where
$$P_j = \begin{bmatrix} a_{1j} \\ \vdots \\ a_{ij} \\ \vdots \\ a_{mj} \end{bmatrix}$$

where the optimality condition is destroyed.

The other case is when the respective p_j is in the basis; then a new B'^{-1} has to be computed in order to check the optimality condition: $c_j - C^T B'^{-1} P_j \leq 0$ for all j. If one of them violates the condition ($c_j - C^T B'^{-1} P_j \geq 0$), the optimality is destroyed.

To find the new B'^{-1}, an elementary matrix E is used such that

$$B' = BE$$
$$B'^{-1} = (BE)^{-1}$$
$$= E^{-1}B^{-1}$$

Suppose P_e is the vector, one of its element a_{ie} is changed:

$$B = [P_1 \quad P_2 \quad \cdots \quad P_e \quad \cdots \quad P_m]$$
$$B' = [P_1 \quad P_2 \quad \cdots \quad P_e' \quad \cdots \quad P_m]$$

$$E = \begin{bmatrix} 1 & 0 & \cdots & r_{1k} & \cdots & 0 \\ 0 & 1 & & r_{2k} & & 0 \\ 0 & 0 & & r_{ek} & & 0 \\ 0 & 0 & & r_{mk} & & 1 \end{bmatrix}$$

$$E^{-1} = \begin{bmatrix} 1 & 0 & \cdots & r_{1k}r_{ek} & \cdots & 0 \\ 0 & 1 & & -r_{2k}r_{ek} & & 0 \\ 0 & 0 & & 1r_{ek} & & 0 \\ 0 & 0 & & -r_{mk}r_{ek} & & 1 \end{bmatrix}$$

which can be easily verified by $E \cdot E^{-1} = I$.

Since $B' = BE$,

$$[P_1 P_2 \cdots P_e' \cdots P_m] = [P_1 P_2 \cdots$$
$$(P_1 r_{1k} + P_2 r_{2k} + \cdots + P_e r_{ek} + \cdots + P_m r_{mk}) \cdots P_m]$$

$$P_e' = BR, \quad \text{where} \quad R = \begin{bmatrix} r_{1k} \\ r_{2k} \\ \vdots \\ r_{ek} \\ \vdots \\ r_{mk} \end{bmatrix}$$

$$R = B^{-1} P_e'$$

Example 9

Let

$$B = \begin{bmatrix} a_{11} & a_{12} \\ a_{21} & a_{22} \end{bmatrix} = \begin{bmatrix} 4 & 1 \\ 1 & 2 \end{bmatrix} \qquad B^{-1} = \begin{bmatrix} \frac{2}{7} & -\frac{1}{7} \\ -\frac{1}{7} & \frac{4}{7} \end{bmatrix}$$

$$BB^{-1} = \begin{bmatrix} 4 & 1 \\ 1 & 2 \end{bmatrix} \begin{bmatrix} 2/7 & -1/7 \\ -1/7 & 4/7 \end{bmatrix} = \begin{bmatrix} 1 & 0 \\ 0 & 1 \end{bmatrix}$$

Now change a_{11} to 3:

$$B' = \begin{bmatrix} 3 & 1 \\ 1 & 2 \end{bmatrix} \qquad R = B^{-1}P_1' = \begin{bmatrix} 2/7 & -1/7 \\ -1/7 & 4/7 \end{bmatrix} \begin{bmatrix} 3 \\ 1 \end{bmatrix} = \begin{bmatrix} 5/7 \\ 1/7 \end{bmatrix}$$

$$E = \begin{bmatrix} 5/7 & 0 \\ 1/7 & 1 \end{bmatrix} \qquad E^{-1} = \begin{bmatrix} \dfrac{1}{5/7} & 0 \\ -\dfrac{1/7}{5/7} & 1 \end{bmatrix} = \begin{bmatrix} 7/5 & 0 \\ -1/5 & 1 \end{bmatrix}$$

$$B'^{-1} = E^{-1}B^{-1} = \begin{bmatrix} 7/5 & 0 \\ -1/5 & 1 \end{bmatrix} \begin{bmatrix} 2/7 & -1/7 \\ -1/7 & 4/7 \end{bmatrix} = \begin{bmatrix} 2/5 & -1/5 \\ -1/5 & 3/5 \end{bmatrix}$$

Check:

$$B'B'^{-1} = \begin{bmatrix} 3 & 1 \\ 1 & 2 \end{bmatrix} \begin{bmatrix} 2/5 & -1/5 \\ -1/5 & 3/5 \end{bmatrix} = \begin{bmatrix} 1 & 0 \\ 0 & 1 \end{bmatrix}$$

5. When new variable (x_{n+1}) is added to the problem, let the respective coefficients vector of x_{n+1} be P_{n+1}. Then if

$$c_{n+1} - z_{n+1} > 0 \quad (c_{n+1} - C^T B^{-1} P_{n+1} > 0)$$

the original optimality will be destroyed and x_{n+1} should be brought into the solution—otherwise, the solution will remain the same.

6. When new constraint ($S = [a_{m+1,1}a_{m+1,2}, \ldots, a_{m+1,m}]$, $SX_B' \le b_{m+1}$) is added to the problem, the original B matrix will be augmented as follows:

$$B' = \begin{bmatrix} a_{11} & a_{12} & \cdots & a_{1m} & 0 \\ \vdots & & & & \\ a_{m1} & a_{m2} & & a_{mm} & 0 \\ \vdots & & & & \\ a_{m+1,1} & a_{m+1,2} & & a_{m+1,m} & 1 \end{bmatrix}$$

$$= \begin{bmatrix} B & 0 \\ S & I \end{bmatrix}$$

Thus

$$B'^{-1} = \begin{bmatrix} B^{-1} & 0 \\ -SB^{-1} & I \end{bmatrix}$$

The new solution can then be computed by the following formula:

$$X'_B = B'^{-1} P'_0, \quad \text{where} \quad P'_0 = \begin{bmatrix} P_0 \\ b_{m+1} \end{bmatrix}$$

and the optimality condition is all $c_j - z'_j \leq 0$, or

$$c_j - C^T B'^{-1} P_j \leq 0$$

DECOMPOSITION ALGORITHM

A linear programming model is set up to describe the objective and constraints of an economic system, and in applying the simplex method to it we hope to find the optimum solution of operating the system. However, a complicated system usually consists of many subsystems and the decision process often starts at the subsystem levels. The suggested decisions then are reviewed and modified by top management to fit the total system's objectives and constraints. Danzig and Wolfe have developed the decomposition method to handle this kind of problem. Baumol and Fabian,* in their paper, give further economic interpretations to the method. In this section we use the Baumol and Fabian numerical example to explain the decomposition algorithm.

Suppose a corporation has two subdivisions. The outputs of division 1 are x_1 and x_2 and the outputs of division 2 are y_1 and y_2. The corporation's objective function and constraint together with the divisions' constraints are as follows.

$$\text{Max } \{F = x_1 + x_2 + 2y_1 + y_2\}$$

* W. J. Baumol and T. Fabian, "Decomposition, Pricing for Decentralization and External Economics," *Management Science*, Vol. 11, Series A (1965), pp. 1–32.

subject to
$$x_1 + 2x_2 + 2y_1 + y_2 \leq 40$$
and
$$x_1 + 3x_2 \qquad \leq 30$$
$$2x_1 + x_2 \qquad \leq 20$$
$$y_1 \qquad \leq 10$$
$$y_2 \leq 10$$
$$y_1 + y_2 \leq 15$$
$$x_1, x_2, y_1, y_2 \geq 0$$

The first constraint is the corporation's constraint. The next two apply to division 1. And the last three apply to division 2. In the objective function, the first two terms are related to division z's activities. When we consider division 1 separately disregarding the corporation's constraint, we have

$$\text{Max } \{F_a = x_1 + x_2\}$$

subject to

$$x_1 + 3x_2 \leq 30$$
$$2x_1 + x_2 \leq 20$$
$$x_1, x_2 \geq 0$$

Using the simplex method to solve this linear programming problem, we can obtain all the extreme points in the feasible region.

c_j		1	1	0	0	
	P_i	P_1	P_2	P_3	P_4	P_0
0	P_3	1	3	1	0	30
0	P_4	2	1	0	1	20
z_j		0	0	0	0	0
$c_j - z_j$		1	1	0	0	

The first extreme point is $x_1 = 0$, $x_2 = 0$, $x_3 = 30$, $x_4 = 20$. (x_3, x_4 are the slack variables.)

If we decide to bring P_2 into the solution, the criteria, Min $\{^{30}/_3, {}^{20}/_1\} = 10$, indicate that P_3 should leave the solution:

c_j		1	1	0	0	
	P_i	P_1	P_2	P_3	P_4	P_0
1	P_2	$\frac{1}{3}$	1	$\frac{1}{3}$	0	10
0	P_4	$\frac{5}{3}$	0	$-\frac{1}{3}$	1	10
z_j		$\frac{1}{3}$	1	$\frac{1}{3}$	0	10
$c_j - z_j$		$\frac{2}{3}$	0	$-\frac{1}{3}$	0	

Thus the second extreme point is $x_1 = 0$, $x_2 = 10$, $x_3 = 0$, $x_4 = 10$.

However, if we choose to bring P_1 instead of P_2 into the solution first, the criteria, Min $\{^{30}/_1, {}^{20}/_2\} = 10$, indicate that P_4 should leave the basic solution. The simplex tableau becomes

c_j		1	1	0	0	
	P_i	P_1	P_2	P_3	P_4	P_0
0	P_3	0	$\frac{5}{2}$	1	$-\frac{1}{2}$	20
1	P_1	1	$\frac{1}{2}$	0	$\frac{1}{2}$	10
z_j		1	$\frac{1}{2}$	0	$\frac{1}{2}$	10
$c_j - z_j$		0	$\frac{1}{2}$	0	$-\frac{1}{2}$	

The third extreme point is $x_1 = 10$, $x_2 = 0$, $x_3 = 20$, $x_4 = 0$.

The next step will be bringing P_2 into the solution. The criteria, Min $\left\{ \dfrac{20}{{}^5/_2}, \dfrac{10}{{}^1/_2} \right\} = 8$, indicate that P_3 should leave the solution.

c_j		1	1	0	0	
	P_i	P_1	P_2	P_3	P_4	P_0
1	P_2	0	1	$\frac{2}{5}$	$-\frac{1}{5}$	8
1	P_1	1	0	$-\frac{1}{5}$	$\frac{3}{5}$	6
z_j		1	1	$\frac{1}{5}$	$\frac{2}{5}$	14
$c_j - z_j$		0	0	$-\frac{1}{5}$	$-\frac{2}{5}$	

The fourth extreme point, which is the optimum point for division 1, is therefore $x_1 = 6$, $x_2 = 8$, $x_3 = 0$, $x_4 = 0$. (If we progress from the second simplex tableau we get the same solution.)

When we consider division 2 separately disregarding the corporations, we have

$$\text{Max } \{F_b = 2y_1 + y_2\}$$

subject to

$$y_1 \leq 10$$
$$y_2 \leq 10$$
$$y_1 + y_2 \leq 15$$
$$y_1, y_2 \geq 0$$

Using the simplex method,

c_j		2	1	0	0	0	
	P_i	P_1	P_2	P_3	P_4	P_5	P_0
0	P_3	1	0	1	0	0	10
0	P_4	0	1	0	1	0	10
0	P_5	1	1	0	0	1	15
z_j		0	0	0	0	0	0
$c_j - z_j$		2	1	0	0	0	

The first extreme point in the feasible region is $y_1 = 0$, $y_2 = 0$, $y_3 = 10$, $y_4 = 10$, $y_5 = 15$ (where y_3, y_4, and y_5 are the slack variables). If we choose P_1 to enter into the solution, the criteria Min $\{^{10}/_1, {}^{15}/_1\} = 10$, indicate that P_3 should leave the basic solution. The simplex tableau becomes

c_j		2	1	0	0	0	
	P_i	P_1	P_2	P_a	P_4	P_5	P_0
2	P_1	1	0	1	0	0	10
0	P_4	0	1	0	1	0	10
0	P_5	0	1	−1	0	1	5
z_j		2	0	2	0	0	20
$c_j - z_j$		0	1	−2	0	0	

The second extreme point is thus $y_1 = 10$, $y_2 = 0$, $y_3 = 0$, $y_4 = 10$, $y_5 = 5$. However, from the first tableau, if we choose P_2 to enter the solution. The criteria, Min $\{^{10}/_1, {}^{15}/_1\} = 10$, will indicate that P_4 should exit. The simplex tableau then becomes

c_j		2	1	0	0	0	
	P_i	P_1	P_2	P_3	P_4	P_5	P_0
0	P_3	1	0	1	0	0	10
1	P_2	0	1	0	1	0	10
0	P_5	1	0	0	-1	1	5
z_j		0	1	0	1	0	10
$c_j - z_j$		2	0	0	-1	0	

The third extreme point is $y_1 = 0$, $y_2 = 10$, $y_3 = 10$, $y_4 = 0$, $y_5 = 5$. Then we bring P_1 into the solution. The criteria, Min $\{^{10}/_1, ^5/_1\} = 5$, indicate that P_5 should exit. The simplex tableau becomes

c_j		2	1	0	0	0	
	P_i	P_1	P_2	P_3	P_4	P_5	P_0
0	P_3	0	0	1	1	-1	5
1	P_2	0	1	0	1	0	10
2	P_1	1	0	0	-1	1	5
z_j		2	1	0	-1	2	20
$c_j - z_j$		0	0	0	1	-2	

The fourth extreme point is $y_1 = 5$, $y_2 = 10$, $y_3 = 5$, $y_4 = 0$, $y_5 = 0$. The optimum position has not been reached. This time we let P_4 enter into the solution. And the criteria, Min $\{^5/_1, ^{10}/_1\} = 5$, indicate that P_3 should exit.

c_j		2	1	0	0	0	
	P_i	P_1	P_2	P_3	P_4	P_5	P_0
0	P_4	0	0	1	1	-1	5
1	P_2	0	1	-1	0	1	5
2	P_1	1	0	1	0	0	10
z_j		2	1	1	0	1	25
$c_j - z_j$		0	0	-1	0	-1	

The fifth extreme point which is the optimum point for division 2 is $y_1 = 10$, $y_2 = 5$, $y_3 = 0$, $y_4 = 5$, $y_5 = 0$. (If we progress from the second simplex tableau of division 2, we will reach the same optimum point.)

Now we have the optimum points for both division 1, (6, 8, 0, 0) and division 2 (10, 5, 0, 5,0). We substitute the values into the corporation's constraint:

$$x_1 + 2x_2 + 2y_1 + y_2 = 6 + 2 \times 8 + 2 \times 10 + 5 = 47 > 40$$

which in this example unfortunately violates the corporation's constraint. Danzig and Wolf suggest that dual or shadow prices be used as guidance for revising the decisions, and find that the final solution will be a linear combination of some of the extreme points of the subdivisions.

Let u_i be the linear combination coefficients for the extreme points of division 1 and v_i be the linear combination coefficients for the extreme points of division 2:

Division 1: $\sum_{i-1}^{4} u_i = 1$
1. (0, 0, 30, 20)
2. (0, 10, 0, 10)
3. (10, 0, 20, 0)
4. (6, 8, 0, 0)

Division 2: $\sum_{i-1}^{5} v_i = 1$
1. (0, 0, 10, 10, 15)
2. (10, 0, 0, 10, 5)
3. (0, 10, 10, 0, 5)
4. (5, 10, 5, 0, 0)
5. (10, 5, 0, 5, 0)

Consider division 1's fourth extreme point and division 2's fifth extreme point, let $u_4 = 1$, $u_1 = 0$ and $v_5 = 1$, $v_1 = 0$. The linear programming model becomes

$$\text{Max } \{0u_1 + (6 + 8)u_4 + 0v_1 + (2 \times 10 + 5)v_5\}$$

subject to

$$0u_1 + (6 + 2 \times 8)u_4 + 0v_1 + (2 \times 10 + 5)v_5 + s = 40$$
$$u_1 + \qquad u_4 \qquad\qquad\qquad\qquad = 1$$
$$v_1 + \qquad\qquad v_5 \quad = 1$$

where s is a nonnegative slack variable. Putting this into a simplex tableau, we have

c_j		0	14	0	25	0	
	P_j	P_{u_1}	P_{u_4}	P_{v_1}	P_{v_5}	P_S	P_0
0	P_S	0	22	0	25	1	40
0	P_{u_1}	1	1	0	0	0	1
0	P_{v_1}	0	0	1	1	0	1
z_j		0	0	0	0	0	0
$c_j - z_j$		0	14	0	25	0	

Suppose we choose to bring u_4 into the solution. The criteria, Min $\{{}^{40}/_{22}, {}^1/_1\} = 1$, indicate that u_1 should exit.

c_j		0	14	0	25	0	
	P_j	P_{u_1}	P_{u_4}	P_{v_1}	P_{v_5}	P_S	P_0
0	P_S	-22	0	0	25	1	18
14	P_{u_4}	1	1	0	0	0	1
0	P_{v_1}	0	0	1	1	0	1
z_j		14	14	0	0	0	14
$c_j - z_j$		-14	0	0	25	0	

Next we bring v_5 into the solution. The criteria, Min $\{{}^{18}/_{25}, {}^1/_1\} = {}^{18}/_{25}$, indicate that s should exit.

c_j		0	14	0	25	0	
	P_j	P_{u_1}	P_{u_4}	P_{v_1}	P_{v_5}	P_S	P_0
25	P_{v_5}	$-{}^{22}/_{25}$	0	0	1	${}^1/_{25}$	${}^{18}/_{25}$
14	P_{u_4}	1	1	0	0	0	1
0	P_{v_1}	${}^{22}/_{25}$	0	1	0	$-{}^1/_{25}$	${}^7/_{25}$
z_j		-8	14	0	25	1	32
$c_j - z_j$		8	0	0	0	-1	

As we learned previously that the dual or shadow prices are $(z_j - c_j)$. In this case, the dual prices are -8 and 1. However, negative dual price (indicating the resource has disutility or it is a nuisance) is nonfeasible. Thus we should bring in another extreme point for consideration. Suppose we choose to consider division 1's second extreme point, the linear programming model becomes

$$\text{Max } 0u_1 + (10 + 0)u_3 + (6 + 8)u_4 + 0v_1 + (2 \times 10 + 5)v_5$$

subject to

$$0u_1 + (10 + 2 \times 0)u_3 + (6 + 2 \times 8)u_4$$
$$+ 0v_1 + (2 \times 10 + 5)v_5 + s = 40$$
$$u_1 + \qquad\qquad u_3 + \qquad u_4 \qquad\qquad\qquad = 1$$
$$v_5 \quad = 1$$

where s is a nonnegative slack variable. Putting this into tableau form

c_j		0	10	14	0	25	0	
	P_j	P_{u_1}	P_{u_3}	P_{u_4}	P_{v_1}	P_{v_5}	P_s	P_0
0	P_s	0	10	22	0	25	1	40
0	P_{u_1}	1	1	1	0	0	0	1
0	P_{v_1}	0	0	0	1	1	0	1
z_j		0	0	0	0	0	0	0
$c_j - z_j$		0	10	14	0	25	0	

If we choose to bring v_5 into the solution, the criteria, Min $\{{}^{40}\!/_{25}, {}^1\!/_1\} = 1$, indicates that v_1 should exit.

c_j		0	10	14	0	25	0	
	P_j	P_{u_1}	P_{u_3}	P_{u_4}	P_{v_1}	P_{v_5}	P_s	P_0
0	P_s	0	10	22	-25	0	1	15
0	P_{u_1}	1	1	1	0	0	0	1
25	P_{v_5}	0	0	0	1	1	0	1
z_j		0	0	0	25	25	0	25
$c_j - z_j$		0	10	14	-25	0	0	

Next if we choose u_4 to enter, the criteria, Min $\{{}^{15}\!/_{22}, {}^1\!/_1\} = {}^{15}\!/_{22}$, indicate that s should exit.

c_j		0	10	14	0	25	0	
	P_j	P_{u_1}	P_{u_3}	P_{u_4}	P_{v_1}	P_{v_5}	P_s	P_0
14	P_{u_4}	0	$^{10}/_{22}$	1	$-^{25}/_{22}$	0	$^1/_{22}$	$^{15}/_{22}$
0	P_{u_1}	1	$^{12}/_{22}$	0	$^{25}/_{22}$	0	$-^1/_{22}$	$^7/_{22}$
25	P_{v_5}	0	0	0	1	1	0	1
z_j		0	$^{70}/_{11}$	14	$^{100}/_{11}$	25	$^7/_{11}$	$^{308}/_{11}$
$c_j - z_j$			$^{40}/_{11}$	0	$-^{100}/_{11}$	0	$-^7/_{11}$	

u_3 should enter and the criteria, Min $\{^{15}/_{10}, {}^7/_{12}\} = {}^7/_{12}$, indicate that u_1 should exit.

c_j		0	10	14	0	25	0	
	P_j	P_{u_1}	P_{u_3}	P_{u_4}	P_{v_1}	P_{v_5}	P_s	P_0
14	P_{u_4}	$-^5/_6$	0	1	$-^{25}/_{12}$	0	$^1/_{12}$	$^5/_{12}$
10	P_{u_3}	$^{22}/_{12}$	1	0	$^{25}/_{12}$	0	$-^1/_{12}$	$^7/_{12}$
25	P_{v_5}	0	0	0	1	1	0	1
z_j		$^{20}/_3$	10	14	$^{50}/_3$	25	$^1/_3$	$^{110}/_3$
$c_j - z_j$		$-^{20}/_3$	0	0	$-^{50}/_3$	0	$-^1/_3$	

Since the dual or shadow prices $z_j - c_j$ ($^{20}/_3$, 0, 0, $^{50}/_3$, 0, $^1/_3$) of the resources are all nonnegative, we reach the optimum position:

$$u_1 = 0, \quad u_2 = 0, \quad u_3 = {}^7/_{12}(10, 0, 20, 0), \quad u_4 = {}^5/_{12}(6, 8, 0, 0)$$
$$v_1 = 0, \quad v_2 = 0, \quad v_3 = 0, \quad v_4 = 0, \quad v_5 = 1(10, 5, 0, 5, 0)$$

With this new solution, both the corporation constraint and the divisional constraints are not violated:

1. $x_1 + 2x_2 + 2y_1 + y_2$
$$= {}^7/_{12}(10 + 2 \times 0) + {}^5/_{12}(6 + 2 \times 8)$$
$$+ (2 \times 10 + 5)$$
$$= {}^{70}/_{12} + {}^{110}/_{12} + 25$$
$$= 40$$

2. $x_1 + 3x_2 = {}^7/_{12}(10 + 3 \times 0) + {}^5/_{12}(6 + 3 \times 8)$
$$= 18\tfrac{1}{3} < 30$$

3. $2x_1 + x_2 = {}^7/_{12}(2 \times 10 + 0) + {}^5/_{12}(2 \times 6 + 8)$
$$= 20$$

4. $y_1 = 10$

5. $y_2 = 5 < 10$

6. $y_1 + y_2 = 10 + 5 = 15$

And the corporation profit is at its allowable maximum $110/_3$.

SUMMARY

In this chapter linear programming models are introduced. Linear programming provides a theoretical framework for analyzing and solving the problems of an organization. The objectives of the organization are represented by a linear objective function and the constraints—such as capital, labor and other resources—within which the organization operates are represented by several linear inequalities. The solution of a linear programming problem may thus be considered as the optimum use of the available scarce resources to achieve the objectives. The simplex method is an algorithm for solving linear programming problems. The initial feasible solution usually starts at the zero-activity level (none of the resources being utilized), and the value of the objective function is equal to zero. Then for each iteration of computation the activity level moves to another extreme point in the feasible region, which improves the value of the objective function until the optimal solution is obtained.

The primal simplex method has its dual. Solving the dual problem is to approach the same optimal solution from the other direction. Thus if the primal is to maximize an objective function, subject to several smaller or equal constraints, its dual is to minimize another objective function subject to several greater or equal constraints. Since the parameters of the objective function of the dual are the coefficients of the constraints in the primal and vice versa, the solution of the dual represents the optimal use of the scarce resources. They are called the shadow prices of the scarce resources.

When the solution has to be integer units, such as numbers of automobiles to be produced, numbers of airplanes to be produced, etc., the integer programming method is to be used. It can be considered as adding more constraints into the original linear programming problem. Also if some of the variables in the solution have to exceed (or be below) some given constants, the bounded-variable method is used. More constraints again are added into the original problem.

The parameters of a linear programming problem and the constraints are subject to change. If change occurs, we may not have to reevaluate the entire problem from the beginning, but merely recompute a few columns in the final simplex tableau either to find the new optimum solution or to verify that the original optimality condition is not violated.

When a system consists of several subsystems and the objectives or constraints of the subsystems and the total system are not the same, decomposition algorithm is developed to find the optimum solution which will be consistent with both the objectives and constraints of the subsystems and those of the total system.

PROBLEMS

1. A factory can produce three different products X, Y, and Z. Each product requires the input of three different raw materials A, B, and C. Each unit of product X can bring \$10 profit, each unit of product Y can bring \$12 profit, and each unit of product Z can bring \$8 profit. The factory presently has available material A, 300 lb, B, 500 lb, and C, 200 lb. For producing X, 1 lb of A, 2 lb of B, and $\frac{1}{2}$ lb of C are required. For producing Y, $1\frac{1}{2}$ lb of A, $1\frac{1}{2}$ lb of B, and $1\frac{1}{2}$ lb of C are required. For producing Z, $\frac{1}{2}$ lb of A, $1\frac{1}{2}$ lb of B, and $\frac{1}{2}$ lb of C are required. In order to maximize profit, how much of X, Y, and Z should the factory produce? Are there any leftovers of materials A, B, and C after the production? What is the maximum total profit the factory can obtain by producing X, Y, and Z?

2. Set Prob. 1 in dual simplex format and compute the shadow prices of materials A, B, and C (the worth of A, B, and C when they are optimally allocated in producing X, Y, and Z).

3. In Prob. 1, if X, Y, and Z cannot be produced in fractional units or if only an integer unit of X, Y, and Z has exchange

and use value, how will the decision vary? What will become the total maximum profit? (Use the Gomory method.)

4. If the factory is required to produce a minimum quantity of Y of 100 units in order to maintain its reputation of producing high-quality goods, how will this change the optimal decision, and how will it affect the total profit?

5. If a new technology is discovered whereby producing a unit of Y requires only 1 lb of A, 2 lb of B, and 1 lb of C, how will this change the optimal decision? How will it affect the total profit?

6. Use the decomposition algorithm to solve the linear programming problem

$$\text{Max}\,\{F = 3x_1 + 2x_2 + y_1 + 4y_2\}$$

subject to

$$2x_1 + x_2 + 5y_1 + 4y_2 \leq 100$$
$$x_1 + 2x_2 \leq 40$$
$$3x_1 + x_2 \leq 30$$
$$y_1 + y_2 \leq 10$$
$$2y_1 + 3y_2 \leq 20$$
$$x_1, x_2, y_1, y_2 \geq 0$$

7. Discuss where in the business world linear programming method would find wide applications and where its applications would be very limited.

SELECTED REFERENCES

Chung, An-Min, *Linear Programming*. Columbus, Ohio. Charles E. Merrill Books, Inc., 1963.

Dantzig, George B., *Linear Programming and Extensions*. Princeton, N.J.: Princeton University Press, 1963.

Garvin, Walter W., *Introduction to Linear Programming*. New York: McGraw-Hill Book Company, 1960.

Hadley, G., *Linear Programming*. Reading, Mass.: Addison-Wesley Publishing Company, Inc., 1962.

Vazsonyi, Andrew, *Scientific Programming in Business and Industry*. New York: John Wiley & Sons, Inc., 1958.

chapter 2

Nonlinear Programming

The simplex method is a very efficient method of solving linear programming problems. Unfortunately in the real world the objectives and constraints cannot always be represented by linear functions—they may be nonlinear. For example, if the objective of a monopolistic firm is to maximize profit, which is the difference between revenue and cost. Revenue is equal to the product of price p and quantity sold x. However, since the firm is in a monopolistic situation, the price is a function of the quantity sold, or $p = f(x)$. Thus the objective function is a nonlinear quadratic function of x. To this date, however, no simple and straightforward method is available for solving nonlinear programming problems. In this section, we assume only the objective function is nonlinear and the constraints are still linear and rely on classical calculus method to illustrate the search procedures over the interior and along the boundaries of the feasible region.

CALCULUS METHOD

Example 1

Max $\{f(x_1, x_2) = 4x_1 + 6x_2 + x_1 x_2 - 2x_1^2 - x_2^2 + 10\}$

subject to

$$x_1 + x_2 \leq 8$$
$$x_1 \leq 3$$
$$x_2 \leq 6$$
$$x_1, x_2 \geq 0$$

The first- and second-order derivatives of the objective function are

$$f_1(x_1, x_2) = 4 + x_2 - 4x_1$$
$$f_2(x_1, x_2) = 6 + x_1 - 2x_2$$
$$f_{11}(x_1, x_2) = -4$$
$$f_{22}(x_1, x_2) = -2$$
$$f_{12}(x_1, x_2) = 1$$
$$f_{21}(x_1, x_2) = 1$$

Since

$$f_{11} < 0, \quad \begin{vmatrix} f_{11} & f_{12} \\ f_{21} & f_{22} \end{vmatrix} = \begin{vmatrix} -4 & 1 \\ 1 & -2 \end{vmatrix} = 7 > 0$$

it satisfies the maximum condition. Set

$$f_1(x_1, x_2) = 0 \quad \text{and} \quad f_2(x_1, x_2) = 0$$
$$4 + x_2 - 4x_1 = 0$$
$$6 + x_1 - 2x_2 = 0$$

Solving the simultaneous equations, we get

$$x_1 = 2, \, x_2 = 4$$

Substituting $x_1 = 2$ and $x_2 = 4$ in the constraints, they satisfy all conditions, and thus ($x_1 = 2$, $x_2 = 4$) is the optimum solution. The value of the objective function is $f(2, 4) = 4(2) + 6(4) + (2)(4) - 2(2)^2 - (4)^2 + 10 = 26$.

Now, changing the first constraint to

$$x_1 + x_2 \leq 5$$

makes the solution ($x_1 = 2$, $x_2 = 4$) nonfeasible, since it lies outside the feasible region. In this problem all the constraints are still linear. However, the objective function is nonlinear but concave: thus the optimum solution may not be one of the extreme points but may lie on the boundaries of the feasible region. We must therefore check each boundary to determine the maximum values of the objective function attainable and compare them to get the optimum solution.

1. The first boundary is $x_1 = 0$, and the original problem becomes

$$\text{Max} \{f(0, x_2) = 6x_2 - x_2^2 + 10\}$$

subject to

$$x_2 \leq 5$$
$$x_2 \leq 6 \quad \text{(redundant)}$$
$$x_2 \geq 0$$

The first- and second-order derivatives are

$$f_2(0, x_2) = 6 - 2x_2$$
$$f_{22}(0, x_2) = -2$$

Since the second-order derivative is negative, it satisfies the maximum condition. Setting the first derivative equal to zero,

$$x_2 = 3$$

the respective value of the objective function becomes

$$f(0, 3) = 6(3) - (3)^2 + 10 = 19$$

2. The second boundary is $x_2 = 0$, and the original problem becomes

$$\text{Max} \quad \{f(x_1, 0) = 4x - 2x_1^2 + 10\}$$

subject to

$$x_1 \leq 5 \quad \text{(redundant)}$$
$$x_1 \leq 3$$
$$x_1 \geq 0$$

The first- and second-order derivatives are

$$f_1(x_1, 0) = 4 - 4x_1$$
$$f_{11}(x_1, 0) = -4$$

Since the second-order derivative is negative, it satisfies the maximum condition.
Setting the first derivative equal to zero, we obtain

$$x_1 = 1$$

and the respective value of the objective function becomes

$$f(1,0) = 4(1) - 2(1)^2 + 10 = 12$$

3. The third boundary is $x_1 = 3$, the original problem becomes

$$\text{Max} \quad \{f(3, x_2) = 9x_2 - x_2^2 + 4\}$$

subject to

$$x_2 \leq 2$$
$$x_2 \leq 6 \quad \text{(redundant)}$$
$$x_2 \geq 0$$

The first- and second-order derivatives are

$$f_2(3, x_2) = 9 - 2x_2$$
$$f_{22}(3, x_2) = -2$$

Since the second-order derivative is negative, it satisfies the maximum condition.

Setting the first derivative equal to zero, we get

$$x_2 = 4.5$$

However, the first constraint limits $x_2 \leq 2$; therefore the maximum value x_2 can take is 2, and the respective value of the objective function is

$$f(3,2) = 9(2) - (2)^2 + 4 = 18$$

4. The fourth boundary is $x_2 = 6$, and the original problem becomes

$$\text{Max} \{f(x_1, 6) = 10x_1 - 2x_1^2 + 10\}$$

subject to

$$x_1 \leq -1$$
$$x_1 \leq 3 \quad \text{(redundant)}$$
$$x_1 \geq 0$$

However, the first constraint is contradictory to the nonnegativity requirement of the solution, therefore there is no feasible solution on this boundary line. In Fig. 2-1, we can see the line $x_2 = 6$ is not in the feasible region.

5. The fifth boundary is $x_1 + x_2 = 5$, or $x_2 = 5 - x_1$, the original problem becomes

$$\text{Max} \quad \{f(x_1) = 4x_1 + 6(5 - x_1) + x(5 - x_1)$$
$$-2x_1^2 - (5 - x_1)^2 + 10\}$$

or

$$\text{Max} \{f(x_1) = 13x_1 - 4x_1^2 + 15\}$$

subject to

$$x_1 + (5 - x_1) \leq 5 \text{ or } 5 \leq 5 \quad \text{(redundant)}$$
$$x_1 \leq 3$$
$$5 - x_1 \leq 6 \text{ or } x \geq -1 \quad \text{(redundant)}$$
$$x_1 \geq 0$$

The first- and second-order derivatives of the objective function are

$$f_1(x_1) = 13 - 8x_1$$
$$f_{11}(x_1) = -8$$

Since the second-order derivative is negative, it satisfies the maximum condition.

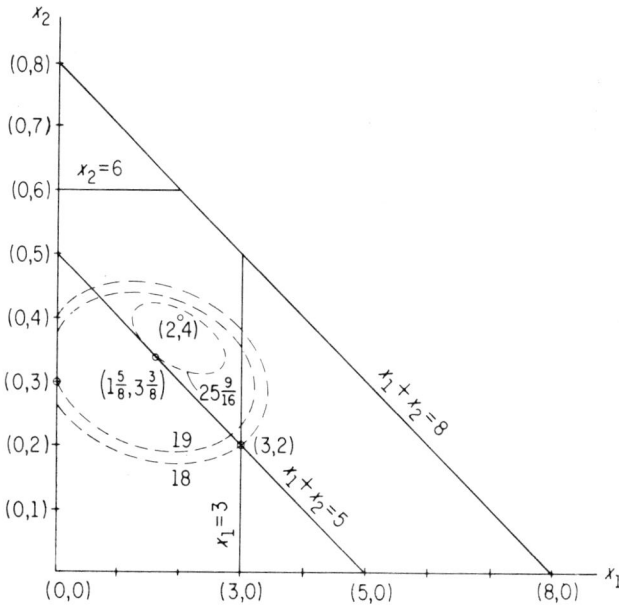

Fig. 2-1

Setting the first derivative equal to zero, we get $x_1 = 1\frac{5}{8}$, which is consistent with all the constraints, and $x_2 = 5 - 1\frac{5}{8} = 3\frac{3}{8}$. The respective value of the objective function is

$$f\left(1\frac{5}{8}, 3\frac{3}{8}\right) = 13\left(\frac{13}{8}\right) - 4\left(\frac{13}{8}\right)^2 + 15 = 25\frac{9}{16}$$

Comparing the values of the objective function at the optimum points on each boundary, $f(0, 3) = 19$, $f(1, 0) = 12$, $f(3, 2) = 18$, and $f(1\frac{5}{8}, 3\frac{3}{8}) = 25\frac{9}{16}$. The last value is the largest, and thus the global optimum position is at $(1\frac{5}{8}, 3\frac{3}{8})$, so that the solution of the nonlinear programming model is

$$x_1 = 1\frac{5}{8}, x_2 = 3\frac{3}{8}$$

The solution may be seen graphically in Fig. 2-1.

LAGRANGE MULTIPLIERS

When we want to maximize or minimize an objective function subject to one or more equality constraints, we may transform the problem into the maximization or minimization of a single function by joining the objective function with the constraints by Lagrange multipliers.

Example 2
$$\text{Max} \{f(x_1, x_2) = 10e^{-.5x_1} + 5e^{-.2x_2}\}$$

subject to

$$x_1 + x_2 = 10 \qquad x_1, x_2 \geq 0$$

We may change the problem into a Lagrangean function as follows:

$$\text{Max} \{L(x_1, x_2) = 10e^{-.5x_1} + 5e^{-.2x_2} + \lambda(x_1 + x_2 - 10)\}$$

Taking first-order partial derivatives with respect to x_1, x_2, and λ, we obtain

$$\frac{\partial L}{\partial x_1} = 10e^{-.5x_1}(-.5) + \lambda = -5e^{-.5x_1} + \lambda$$

$$\frac{\partial L}{\partial x_2} = 5e^{-.2x_2}(-.2) + \lambda = -e^{-.2x_2} + \lambda$$

$$\frac{\partial L}{\partial \lambda} = x_1 + x_2 - 10$$

If we set the partial derivatives equal to zero, the third equation restates the constraint $x_1 + x_2 = 10$ and the first and second equations give the following results:

$$\lambda = 5e^{-.5x_1^0}$$
$$\lambda = e^{-.2x_2^0}$$

where x_1^0, x_2^0 represent optimum values of x_1 and x_2. Thus

$$5e^{-.5x_1^0} = e^{-.2x_2^0}$$
$$\log 5 - .5x_1^0 = -.2x_2^0$$

However,

$$x_1 = 10 - x_2$$
$$\log 5 - .5(10 - x_2^0) = -.2x_2^0$$
$$\log 5 - 5 + .5x_2^0 = -.2x_2^0$$
$$x_2^0 = \frac{5 - \log 5}{.7}$$
$$= \frac{5 - 1.6094}{.7}$$
$$= 4.85$$
$$x_1^0 = 5.15$$
$$f(x_1^0, x_2^0) = 10e^{-2.57} + 5e^{-0.97}$$
$$= 2.66$$

THE KUHN-TUCKER CONDITIONS

As indicated previously, the nonlinear objective function has to be in some specific form in order to solve the problem by the calculus method. In this section the necessary and sufficient conditions for arriving at an optimum solution to a nonlinear programming problem are more clearly stated as the Kuhn-Tucker conditions and saddle-point equivalence. A *sadde point* is defined as a point which is not only the maximum point of a function with respect to one set of variables, but also the minimum point of the same function with respect to another set of variables. The primal and dual of a linear programming problem is one of the saddle-point cases.

The Kuhn-Tucker conditions state that if $f(x, u)$ is a differentiable function, then for a point $(\hat{x}, \hat{u})$ to be a saddle point of $f(x, u)$, the necessary conditions are

1. When $x > 0$,

$$\frac{\partial f}{\partial x} = 0$$

but when $x = 0$,

$$\frac{\partial f}{\partial x} \leq 0$$

Since the saddle point $(\hat{x}, \hat{u})$ represents a maximum point with respect to x, and since x can only have nonnegative values, we may see intuitively that the above statement is true in Fig. 2-2.

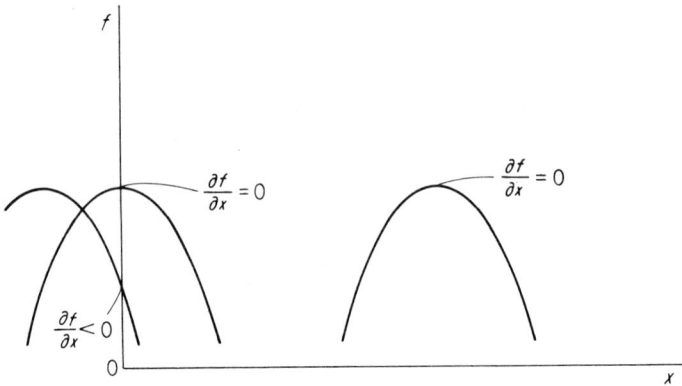

Fig. 2-2

2. When $u > 0$,

$$\frac{\partial f}{\partial u} = 0$$

but when $u = 0$,

$$\frac{\partial f}{\partial u} \geq 0$$

Since the saddle point $(\hat{x}, \hat{u})$ also represents a minimum point with respect to u, and since u can have only nonnegative values, we may see intuitively that the above statement is true in Fig. 2-3.

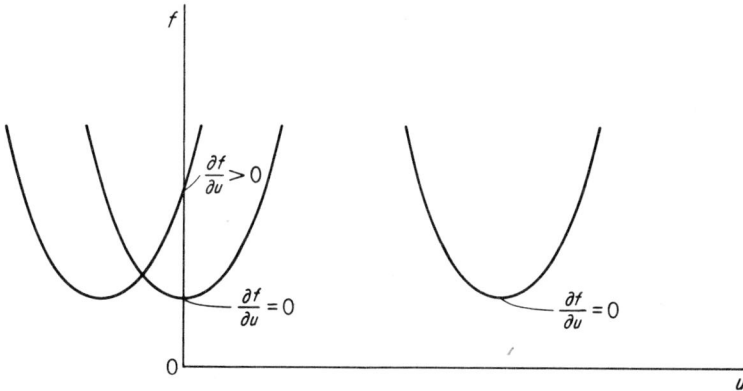

Fig. 2-3

The application of the conditions may be seen through an example:*

$$\text{Max}\,\{f(x_1, x_2) = -c_1 e^{-k_1 x_1} - c_2 e^{-k_2 x_2}\}$$

where

$$c_1, k_1, c_2, k_2 > 0$$

subject to

$$x_1 + x_2 \leq 1$$
$$x_1, x_2 \geq 0$$

Using a Lagrangean multiplier (λ)—equivalent to the variable u we used in the above section—to include the constraint into the objective function, we get

$$\text{Max}\quad \{L(x_1, x_2, \lambda) = -c_1 e^{-k_1 x_1} - c_2 e^{-k_2 x_2}$$
$$+ \lambda(1 - x_1 - x_2)\}$$

$$\frac{\partial L}{\partial x_1} = (-c_1)(e^{-k_1 x_1})(-k_1) - \lambda = c_1 k_1 e^{-k_1 x_1} - \lambda$$

*Using the example in C. R. Carr and C. W. Howe, *Quantitative Decision Procedures in Management and Economics* (New York: McGraw-Hill Book Company, 1964), p. 262.

When $x_1 > 0$,

$$c_1 k_1 e^{-k_1 \hat{x}_1} - \hat{\lambda} = 0$$

When $x_1 = 0$,

$$c_1 k_1 e^{-k_1 \hat{x}_1} - \hat{\lambda} \leq 0$$

$$\frac{\partial L}{\partial x_2} = (-c_2)(e^{-k_2 x_2})(-k_2) - \lambda = c_2 k_2 e^{-k_2 x_2} - \lambda$$

When $\hat{x}_2 > 0$,

$$c_2 k_2 e^{-k_2 \hat{x}_2} - \hat{\lambda} = 0$$

When $\hat{x}_2 = 0$,

$$c_2 k_2 e^{-k_2 \hat{x}_2} - \hat{\lambda} \leq 0$$

$$\frac{\partial L}{\partial \lambda} = 1 - x_1 - x_2$$

When $\hat{\lambda} > 0$,

$$1 - \hat{x}_1 - \hat{x}_2 = 0$$

When $\hat{\lambda} = 0$,

$$1 - \hat{x}_1 - \hat{x}_2 \geq 0$$

1. If $\hat{x}_1 = 0$ and $\hat{x}_2 > 0$,

$$c_1 k_1 e^{-k_1 \hat{x}_1} - \hat{\lambda} = c_1 k_1 - \hat{\lambda} \leq 0, \quad \hat{\lambda} \geq c_1 k_1$$

and

$$c_2 k_2 e^{-k_2 \hat{x}_2} - \hat{\lambda} = 0$$

Since $\hat{\lambda} > 0$,

$$1 - \hat{x}_1 - \hat{x}_2 = 0, \quad \hat{x}_2 = 1$$
$$c_2 k_2 e^{-k_2} - \hat{\lambda} = 0, \quad \hat{\lambda} = c_2 k_2 e^{-k_2}$$

$$c_1 k_1 \leq c_2 k_2 e^{-k_2}, \quad \frac{c_1 k_1}{c_2 k_2} \leq e^{-k_2}$$

or

$$\log_e \frac{c_1 k_1}{c_2 k_2} \leq -k_2$$

which is the condition for $\hat{x}_1 = 0$, $\hat{x}_2 = 1$ to be the optimum solution.

2. If $\hat{x}_1 > 0$ and $\hat{x}_2 = 0$,

$$c_1 k_1 e^{-k_1 \hat{x}_1} - \hat{\lambda} = 0$$

and

$$c_2 k_2 e^{-k_2 \hat{x}_2} - \hat{\lambda} = c_2 k_2 - \hat{\lambda} \leq 0, \quad \hat{\lambda} \geq c_2 k_2$$

Since $\hat{\lambda} > 0$,

$$1 - \hat{x}_1 - \hat{x}_2 = 0, \quad \hat{x}_1 = 1$$

$$c_1 k_1 e^{-k_1} - \hat{\lambda} = 0, \quad \hat{\lambda} = c_1 k_1 e^{-k_1}$$

$$c_2 k_2 \leq c_1 k_1 e^{-k_1}, \quad \frac{c_1 k_1}{c_2 k_2} \geq e^{k_1}$$

or

$$\log_e \frac{c_1 k_1}{c_2 k_2} \geq k_1$$

which is the condition for $\hat{x}_1 = 1$, $\hat{x}_2 = 0$ to be the optimum solution.

3. If $\hat{x}_1 > 0$ and $\hat{x}_2 > 0$,

$$c_1 k_1 e^{-k_1 \hat{x}_1} - \hat{\lambda} = 0$$

and

$$c_2 k_2 e^{-k_2 \hat{x}_2} - \hat{\lambda} = 0$$

Thus

$$c_1 k_1 e^{-k_1 \hat{x}_1} = c_2 k_2 e^{-k_2 \hat{x}_2}$$

$$\frac{c_1 k_1}{c_2 k_2} = e^{k_1 \hat{x}_1 - k_2 \hat{x}_2}$$

Since $\hat{\lambda}$ cannot equal zero, otherwise

$$c_1 k_1 e^{-k_1 \hat{x}_1} = 0, \quad e^{-k_1 \hat{x}_1} = 0$$

with $0 < \hat{x}_1 < 1$, $e^{-k_1 \hat{x}_1}$ does not equal zero; thus

$$\hat{\lambda} > 0, \quad 1 - \hat{x}_1 - \hat{x}_2 = 0, \quad \hat{x}_2 = 1 - \hat{x}_1$$

$$\frac{c_1 k_1}{c_2 k_2} = e^{k_1 \hat{x}_1 - k_2 (1 - \hat{x}_1)}$$

$$\log_e \frac{c_1 k_1}{c_2 k_2} = -k_2 + \hat{x}_1 (k_1 + k_2)$$

$$\hat{x}_1 = \frac{k_2 + \log_e \dfrac{c_1 k_1}{c_2 k_2}}{k_1 + k_2}, \quad \hat{x}_2 = \frac{k_1 - \log_e \dfrac{c_1 k_1}{c_2 k_2}}{k_1 + k_2}$$

Since $0 < \hat{x}_1 < 1$,

$$0 < \frac{k_2 + \log_e \frac{c_1 k_1}{c_2 k_2}}{k_1 + k_2} < 1$$

$$0 < k_2 + \log_e \frac{c_1 k_1}{c_2 k_2} < k_1 + k_2$$

$$-k_2 < \log_e \frac{c_1 k_1}{c_2 k_2} < k_1$$

which is the condition for

$$\hat{x}_1 = \frac{k_2 + \log_e \frac{c_1 k_1}{c_2 k_2}}{k_1 + k_2}$$

and

$$\hat{x}_2 = \frac{k_1 - \log_e \frac{c_1 k_1}{c_2 k_2}}{k_1 + k_2}$$

to be the optimum solution.

4. If $\hat{x}_1 = 0$ and $\hat{x}_2 = 0$,

$$c_1 k_1 - \hat{\lambda} \le 0, \quad \hat{\lambda} \ge c_1 k_1$$
$$c_2 k_2 - \hat{\lambda} \le 0, \quad \hat{\lambda} \ge c_2 k_2$$

But $1 - \hat{x}_1 - \hat{x}_2 = 1 > 0$, which implies $\hat{\lambda} = 0$, which in turn contradicts the above condition; therefore no such solution can exist.

In conclusion, the optimum solution of this problem depends on the value of $\log_e \frac{c_1 k_1}{c_2 k_2}$:

QUADRATIC PROGRAMMING

When the objective function is a second-degree poly-nomial in the x variables and the constraints are still all linear, we call the problem a *quadratic programming prob-lem*. The problem can be solved by the simplex method only when the objective function is strictly concave on a convex set of feasible region and if the Kuhn-Tucker conditions are satisfied.

We state the quadratic programming problem in matrix notation:

$$\text{Max} \quad \{f(X) = B^T X = \tfrac{1}{2} X^T C X\}$$

subject to

$$AX \leq P_0$$
$$X \geq 0$$

The Lagrangean function will be

$$\text{Max} \quad \{L(X, U) = B^T X + \tfrac{1}{2} X^T C X + U^T(P_0 - AX)\}$$

According to the Kuhn-Tucker conditions,

$$\frac{\partial L}{\partial X} = B + CX - A^T U \leq 0 \quad (\text{if} < \text{holds}, X = 0)$$

$$\frac{\partial L}{\partial U} = P_0 - AX \geq 0 \quad (\text{if} > \text{holds}, U = 0)$$

Changing the first derivatives into equation forms, we get

$$B + CX - A^T U + V = 0$$
$$P_0 - AX - W = 0$$

where V and W are positive slack variables. Arranging the result in a simplex tableau, we obtain

X	U	V	W	
C	$-A^T$	I	0	$-B$
A	0	0	I	P_0

$(-B)$ would make the initial solution not feasible, so we may change it into positive values by adding artificial vari-ables Z to the tableau.

$$
\begin{array}{ccccc|c}
X & U & V & W & Z & \\
\hline
-C & A^T & -I & 0 & I & B \\
A & 0 & 0 & I & 0 & P_0
\end{array}
$$

We then may apply the simplex method by first driving the artificial variables out of the initial solution to solve the problem.

Example 3

Max $\{f(x_1, x_2) = 4x_1 + 6x_2 + x_1 x_2 - 2x_1^2 - x_2^2\}$

subject to

$$
\begin{aligned}
x_1 + x_2 &\le 8 \\
x_1 &\le 3 \\
x_2 &\le 6 \\
x_1, x_2 &\ge 0
\end{aligned}
$$

Putting the objective function into matrix form,

$$
f(x_1, x_2) = (4, 6) \begin{bmatrix} x_1 \\ x_2 \end{bmatrix} + \tfrac{1}{2}(x_1 x_2) \begin{bmatrix} -4 & 1 \\ 1 & -2 \end{bmatrix} \begin{bmatrix} x_1 \\ x_2 \end{bmatrix}
$$

Thus

$$
B = \begin{bmatrix} 4 \\ 6 \end{bmatrix} \qquad C = \begin{bmatrix} -4 & 1 \\ 1 & -2 \end{bmatrix}
$$

$$
A = \begin{bmatrix} 1 & 1 \\ 1 & 0 \\ 0 & 1 \end{bmatrix} \qquad P_0 = \begin{bmatrix} 8 \\ 3 \\ 6 \end{bmatrix}
$$

$$
\begin{bmatrix}
C & -A^T & I & 0 & \vdots & -B \\
A & 0 & 0 & I & \vdots & P_0
\end{bmatrix}
$$

$$
=
\begin{array}{c|ccccccccccc}
 & x_1 & x_2 & u_1 & u_2 & u_3 & v_1 & v_2 & w_1 & w_2 & w_3 & \begin{matrix}-B\\P_0\end{matrix} \\
\hline
 & -4 & 1 & -1 & -1 & 0 & 1 & 0 & 0 & 0 & 0 & -4 \\
 & 1 & -2 & -1 & 0 & -1 & 0 & 1 & 0 & 0 & 0 & -6 \\
\hline
 & 1 & 1 & 0 & 0 & 0 & 0 & 0 & 1 & 0 & 0 & 8 \\
 & 1 & 0 & 0 & 0 & 0 & 0 & 0 & 0 & 1 & 0 & 3 \\
 & 0 & 1 & 0 & 0 & 0 & 0 & 0 & 0 & 0 & 1 & 6
\end{array}
$$

We then change the signs of the elements in the first two rows and add artificial variables z_1 and z_2 into the tableau to obtain an initial solution. Then assign positive values, such as 1's as pseudo objective function coefficients to z_1 and z_2 and zero to rest of the variables and using minimizing criteria to drive z_1 and z_2 out of the solution:

x_1	x_2	u_1	u_2	u_3	v_1	v_2	w_1	w_2	w_3	z_1	z_2				
0	0	0	0	0	0	0	0	0	0	1	1			c_j	
x_1	x_2	u_1	u_2	u_3	v_1	v_2	w_1	w_2	w_3	z_1	z_2	P_0	Basis		
4	−1	1	1	0	−1	0	0	0	0	1	0	4	z_1	1	$\frac{1}{4} = 1 \rightarrow$
−1	2	1	0	1	0	−1	0	0	0	0	1	6	z_2	1	
1	1	0	0	0	0	0	1	0	0	0	0	8	w_1	0	$\frac{8}{1} = 8$
1	0	0	0	0	0	0	0	1	0	0	0	3	w_2	0	$\frac{3}{1} = 3$
0	1	0	0	0	0	0	0	0	1	0	0	6	w_3	0	
3	1	2	1	1	−1	−1	0	0	0	1	1		z_j		
−3	−1	−2	−1	−1	1	1	0	0	0	0	0		$c_j - z_j$		

(arrow under x_1)

x_1	x_2	u_1	u_2	u_3	v_1	v_2	w_1	w_2	w_3	z_1	z_2				
0	0	0	0	0	0	0	0	0	0	1	1			c_j	
x_1	x_2	u_1	u_2	u_3	v_1	v_2	w_1	w_2	w_3	z_1	z_2	P_0	Basis		
1	$-\frac{1}{4}$	$\frac{1}{4}$	$\frac{1}{4}$	0	$-\frac{1}{4}$	0	0	0	0	$\frac{1}{4}$	0	1	x_1	0	
0	$\frac{7}{4}$	$\frac{5}{4}$	$\frac{1}{4}$	1	$-\frac{1}{4}$	−1	0	0	0	$\frac{1}{4}$	1	7	z_2	1	$\frac{7}{\frac{7}{4}} = 4 \rightarrow$
0	$\frac{5}{4}$	$-\frac{1}{4}$	$-\frac{1}{4}$	0	$\frac{1}{4}$	0	1	0	0	$-\frac{1}{4}$	0	7	w_1	0	$\frac{7}{\frac{5}{4}} = \frac{28}{5}$
0	$\frac{1}{4}$	$-\frac{1}{4}$	$-\frac{1}{4}$	0	$\frac{1}{4}$	0	0	1	0	$-\frac{1}{4}$	0	2	w_2	0	$\frac{2}{\frac{1}{4}} = 8$
0	1	0	0	0	0	0	0	0	1	0	0	6	w_3	0	6
0	$\frac{7}{4}$	$\frac{5}{4}$	$\frac{1}{4}$	1	$-\frac{1}{4}$	−1	0	0	0	$\frac{1}{4}$	1		z_j		
0	$-\frac{7}{4}$	$-\frac{5}{4}$	$-\frac{1}{4}$	−1	$\frac{1}{4}$	1	0	0	0	$\frac{3}{4}$	0		$c_j - z_j$		

(arrow under x_2)

x_1	x_2	u_1	u_2	u_3	v_1	v_2	w_1	w_2	w_3	P_0	Basis
1	0	$\frac{3}{7}$	$\frac{2}{7}$	$\frac{1}{7}$	$-\frac{2}{7}$	$-\frac{1}{7}$	0	0	0	2	x_1
0	1	$\frac{5}{7}$	$\frac{1}{7}$	$\frac{4}{7}$	$-\frac{1}{7}$	$-\frac{1}{7}$	0	0	0	4	x_2
0	0	$-\frac{8}{7}$	$-\frac{3}{7}$	$-\frac{5}{7}$	$\frac{3}{7}$	$\frac{5}{7}$	1	0	0	2	w_1
0	0	$-\frac{3}{7}$	$-\frac{2}{7}$	$-\frac{1}{7}$	$\frac{2}{7}$	$\frac{1}{7}$	0	1	0	1	w_2
0	0	$-\frac{5}{7}$	$-\frac{1}{7}$	$-\frac{1}{7}$	$\frac{1}{7}$	$\frac{4}{7}$	0	0	1	2	w_3

The optimal solution is therefore $x_1 = 2$, $x_2 = 4$ and the slacks of the three constraints are $w_1 = 2$, $w_2 = 1$, and

$w_3 = 2$, which checks with the previous Examples in the beginning of this section, using the calculus method to solve the problem.

GRADIENT METHOD

A similar method to solve the quadratic programming problem is the gradient method developed by M. Frank and P. Wolfe.* A gradient vector is used to determine the direction of maximum increase in the value of a linear function.

Given the linear function

$$f(X) = c_1 x_1 + c_2 x_2 + \cdots + c_n x_n$$

the gradient vector of the function is

$$\left[\frac{\partial f(X)}{\partial x_1} \frac{\partial f(X)}{\partial x_2}, \ldots, \frac{\partial f(X)}{\partial x_n} \right] = [c_1, c_2 \cdots c_n]$$

Example 4
Given

$$f(X) = 3x_1 + 2x_2$$

the gradient vector is

$$\left[\frac{\partial f(X)}{\partial x_1}, \frac{\partial f(X)}{\partial x_2} \right] = [3, 2]$$

Let $f(X) = k$. Then

$$3x_1 + 2x_2 = k$$

$$x_2 = \frac{k}{2} - \frac{3}{2} x_1$$

where $k/2$ is the intercept and $-3/2$ is the slope of the linear function. The slope represents a constant ratio between x_2 and x_1. As the line moves out according to the direction of the gradient vector, the value of the function will increase at the maximum rate (see Fig. 2-4).

Now for the quadratic objective function

$$f(X) = B^T X + X^T C X$$

*M. Frank and P. Wolfe, "An Algorithm for Quadratic Programming," *Naval Research Logistics Quarterly*, Vol. III, Nos. 1 and 2 (1956).

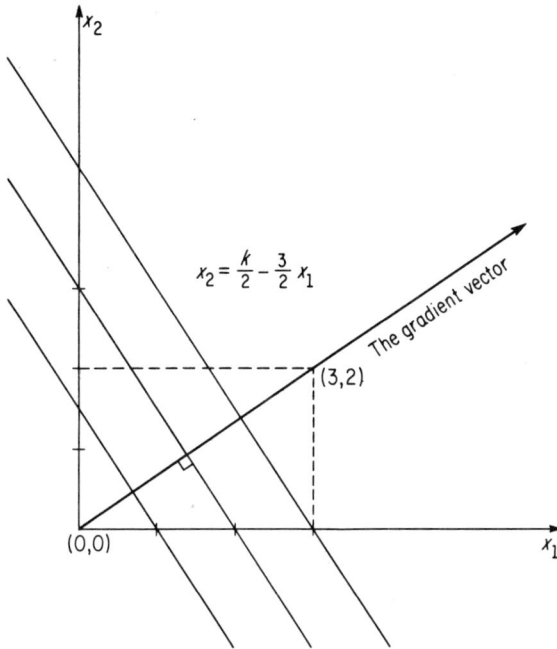

Fig. 2-4

Two-variable case:

$$f(x_1, x_2) = b_1 x_1 + b_2 x_2 + c_{11} x_1^2 + c_{22} x_2^2 + 2c_{12} x_1 x_2$$

$$= [b_1, b_2] \begin{bmatrix} x_1 \\ x_2 \end{bmatrix} + [x_1 \quad x_2] \begin{bmatrix} c_{11} & c_{12} \\ c_{12} & c_{22} \end{bmatrix} \begin{bmatrix} x_1 \\ x_2 \end{bmatrix}$$

The gradient vector is

$$\partial f(X) = \left[\frac{\partial f(X)}{\partial x_1}, \ldots, \frac{\partial f(X)}{\partial x_n} \right]$$

$$= B + 2X^T C$$

For the two-variable case,

$$\partial f(x_1, x_2) = b_1 + 2c_{11} x_1 + 2c_{12} x_2 + b_2 + 2c_{22} x_2 + 2c_{12} x_1$$

$$= \begin{bmatrix} b_1 \\ b_2 \end{bmatrix} + 2 \left\{ [x_1 \quad x_2] \begin{bmatrix} c_{11} & c_{22} \\ c_{12} & c_{22} \end{bmatrix} \right\}$$

Wolfe's algorithm may be understood as follows. If the quadratic objective function is concave and the constraints are linear, a point X_0 is the unique global maximum, if the hyperplane passing through X_0 and normal to the quadient vector at X_0 touches the constraint set in the vicinity of X_0 and only at X_0.

Definition of concavity: A function is concave if any two points X_p and X_q in the n-dimensional vector space satisfy the following relationship

$$f[aX_p + (1 - a)X_q] \geq af(X_p) + (1 - a)f(X_q)$$

where $0 \leq a \leq 1$.

Also, it is proved that the quadratic form must be negative semi-definite. In other words, the successively higher-ordered determinant of the coefficients along the diagonal must be alternatively nonpositive and nonnegative.

$$c_{11} \leq 0, \quad \begin{vmatrix} c_{11} & c_{12} \\ c_{12} & c_{22} \end{vmatrix} \geq 0 \cdots$$

Thus to maximize a concave quadratic objective function we set

$$\text{Max} \quad \{f(X) = BX + X^T CX\}$$

subject to linear constraints

$$AX \leq P_0$$
$$X \geq 0$$

The gradient vector of the objective function is

$$\partial f(X) = \left[\frac{\partial f(X)}{\partial x_1} \cdots \frac{\partial f(X)}{\partial x_n} \right] = [B + 2X^T C]$$

If X_0 is the global maximum, it can be shown geometrically that the projection of X_0 along the gradient vector has the maximum length.* Thus the problem becomes

$$\text{Max} \quad \{\partial f(X) \cdot X\} \quad \text{(projection along the gradient vector)}$$

The primal is

$$\text{Max} \quad \{\partial f(X) \cdot X\}$$

subject to

$$AX \leq P_0$$
$$X \geq 0$$

*A. M. Chung, *Linear Programming* (Columbus, Ohio: Charles E. Merrill Publishing Co., 1963), pp. 317–318.

or

$$AX + X_s = P_0$$
$$X, X_s \geq 0$$

where X_s represents the slack variables, and the dual is

$$\text{Min} \quad \{WP_0\}$$

subject to

$$WA \geq \partial f(X)$$
$$W \geq 0$$

or

$$WA - W_s = \partial f(X)$$
$$W, W_s \geq 0$$

where W_s represents the slack variables. Since the primal and the dual will yield the same solution at the optimum,

$$\partial f(X_0)X_0 = W_0 P_0$$

Combining these together,

$$
\begin{aligned}
\text{Max} \quad g(X, W) &= \partial f(X)X - WP_0 \\
&= (WA - W_s)X - WP_0 \\
&= W(AX - P_0) - W_s X \\
&= -(WX_s + W_s X) \\
&= -\tfrac{1}{2}(W_s X + WX_s + X_s^T W^T + X^T W_s^T) \\
&= -\tfrac{1}{2}[W_s\ W\ X_s^T\ X^T] \begin{bmatrix} X \\ X_s \\ W^T \\ W_s^T \end{bmatrix}
\end{aligned}
$$

Thus $[W_s\, W X_s^T X^T]$ may be considered as the coefficients for evaluation, and when $g(X, W)$ equals zero; the optimum condition is reached, and the constraints are

$$AX + X_s = P_0$$
$$WA - W_s = B + 2X^T C$$

or

$$
\begin{bmatrix} A & I & 0 & 0 \\ -2C & 0 & A^T & -I \end{bmatrix} \begin{bmatrix} X \\ X_s \\ W^T \\ W_s^T \end{bmatrix} = \begin{bmatrix} P_0 \\ B \end{bmatrix}
$$

$$X, X_s, W, W_s \geq 0$$

Example 5

$$\text{Max} \quad f(x_1, x_2) = 4x_1 + 6x_2 + x_1 x_2 - 2x_1^2 - x_2^2$$

$$= (4, 6)\begin{bmatrix} x_1 \\ x_2 \end{bmatrix} + (x_1, x_2)\begin{bmatrix} -2 & \tfrac{1}{2} \\ \tfrac{1}{2} & -1 \end{bmatrix}\begin{bmatrix} x_1 \\ x_2 \end{bmatrix}$$

subject to

$$x_1 + x_2 \le 8$$
$$x_1 \le 3$$
$$x_2 \le 6$$
$$x_1, x_2 \ge 0$$

or

$$x_1 + x_2 + x_3 = 8$$
$$x_1 + x_4 = 3$$
$$x_2 + x_5 = 6$$
$$x_1, x_2, x_3, x_4, x_5 \ge 0$$

Thus

$$A = \begin{bmatrix} 1 & 1 \\ 1 & 0 \\ 0 & 1 \end{bmatrix} \quad C = \begin{bmatrix} -2 & \tfrac{1}{2} \\ \tfrac{1}{2} & -1 \end{bmatrix} \quad -2C = \begin{bmatrix} 4 & -1 \\ -1 & 2 \end{bmatrix}$$

$$P_0 = \begin{bmatrix} 8 \\ 3 \\ 6 \end{bmatrix} \quad B = \begin{bmatrix} 4 \\ 6 \end{bmatrix}$$

The first tableau is

Basis	P_1	P_2	P_3	P_4	P_5	P_6	P_7	P_8	P_9	P_{10}	P_0
P_3	1	1	1	0	0	0	0	0	0	0	8
P_4	1	0	0	1	0	0	0	0	0	0	3
P_5	0	1	0	0	1	0	0	0	0	0	6
P_7	4	-1	0	0	0	1	1	0	-1	0	4
P_8	-1	2	0	0	0	1	0	1	0	-1	6

At this stage the feasible solution is

$$x_1 = 0, x_2 = 0, x_3 = 8, x_4 = 3, x_5 = 6$$
$$w_1 = 0, w_2 = 4, w_3 = 6, w_4 = 0, w_5 = 0$$

using $[w_4, w_5, w_1, w_2, w_3, x_3, x_4, x_5, x_1, x_2] = [0, 0, 0, 4, 6, 8, 3, 6, 0, 0]$ as evaluation measure.

Similar to c_j		0	0	0	4	6	8	3	6	0	0		
Basis		P_1	P_2	P_3	P_4	P_5	P_6	P_7	P_8	P_9	P_{10}	P_0	
0	P_3	1	1	1	0	0	0	0	0	0	0	8	$8/1$
4	P_4	1	0	0	1	0	0	0	0	0	0	3	
6	P_5	0	1	0	0	1	0	0	0	0	0	6	$6/1$
3	P_7	4	−1	0	0	0	1	1	0	−1	0	4	
6	P_8	−1	2	0	0	0	1	0	1	0	−1	6	$6/2 = 3 \rightarrow$
Similar to z_j		16	24	0	4	6	9	3	6	−3	−6		
Similar to $c_j - z_j$		−16	−24	0	0	0	−1	0	0	3	6		

Since

$$g(X, W) = -(x_3 w_1 + x_4 w_2 + x_5 w_3 + x_1 w_4 + x_2 w_5)$$
$$= -(8 \cdot 0 + 3 \cdot 4 + 6 \cdot 6 + 0 \cdot 0 + 0 \cdot 0)$$
$$= -48 \neq 0$$

Because the optimum solution has not been reached, we bring P_2 into the basis, and the constraint criteria indicates that P_8 should exit.

The second tableau is thus

Similar to c_j		0	0	0	4	6	8	3	6	0	0		
Basis		P_1	P_2	P_3	P_4	P_5	P_6	P_7	P_8	P_9	P_{10}	P_0	
0	P_3	$3/2$	0	1	0	0	$-1/2$	0	$-1/2$	0	$1/2$	5	$\frac{5}{3/2} = {}^{10}/_3$
4	P_4	1	0	0	1	0	0	0	0	0	0	3	3
6	P_5	$1/2$	0	0	0	1	$-1/2$	0	$-1/2$	0	$1/2$	3	$\frac{3}{1/2} = 6$
3	P_7	$7/2$	0	0	0	0	$3/2$	1	$1/2$	−1	$-1/2$	7	$\frac{7}{7/2} = 2 \rightarrow$
0	P_2	$-1/2$	1	0	0	0	$1/2$	0	$1/2$	0	$-1/2$	3	
Similar to z_j		$^{35}/_2$	0	0	4	6	$3/2$	3	$-3/2$	−3	$3/2$		
Similar to $c_j - z_j$		$-^{35}/_2$	0	0	0	0	$^{13}/_2$	0	$^{15}/_2$	3	$-3/2$		

Since

$$g(X, W) = (x_3 w_1 + x_4 w_2 + x_5 w_3 + x_1 w_4 + x_2 w_5)$$
$$= -(5 \cdot 0 + 3 \cdot 7 + 3 \cdot 0 + 0 \cdot 0 + 3 \cdot 0)$$
$$= -21 \neq 0$$

The optimum solution has not been reached, so we bring P_1 into the basis, and the constraint criteria indicates that P_7 should exit.

The next tableau is

c_j	0	0	0	4	6	8	3	6	0	0	
Basis	P_1	P_2	P_3	P_4	P_5	P_6	P_7	P_8	P_9	P_{10}	P_0
P_3	0	0	1	0	0	$-8/7$	$-3/7$	$5/7$	$3/7$	$5/7$	2
P_4	0	0	0	1	0	$-3/7$	$2/7$	$1/7$	$2/7$	$1/7$	1
P_5	0	0	0	0	1	$-5/7$	$1/7$	$4/7$	$1/7$	$4/7$	2
P_1	1	0	0	0	0	$3/7$	$2/7$	$1/7$	$-2/7$	$-1/7$	2
P_2	0	1	0	0	0	$5/7$	$1/7$	$4/7$	$-1/7$	$-4/7$	4

$$P_0 = \begin{vmatrix} 3 \\ 6 \end{vmatrix} \qquad B = \begin{vmatrix} \\ 6 \end{vmatrix}$$

Now

$$g(X, W) = -(x_3 w_1 + x_4 w_2 + x_5 w_3 + x_1 w_4 + x_2 w_5)$$
$$= -(2 \cdot 0 + 1 \cdot 0 + 2 \cdot 0 + 2 \cdot 0 + 4 \cdot 0)$$
$$= 0$$

The optimum solution has been reached

$$x_1^0 = 2, \; x_2^0 = 4, \; x_3^0 = 2, \; x_4^0 = 1, \; x_5^0 = 2$$
$$f(x_1^0, x_2^0) = 8 + 24 + 8 - 8 - 16 = 16$$

and

$$x_1^0 + x_2^0 + x_3^0 = 2 + 4 + 2 = 8$$
$$x_1^0 + x_4^0 = 2 + 1 = 3$$
$$x_2^0 + x_5^0 = 4 + 2 = 6$$

which meet all the constraints.

DYNAMIC PROGRAMMING

In the preceding section we have discussed mathematical techniques that will help us to find the optimum decision when given an objective function with several constraints. However, in the real world we sometimes have to make consecutive decisions, where the objective is to optimize the overall returns of several consecutive time periods. The mathematical technique for this kind of multistage decision rule is called *dynamic programming.*

Richard Bellman* contributes significantly to the development of dynamic programming by his principle of optimality: "An optimal policy has the property that, whatever the initial state and initial decision are, the remaining decisions must constitute an optimal policy with respect to the state resulting from the first decision." Based on this principle, the *backward induction method* is developed.

Example 6

Suppose a traveling salesman needs to travel from city A to city B and the alternative routes he can take are represented by the following network, with the mileage specified between each pair of intersections.

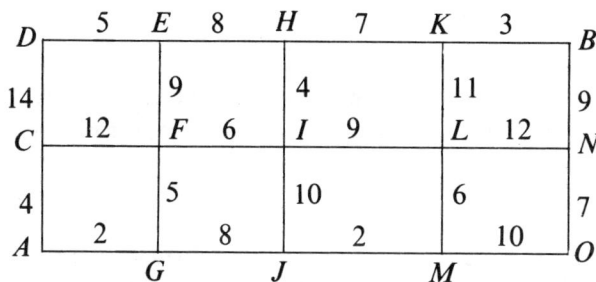

Using the backward induction method, the diagram shown in Fig. 2-5 is drawn starting from B to A.

The number at each intersection represents the distance between that intersection and the terminal point B. If more than one number is shown at an intersection, they indicate the mileage of alternative routes to B. After we calculate all the mileages between each intersection and the

*R. Bellman, *Dynamic Programming* (Princeton, N. J.: Princeton University Press, 1957).

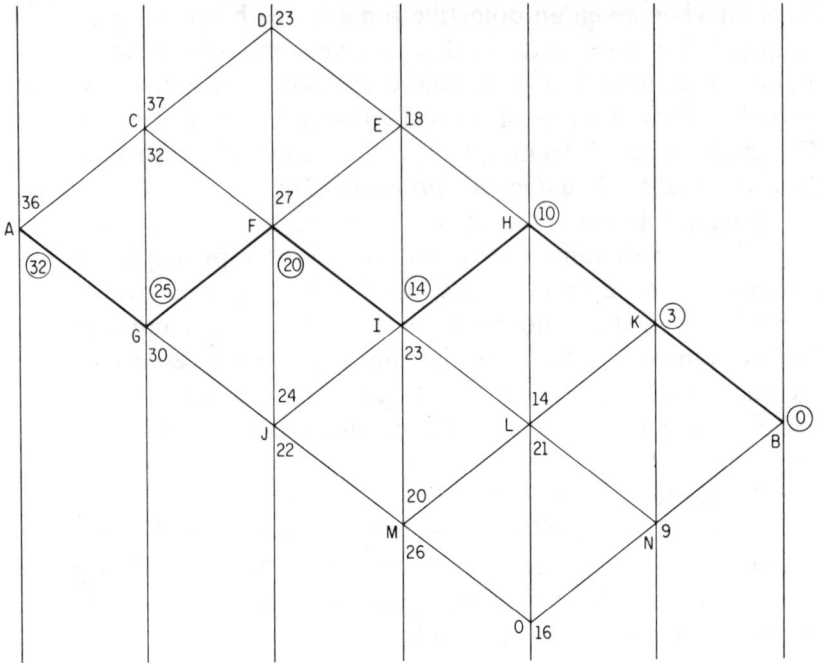

Fig. 2-5

terminal *B*, we start from *A* and select the shortest route
to *B*, which is *A–G–F–I–H–K–B* and the total mileage is 32.

Example 7

A merchant rents an empty warehouse from its owner
to engage in buying and selling a commodity. Assume that
he makes decisions only about whether he wants to buy at
the beginning of each month, and if he decides to buy he
buys only a whole warehouse load, provided that the warehouse is empty at the time. He makes decisions regarding
sale only at the 15th of each month, and if he decides to sell,
he sells only a whole warehouse load, provided that the
warehouse is full at the time. Further, we assume that the
merchant operates for four months, and at the beginning of
the fifth month he returns the empty warehouse to its owner.
Given the information in the table, and applying the backward induction method, the resulting diagram will be
formed.

Month	Buying Price per Warehouse Load (in thousands)	Selling Price per Warehouse Load (in thousands)
1	$10	20
2	9	9
3	15	12
4	8	10

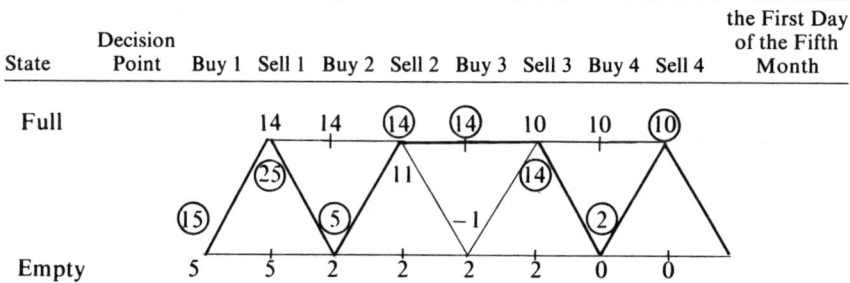

State	Decision Point	Buy 1	Sell 1	Buy 2	Sell 2	Buy 3	Sell 3	Buy 4	Sell 4	the First Day of the Fifth Month

Full

14   14   (14)   (14)   10   10   (10)

(25)   11   (14)

(15)   (5)   -1   (2)

Empty   5   5   2   2   2   2   0   0

The dollar figure (in thousands) written at each decision point represents the net result of the operation from that decision point to the terminal point (the first day of the fifth month) in accordance with the alternative decision routes. The result indicates that the optimum set of decisions for the six-months operation will be (1) buy at the beginning of the first period, (2) sell in the middle of the first period, (3) buy at the beginning of the second period, (4) don't sell in the middle of the second period, (5) don't buy at the beginning of the third period, (6) sell in the middle of the third period, (7) buy at the beginning of the fourth period, and (8) sell in the middle of the fourth period. The profit of the total operation will be $15,000 minus the rent of the warehouse.

The method may be stated in a more precise mathematical form, as illustrated in the following example.

Example 8

A merchant operates a warehouse for selling and buying a given commodity. The warehouse can store a maximum of 1,000 units of the commodity. He starts with an initial stock of 500 units and plans to operate for a period of four months. He estimates that the selling and buying prices of the commodity in the four months will be as follows.

i	Buying Price (c_i)	Selling Price (p_i)
1	$10	$12
2	9	9
3	11	13
4	15	17

Assume that he can sell only what he has in the warehouse, and when he decides to buy in a particular month, the stock will be received at the beginning of the following month. Let x_i be the quantity sold in the ith month and y_i the quantity received in the ith month. By the principle of optimality, the decision rule for the last month may be expressed by the following mathematical formulation:

$$f_1(S_4) = \max \ \{p_4 x_4 - c_4 y_4\}$$
$$0 \le x_4 \le S_4$$
$$0 \le y_4 \le T - (S_4 - x_4)$$

where f_1 represents the decision function of the fourth month which we have to examine first according to the backward induction method, S_4 is the stock available in the warehouse at the beginning of the fourth month, ($p_4 x_4 - c_4 y_4$) represents revenue minus cost during the fourth month. x_4 has to be nonnegative and cannot exceed the amount available in the warehouse. y_4 also has to be non-negative and the merchant can buy only up to the quantity which can be stored in the available empty space in the warehouse. The empty space is computed as the total warehouse capacity T minus the difference between the beginning inventory of the month and the quantity sold that month.

Looking at the equation, we see that in order to maximize $f_1(S_4)$, x_4 should be as large as possible and y_4 as small as possible. Thus the optimum policy should be

$$x_4^0 = S_4 \qquad \text{and} \qquad y_4^0 = 0$$

and

$$f_1^0(S_4) = p_4 S_4 \text{ or } 17 S_4$$

The decision rule for the third month should take consideration of the fourth month, since the merchant is attempting to maximize the overall returns. Therefore it should be as follows:

$$f_2(S_3) = \max \quad \{p_3x_3 - c_3y_3 + f_1(S_4)\}$$

Since the beginning inventory of the fourth month is equal to the beginning inventory of the third month plus the quantity received in the third month minus the quantity sold in the third month, the decision function may be written as

$$f_2(S_3) = \max \quad \{p_3x_3 - c_3y_3 + f_1(S_3 + y_3 - x_3)\}$$

The optimum policy for the fourth month is known to be $f_1^0 = p_4S_4$, so that

$$f_2(S_3) = \max \quad \{p_3x_3 - c_3y_3 + p_4(S_3 + y_3 - x_3)\}$$
$$= \max \quad \{(p_3 - p_4)x_3 + (p_4 - c_3)y_3 + p_4S_3\}$$
$$0 \le x_3 \le S_3$$
$$0 \le y_3 \le T - (S_3 - x_3)$$

Substituting the estimated buying and selling prices into the equation, we obtain

$$f_2(S_3) = \max \quad \{(13 - 17)x_3 + (17 - 11)y_3 + 17S_3\}$$
$$= \max \quad \{-4x_3 + 6y_3 + 17S_3\}$$
$$0 \le x_3 \le S_3$$
$$0 \le y_3 \le T - (S_3 - x_3)$$

In order to maximize f_2, y_3 should be as large as possible, or $y_3^0 = T$, which makes $S_3 - x_3 = 0$ or $x_3^0 = S_3$. The optimum policy is therefore

$$f_2^0(S_3) = -4S_3 + 6T + 17S_3$$
$$= 13S_3 + 6T$$

The decision rule for the second month, taking consideration of the third and fourth month, is likewise

$$f_3(S_2) = \max \quad \{p_2x_2 - c_2y_2 + f_2(S_3)\}$$
$$= \max \quad \{p_2x_2 - c_2y_2 + (13S_3 + 6T)\}$$
$$= \max \quad \{p_2x_2 - c_2y_2 + 13(S_2 + y_2 - x_2) + 6T\}$$
$$= \max \quad \{9x_2 - 9y_2 + 13S_2 + 13y_2 - 13x_2 + 6T\}$$
$$= \max \quad \{-4x_2 + 4y_2 + 13S_2 + 6T\}$$
$$0 \le x_2 \le S_2$$
$$0 \le y_2 \le T - (S_2 - x_2)$$

In order to maximize f_3, $y_2^0 = T$, $x_2^0 = S_2$, and the optimum policy is

$$f_3^0(S_2) = -4S_2 + 4T + 13S_2 + 6T$$
$$= 9S_2 + 10T$$

The decision rule for the first month, taking consideration of the entire four-month period, is

$$f_4(S_1) = \max \{p_1 x_1 - c_1 y_1 + f_3(S_2)\}$$
$$= \max \{p_1 x_1 - c_1 y_1 + 9S_2 + 10T\}$$
$$= \max \{12x_1 - 10y_1 + 9(S_1 + y_1 - x_1) + 10T\}$$
$$= \max \{3x_1 - y_1 + 9S_1 + 10T\}$$
$$0 \le x_1 \le S_1$$
$$0 \le y_1 \le T - (S_1 - x_1)$$

In order to maximize f_4, x_1 should be made as large as possible and y_1 as small as possible. Thus $x_1^0 = S_1$, $y_1^0 = 0$ and the optimum policy is

$$f_4^0(S_1) = 3S_1 - 0 + 9S_1 + 10T$$
$$= 12S_1 + 10T$$

Since the beginning inventory in the first month is $S_1 = 500$ and total capacity of the warehouse is $T = 1,000$, the multistage decisions are

Month	Beginning Inventory (S_i)	Sell (x_i^0)	Buy (y_i^0)
1	500	500	0
2	0	0	1,000
3	1,000	1,000	1,000
4	1,000	1,000	0

and the total maximum profit is

$$f_4^0(500) = 12S_1 + 10T = 12 \times 500 + 10 \times 1,000$$
$$= \$16,000$$

A similar method for analyzing multistage decision problems is the *forward induction method*, which enables us to start from the first period and then work toward the last period, one period after another. An example will illustrate the algorithm.

Example 9

A firm produces a commodity for three consecutive months. A production run is made at the beginning of each month. The producing cost of the commodity is x^2, where x is the number of units produced. The carrying cost for each unit per month is \$1. If the estimated demand for the commodity during the three months is

$$y_1 = 100 \qquad y_2 = 110 \qquad y_3 = 120$$

and if the initial inventory (S_0) is zero and the inventory at the end of the third month (S_3) also zero, what should be the quantities produced in each month?

Solution:

The total cost for the first month is the sum of the production cost and inventory cost:

$$F_1(S_1, x_1) = f_1(S_1, x_1) = x_1^2 + S_1; \quad x_1, S_1 \geq 0$$

where F is the cumulative cost and f the cost of the month. Since $S_0 + x_1 - y_1 = S_1$ (beginning inventory + production − demand = ending inventory), or $x_1 = y_1 + S_1 - S_0$,

$$F_1(S_1, x_1) = (y_1 + S_1 - S_0)^2 + S_1$$

The total cost for the first two months is

$$
\begin{aligned}
F_2(S_2, x_2, x_1) &= f_2(S_2, x_2) + F_1(S_1, x_1) \\
&= x_2^2 + S_2 + (y_1 + S_1 - S_0)^2 + S_1
\end{aligned}
$$

Since $S_1 + x_2 - y_2 = S_2$ or $S_1 = y_2 - x_2 + S_2$,

$$
\begin{aligned}
F_2(S_2, x_2, x_1) = {}& x_2^2 + S_2 \\
& + (y_1 + y_2 - x_2 + S_2 - S_0)^2 + (y_2 - x_2 + S_2)
\end{aligned}
$$

To find optimum x_2, we use the calculus method:

$$\frac{dF_2}{dx_2} = 2x_2 - 2(y_1 + y_2 - x_2 + S_2 - S_0) - 1 = 0$$

$$x_2^0 = \frac{1}{2}(y_1 + y_2 + S_2 - S_0) + \frac{1}{4}$$

Thus the minimum value of F_2 is

$$F_2^0(S_2, x_2, x_1) = [\tfrac{1}{2}(y_1 + y_2 + S_2 - S_0) + \tfrac{1}{4}]^2 + S_2$$
$$+ [\tfrac{1}{2}(y_1 + y_2 + S_2 - S_0) - \tfrac{1}{4}]^2$$
$$+ [\tfrac{1}{2}(y_2 + S_2 - y_1 + S_0) - \tfrac{1}{4}]$$

The total cost for the three months is

$$F_3(S_3, x_3, x_2, x_1) = f_3(S_3, x_3) + F_2(S_2, x_2, x_1)$$
$$= x_3^2 + S_3$$
$$+ [\tfrac{1}{2}(y_1 + y_2 + S_2 - S_0) + \tfrac{1}{4}]^2$$
$$+ [\tfrac{1}{2}(y_1 + y_2 + S_2 - S_0) - \tfrac{1}{4}]^2$$
$$+ [\tfrac{1}{2}(y_2 - 3S_2 - y_1 + S_0) - \tfrac{1}{4}]$$

Since $S_2 + x_3 - y_3 = S_3$ or $S_2 = y_3 - x_3 + S_3$,

$$F_3(S_3, x_3, x_2, x_1) = x_3^2 + S_3$$
$$+ [\tfrac{1}{2}(y_1 + y_2 + y_3 - x_3 + S_3 - S_0) + \tfrac{1}{4}]^2$$
$$+ [\tfrac{1}{2}(y_1 + y_2 + y_3 - x_3 + S_3 - S_0) - \tfrac{1}{4}]^2$$
$$+ [\tfrac{1}{2}(y_2 - y_1 + S_0) - \tfrac{3}{2}(y_3 - x_3 + S_3) - \tfrac{1}{4}]$$

To find optimum x_3, we use the calculus method:

$$\frac{dF_3}{dx_3} = 2x_3 - [\tfrac{1}{2}(y_1 + y_2 + y_3 - x_3 + S_3 - S_0) + \tfrac{1}{4}]$$
$$- [\tfrac{1}{2}(y_1 + y_2 + y_3 - x_3 + S_3 - S_0) - \tfrac{1}{4}] + \tfrac{3}{2} = 0$$
$$x_3^0 = \tfrac{1}{3}(y_1 + y_2 + y_3 + S_3 - S_0) - \tfrac{1}{2}$$

Given $S_0 = 0$, $S_3 = 0$, $y_1 = 100$, $y_2 = 110$, and $y_3 = 120$, the optimum quantities to be produced at the beginning of each month should be

$$x_3^0 = \tfrac{1}{3}(y_1 + y_2 + y_3 + S_3 - S_0) - \tfrac{1}{2}$$
$$= \tfrac{1}{3}(100 + 110 + 120) - \tfrac{1}{2} = 109\tfrac{1}{2} \text{ units}$$
$$S_2 = y_3 - x_3 + S_3$$
$$= 120 - 109\tfrac{1}{2} = 10\tfrac{1}{2} \text{ units}$$
$$x_2^0 = \tfrac{1}{2}(y_1 + y_2 + S_2 - S_0) + \tfrac{1}{4}$$
$$= \tfrac{1}{2}(100 + 110 + 10\tfrac{1}{2}) + \tfrac{1}{4}$$
$$= 110\tfrac{1}{2} \text{ units}$$
$$S_1 = y_2 - x_2 + S_2$$
$$= 110 - 110\tfrac{1}{2} + 10\tfrac{1}{2} = 10 \text{ units}$$
$$x_1^0 = y_1 + S_1 - S_0 = 100 + 10 = 110 \text{ units}$$

and the minimum cost for the entire period will be

$$F_3^0(S_3, x_3, x_2, x_1) = (109\tfrac{1}{2})^2 + 0 + (110\tfrac{1}{2})^2$$
$$+ 10\tfrac{1}{2} + (110)^2 + 10 = \$35,321$$

Compare to the policy of producing only the amount that each month demands:

$$\text{Total cost} = (100)^2 + 0 + (110)^2 + 0$$
$$+ (120)^2 + 0 = \$35,500$$

The optimum policy of producing $x_1^0 = 110$, $x_2^0 = 110\tfrac{1}{2}$, $x_3^0 = 109\tfrac{1}{2}$ incurs less cost.

SUMMARY

When the objectives of an organization cannot be represented by a linear function, the problem becomes a nonlinear programming problem. In the case of quadratic objective function, the simplex method can be salvaged and still be useful to find the optimum solution by maximizing a concave quadratic function or minimizing a convex quadratic function. Calculus methods may also solve some nonlinear programming problems, if the objective function satisfies certain conditions. If the conditions are not satisfied and/or the constraints are also nonlinear, then calculus methods and simplex methods cannot assure us of finding the optimum solution. Numerical methods or computer simulation methods may provide a better alternative.

In case the decisions are required on a continuing basis and the objective is to optimize or maximize total profit, not just for one stage but for multistages, the situation becomes a dynamic programming problem. Bellman's optimality condition then applies. The *backward induction method* is developed to solve this type of problem. (Another similar method is called the *forward induction method*.)

PROBLEMS

1. A firm is considering the production of two new products X and Y. The unit profit of each product depends on the quantity produced. For product X, the profit function is

$100q_x - q_x^2$, where q_x is the quantity of X produced. For product Y, the profit function is $80q_y - \frac{1}{2}q_y^2$, where q_y is the quantity of Y produced. In producing X and Y, two raw materials A and B are required. Each unit of X requires 1 unit of A and 2 units of B, and each unit of Y requires 2 units of A and $1\frac{1}{2}$ units of B. The firm can obtain only 100 units of A and 150 units of B. How many X and Y should the firm produce in order to maximize the total profit, and what is the total maximum profit? (Use calculus methods.)

2. Use calculus methods and LaGrange multiplier to find the optimum solution of the following problem.

$$\text{Max } \{f(x_1, x_2) = 2e^{-x_1} + 3e^{-x_2/2}\}$$

subject to

$$2x_1 + 3x_2 = 20$$
$$x_1, x_2 \geq 0$$

3. Does the following problem satisfy the Kuhn-Tucker condition? If so, find the optimum solution.

$$\text{Max } \{f(x_1, x_2) = e^{-2x_1} + 2e^{-x_2}\}$$

subject to

$$5x_1 + 2x_2 \leq 100$$
$$x_1, x_2 \geq 0$$

4. Solve the following quadratic programming problem by simplex algorithm.

$$\text{Max} \{f(x_1, x_2) = 2x_1 + 3x_2 + x_1x_2 - 4x_1^2 - 2x_2^2 + 20\}$$

subject to

$$x_1 + 2x_2 \leq 10$$
$$3x_1 + x_1 \leq 8$$
$$x_1, x_2 \geq 0$$

5. The marketing research group of a firm estimates the sales forecast for next 6 months as follows:

Months	1	2	3	4	5	6
Sales forecast	100	110	95	90	120	130

The current production level is 95 units per month. Change of level of production from one month to the next will cost the firm dollars which amounts to five times the difference in units produced. Any unit not sold in the month it is produced will cost the firm $10. What should be the firm's decision as to the quantity to produce in the six months in order to minimize total cost and at the same time to meet the demand? (Use the backward induction method.)

SELECTED REFERENCES

Bellman, Richard, and Stuart Dreyfus, *Applied Dynamic Programming*. Princeton, N. J.: Princeton University Press, 1962.

Carr, C. R., and C. W. Howe, *Quantitative Decision Procedures in Management and Economics*. New York: McGraw-Hill Book Company, 1964.

Graves, R. L., and P. Wolfe (eds.), *Recent Advances in Mathematical Programming*. New York: McGraw-Hill Book Company, 1963.

Hadley, G., *Nonlinear Programming and Dynamic Programming*. Reading, Mass.: Addison-Wesley Publishing Company, Inc., 1964.

Howard, Ronald A., *Dynamic Programming and Markov Processes*. Cambridge, Mass.: M.I.T. Press, 1960.

Elementary Game Theory

In a market economy, there is always competition. Its advantage is that it keeps the cost down and the price low. Ultimately, the benefit is passed on to the final consumers. However, during the process of competition the competitors have to watch every move that the others make and be able to choose the optimum strategy in order not to lose. Mathematical theory has been developed to describe some cases of this kind of conflicting interests. The theory is generally called *game theory*.

A set of terms is used in introducing the theory, here listed with their definitions.

1. *Game*: a set of rules for play.
2. *Play*: a single course of action chosen by a player from the list of courses available to him. The choices are assumed to be made simultaneously so that no player knows his opponent's choices until he is already committed to his own.
3. *Players*: a finite number of competitors.
4. *Strategy*: the player's method or plan of making his choices during play. It is his decision rule.
   (a) *Pure strategy*: a decision rule, in advance of all plays, always to choose a particular course of action.
   (b) *Mixed strategy*: a set of choices for all plays in advance according to certain probability distribution.

5. *Finite or infinite games*: If the number of plays in a game is definite, it is a finite game; otherwise it is an infinite game.

6. *Payoff*: the agreement about payments among players at the end of the game. The player's objective is assumed to be maximizing gain or minimizing loss.

7. *Zero-sum or nonzero-sum game*: If the agreement of the game is such that the sum of the payment among players is zero, then the game is a zero-sum game. Otherwise it is a nonzero-sum game. A zero-sum game does not create value, it just redistributes the original total value.

8. *Perfect or imperfect information*: When the player is informed of all the plays made by his competitors and the exact amount of payoffs associated with each play, he has perfect information. Otherwise he has only imperfect information.

TWO-PERSON ZERO-SUM GAME

When there are only two players and the sum of the payment among the players is zero, it is a two-person zero-sum game.

Example 1

If there are two players A and B, A has 2 choices and B has 3 choices for each play. Assume that for each alternative A and B chooses to play, B has to pay A the following amount:

		B 1	2	3
A	1	3	3	2
	2	−1	4	0

For a zero-sum game, B's payoff matrix necessarily
has to be

$$A$$

		1	2
	1	-3	1
B	2	-3	-4
	3	-2	0

which is the exact reverse of A's payoff matrix. Thus A's
payoff matrix provides sufficient information in considering the game's strategy.

With the information provided by A's payoff matrix,
and with both A and B assuming that the opponent will act
rationally (that is, A will maximize gain and B will minimize
loss), we can reach the following conclusions.

1. When A chooses the first alternative, A will expect B
   to choose the third alternative, since the loss for B
   will be 2 and it is the minimum loss among all B's
   alternatives.

2. When A chooses the second alternative, A will expect B to choose the first alternative, since the loss
   for B will be -1 (B gains 1) and it is the minimum
   loss among all B's alternatives.

3. Between the two alternatives, A will reason that if
   he chooses the first alternative, he will at least be
   sure to gain 2 from B. This approach is called the
   maximin strategy—that is, A tries to maximize the
   minimum gains expected in choosing all alternatives. (A may adopt other strategies; a more risky
   one is taking a gambler's approach, wherein A
   chooses the second alternative, expecting B to
   choose the second alternative which will make A
   gain 4. However, with the assumption of perfect
   information and with each side expecting the opponent to act in his own best interest, the maximin
   strategy should be adopted by A).

From player B's point of view, the following conclusions are reached.

1. When B chooses the first alternative, B will expect A to choose the first alternative, since 3 will be the maximum gain A can expect.

2. When B chooses the second alternative, B will expect A to choose the second alternative, since 4 will be the maximum gain A can expect.

3. When B chooses the third alternative, B will expect A to choose the first alternative, since 2 is the maximum gain A can expect.

4. Comparing the maximum gains that his opponent will get with respect to his choices, B will choose the third alternative. In that way A can gain only 2, which is the minimum among the three. For B, this is the *minimax strategy*—that is, B tries to minimize the maximum gains which may go to A.

In the above example, A will choose the first alternative and B will choose the third alternative. A's maximin strategy coincides with B's minimax strategy, the game will be stable and the value of the game will be 2 for each play. The condition is called a *saddle point* and the strategy a *pure strategy*:

$$\max_{i} \min_{j} a_{ij} = \min_{j} \max_{i} a_{ij}$$

Where i indicates row, j indicates column, and a_{ij} is the entry of A's payoff matrix.

Also, observe column 2 and column 3 of A's *payoff* matrix. All the *payoff* values in column 2 are greater than the respective values in column 3. Thus B has no cause to choose the second alternative, since the third alternative is always better than the second. We call the situation *dominance*—that is, column 3 dominates column 2, and the payoff matrix may be reduced to the following:

		B	
		1	3
A	1	3	2
	2	−1	0

Now if A's payoff matrix is changed to the following:

	B	
A	1	2
1	-1	2
2	3	0

the minimum value in row 1 is -1 and the minimum value in row 2 is 0, thus A will choose the second alternative. The maximum value in column 1 is 3, the maximum value in column 2 is 2, and thus B will choose the second alternative. However, when A perceives that B keeps on choosing the second alternative, he will change to the first alternative in order to gain 2. After a while when B discerns A's change of strategy, he will switch to the first alternative so that B will gain 1. Therefore the game is not stable, because no saddle point exists.

The problem may be solved by a set of linear equations. Let x_1 and x_2 be the probabilities of A's choosing first or second alternatives, y_1 and y_2 the probabilities of B's choosing first or second alternatives, and v be the expected value of the game. From A's point of view,

$$-1x_1 + 3x_2 \geq v$$
$$2x_1 + 0x_2 \geq v$$

From B's point of view,

$$-1y_1 + 2y_2 \leq v$$
$$3y_1 + 0y_2 \leq v$$

Also, by definition,

$$x_1 + x_2 = 1 \quad \text{and} \quad y_1 + y_2 = 1$$

By bringing together A's and B's conflicting interest, we get a set of linear equations

$$-x_1 + 3x_2 = v$$
$$2x_1 = v$$
$$-y_1 + 2y_2 = v$$
$$3y_1 = v$$

The solution is $y_1 = \frac{1}{3}, y_2 = \frac{2}{3}, x_1 = \frac{1}{2}, x_2 = \frac{1}{2}$, and $v = 1$.

The strategy is then: Half the time A should choose the first alternative and half the time choose the second alternative; B one-third of the time should choose the first alternative and two-thirds of the time should choose the second alternative. If they use this strategy and play a large number of times, the expected value of game will be 1 per each play—that is, each play A will gain 1 and B will lose 1 on the average. The above may be illustrated graphically.

Since

$$x_2 = 1 - x_1$$

The inequalities

$$-1x_1 + 3x_2 \geq v$$
$$2x_1 + 0x_2 \geq v$$

may be rewritten as

$$-x_1 + 3(1 - x_1) \geq v$$
$$2x_1 \geq v$$

or

$$4x_1 + v \leq 3$$
$$-2x_1 + v \leq 0$$

Graphically, they are as shown in Fig. 3-1.

The shaded area in the figure is the feasible area and the maximum attainable v for A is 1. The associated x_1

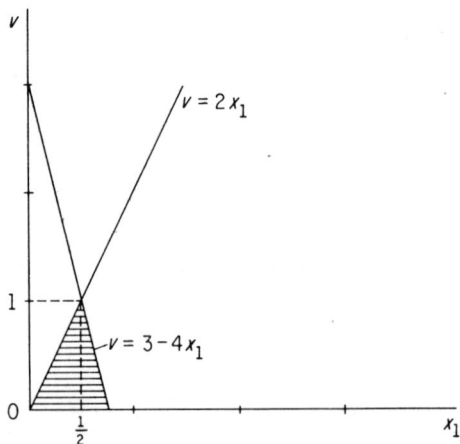

Fig. 3-1

is $\frac{1}{2}$. Thus $x_2 = 1 - x_1 = \frac{1}{2}$. And since $y_2 = 1 - y_1$, the inequalities

$$-1y_1 + 2y_2 \leq v$$
$$3y_1 + 0y_2 \leq v$$

may be rewritten as

$$-y_1 + 2(1 - y_1) \leq v$$
$$3y_1 \leq v$$

or

$$3y_1 + v \geq 2$$
$$-3y_1 + v \geq 0$$

The shaded area in Fig. 3-2 is the feasible region and the minimum attainable v for B is 1. The associated y_1 is $\frac{1}{3}$, and $y_2 = 1 - y_1 = \frac{2}{3}$.

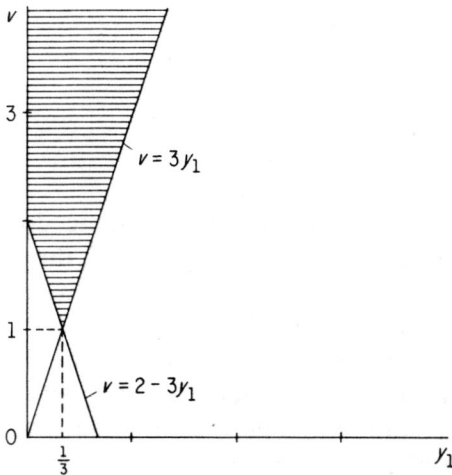

Fig. 3-2

A rule-of-thumb method of finding the mixed strategy of the players of a two-person zero-sum game is by taking the difference of the elements in the other row or column. And the ratio of this difference with the sum of the differences will yield the probabilities of the mixed strategy. For example,

$$B$$

$$3 - 0 = 3 \qquad x_1 = \frac{3}{3+3} = \frac{1}{2}$$

$$2 - (-1) = 3 \qquad x_2 = \frac{3}{3+3} = \frac{1}{2}$$

$$2 - 0 = 2 \qquad 3 - (-1) = 4$$

$$y_1 = \frac{2}{2+4} \qquad y_2 = \frac{4}{2+4}$$

$$= \frac{1}{3} \qquad\qquad = \frac{2}{3}$$

The value of the game is equal to the sum of the product of the probabilities and the elements of any respective row or column. Thus

$$v = \tfrac{1}{2}(-1) + \tfrac{1}{2}(3) = 1$$

GAMES IN EXTENSIVE FORM (WITH CONSECUTIVE MOVES)

When the two players in a game do not play at the same time, but one makes a play after the other has already made a play, the game is said to be in *extensive form*. There are two possible situations.

1. The player has perfect information.

Rule: A game in extensive form with perfect information is equivalent to a zero-sum game with a saddle point. For example, the payoff matrix of player P_1 in a two-person zero-sum game is as follows:

		$(11,21)$	$(11,22)$	$(12,21)$	$(12,22)$
P_1	1	-1	-1	1	1
	2	1	-1	1	-1

The matrix indicates that the second player P_2 may have four different strategies, namely $(11, 21)$, $(11, 22)$, $(12, 21)$, $(12, 22)$. However, in this case P_2 will always prefer the second strategy. That is, when he sees P_1 choose the first alternative he will choose the first alternative, and when he sees P_1 choose the second alternative he will choose the second alternative, so that P_2 always gains 1 in each play. Thus the strategy is a pure strategy, which may be represented by the following tree diagram.

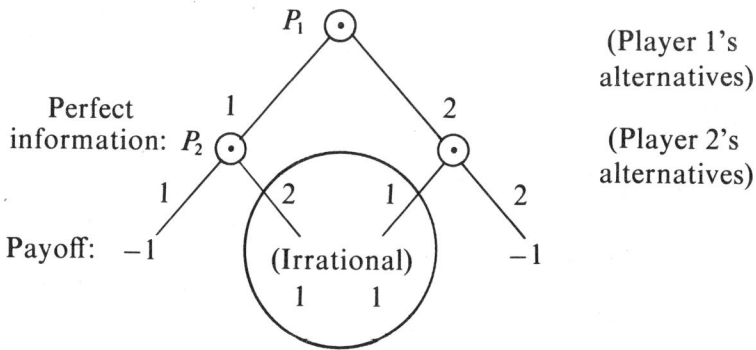

2. The player has imperfect information.

Rule: A game in extensive form with imperfect information is equivalent to a zero-sum game with mixed strategy. In the previous example, if P_2 does not have information on P_1, the diagram changes to the following:

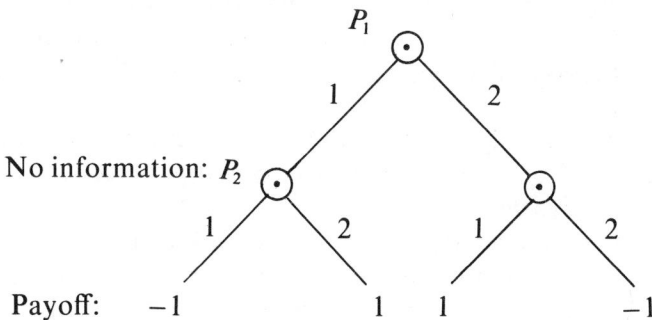

And the payoff matrix for P_1 becomes as follows:

$$P_2$$

		1	2
P_1	1	-1	1
	2	1	-1

which has no saddle point and P_2 should follow a mixed strategy of choosing the first alternative half the time and choosing the other alternative half the time in order to maximize his expected gain (or minimize his expected loss).

NONZERO-SUM GAMES

There are instances whence the sum of the payoffs of the players in a game does not equal to zero, the game then becomes a nonzero-sum game.

Using a two person's game as an illustration, the payoff matrix may be as follows:

$$B$$

		1	2
A	1	$(2, 2)$	$(-2, 4)$
	2	$(4, -2)$	$(0, 0)$

In each cell of the matrix, the first number is player A's payoff, the second number is player B's payoff. For example, if player A chooses the first alternative and player B chooses the second alternative, player A looses 2 and player B gains 4.

How the player's play the game depends on their objectives. The following are three possible objectives and their respective decisions.

1. Each player tries to maximize his own payoff but knows the other player is intelligent and rational, so both agree to maximize the sum of their payoffs. In this example, player A chooses the first alternative,

player B chooses the first alternative, and the total payoff is 4.

2. Each player tries to maximize his own payoff and expects the other player to make the wrong choice. Thus in the example player A chooses the second alternative, expecting player B to choose the first alternative, which will give player A a payoff of 4. Player B chooses the second alternative, expecting player A to choose the first alternative, which will give player B a payoff of 4.

3. Each player wants to ruin the other player and expects the other player to make mistakes. The objective may be defined as to maximize the difference of one player's payoff and the other player's payoff. In the example, player A chooses the second alternative, expecting player B to choose the first alternative, so that the difference of the payoffs will be 6. Player B chooses the second alternative, expecting player A to choose the first alternative, so that the difference of the payoffs will be 6.

Also, we may consider that for a two-person nonzero-sum game, there is a third person involved. For example, the choices and payoffs of A and B are given as follows:

\multicolumn{2}{c}{Choices}		\multicolumn{2}{c}{Payoffs}	
A	B	A	B
a_1	b_1	2	-1
a_1	b_2	-1	1
a_2	b_1	1	2
a_2	b_2	-4	-2

Then for A, the choices and payoffs may be represented by the regular two-person game matrix:

	b_1	b_2
a_1	2	-1
a_2	1	-4

which has a saddle point at (a_1, b_2) and the value of the game for A is -1. But for B the matrix is

A

	a_1	a_2
b_1	-1	2
b_2	1	-2

B

which has no saddle point. Let the probability of B choosing b_1 be y, than the probability of B choosing b_2 is $(1 - y)$.

$$y(-1) + (1 - y)(1) = y(2) + (1 - y)(-2)$$
$$y = \tfrac{1}{2}, (1 - y) = \tfrac{1}{2}$$

The value of the game for B then is $\tfrac{1}{2}(-1) + \tfrac{1}{2}(1) = 0$.

We may add a third player C to the game, thus transforming it to zero-sum. The payoff matrix for C is computed as the negative of the sum of A and B's payoffs:

B

	(a_1, b_1)	(a_1, b_2)	(a_2, b_1)	(a_2, b_2)
C c	-1	0	-3	6

The matrix has a saddle point (c, a_2, b_1) and the value of the game for C is -3. It also indicates that if A and B will cooperate—that is, A chooses a_2 and B chooses b_1; together they can win 3 per each play.

THE PRISONER'S DILEMMA

One of the applications of the two-person game is the *prisoner's dilemma*. The problem is formed in the following situation.

Two suspects alleged to be partners in a crime are arrested and placed in separate rooms to be interrogated. Each prisoner has two alternatives: (1) to confess to the crime the police are sure they have done, and (2) not to confess. If they both do not confess, they will be booked on some minor charges. If they both confess, they will be prosecuted but will be recommended for less than the most severe sentence. But if one confesses and the other does not, then the confessor will receive lenient treatment while the latter will get most severe punishment.

The game matrix may be set up as follows:

Prisoner B

Prisoner A	Confess	Not confess
Confess	2 years each	3 months for A, 5 years for B
Not confess	5 years for A, 3 months for B	6 months each.

Or, according to the evaluations of both prisoners, values may put in the matrix to make it a payoff matrix:

B

A	1	2
1	$(0,0)$	$(-3,2)$
2	$(2,-3)$	$(1,1)$

which indicates that if A chooses the first strategy and B also chooses the first strategy then both will gain nothing, but if they both choose the second strategy then both will gain 1. But if A chooses the first strategy and B chooses the second strategy, then A will lose 3 while B will gain 2, or if A choose the second strategy and B chooses the first strategy, then A will gain 2 while B will lose 3.

As we can see in this example, for A the second strategy (not confess) is always better than the first one (dominance—because $2 > 0$, $1 > -3$) and for B the second strategy (not confess) is also always better than the first one ($2 > 0$, $1 > -3$). Thus, if both A and B are rational (*cooperative* is the adjective generally used in this kind of problem), both of them should stick to the second strategy —that is, not confess. However, human behavior indicates in some cases that one prisoner might try to take advantage of his partner's loyalty and decide to confess, or in the extreme case both may decide to confess. So the prisoner's dilemma becomes an interesting problem on which to do empirical experiments, such as the two storeowner's decisions on whether to maintain their regular prices or launch a price war or similar action.

Extending the two-person game to more-than-two-person games will make the situation much more complicated, since besides competition we now have possibility of collusion among some of the players.

Example 2

Three players P_1, P_2, and P_3 each has two alternatives and the payoffs are as follows:

P_1's alternatives

P_2's alternatives

P_3's alternatives

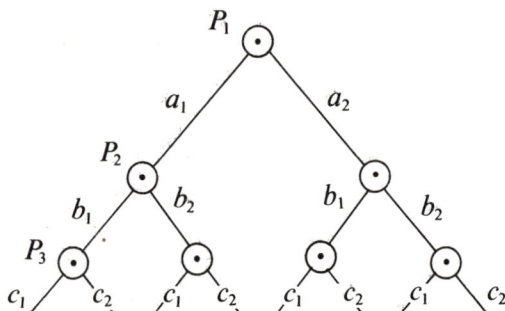

Payoffs:

P_1	2	−1	−1	0	3	−2	0	−1
P_2	1	1	−2	2	−2	0	−1	1
P_3	−3	0	3	−2	−1	2	1	0

Case 1. P_2 and P_3 are colluded.

The payoff matrix for P_1 is as follows:

		$P_2 P_3$			
		$(b_1 c_1)$	$(b_1 c_2)$	$(b_2 c_1)$	$(b_2 c_2)$
P_1	a_1	2	−1	−1	0
	a_2	3	−2	0	−1

The solution has a saddle point in which P_1 chooses a_1, P_2 chooses b_1, and P_3 chooses c_2. The value of the game for P_1 is −1 for P_2 and P_3 together is 1.

Case 2. P_1 and P_2 are colluded.

The payoff matrix for P_3 is as follows:

$$P_1 P_2$$

	$(a_1 b_1)$	$(a_1 b_2)$	$(a_2 b_1)$	$(a_2 b_2)$	
c_1	-3	3	-1	1	$\frac{1}{4}$
c_2	0	-2	2	0	$\frac{3}{4}$
	$\frac{5}{8}$	$\frac{3}{8}$			

(P_3 labels the left row axis.)

For P_1 and P_2, strategies $(a_2 b_1)$ and $(a_2 b_2)$ are inferior to (dominated by) strategy $(a_1 b_1)$. However, no saddle point exists,·and the solution is a mixed strategy with P_3 playing c_1, one-quarter of the time and playing c_2, three-quarters of the time. P_1, P_2 choose $(a_1 b_1)$ $\frac{5}{8}$ of the time and $(a_1 b_2)$ $\frac{3}{8}$ of the time. The value of the game for P_3 is $-\frac{3}{4}$ and for P_1 and P_2 together is $\frac{3}{4}$.

Case 3. P_1 and P_3 are colluded.

The payoff matrix for P_2 is as follows:

$$P_1 P_3$$

	$(a_1 c_1)$	$(a_1 c_2)$	$(a_2 c_1)$	$(a_2 c_2)$	
b_1	1	1	-2	0	$\frac{1}{4}$
b_2	-2	2	-1	1	$\frac{3}{4}$
	$\frac{1}{4}$		$\frac{3}{4}$		

(P_2 labels the left row axis.)

For P_1 and P_3, strategies $(a_1 c_2)$ and $(a_2 c_2)$ are inferior to strategy $(a_2 c_1)$. The solution is a mixed strategy with P_2 playing b_1 one-quarter of the time and playing b_2 three-quarters of the time. P_1, P_3 choose $(a_1 c_1)$ one-quarter of the time and $(a_2 c_1)$ three-quarters of the time. The value of the game for P_2 is $-1\frac{1}{4}$, and for P_1 and P_3 together is $1\frac{1}{4}$.

SUMMARY

Game theory is used to analyze the competitions among business firms and other organizations. The simplest form of game is the two-person zero-sum game, which assumes that there are only two players in the game and that their interests directly conflict with each other. One player's gain is the others' loss, and this termination is called the payoff. Each player has several choices to play the game and each combination of choices gives one payoff. The aim of the game is to find the optimum strategy for both players to maximize gain or minimize loss. If two optimum strategies coincide, it is called a saddle point or *pure strategy*. If they do not coincide, the strategy is to play different alternatives with assigned probabilities, called *mixed strategy*. If the game goes on forever, the mixed strategy will bring maximum expected gain or minimum expected loss per play. When one player's gain does not equal other's loss, the game becomes nonzero-sum game.

Extending the two-person game to more than two persons, we encounter the possibility of collusion among the players besides competition. For example, in the three-person game it is possible for any two players to gang together against the third player.

More complicated game situations are difficult to solve by analytical methods. Monte Carlo or other computer-simulation methods (discussed in Chapter 9) may be used to compare alternative strategies.

PROBLEMS

1. Given the payoff matrix of *A* as the following, determine the minimax strategy for *A* and maximin strategy for *B*, and the value of the game.

		B 1	2	3
A	1	4	3	2
	2	7	2	1
	3	5	4	6

2. Find the solution of the following game.

$$B$$

		1	2	3
A	1	1	3	9
	2	6	5	2

3. A and B play a game in which each player shows either one or two fingers. If the sum of the fingers shown is even, B pays A a dollar. If the sum is odd, A pays B eighty cents. Find the best strategy for each player and the value of the game.

4. At a road intersection are two gasoline stations. Each morning the station manager set the price of the gasoline for the day. He may set the price at the normal price or set it five cents per gallon lower. If both set the price at the normal price level, station A will earn a daily profit of $100 and station B $150. If station A lowers the price it will earn $100 more and station B will earn only $75. If station B lowers the price, station B will earn $100 more and station A will earn only $25. If both stations lower the price, station A will earn only $75 and station B $100. What will be the optimum strategies for each station manager?

5. The alternatives and payoffs of three players A, B, and C are as follows:

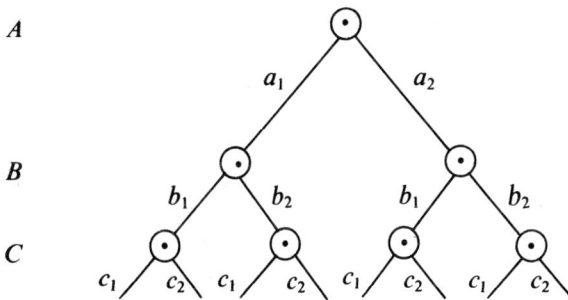

Payoffs								
A	3	-1	2	4	1	2	0	-1
B	2	-2	0	-1	1	-3	-3	-1
C	-5	3	-2	-3	-2	1	3	2

Analyze their strategies and respective values of the game.

6. A couple goes on a camping trip. The problem occurs when they need to choose a camping site. The husband likes high altitude but the wife prefers low altitude. They both agree that they should camp at one of the intersections of the roads. Assume the roads go either north-south or east-west, and that the husband makes the choice of one of the east-west roads and the wife makes the choice of one of the north-south roads. The altitude of all the intersections are as follows:

North-South Roads

		1	2	3	4
	1	750	200	550	100
East-West	2	200	200	300	400
Roads	3	500	300	400	400
	4	300	200	150	650

What should be the strategies of the husband and the wife?

7. The choices and payoffs of a two-person game is given below.

Choices		Payoffs	
A	B	A	B
a_1	b_1	2	1
a_1	b_2	-1	1
a_2	b_1	1	0
a_2	b_2	-2	-1

What is the solution of the game?

8. In a nonzero-sum game with the payoffs for the players as follows:

		B	
		1	2
A	1	(10, 10)	(80, 0)
	2	(0, 100)	(5, 5)

What possible strategies can the players take? Discuss the motivation and consequences.

9. Two firms producing the same product are competing in n sales markets. Assume that the potential demand in the sales markets are known to be D_i, $(i = 1, 2 \ldots, n)$ and that the two firms' sales promotion budgets are K_1 and K_2 respectively. If the objective of both firms is to maximize sales, and if sales are expected to be in proportion to the amount of promotion expenditures, how can this problem be solved in a gaming structure, and what should be the strategies of the firms?

10. Two grocery chains A and B are considering building new stores in the triangular area formed by three cities. The distance between the cities and the population distribution of the triangular area is indicated by the diagram.

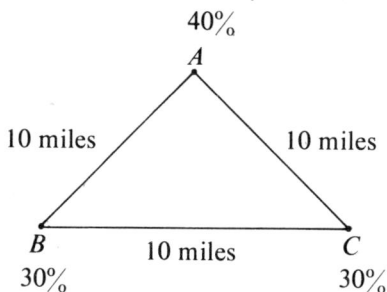

If store A is closer to a city than store B, store A will get 70 percent of the business of the city. If store B is closer, store B will get 60 percent of the business of the city. If they are equal distance, store A and store B's share of the business of the city will be 55 and 45 percent respectively. Set up the problem into a two-person game matrix. Find optimal strategies for A and B store to choose sites and the value of the game.

SELECTED REFERENCES

Blackwell, D., and M. A. Girshick, *Theory of Games and Statistical Decisions.* New York: John Wiley & Sons, Inc., 1954.

Luce, R. D., and H. Raifta, *Games and Decisions.* New York: John Wiley & Sons, Inc., 1957.

McKinsey, J. C. C., *Introduction to the Theory of Games.* New York: McGraw-Hill Book Company, 1952.

Vajda, S., *The Theory of Games and Linear Programming.* New York: John Wiley & Sons, Inc., 1956.

Von Neumann, J., and O. Morgenstern, *Theory of Games and Economic Behavior.* 2d ed.   Princeton, N. J.: Princeton University Press, 1947.

chapter 4

Classical Statistics

In search for truth in a universe we need to collect data. After proper data is collected, we need to arrange or classify it in such a way that it will reveal the true characteristics of the universe which we are interested in learning. Also, we need to inform others of our discoveries. At the same time we expect that the others will inform us of their discoveries, too. This mutual exchange of information will facilitate our joint effort in the search for knowledge. This section will introduce statistical methods of describing information.

Suppose we want to describe the age of the employees of a firm. First thing we will mention may be the average age of the employees—say thirty years. This will give some idea about the central location of the age of the employees of the firm. However, this does not really give enough information for others to have an unmistakable notion about the age of the employees. The employees may *all* be thirty years old, or half of them may be twenty years old and the other half forty years old. There are many other combinations which will result in an average employee age of thirty years. So the second parameter we will use to describe the age of the employees should indicate the *variation* of the individual employee's age from the average age. Some of them may exceed the average age, and then we will have a positive difference. Some of them may be below the average, and then we will have a negative difference. We may use the sum of the square of differences divided by the number of employees as a measure of the variation. (The square will make all terms positive, so that the negative difference will not offset the positive difference, and when divided by the number of employees will enable us to compare the age of employees of firms with different numbers of employees.)

But we still have not given the exact information. The exact information will contain a list of all the employees and their respective ages. However, if the list is unorganized, the information may not be immediately meaningful. So we may list the relevant ages in ascending order starting with the youngest age, say 20, and moving up to the oldest age, say 65, and counting the number of employees whose ages fall into each age bracket. The result is a frequency table. The age brackets may be of one-year intervals, five-year intervals, ten-year intervals, or other classifications which may fit our research purpose.

The following are different measures of central location and variation.

MEASURES OF CENTRAL LOCATION

1. *Median:* the middle measurement after the measurements have been arranged in order of magnitude. If the total number of the measurements is an even number, then the median is half of the sum of the two middle measurements. For example, if we have the following measurements already arranged in ascending order:

1   5   10   14   17   21

$$\text{Median} = \frac{10 + 14}{2} = 12$$

2. *Mode:* the measure with the maximum frequency, if there is one. There may be more than one mode in a frequency distribution. For example, in the following frequency distribution

Variable	Frequency
1	5
3	10

5	18
7	23
9	12

the mode is 7, since it has the maximum frequency of 23.

3. *Mean:* the measure of central location. It is computed by summing up all the measurements, then dividing by the number of measurements:

$$\overline{X} = \frac{\sum_{i=1}^{N} X_i}{N}$$

MEASURES OF VARIATION

1. *Range:* the difference between the largest and smallest measurements of the entire population. The range is very easy to compute. However, when extreme values are included in the sample, it may give a false impression of the variation.

2. *Mean deviation:* the sum of the absolute difference of each individual measurement with the mean divided by the number of measurements:

$$\frac{\sum_{i=1}^{N} |X_i - \overline{X}|}{N}$$

3. *Variance and standard deviation:* the difference of each individual measurement with the mean is squared before they are summed up and divided by the number of measurements, so that we obtain a measure of variation called *variance:*

$$\text{Variance} = \frac{\sum_{i=1}^{N} (X_i - \overline{X})^2}{N}$$

The square root of variance is called *standard deviation* (S.D.):

$$\text{S.D.} = \frac{\sum_{i=1}^{N} (X_i - \overline{X})^2}{N}$$

Because of certain desirable theoretical properties possessed by mean and variance (or standard deviation) which make them more suitable for statistical analysis, they are used more often as measures of location and variation.

THEORETICAL FREQUENCY DISTRIBUTIONS

Some of the actual frequency distributions, when the number of observations or measurements increases infinitely, will approach some mathematical models called *theoretical frequency distributions.* Because the properties of the theoretical distributions have been explored and discovered, it would be convenient for us if we could find a theoretical distribution which would fit our empirical data. In this section we will introduce some well-known theoretical distributions.

1. Discrete distributions, where the random variable takes only discrete or integer values.

(a) *Uniform distribution,* where the probabilities of the random variable assuming the values of a given set of integers are all equal. If the given set of integers are $x = 0, 1, 2, \ldots, n$, the probability distribution is

$$f(x) = \frac{1}{n + 1}$$

The mean is

$$u = \sum_{x=0}^{n} xf(x) = \sum_{x=0}^{n} x \left(\frac{1}{n + 1}\right)$$

$$= \frac{0 + 1 + 2 \cdots + n}{n + 1}$$

$$= \frac{n(n + 1)/2}{n + 1}$$

$$= \frac{n}{2}$$

and the variance is

$$\sigma^2 = \sum_{x=0}^{n} (x - u)^2 f(x)$$

$$= \sum_{x=0}^{n} x^2 f(x) - 2u \sum_{x=0}^{n} xf(x) + u^2 \sum_{x=0}^{n} f(x)$$

$$= \frac{0^2 + 1^2 + 2^2 \cdots + n^2}{n + 1} - 2 \left(\frac{n}{2}\right)\left(\frac{n}{2}\right) + \left(\frac{n}{2}\right)^2$$

$$= \frac{n(n + 1)(2n + 1)}{6(n + 1)} - \left(\frac{n}{2}\right)^2$$

$$= \frac{n(n + 2)}{12} = \frac{n^2}{12} + \frac{n}{6}$$

(b) *Binomial distribution.* The distribution is origi-
nated from Bernoulli trials, which are repeated
trials with two possible outcomes. If we define
one outcome as success with probability of p and
the other outcome as failure with probability of
q, then $q = 1 - p$. And for each experiment,
if the number of trials is n, the probability
distribution is

$$f(x) = \binom{n}{x} p^x (1 - p)^{n-x} \quad \text{where} \quad \binom{n}{x} = \frac{n!}{x!(n - x)!}$$

The mean is

$$u = \sum_{x=0}^{n} xf(x) = \sum_{x=0}^{n} x \frac{n!}{x!(n - x)!} p^x (1 - p)^{n-x}$$

$$= \sum_{x=0}^{n} \frac{n!}{(x - 1)!(n - x)!} p^x (1 - p)^{n-x}$$

$$= np \sum_{x-1=0}^{n-1} \frac{(n - 1)!}{(x - 1)![(n - 1) - (x - 1)]!}$$
$$\cdot p^{x-1} (1 - p)^{(n-1)-(x-1)}$$

$$= np \quad \left[\text{since} \sum_{x=0}^{n} f(x) = 1 \text{ and } \sum_{x-1=0}^{n-1} f(x - 1) = 1\right]$$

and the variance is

$$\sigma^2 = \sum_{x=0}^{n} (x - u)^2 f(x)$$

$$= \sum_{x=0}^{n} x^2 f(x) - 2u \sum_{x=0}^{n} xf(x) + u^2 \sum_{x=0}^{n} f(x)$$

$$= \sum_{x=0}^{n} x^2 f(x) - (np)^2$$

but

$$x(x - 1) = x^2 - x \quad \text{and} \quad x^2 = x(x - 1) + x$$

Thus

$$\sum_{x=0}^{n} x^2 f(x) = \sum_{x=0}^{n} x(x - 1)f(x) + \sum_{x=0}^{n} xf(x)$$

$$= \sum_{x=0}^{n} x(x - 1) \frac{n!}{x!(n - x)!} \cdot p^x(1 - p)^{n-x} + np$$

$$= n(n - 1)p^2$$

$$\cdot \sum_{x-2=0}^{n-2} \frac{(n - 2)!}{(x - 2)!(n - 2) - (x - 2)!} \cdot p^{x-2}(1 - p)^{(n-2)-(x-2)} + np$$

$$= n(n - 1)p^2 + np$$

Since

$$\sum_{x-2=0}^{n-2} f(x - 2) = 1$$

therefore

$$\sigma^2 = n(n - 1)p^2 + np - n^2 p^2$$
$$= n^2 p^2 - np^2 + np - n^2 p^2$$
$$= np(1 - p)$$

(c) *Poisson distribution.* When the number of Bernoulli trials is very large, and the probability of success is very small ($n \to \infty$, $p \to 0$), the binomial distribution regresses to a distribution called the *Poisson distribution:*

$$f(x) = \frac{e^{-\lambda}\lambda^x}{x!}$$

where $\lambda = np$. Substituting $p = \lambda/n$ in the binomial distribution, we obtain

$$f(x) = \frac{n!}{x!(n - x)!}\left(\frac{\lambda}{n}\right)^x \left(1 - \frac{\lambda}{n}\right)^{n-x}$$

$$= \left(\frac{\lambda^x}{x!}\right)\left(1 - \frac{\lambda}{n}\right)^n$$

$$\cdot \frac{n(n - 1) \cdots (n - x + 1)}{n^x}\left(1 - \frac{\lambda}{n}\right)^{-x}$$

When $n \rightarrow \infty$,

$$\frac{n(n - 1) \cdots (n - x + 1)}{n^x}$$

$$= \frac{n}{n} \cdot \frac{n - 1}{n} \cdots \frac{n - x + 1}{n} = 1$$

and

$$\left(1 - \frac{\lambda}{n}\right)^{-x} = 1$$

Thus

$$f(x) = \frac{\lambda^x}{x!} \left(1 - \frac{\lambda}{n}\right)^n$$

From Taylor's expansion, we know that

$$e^x = \lim_{n \to \infty} \left(1 + \frac{x}{n}\right)^n$$

For the Poisson distribution the function is therefore

$$f(x) = \frac{\lambda^x}{x!} e^{-\lambda}$$

$$= \frac{e^{-\lambda} \lambda^x}{x!} \qquad x = 0, 1, \ldots, \infty$$

The mean is

$$u = \sum_{x=0}^{\infty} x f(x)$$

$$= \sum_{x=0}^{\infty} x \frac{e^{-\lambda} \lambda^x}{x!}$$

$$= \lambda \sum_{x-1=0}^{\infty} \frac{e^{-\lambda} \lambda^{x-1}}{(x - 1)!}$$

Since $\Sigma f(x) = 1$,

$$u = \lambda$$

The variance is

$$\sigma^2 = \sum_{x=0}^{\infty} (x - u)^2 f(x)$$

$$= \sum_{x=0}^{\infty} (x^2 - 2ux + u^2) f(x)$$

$$= \sum_{x=0}^{\infty} x^2 f(x) - u^2$$

$$= \sum_{x=0}^{\infty} x(x-1)f(x) + \sum_{x=0}^{\infty} xf(x) - \lambda^2$$

$$= \sum_{x=0}^{\infty} x(x-1)\frac{e^{-\lambda}\lambda^x}{x!} + \lambda - \lambda^2$$

$$= \lambda^2 \sum_{x-2=0}^{\infty} \frac{e^{-\lambda}\lambda^{x-2}}{(x-2)!} + \lambda - \lambda^2$$

$$= \lambda^2 + \lambda - \lambda^2 = \lambda$$

Note that for Poisson distribution the variance is equal to the mean and for binomial distribution, because $0 \le (1-p) \le 0$, thus generally the variance is smaller than the mean.

(d) *Geometric distribution.* The random variable of a geometric distribution may be viewed as the number of trials required to get the first success. The function is thus

$$f(x) = p(1-p)^{x-1} \qquad x = 1, 2, \ldots, \infty$$

The mean is

$$u = \sum_{x=1}^{\infty} xf(x) = \sum_{x=1}^{\infty} xp(1-p)^{x-1}$$

$$= 1 \cdot p(1-p)^0 + 2p(1-p) + 3p(1-p)^2$$
$$+ \cdots + np(1-p)^{n-1} + \cdots$$

$$= p[1 + 2(1-p) + 3(1-p)^2 + \cdots$$
$$+ n(1-p)^{n-1} + \cdots]$$

Let

$$S = 1 + 2q + 3q^2 + \cdots + nq^{n-1}$$
$$qS = q + 2q^2 + \cdots + (n-1)q^{n-1} + nq^n$$
$$S - qS = 1 + q + q^2 + \cdots + q^{n-1} \qquad - nq^n$$
$$= \frac{1 - q^{n-2}}{1 - q} - nq^n$$

When $q < 1$ and $n \to \infty$; q^n and $q^{n-2} \to 0$,

$$S - qS = \frac{1}{1-q}$$

$$S = \frac{1}{(1 - q)^2}$$

Thus

$$u = p \, \frac{1}{p^2}$$

$$= \frac{1}{p}$$

The variance is

$$\sigma^2 = \sum_{x=1}^{\infty} (x - u)^2 f(x) = \sum_{x=1}^{\infty} x^2 f(x) - u^2$$
$$= 1^2 \cdot p(1 - p)^0 + 2^2 p(1 - p) + 3^2 p(1 - p)^2$$
$$+ \cdots + n^2 p (1 - p)^{n-1} + \cdots - u^2$$
$$= p[1 + 4(1 - p) + 9(1 - p)^2 + \cdots$$
$$+ n^2(1 - p)^{n-1} + \cdots] - u^2$$

Let

$$S = 1 + 4q + 9q^2 + \cdots + n^2 q^{n-1}$$
$$qS = q + 4q^2 + \cdots + (n - 1)^2 q^{n-1} + n^2 q^n$$
$$S - qS = 1 + 3q + 5q^2 + \cdots$$
$$+ (2n - 1) q^{n-1} - n^2 q^n$$
$$= (2 - 1) + (4 - 1) q + (6 - 1) q^2 + \cdots$$
$$+ (2n - 1) q^{n-1} - n^2 q^n$$
$$= 2(1 + 2q + 3q^2 + \cdots + nq^{n-1})$$
$$- (1 + q + q^2 + \cdots + q^{n-1}) - n^2 q^n$$
$$= 2 \, \frac{1}{(1 - q)^2} - \left(\frac{1 - q^{n-2}}{1 - q} \right) - n^2 q^n$$

When $q < 1$ and $n \rightarrow \infty$; q^n and $q^{n-2} \rightarrow 0$,

$$S - qS = \frac{2}{(1 - q)^2} - \frac{1}{1 - q}$$

$$S = \frac{2}{(1 - q)^3} - \frac{1}{(1 - q)^2}$$

Therefore

$$\sigma^2 = p\left(\frac{2}{p^3} - \frac{1}{p^2} \right) - \left(\frac{1}{p} \right)^2$$

$$= \frac{2}{p^2} - \frac{1}{p} - \frac{1}{p^2}$$

$$= \frac{1 - p}{p^2}$$

There are other more complicated theoretical discrete distributions, such as the *hypogeometric distribution*,

$$f(x) = \frac{\binom{Np}{x}\binom{Nq}{n-x}}{\binom{N}{n}} \qquad u = np \qquad \sigma^2 = np(1-p)\left(\frac{N-n}{N-1}\right)$$

where N is the size of a finite population, n the sample size, p the probability of success, and q the probability of failure.

There is also the *negative binomial distribution:*

$$f(x) = \binom{r + x - 1}{x} p^r (1 - p)^x$$

which indicates the number of failures (x) before r successes are reached. If set $p = \alpha/+1$,

$$u = \frac{r}{\alpha} \qquad \sigma^2 = \frac{r}{\alpha} + \frac{r}{\alpha^2}$$

The detailed discussion of their characteristics may be found in advanced mathematics text or articles.

2. Continuous distributions where the random variable may take any real values.

(a) *The rectangular distribution*, similar to the uniform distribution only its random variable may take any real values:

$$f(x) = \frac{1}{a} \quad \text{range of } x, \text{ from 0 to } a$$

The means is

$$u = \int_0^a xf(x)\, dx = \frac{1}{a} \int_0^a x\, dx = \frac{1}{a} \cdot \left.\frac{x^2}{2}\right|_0^a$$

$$= \frac{1}{a}\left(\frac{a^2}{2}\right) = \frac{a}{2}$$

The variance is

$$\sigma^2 = \int_0^a (x - u)^2 f(x)\, dx$$

$$= \int_0^a x^2 f(x)\, dx - 2u \int_0^a xf(x)\, dx$$

$$+ u^2 \int_0^a f(x)\, dx$$

$$= \frac{1}{a} \int_0^a x^2\, dx - u^2$$

$$= \frac{1}{a} \left(\frac{x^3}{3} \Big|_0^a \right) - \left(\frac{a}{2} \right)^2 = \frac{a^2}{3} - \frac{a^2}{4} = \frac{a^2}{12}$$

(b) *The exponential distribution*, where the random variable may be viewed as the intervals between consecutive Poisson variates:

$$f(x) = ae^{-ax} \quad a > 0 \text{ and range of } x, \text{ from } 0 \text{ to } \infty$$

The mean is

$$u = \int_0^\infty xf(x)\, dx = \int_0^\infty xae^{-ax}\, dx$$

$$= - \int_0^\infty xde^{-ax}$$

$$= - \left[xe^{-ax} \Big|_0^\infty - \int_0^\infty e^{-ax}\, dx \right]$$

$$= 0 + \frac{1}{-a} e^{-ax} \Big|_0^\infty$$

$$= \frac{1}{a}$$

The variance is

$$\sigma^2 = \int_0^\infty (x - u)^2 f(x)\, dx$$

$$= \int_0^\infty x^2 f(x)\, dx - u^2 \int_0^\infty f(x)\, dx$$

$$= \int_0^\infty x^2 ae^{-ax}\, dx - \frac{1}{a^2}$$

$$= - \int x^2 de^{-ax} - \frac{1}{a^2}$$

$$= - \left[x^2 e^{-ax} \Big|_0^\infty - \int_0^\infty e^{-ax}\, dx^2 \right] - \frac{1}{a^2}$$

$$= 0 + 2\int_0^\infty xe^{-ax}\,dx - \frac{1}{a^2}$$

$$= -\frac{2}{a}\int_0^\infty xde^{-ax} - \frac{1}{a^2}$$

$$= \frac{2}{a}\cdot\frac{1}{a} - \frac{1}{a^2}$$

$$= \frac{1}{a^2}$$

(c) *Normal distribution.* When the n is large and p is not small, a binomial distribution may be approximated by a normal distribution. The function form is

$$f(x) = \frac{1}{\sigma\sqrt{2\pi}}e^{-\frac{1}{2}\frac{(x-u)^2}{\sigma^2}}$$

where u is the mean and σ^2 is the variance, and the range of x is from $-\infty$ to ∞.

Moment-Generating Function

Since the discussion of normal distribution and small sample distributions involves the use of moment-generating functions, it will be appropriate to introduce these here. For a continuous variable, the function is defined as

$$M_y(t) = \int_{-\infty}^\infty e^{yt}f(y)\,dy$$

and the properties of the function are

(1) $M_{cf(y)}(t) = M_{f(y)}(ct)$

(2) $M_{f(y)+c}(t) = e^{ct}M_{f(y)}(t)$

where c is a constant.

The first moment of a probability function is the mean and may be found by taking first derivative of the moment-generating function with respect to t and let t approach zero. In the case of the normal distribution, let

$$y = \frac{x-u}{\sigma}\qquad dy = \frac{1}{\sigma}\,dx$$

$$M_y(t) = \int_{-\infty}^{\infty} e^{yt} \frac{1}{\sqrt{2\pi}} e^{-\frac{y^2}{2}} dy$$

$$= \int_{-\infty}^{\infty} \frac{1}{\sqrt{2\pi}} e^{-\frac{y^2}{2}+yt} dy$$

$$= \int_{-\infty}^{\infty} \frac{1}{\sqrt{2\pi}} e^{-\left(\frac{y^2}{2}-2\left(\frac{y}{\sqrt{2}}\right)\left(\frac{t}{\sqrt{2}}\right)+\frac{t^2}{2}\right)+\frac{t^2}{2}} dy$$

$$= \int_{-\infty}^{\infty} \frac{1}{\sqrt{2\pi}} e^{-\frac{1}{2}(y-t)^2+\frac{t^2}{2}} dy$$

$$= \frac{e^{\frac{t^2}{2}}}{\sqrt{2\pi}} \int_{-\infty}^{\infty} e^{-\frac{1}{2}(y-t)^2} dy$$

Since in calculus we found

$$\int_{-\infty}^{\infty} e^{-\frac{1}{2}z^2} dz = \sqrt{2\pi}$$

Let

$$z = y - t \qquad dz = dy$$

$$M_y(t) = \frac{e^{\frac{t^2}{2}}}{\sqrt{2\pi}} \sqrt{2\pi} = e^{\frac{t^2}{2}}$$

$$M_{(x-u)/\sigma}(t) = e^{\frac{t^2}{2}}$$

Treating $1/\sigma$ as a constant, we get

$$M_{x-u}\left(\frac{t}{\sigma}\right) = e^{\frac{t^2}{2}}$$

$$M_{x-u}(t) = e^{\frac{\sigma^2 t^2}{2}}$$

Treating $(-u)$ as a constant, we get

$$M_x(t) = e^{ut+1/2\sigma^2 t^2}$$

$$\text{Mean} = \frac{dM_x(t)}{dt}\Big|_{t=0} = (e^{ut+1/2\sigma^2 t^2})(u + \sigma^2 t)\big|_{t=0}$$

$$= u$$

The second moment is the variance and may be found by taking the second derivative of the moment-generating function $M_{x-u}(t)$ with respect to t and let t approach zero:

$$\text{Variance} = \left. \frac{d^2 M_{x-u}(t)}{dt^2} \right|_{t=0}$$

$$= \left. \frac{d}{dt} \left[e^{\frac{\sigma^2 t^2}{2}} \sigma^2 t \right] \right|_{t=0}$$

$$= \left. \left[e^{\frac{\sigma^2 t^2}{2}} (\sigma^2) + (\sigma^2 t) e^{\frac{\sigma^2 t^2}{2}} (\sigma^2 t) \right] \right|_{t=0}$$

$$= \sigma^2$$

When $u = 0$, $\sigma^2 = 1$, normal distribution becomes the standard normal distribution, its variable is usually denoted by z:

$$f(z) = \frac{1}{\sqrt{2\pi}} e^{-\frac{1}{2}z^2}$$

Central Limit Theorem

A theorem which is closely related to standard normal distribution is the *central limit theorem*. If x has a distribution with mean u and standard distribution σ for which the moment-generating function exists, then the variable $z = (\bar{x} - u)/(\sigma/\sqrt{n})$ has a distribution that approaches the standard normal distribution as n becomes infinite.

This theorem has important applications in the estimation of the parameters of a population, when only sample observations or values are available.

ESTIMATION

Estimation of Population Mean u

Let x = value of a random variable; $\bar{x}$ = average of sample values; n = sample size; and σ^2 = population variance.

If $n = 25$, $\sigma = 20$, and $x = 170$, the interval estimate of u with 95 percent confidence is

$$\bar{x} \pm z_{.05} \frac{\sigma}{\sqrt{n}} = 170 \pm 1.96 \left(\frac{20}{\sqrt{25}} \right)$$

$$= 170 \pm 7.84$$

where 1.96 indicates the probability of .95 that a normal variable will assume some value within 1.96 standard deviation of its mean.

Now if we want to control the accuracy of the estimate in an interval of ($\bar{x} \pm 5$), then the required sample size will be

$$1.96 \, \frac{20}{\sqrt{n}} = 5,$$

$$n = 62 \, (\text{approx.})$$

Estimation of Population Proportion p

Let n = sample size; x = a random variable representing the number of successes in n; $p' = x/n$, the sample proportion; and $\sigma^2 = npq$, according to the binomial distribution.

If $n = 400$ (large sample), $x = 80$, and $p' = 80/400 = .2$. When the binomial distribution is approximated by standard normal distribution, we get

$$z = \frac{x - u}{\sigma} = \frac{x - np}{\sqrt{npq}} = \frac{(x/n) - p}{\sqrt{pq/n}}$$

With large sample, p may be substituted by p'. The interval estimate of p with 95 percent of confidence is thus

$$p' \pm z_{.05} \sqrt{\frac{p'q'}{n}} = .2 \pm 1.96 \sqrt{\frac{(.2)(.8)}{400}}$$

$$= .2 \pm .0392$$

Now if the interval is allowed to be ($p \pm .05$), then the required sample size is

$$1.96 \sqrt{\frac{(.2)(.8)}{n}} = .05$$

$$n = 246 \, (\text{approx.})$$

TESTING HYPOTHESES

In many instances we do not know the true value of a parameter, such as mean or proportion, so we make guesses or *hypotheses*. Hypotheses may differ. If we have two different hypotheses about the true value of a parameter we need some way of testing them to find out which has the greater probability of being true.

When we test a hypothesis H_0 against an alternative hypothesis H_1 based on sample observations, two types of error may occur:

Facts Decisions	H_0 True	H_1 True
H_0 accepted H_1 accepted	Correct decision Type I error	Type II error Correct decision

The probability of making a Type I error is called α, and the probability of making a Type II error is called β. Though we cannot eliminate the errors completely, we may control the probabilities of making these errors by taking an appropriate number of sample observations and by setting appropriate critical regions.

Testing a Mean

A hypothesis H_0 of a population mean is to be tested against an alternative hypothesis H_1:

$$H_0: \quad u = 10(u_0)$$

$$H_1: \quad u = 12(u_1)$$

The value u_1 is greater than u_0, and the critical region therefore is on the right tail of the normal distribution. A sample $n = 400$ is taken, and the sample mean $\bar{x} = 10.5$, while the sample variance $s^2 = 100$. Transforming the variate $\bar{x}$ to standard normal variate, we obtain

$$z_0 = \frac{\bar{x} - u_0}{s/\sqrt{n}} = \frac{10.5 - 10}{10/20} = 1$$

If the error probability of rejecting u_0 when u_0 is true is .05, the decision point according to the standard normal distribution table is

$$z = 1.64$$

Since 1 is on the left-hand side of 1.64 (that is not in the critical region), the decision rule indicates that we have no evidence to reject H_0 in favor of H_1.

Testing a Proportion

Again, we have a null hypothesis H_0, but this time it is of a population proportion to be tested against an alternative hypothesis H_1.

$$H_0 : p = .5\,(p_0)$$
$$H_1 : p = .4\,(p_1)$$

Since p_1 is smaller than p_0, the critical region is on the left tail of the normal distribution.

If a sample of $n = 2{,}500$ is taken, the sample proportion is found to be

$$p' = .42$$

Transforming the variate p' into standard normal variate,

$$z_0 = \frac{p' - p}{\sqrt{p'q'/n}} \quad \frac{.42 - .5}{\sqrt{(.42)(.58)/2{,}500}} = -8.1 \text{ (approx.)}$$

If the error probability of rejecting u_0 when u_0 is true is .05, the decision point according to the standard normal distribution table is

$$z = -1.64$$

Since -8.1 is on the left-hand side of -1.64 (which is in the critical region), the decision rule calls for rejecting H_0 with the error probability of 5 percent.

Testing the Difference of Two Means

If we have to test the means of two populations (u_1, u_2) to verify whether they are equal or different, we take samples from each population and set up the null hypothesis that $u_1 = u_2$ or $u_1 - u_2 = 0$ and the alternative hypothesis that $u_1 \neq u_2$ or $u_1 - u_2 \neq 0$.

Let n_1 be the number of samples taken from the first population, n_2 the number of samples taken from the second population, σ_1 the standard deviation of the first population and σ_2 the standard deviation of the second population. Then the distribution of the differences of the sample means $\bar{x}_1 - \bar{x}_2$ (where $\bar{x}_1$ is the sample mean of samples taken from the first population and $\bar{x}_2$ the sample mean of samples taken from the second population) will be normally distributed with mean equals to $u_1 - u_2$ and standard deviation equal to

$$\sigma_{\bar{x}_1 - \bar{x}_2} = \sqrt{\sigma_{\bar{x}_1^2} + \sigma_{\bar{x}_2^2}} = \sqrt{\frac{\sigma_1^2}{n_1} + \frac{\sigma_2^2}{n_2}}$$

When the sample sizes are sufficiently large, σ_1^2 and σ_2^2 may be substituted by sample standard deviations s_1^2 and s_2^2.

Example 1

Random samples of size one hundred each are taken from two different brands of light bulbs, brand A and brand B. The average life of the hundred bulbs of brand A is 1,600 hr and the standard deviation is 100 hr. The average life of the hundred bulbs of brand B is 1,550 hr and the standard deviation is 90 hr. We want to decide whether the two brands of bulbs are different in quality.

The null hypothesis is

$$u_1 = u_2 \qquad \text{or} \qquad u_1 - u_2 = 0$$

The standard deviation of the distribution of the differences of the sample means is

$$\sigma_{\bar{x}_1 - \bar{x}_2} = \sqrt{\frac{s_1^2}{n_1} + \frac{s_2^2}{n_2}}$$
$$= \sqrt{\frac{10,000}{100} + \frac{8,100}{100}}$$
$$= 13.6$$

The difference of the sample mean is

$$\bar{x}_1 - \bar{x}_2 = 1,600 - 1,550 = 50$$

Converting to standard normal variate (see Fig. 4-1),

$$z = \frac{(\bar{x}_1 - \bar{x}_2) - (u_1 - u_2)}{\sigma_{x_1} - x_2}$$
$$= \frac{50 - 0}{13.6}$$
$$= 3.6$$

If α is set at .05 (apparently 3.6 is greater than 1.96), we will reject the null hypothesis and conclude that there is signifi-

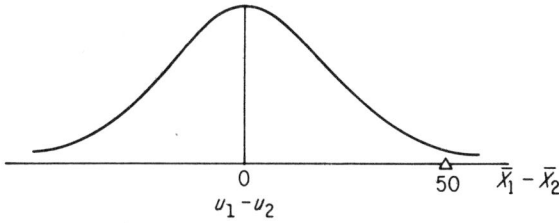

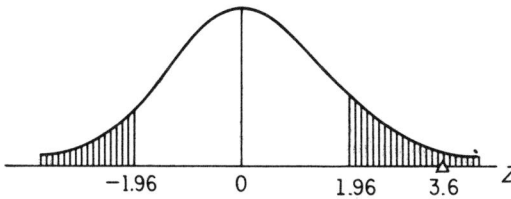

Fig. 4-1

cant difference between brand *A* and brand *B* in their life expectancy.

Testing the Difference of Two Proportions

Sometimes we may determine whether two populations differ with respect to a certain attribute by testing the difference of proportions. The null hypothesis will be $p_1 = p_2$ or $p_1 - p_2 = 0$ and the alternative hypothesis will be $p_1 \neq p_2$ or $p_1 - p_2 \neq 0$ (where p_1 and p_2 are the population proportions). The standard deviation of the distribution of the differences of sample proportions is

$$\sigma_{p_1' - p_2'} = \sqrt{\frac{p_1'(1 - p_1')}{n_1} + \frac{p_2'(1 - p_2')}{n_2}}$$

where p_1' and p_2' are the sample proportions.

Example 2

Random samples of size one hundred each are taken from two truckloads of oranges. Out of the hundred oranges taken from the first truck, eighty of them are juicy; the rest are quite dry, and out of the hundred oranges taken from the second truck ninety are juicy. We want to determine whether the two truckloads of oranges are of similar quality. The null hypothesis is

$$p_1 - p_2 = 0$$

The sample proportions are

$$p_1' = \frac{80}{100} = .8$$

$$p_2' = \frac{90}{100} = .9$$

The standard deviation is

$$\sigma_{p_1 - p_2'} = \sqrt{\frac{(.8)(.2)}{100} + \frac{(.9)(.1)}{100}}$$

$$= .05$$

The difference of the sample mean is

$$p_1' - p_2' = .8 - .9 = -.1$$

Converting to standard normal variate (see Fig. 4-2),

$$z = \frac{(p_1' - p_2') - (p_1 - p_2)}{\sigma_{p_1' - p_2'}}$$

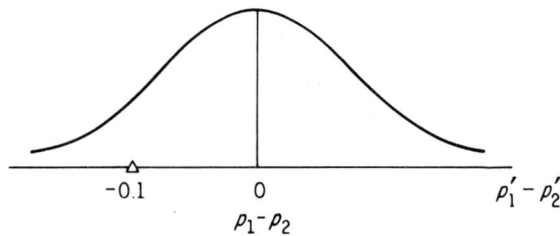

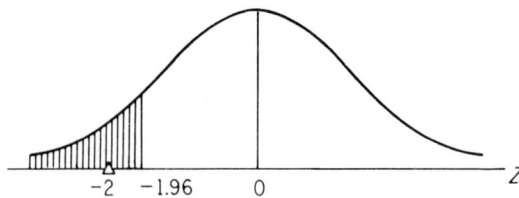

Fig. 4-2

$$= \frac{-.1}{.05}$$

$$= -2$$

If α is set at .05, the critical value is -1.96 which is very close to -2, so we may want to take more samples for another test before we come to a decision.

*Operating Characteristic.** The above examples only illustrate the probability of making a Type I error. We may set α very small, so that the probability of making Type I error could be minimized. However, this may increase the probability of making Type II error. Thus, it is also necessary to study the size of the Type II error. This may be done by computing the *operating characteristic curve*.

Example 3
Suppose we need to test the difference of two means. The two hypotheses are

$$H_0: \quad \mu_1 - \mu_2 = 0$$

$$H_1: \quad \mu_1 - \mu_2 = 2$$

Sample sizes: $n_1 = 100$, $n_2 = 100$
Sample variances: $s_1^2 = 9, s_2^2 = 16$
Sample means: $\bar{x}_1 = 30, \bar{x}_2 = 29$

The formula for transforming the original value to standard normal variate (see Fig. 4-3) is

$$z = \frac{(\bar{x}_1 - \bar{x}_2) - (\mu_1 - \mu_2)}{\sigma_{\bar{x}_1 - \bar{x}_2}}$$

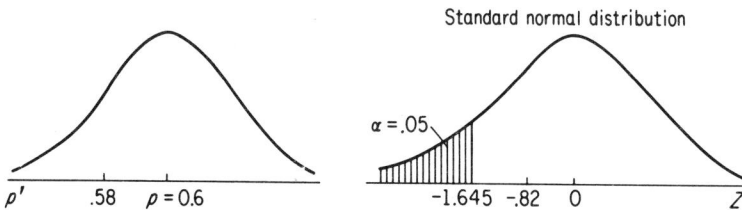

Standard normal distribution

$\alpha = .05$

p' .58 $p = 0.6$ -1.645 $-.82$ 0 Z

Fig. 4-3

*This portion is adapted from K. Chu, *Principles of Econometrics.* Scranton, Pa.: International Textbook Company, 1968.

where

$$\sigma_{\bar{x}_1 - \bar{x}_2} = \sqrt{\frac{s_1^2}{n_1} + \frac{s_2^2}{n_2}}$$

In this example,

$$z = \frac{1 - 0}{\sqrt{\dfrac{9}{100} + \dfrac{16}{100}}} = 2$$

If α is set equal to .025, the critical region is on the right of $z = 1.96$. Since 2 is in the critical region, the decision would be to accept H_1: $\mu_1 - \mu_2 = 2$.

But now we can also calculate the probability of making a Type II error, β, when using this decision rule. The value 1.96, when transformed to the $(\bar{x}_1 - \bar{x}_2)$ scale (see Fig. 4-4), becomes

$$(\mu_1 - \mu_2) + 1.96\,\sigma_{\bar{x}_1 - \bar{x}_2} = 0 + (1.96)\left(\sqrt{\frac{9}{100} + \frac{16}{100}}\right) = 0.98$$

$$z = \frac{0.98 - 2}{\sqrt{\dfrac{9}{100} + \dfrac{16}{100}}} = -2.04$$

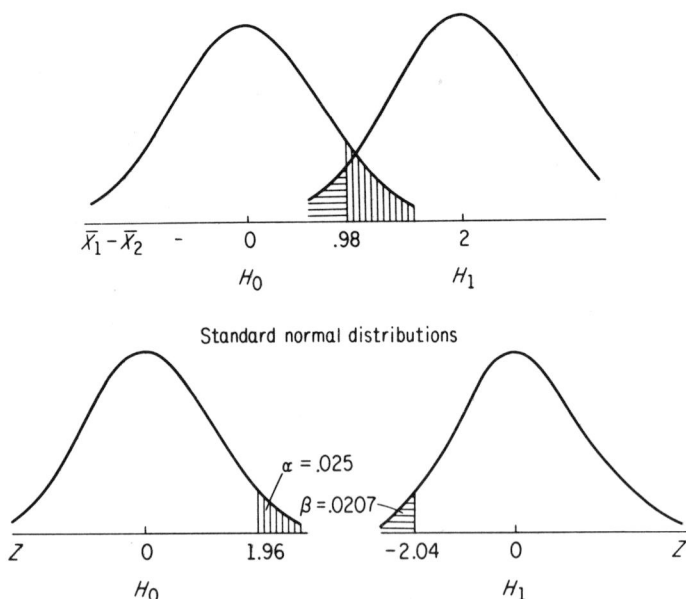

Standard normal distributions

Fig. 4-4

From a standard normal distribution table, we find that $\beta = .5 - .4793 = .0207$.

If the alternative hypotheses of $(\mu_1 - \mu_2)$ are many, we can follow the above procedure to compute β for each alternative hypothesis, thus obtaining an operating characteristic curve as shown in Fig. 4-5.

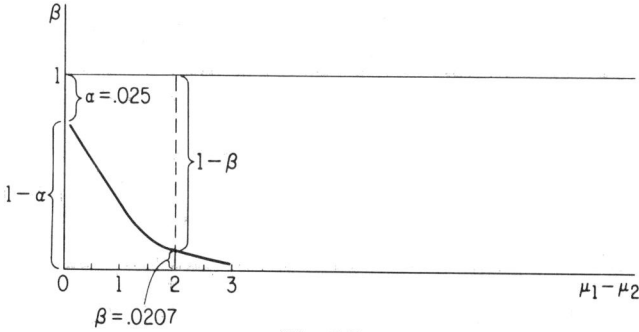

Fig. 4-5

If sample size remains the same, choosing a larger critical region means decreasing the β value at the expense of increasing the α value, or vice versa. When we need to decrease both the α value and the β value, we will have to take larger samples.

Chi-square Distribution

Chi-square (χ^2) distribution is widely used in connection with radial error and testing goodness-of-fit problems. The function is

$$f(\chi^2) = \frac{(\chi^2)^{(n/2)-1} e^{-(x^2/2)}}{2^{n/2}\, \Gamma^{n/2}}$$

where $\Gamma(x)$ denotes the gamma or factorial function of x, which has the property $\Gamma(x + 1) = x\Gamma(x)$, and n is the degree of freedom, which equals the number of independent variables involved. Chi-square distribution is useful in statistics because its variable can be interpreted as the sum of standard normal variates:

$$\chi^2(n) = \sum_{i=1}^{n} z_i^2 = \sum_{i=1}^{n} \left(\frac{x_i - u}{\sigma}\right)^2$$

In small samples, σ^2 is substituted by sample variance s:

$$ns^2 = \sum_{i=1}^{n} (x_i - \bar{x})^2 = \sum_{i=1}^{n} [(x_i - u) - (\bar{x} - u)]^2$$

$$= \sum_{i=1}^{n} (x_i - u)^2 - n(\bar{x} - u)^2$$

where $\bar{x}$ is the sample mean. Dividing both sides by σ^2,

$$\frac{ns^2}{\sigma^2} = \sum_{i=1}^{n} \left(\frac{x_i - u}{\sigma}\right)^2 - \frac{n(\bar{x} - u)^2}{\sigma^2}$$

$$= \sum_{i=1}^{n} \left(\frac{x_i - u}{\sigma}\right)^2 - \left(\frac{\bar{x} - u}{\sigma/\sqrt{n}}\right)^2$$

Using the moment-generating function,

$$M_{ns^2/\sigma^2}(t) = \frac{M_{\sum_{i=1}^{n}\left(\frac{x_i-u}{\sigma}\right)^2}(t) \quad (n \text{ degrees of freedom})}{M_{\frac{\bar{x}-u}{\sigma/\sqrt{n}}}(t) \qquad (1 \text{ degree of freedom})}$$

Thus ns^2/σ^2 possesses a χ^2 distribution with $(n - 1)$ degrees of freedom.

Example 4

Test a hypothetical value of population variance σ^2 against an alternative hypothesis:

$$H_0: \quad \sigma^2 = 30$$
$$H_1: \quad \sigma^2 > 30$$

If we take a sample of size 25 and a sample variance of 40, ns^2/σ^2 possesses a χ^2 distribution with 24 degrees of freedom. From the chi-square distribution table, when error probability is 0.05, the decision point or critical value of χ^2 is 36.4.

Now in this problem the sample χ^2 value is

$$\chi_0^2 = \frac{ns^2}{\sigma^2} = \frac{25 \cdot 40}{30} = 33.3$$

The hypothesis $H_0: \sigma^2 = 30$ is accepted. (*Note:* If the probability of rejecting H_0 erroneously is allowed to be greater, which will at the same time reduce the error probability of rejecting a true H_1, say $\alpha = 0.2$, then the critical value of χ^2 becomes 29.6, the decision rule will change to reject H_0.)

"Student's" t Distribution

When sample is small and population variance is unknown, standard normal distribution cannot be used. "Student's" t distribution with the same mean but larger variance is used instead. (The name "Student" comes from a pseudonym used by William S. Gossett, who developed the procedure in the early 1900's.)

The function is

$$f(t) = c\left(1 + \frac{t^2}{n}\right)^{-\frac{1}{2}(n+1)}$$

where c is a constant and n is the degree of freedom. The variable t may be interpreted as the ratio of $x\sqrt{n}/\chi_n^2$, where z is the standard normal variate and χ_n^2 is a χ^2 variate with n degrees of freedom.

Example 5

Testing a mean with a small sample:

H_0: $u = 10(u_0)$

H_1: $u \neq 10(u_1)$ (two-tailed critical region)

A small sample $n = 25$ is taken, the sample mean is $\bar{x} = 11$, and the sample variance is $s^2 = 49$. The transformation is

$$t_0 = \frac{\bar{x} - u_0}{s/\sqrt{n}} = \frac{11 - 10}{7/5} = 0.71$$

Let the error probability $\alpha = .05$, the decision point according to the t distribution table with 24 degrees of freedom is

$$t = 2.06 \quad \text{or} \quad -2.06$$

Since 0.71 is not in the critical region, we have no evidence of rejecting H_0: $u = 10$.

The F Distribution

In order to compare the variances of different samples (when the samples sizes are small) and determine where the variances are significantly different or may be accepted as the same, the F distribution is used. The function is

$$f(F) = c \frac{F^{\frac{1}{2}(n_1 - 2)}}{(n_2 + n_1 F)^{\frac{1}{2}(n_1 + n_2)}}$$

The variable of the F distribution may be interpreted as the ratio of two χ^2 distributions:

$$F = \frac{\chi^2_{n_1}/n_1}{\chi^2_{n_2}/n_2}$$

where n_1 is the degrees of freedom of $\chi^2_{n_1}$ distribution and n_2 is the degrees of freedom of $\chi^2_{n_2}$ distribution.

Example 6
Testing the equality of variances:

$$H_0: \quad \sigma_x = \sigma_y$$
$$H_1: \quad \sigma_x \neq \sigma_y$$

Take samples $n_x = 10$, $n_y = 10$, and find sample variances $s_x^2 = 30$, $s_y^2 = 5$. From the F distribution table, with 9.9 degrees of freedom and error probability 5 percent, the critical value of F is

$$F = 4.5$$

Since in this example, the F value is

$$F_0 = \frac{s_x^2}{s_y^2} = \frac{30}{5} = 6$$

Since F_0 is in the critical region, we reject $H_0: \sigma_x^2 = \sigma_x^2$ in favor of $H_1: \sigma_x^2 \neq \sigma_y^2$.

ANALYSIS OF VARIANCE*

Analysis of variance is a method to test whether two or more samples differ significantly with respect to some property. The simplest type of an analysis of variance model is to classify observations into different groups on the basis of a single property and use the ratio of the variance

*This portion is taken from K. Chu, *Principles of Econometrics*. Scranton, Pa.: International Textbook Company, 1968.

between the groups and the average variances within the groups to test whether these groups differ significantly with respect to that property. The ratio is known as the F ratio, which is associated with the F distribution. The testing procedure can best be seen through an example.

Example 7

Bath soaps made of the same formula are put in three different wrappings and sold at the same price. The result of eight months' sales is as follows:

Soap A Sales			Soap B Sales			Soap C Sales		
X_1	x_1	x_1^2	X_2	x_2	x_2^2	X_3	x_3	x_3^2
100	0	0	120	15	225	90	−8	64
98	−2	4	115	10	100	100	2	4
102	2	4	105	0	0	90	−8	64
95	−5	25	100	−5	25	115	17	289
90	−10	100	110	5	25	89	−9	81
110	10	100	105	0	0	105	7	49
105	5	25	95	−10	100	100	2	4
100	0	0	90	−15	225	95	−3	9
800		258	840		700	784		564

We want to test the hypotheses to determine whether different wrappings of the same bath soap have any effect on its sales.

The group means are

$$\overline{X}_1 = \frac{\Sigma X_1}{n} = 100 \qquad \overline{X}_2 = \frac{\Sigma X_2}{n} = 105 \qquad \overline{X}_3 = \frac{\Sigma X_3}{n} = 98$$

The group variances:

$$S_1^2 = \frac{\Sigma x_1^2}{n-1} = 36.8 \quad S_2^2 = \frac{\Sigma x_2^2}{n-1} = 100 \quad S_3^2 = \frac{\Sigma x_3^2}{n-1} = 80.5$$

The average variance within the three groups is

$$V_1 = \frac{S_1^2 + S_2^2 + S_3^2}{3} = 72.4$$

The total mean of all the observations:

$$\overline{\overline{X}} = \frac{\overline{X}_1 + \overline{X}_2 + \overline{X}_3}{3} = 101$$

The variance of all the observations:

$$\sigma_{\bar{X}}^2 = \frac{(\bar{X}_1 - \bar{\bar{X}})^2 + (\bar{X}_2 - \bar{\bar{X}})^2 + (\bar{X}_3 - \bar{\bar{X}})^2}{3 - 1} = 13$$

Since the variance of sample means is equal to the variance of the variable divided by the sample size ($\sigma_{\bar{X}}^2 = \sigma^2/n$), the variance between these groups is therefore

$$V_2 = n\sigma_{\bar{X}}^2 = 8 \times 13 = 104$$

The F ratio then can be computed as

$$F = \frac{V_2}{V_1} = \frac{104}{72.4} = 1.44$$

Since the degree of freedom for the numerator is 2 ($c - 1$, where c is the number of the groups), the degree of freedom for the denominator is 21 [$c(r - 1)$, where r is the number of observations in each group], and from the F distribution table, the 5 percent critical value of F corresponding to the degree of freedom (2, 21) is 3.45. Apparently, the computed F value 1.44 is smaller than 3.47. The analysis thus indicates that we have no significant evidence to reject the hypothesis that different wrappings have no effect on the sales of the bath soap.

For testing samples with more than one classification variable, e.g. the effect of different formulas and different wrappings on the sale of bath soap, the total variance is decomposed into more than two components. In the case of two variables of classification, the total variance is decomposed into the row variance (one classification), the column variance (the other classification), and the residual variance.

$$\sum_{i=1}^{r} \sum_{j=1}^{c} (X_{ij} - \bar{\bar{X}})^2 = \sum_{i=1}^{r} \sum_{j=1}^{c} (\bar{X}_i - \bar{\bar{X}})^2 + \sum_{i=1}^{r} \sum_{j=1}^{c} (\bar{X}_j - \bar{\bar{X}})^2$$

$$+ \sum_{i=1}^{r} \sum_{j=1}^{c} (X_{ij} - \bar{X}_i - \bar{X}_j + \bar{\bar{X}})^2$$

where r is the number of rows, c is the number of columns, X_{ij} are the observations, $\bar{X}_i$ is the mean of the ith row, $\bar{X}_j$ is the mean of the jth column, and $\bar{\bar{X}}$ is the total mean.

Thus the row variance is

$$V_r = c \frac{\sum\limits_{i=1}^{r} (\bar{X}_i - \bar{\bar{X}})^2}{r - 1}$$

The column variance is

$$V_c = r \frac{\sum\limits_{j=1}^{c} (\bar{X}_j - \bar{\bar{X}})^2}{c - 1}$$

and the residual variance is

$$V_e = \frac{\sum\limits_{i=1}^{r} \sum\limits_{j=1}^{c} (X_{ij} - \bar{X}_i - \bar{X}_j + \bar{\bar{X}})^2}{(r - 1)(c - 1)}$$

The F ratio for testing the hypothesis to determine whether the column means are equal is

$$F_1 = \frac{V_c}{V_e} = \frac{r(r - 1) \sum\limits_{j=1}^{c} (\bar{X}_j - \bar{\bar{X}})^2}{\sum\limits_{i=1}^{r} \sum\limits_{j=1}^{c} (X_{ij} - \bar{X}_i - \bar{X}_j + \bar{\bar{X}})^2}$$

where the degree of freedom for the numerator is $c - 1$ and the degree of freedom for the denominator is $(r - 1)(c - 1)$. The F ratio for testing the hypothesis whether the row means are equal is

$$F_2 = \frac{V_r}{V_e} = \frac{c(c - 1) \sum\limits_{i=1}^{r} (\bar{X}_i - \bar{\bar{X}})^2}{\sum\limits_{i=1}^{r} \sum\limits_{j=1}^{c} (X_{ij} - \bar{X}_i - \bar{X}_j + \bar{\bar{X}})^2}$$

where the degree of freedom for the numerator is $r - 1$ and the degree of freedom for the denominator is $(r - 1)(c - 1)$.

Example 8

A soap manufacturer produces four different kinds of bath soap and uses three different kinds of wrappings on each of them before putting them on the market, the annual sales of the soap are

Formula \ Wrapping	A	B	C
1	3,105	3,092	3,118
2	2,880	2,905	2,895
3	3,001	3,014	2,995
4	2,612	2,603	2,598

We use F ratios to test whether different formulas and different wrappings have significant effect on the sales volume,

$$\sum_{i=1}^{4} \sum_{j=1}^{3} X_{ij} = 34{,}818 \qquad \sum_{i=1}^{4} \sum_{j=1}^{3} X_{ij}^2 = 101{,}445{,}842$$

$$\sum_{j=1}^{3} \left(\sum_{i=1}^{4} X_{ij} \right)^2 = 404{,}097{,}836 \qquad \sum_{i=1}^{4} \left(\sum_{j=1}^{3} X_{ij} \right)^2 = 304{,}334{,}694$$

$$\sum_{j=1}^{3} (\bar{X}_j - \bar{\bar{X}})^2 = \frac{404{,}097{,}836}{4^2} - \frac{(34{,}818)^2}{3 \cdot 4^2} = 15$$

$$\sum_{i=1}^{4} (\bar{X}_i - \bar{\bar{X}})^2 = \frac{304{,}334{,}694}{3^2} - \frac{(34{,}818)^2}{4 \cdot 3^2} = 140{,}160$$

$$\sum_{i=1}^{4} \sum_{j=1}^{5} (X_{ij} - \bar{\bar{X}})^2 = 101{,}445{,}842 - \frac{(34{,}818)^2}{4 \cdot 3} = 421{,}420$$

$$\sum_{i=1}^{4} \sum_{j=1}^{5} (X_{ij} - \bar{X}_i - \bar{X}_j + \bar{\bar{X}})^2$$
$$= 421{,}420 - 3(140{,}160) - 4(15) = 880$$

To test the column variance,

$$F_1 = \frac{4 \cdot 3 \cdot 15}{880} = 0.2$$

with degrees of freedom $(2, 6)$. From the F distribution table, we will find that the 5 percent critical value of F corresponding the degrees of freedom $(2, 6)$ is 5.14. Since F_1 is smaller than 5.14 (not in the critical region), we have no reason to reject the hypothesis that different wrappings have no effect on sales. To test the row variance,

$$F_2 = \frac{3 \cdot 2 \cdot 140{,}160}{880} = 955.6$$

with degrees of freedom $(3, 6)$. From the F distribution table, we will find that the 5 percent critical value of F corresponding the degrees of freedom $(2, 6)$ is 4.76. Since F_2 is greater than 4.76 (in the critical region), we reject the hypothesis that different formulas have no effect on sales.

We have listed above only some basic theoretical distributions. There exist many more complicated theoretical probability distributions. Some of these are made by changing the scale from ordinary to logarithm, such as the log-normal distribution. The function becomes

$$f(x) = \frac{1}{\sqrt{2\pi}\,\sigma} e^{-\frac{1}{2}\left(\frac{\log x - \mu}{\sigma}\right)^2}$$

where

$$\mu = \frac{\sum_{i=1}^{n} \log x_i}{n} \qquad \sigma^2 = \sum_{i=1}^{n} \frac{(\log x_i - \mu)^2}{n}$$

Some are made by adding up several similar distributions to form a new probability distribution, such as the kth Erlang distribution. The random variable x of the kth Erlang distribution with parameter μ is the sum of the k random variables $(x_1 + x_2 + \cdots + x_k)$ of k independent exponential distributions with mean all equal to $1/k\mu$.

ANALYSIS OF COVARIANCE

The method of testing the effect of one variable, separated from the effects of a second variable is called the analysis of co-variance. The second variable is usually referred to as the control variable. Similar to analysis of variance, the analysis of covariance procedure also leads to a test for difference in means by separation of a total sum of products into within-groups sum of products and among-groups sum of products.

$$\sum_{i=1}^{g} \sum_{j=1}^{n} (X_{ij} - \bar{\bar{X}})(Y_{ij} - \bar{\bar{Y}}) = \sum_{i=1}^{g} \sum_{j=1}^{n} (X_{ij} - \bar{X}_i)(Y_{ij} - \bar{Y}_i)$$

$$+ n \sum_{i=1}^{g} (\bar{X}_i - \bar{\bar{X}})(\bar{Y}_i - \bar{\bar{Y}})$$

where g is the number of groups, n the number of observations in the groups, $\bar{X}_i$, $\bar{Y}_i$ are the group means and $\bar{\bar{X}}$, $\bar{\bar{Y}}$ are the total means. The equation may be reduced to the following for easier computation:

$$\sum_{i=1}^{g}\sum_{j=1}^{n} X_{ij}Y_{ij} - \frac{\left(\sum_{i=1}^{g}\sum_{j=1}^{n} X_{ij}\right)\left(\sum_{i=1}^{g}\sum_{j=1}^{n} Y_{ij}\right)}{n \times g}$$

$$= \left[\sum_{i=1}^{g}\sum_{j=1}^{n} X_{ij}Y_{ij} - \frac{\sum_{i=1}^{g}\left(\sum_{j=1}^{n} X_{ij} \times \sum_{j=1}^{n} Y_{ij}\right)}{n}\right]$$

$$+ \left[\frac{\sum_{i=1}^{g}\left(\sum_{j=1}^{n} X_{ij} \times \sum_{j=1}^{n} Y_{ij}\right)}{n} - \frac{\left(\sum_{i=1}^{g}\sum_{j=1}^{n} X_{ij}\right)\left(\sum_{i=1}^{g}\sum_{j=1}^{n} Y_{ij}\right)}{n \times g}\right]$$

Next, by treating X as the control variable, the linear regression coefficient of Y on X is computed by the following,

$$y = \hat{b}x + e$$

$$\hat{b} = \frac{\Sigma xy}{\Sigma x^2}$$

where $y = Y - \bar{\bar{Y}}$, $x = X - \bar{\bar{X}}$, and e is the residual or the difference of actual observation and regression quantity of Y based on X,

$$\begin{aligned}
\Sigma e^2 &= \Sigma(y - \hat{y})^2 \\
&= \Sigma(y - \hat{b}x)^2 \\
&= \Sigma y^2 - 2\hat{b}\Sigma xy + \hat{b}^2\Sigma x^2 \\
&= \Sigma y^2 - \frac{(\Sigma xy)^2}{\Sigma x^2}
\end{aligned}$$

The formulas for computing the sums of products are listed in the table on p. 151.

The sum of products divided by degrees of freedom gives the mean square.

And the F value for the analysis of covariance is the ratio of the among-groups mean square and the within-groups mean square.

A numerical example will illustrate the computation procedure.

	Degrees of Freedom	Σx^2	Σy^2	Σxy
Total	$ng - 1$	$\Sigma_i \Sigma_j X_{ij}^2 - \dfrac{(\Sigma_i \Sigma_j X_{ij})^2}{ng}$	$\Sigma_i \Sigma_j Y_{ij}^2 - \dfrac{(\Sigma_i \Sigma_j Y_{ij})^2}{ng}$	$\Sigma_i \Sigma_j X_{ij} Y_{ij} - \dfrac{(\Sigma_i \Sigma_j X_{ij})(\Sigma_i \Sigma_j Y_{ij})}{ng}$
Among groups	$g - 1$	$\dfrac{\Sigma_i (\Sigma_j X_{ij})^2}{n} - \dfrac{(\Sigma_i \Sigma_j X_{ij})^2}{ng}$	$\dfrac{\Sigma_i (\Sigma_j Y_{ij})^2}{n} - \dfrac{(\Sigma_i \Sigma_j Y_{ij})^2}{ng}$	$\dfrac{\Sigma_i (\Sigma_j X_{ij} \times \Sigma_j Y_{ij})}{n} - \dfrac{(\Sigma_i \Sigma_j X_{ij})(\Sigma_i \Sigma_j Y_{ij})}{ng}$
Within groups	$g(n - 1)$	The difference of "Total" and "Among groups"		

	Degrees of Freedom	Σe^2
Total	$ng - 2$	$\left[\Sigma_i \Sigma_j Y_{ij}^2 - \dfrac{(\Sigma_i \Sigma_j Y_{ij})^2}{ng}\right] - \dfrac{\left[\Sigma_i \Sigma_j X_{ij} Y_{ij} - \dfrac{(\Sigma_i \Sigma_j X_{ij})(\Sigma_i \Sigma_j Y_{ij})}{ng}\right]^2}{\left[\Sigma_i \Sigma_j X_{ij}^2 - \dfrac{(\Sigma_i \Sigma_j X_{ij})^2}{ng}\right]}$
Among groups	$g - 1$	$\left[\dfrac{\Sigma_i (\Sigma_j Y_{ij})^2}{n} - \dfrac{(\Sigma_i \Sigma_j Y_{ij})^2}{ng}\right] - \dfrac{\left[\dfrac{\Sigma_i (\Sigma_j X_{ij} \times \Sigma_j Y_{ij})}{n} - \dfrac{(\Sigma_i \Sigma_j X_{ij})(\Sigma_i \Sigma_j Y_{ij})}{ng}\right]^2}{\left[\dfrac{\Sigma_i (\Sigma_j X_{ij})^2}{n} - \dfrac{(\Sigma_i \Sigma_j X_{ij})^2}{ng}\right]}$
Within groups	$g(n - 1) - 1$	The difference of "Total" and "Among groups"

Group 1		Group 2		Group 3	
X	Y	X	Y	X	Y
4	12	5	15	2	6
3	10	4	14	3	7
2	9	4	13	4	9
3	11	6	16	2	7
12	42	19	58	11	29

The sums of products are:

1. for Σx^2

Total: $4^2 + 3^2 + 2^2 + 3^2 + 5^2 + 4^2 + 4^2 + 6^2$

$$+ 2^2 + 3^2 + 4^2 + 2^2 - \frac{(12 + 19 + 11)^2}{4 \cdot 3}$$

$$= 164 - \frac{1764}{12} = 17$$

Among groups: $\dfrac{12^2 + 19^2 + 11^2}{4} - \dfrac{(12 + 19 + 11)^2}{4 \cdot 3}$

$$= \frac{626}{4} - \frac{1764}{12} = 9.5$$

Within groups: $17 - 9 \cdot 5 = 7.5$

2. for Σy^2

Total: $12^2 + 10^2 + 9^2 + 11^2 + 15^2 + 14^2 + 13^2$

$$+ 16^2 + 6^2 + 7^2 + 9^2 + 7^2 - \frac{(42 + 58 + 29)^2}{4 \cdot 3}$$

$$= 1507 - \frac{16641}{12} = 120.25$$

Among groups: $\dfrac{42^2 + 58^2 + 29^2}{4} - \dfrac{(42 + 58 + 29)^2}{4.3}$

$$= \frac{5969}{4} - \frac{16641}{12} = 105.5$$

$$(\text{d.f.} = 2)$$

Within groups: $120.25 - 105.5 = 14.75$ (d.f. $= 9$)

3. for Σxy

Total: $4(12 + 3(10) + 2(9) + 3(11) + 5(15)$
$$+ 4(14 + 4(13) + 6(16) + 2(6) + 3(7)$$

$+ 4(9) + 2(7) \cdot \dfrac{(12 + 19 + 11)(42 + 58 + 29)}{4.3}$

$$= 491 - \frac{5418}{12} = 39.5$$

Among groups: $\dfrac{12(42)}{4} + \dfrac{19(58)}{4}$

$$+ \dfrac{11(29)}{4} - \dfrac{(12 + 19 + 11)(42 + 58 + 29)}{4.3}$$

$$= \dfrac{1925}{4} - \dfrac{5418}{12} = 29.75$$

Within groups: $39.5 - 29.75 = 9.75$

4. for Σe^2

Total: $120.25 - \dfrac{39.5}{17} = 117.93$

Among groups: $105.5 - \dfrac{29.75}{9.5} = 102.37$ (d.f. = 2)

Within groups: $117.93 - 102.37 = 15.56$ (d.f. = 8)

$$F = \dfrac{102.37/2}{15.56/8} = \dfrac{51.18}{1.94} = 26.4$$

Compare to $F_{.95}(2,8) = 4.46$, $F_{.99}(2,8) = 8.65$, there are significant differences in Y means among the groups after the Y values have been adjusted by the regression of Y on X in each group.

Following the analysis of variance of the Y values only without using the X values, the F ratio would be

$$\dfrac{105.5/2}{14.75/9} = \dfrac{52.75}{1.64} = 32.1$$

The larger value of F in this case is the result of overlooking the effect of X on Y.

Neyman-Pearson Theorem for Testing Hypotheses

The best means of testing two hypotheses may be viewed as a test with a given Type I error of size α, and at the same time minimizing the size of the Type II error β.

Neyman-Pearson Theorem. The theorem states that if there exists a critical region of size α and a constant K such that

$$\frac{\prod_{i=1}^{n} f(x_i; u_1)}{\prod_{i=1}^{n} f(x_i; u_0)} \geq K \text{ inside of the critical region}$$

and

$$\frac{\prod_{i=1}^{n} f(x_i; u_1)}{\prod_{i=1}^{n} f(x_i; u_0)} < K \text{ outside of the critical region}$$

Thus the critical region is the best critical region of size (where n is the sample size and f is the probability distribution of random variable x).

Example 9

Suppose we have two hypotheses

$$H_0: \quad u = 1(u_0)$$

$$H_1: \quad u = 2(u_1)$$

Sample size $n = 100$; standard deviation of x, $\sigma = 3$ and x is normally distributed. We then have

$$f(x; u) = \frac{e^{-\frac{1}{2}(x-u)^2}}{\sqrt{2\pi}}$$

Then

$$\prod_{i=1}^{n} f(x_i; u_1) = (2\pi)^{-\frac{n}{2}} e^{-\frac{1}{2} \sum_{i=1}^{n} (x_i - u_1)^2}$$

$$\prod_{i=1}^{n} f(x_i; u_0) = (2\pi)^{-\frac{n}{2}} e^{-\frac{1}{2} \sum_{i=1}^{n} (x_i - u_0)^2}$$

When inside the critical region, we have

$$\frac{\prod_{i=1}^{n} f(x_i; u_1)}{\prod_{i=1}^{n} f(x_i; u_0)} \geq k$$

In this case,

$$\frac{(2\pi)^{-\frac{n}{2}} e^{-\frac{1}{2}\sum_{i=1}^{n}(x_i - u_1)^2}}{(2\pi)^{-\frac{n}{2}} e^{-\frac{1}{2}\sum_{i=1}^{n}(x_i - u_0)^2}} = e^{\frac{1}{2}\left[\sum_{i=1}^{n}(x_i - u_0)^2 - \sum_{i=1}^{n}(x_i - u_1)^2\right]} \geq k$$

$$\sum_{i=1}^{n}(x_i - u_0)^2 - \sum_{i=1}^{n}(x_i - u_1)^2 \geq 2\log k$$

$$2(u_1 - u_0)\sum_{i=1}^{n} x_i \geq 2\log k + n(u_1^2 - u_0^2)$$

When both sides are divided by n,

$$\bar{x} \geq \frac{2\log k + n(u_1^2 - u_0^2)}{2n(u_1 - u_0)}$$

Substituting the numerical values,

$$\bar{x} \geq \frac{2\log k + 100(4 - 1)}{2 \cdot 100(2 - 1)}$$

$$\bar{x} \geq \frac{2\log k + 300}{200}$$

If we set $k = 1$, $\log k = 0$, then

$$\bar{x} = 1.5$$

Therefore the best critical region is in the right tail of the normal curve (see Fig. 4-6). Transforming into the scale of standard normal distribution:

$$z_1 = \frac{1.5 - u_0}{\sigma/\sqrt{n}}$$

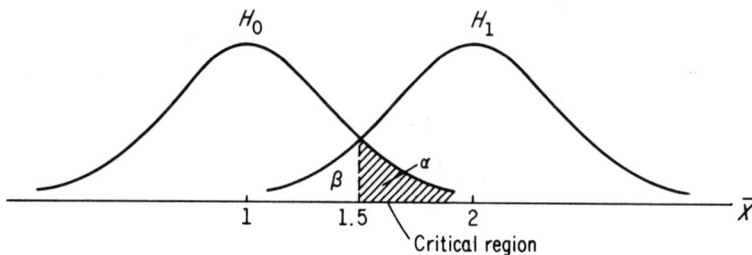

Fig. 4-6

$$= \frac{.5}{3/\sqrt{100}} = 1.66, \quad \alpha \approx .05$$

$$x_2 = \frac{1.5 - u_1}{\sigma/\sqrt{n}}$$

$$= \frac{-.5}{3/\sqrt{100}} = 1.66, \quad \beta \approx .05$$

SEQUENTIAL ANALYSIS

In making decisions, the method outlined above indicates that the sample size is predetermined and fixed. This might not be an economical way to take samples, because the predetermined sample size may be more than enough. An improved method is to examine the samples one at a time, and each time after a sample is examined we may make one of the following decisions:

1. Accept the hypothesis.
2. Reject the hypothesis.
3. Postpone the final decision by taking another sample.

Thus the sample size is a variable and we need two constants for the decision rule. It has been proved that the two constants are approximately equal to $\beta/(1 - \alpha)$, $(1 - \beta)/\alpha$.

The decision rules become

(1) If $\dfrac{\displaystyle\prod_{i=1}^{y} f(x_i, u_1)}{\displaystyle\prod_{i=1}^{y} f(x_i, u_0)} \leq \dfrac{\beta}{1 - \alpha};$ accept H_0 (reject H_1).

(2) If $\dfrac{\displaystyle\prod_{i=1}^{y} f(x_i, u_1)}{\displaystyle\prod_{i=1}^{y} f(x_i, u_0)} \geq \dfrac{1 - \beta}{\alpha};$ reject H_0 (accept H_1).

(3) If $\dfrac{\beta}{1 - \alpha} < \dfrac{\displaystyle\prod_{i=1}^{y} f(x_i, u_1)}{\displaystyle\prod_{i=1}^{y} f(x_i, u_0)} < \dfrac{1 - \beta}{\alpha};$

take another sample.

Example 10
Suppose we have two hypotheses

$$H_0: \quad u = 1(u_0)$$

$$H_1: \quad u = 2(u_1)$$

and that $\alpha = .05$, $\beta = .1$, with x normally distributed:

$$f(x, u) = \frac{e^{-\frac{1}{2}(x-u)^2}}{\sqrt{2\pi}}$$

$$\frac{\beta}{1 - \alpha} = \frac{.1}{1 - .05} \qquad \frac{1 - \beta}{\alpha} = \frac{1 - .1}{.05}$$

$$\frac{\prod\limits_{i=1}^{y} f(x_i, u_1)}{\prod\limits_{i=1}^{y} f(x_i, u_0)} = \frac{\prod\limits_{i=1}^{y} e^{-\frac{1}{2}(x_i - u_1)^2}}{\prod\limits_{i=1}^{y} e^{-\frac{1}{2}(x_i - u_0)^2}}$$

$$= e^{(u_1 - u_0) \sum\limits_{i=1}^{y} x_i + \frac{y}{2}(u_0^2 - u_1^2)}$$

Decision rule (1):

If $\dfrac{\prod\limits_{i=1}^{y} f(x_i, u_1)}{\prod\limits_{i=1}^{y} f(x_i, u_0)} \leq \dfrac{\beta}{1 - \alpha}$; accept H_0: $u = 1$

$$e^{(2-1) \sum\limits_{i=1}^{y} x_i + \frac{y}{2}(1^2 - 2^2)} \leq \frac{.1}{1 - .05}$$

$$\sum_{i=1}^{y} x_i - 1.5y \leq \log .105$$

$$\sum_{i=1}^{y} x_i \leq 1.5y - 2.25$$

which means that when we are taking samples one at a time, if we reach a point that the sum of the sample values becomes smaller or equal to $(1.5y - 2.25)$ (y being the number of samples that we have taken), we can stop taking additional sample and accept the hypothesis that $u = 1$.

Decision rule (2):

If
$$\frac{\prod_{i=1}^{y} f(x_i, u_1)}{\prod_{i=1}^{y} f(x_i, u_0)} \geq \frac{1-\beta}{\alpha}; \quad \text{accept } H_1: \quad u = 2$$

$$e^{(2-1)\sum_{i=1}^{y} x_i + \frac{y}{2}(1^2 - 2^2)} \geq \frac{1 - .1}{.05}$$

$$\sum_{i=1}^{y} x_i - 1.5y \geq \log 18$$

$$\sum_{i=1}^{y} x_i \geq 1.5y + 2.89$$

which means that when we are taking samples one at a time, if we reach a point where the sum of the sample values becomes greater than or equal to $(1.5y + 2.89)$, (y being the number of samples that we have taken), we can stop taking additional sample and accept the hypothesis that $u = 2$.

Decision rule (3):

$$1.5y - 2.25 < \sum_{i=1}^{y} x_i < 1.5y + 2.89$$

(y being the number of samples that we have taken), then the advice is to postpone the decision of accepting either hypothesis and taking another sample.

CORRELATION AND REGRESSION*

Thus far we have been concerned with a single variable and its frequency function. Many of the statistical problems, however, involve several variables. Therefore in this section we introduce correlation and regression. *Correlation* is a method for studying two or more variables simultaneously. The purpose is to determine whether they are interrelated. If they are, how and to what extent they are

*This portion is taken from K. Chu, *Principles of Econometrics.* Scranton, Pa.: International Textbook Company, 1968.

interrelated. The term *regression* indicates that we are interested in one particular variable—the *dependent* or *explained* variable. Other variables (the independent or explanatory variables) are studied for their possible effect on this particular variable. Following are some commonly used linear models in estimating relationships among more than two variables.

Two-Variable Linear-Regression Model

Let Y be a variable whose value is determined by another variable X. We call X the *explanatory variable* and Y the *explained variable*, or the variable to be explained. First we test whether we can accept the hypothesis that a linear relationship exists between the two variables. We take a sample of X_i, $Y_i (i = 1, \ldots, n)$ and calculate the linear correlation coefficient r.

$$r = \frac{\Sigma x_i y_i}{n S_x S_y} \qquad (4\text{-}1)$$

where x, y are the deviations from the sample mean and S_x, S_y are sample standard deviations. If x_i and y_i are of the same sign, negative or positive, the sum of the product $\Sigma x_i y_i$ will be large; otherwise it will be small.

Figure 4-7 shows that if the sample points cluster in

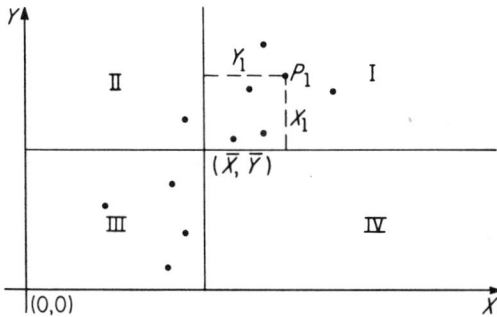

Fig. 4-7

quadrants I and III, it indicates intuitively that a positive correlation exists between X and Y. (If the sample points cluster in quadrants II and IV, it shows a negative correlation between X and Y, and $\Sigma x_i y_i$ will have a negative value.) In the other case, if they scatter evenly in all four quadrants there does not seem to be any correlation between the two variables, and the value of $\Sigma x_i y_i$ will approach zero.

The correlation coefficients between different sets of variables may need to be compared to each other to examine their degrees of correlation. However, X and Y may be in different units; for example, Y may be in dollars and X may be in pounds. Also, the sample size may be different in different cases. Larger sample size will make the value of $\Sigma x_i y_i$ larger. So in order to make r unit free, x is divided by S_x, y is divided by S_y, and the whole term is divided by n to eliminate the effect of different sample size.

When r approaches to zero, there is no linear correlation between Y and X, and when r is different from zero we may test its significance by transforming r to an approximately normal variate by the following formula:

$$Z = \frac{1}{2} \log \left(\frac{1 + r}{1 - r} \right)$$

The mean value of this transformed variable Z is

$$\mu_Z = \frac{1}{2} \log \left(\frac{1 + \rho}{1 - \rho} \right)$$

where ρ is the true value of the linear correlation coefficient. When $\rho = 0$, $\mu_Z = 0$, the standard deviation of the distribution of Z is

$$\sigma_Z = \frac{1}{\sqrt{n - 3}}$$

for sample size n larger than 30.

We then may use the classical statistical method to test the hypothesis that ρ equals zero (which means no linear correlation between Y and X) against an alternative hypothesis that ρ does not equal zero (which means there is a linear correlation between Y and X).

After we have decided to accept the hypothesis that the relationship between Y and X is linear, we then want to estimate the coefficients of the linear equation. The equation may be expressed as

$$\hat{Y} = a + bX$$

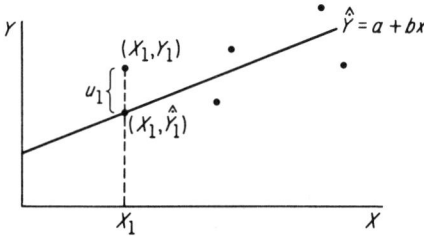

Fig. 4-8

where a is the intercept of the line on the Y-axis, and b is the slope of the line. $\hat{Y}$ is used because the true values of X and Y may not fall on the line. We use Y to denote the true Y value and write

$$Y = a + bX + u$$

where u is the difference between the true Y value and the Y value as specified by the line given X.

The value u may represent either the net effect of the variables not included in the equation or errors of observation and measurement, or it may be a basic and unpredictable element of randomness, etc. and we assume u_i are independent random variables with zero mean and constant variance; that is,

$$E(u_i) = 0, \quad E(u_i^2) = \sigma_u^2 \quad \text{for} \quad i = 1, 2, \ldots, n$$

and

$$E(u_i u_j) = 0 \quad \text{for} \quad i \neq j (i, j = 1, 2, \ldots, n)$$

Now in general we cannot observe all values of X and Y, but can take only a limited number of samples. From the sample values we estimate the true regression line. We write the estimated values of a and b as $\hat{a}$ and $\hat{b}$. Again, the

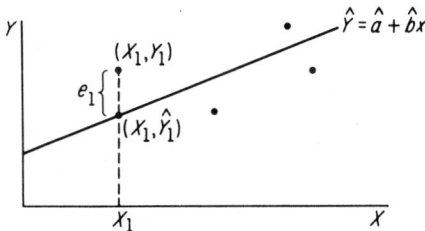

Fig. 4-9

true sample values of X and Y may not fall on the estimated regression line, thus we write

$$Y = \hat{Y} + e = \hat{a} + \hat{b}X + e$$

or

$$y = \hat{y} + e = \hat{b}x + e \tag{4-2}$$

where $\hat{Y}$ is the Y value specified by the estimated regression line, given X, e is the difference between the true sample value of Y and $\hat{Y}$, $y = Y - \overline{Y}$ and $\hat{y} = \hat{Y} - \overline{Y}$.

The Least-Squares Estimators

Suppose we take n pairs of values of X and Y and denote these values by

$$(X_1, Y_1), (X_2, Y_2), \ldots, (X_n, Y_n)$$

Then

$$e_i = Y_i - \hat{Y}_i \quad (i = 1, \ldots, n)$$

The principle of least squares is to make Σe_i^2 as small as possible:

$$\Sigma e_i^2 = \Sigma(Y_i - \hat{Y}_i)^2 = \Sigma(Y_i - a - bX_i)^2$$

A necessary condition that Σe_i^2 be the minimum is that the partial derivatives with respect to a and b should equal to zeros.

$$\frac{\partial}{\partial a} \Sigma e_i^2 = -2\Sigma(Y_i - a - bX_i)$$

$$\frac{\partial}{\partial b} \Sigma e_i^2 = -2\Sigma X_i(Y_i - a - bX_i)$$

When they are set to zeros, the following equations are obtained:

$$\Sigma Y_i = n\hat{a} + \hat{b}\Sigma X_i \tag{4-3}$$

$$\Sigma X_i Y_i = \hat{a}\Sigma X_i + \hat{b}\Sigma X_i^2 \tag{4-4}$$

These equations are called *normal equations*. Solving for b,

$$\hat{b} = \frac{\begin{vmatrix} n & \Sigma Y \\ \Sigma X & \Sigma XY \end{vmatrix}}{\begin{vmatrix} n & \Sigma X \\ \Sigma X & \Sigma X^2 \end{vmatrix}} = \frac{n\Sigma XY - (\Sigma X)(\Sigma Y)}{n\Sigma X^2 - (\Sigma X)^2}$$

$$\hat{a} = \overline{Y} - \hat{b}\overline{X}$$

Let $x = X - \overline{X}$ and $y = Y - \overline{Y}$. Then the normal equations become

$$\Sigma(y + \overline{Y}) = n\hat{a} + \hat{b}\Sigma(x + \overline{X})$$
$$\Sigma(x + \overline{X})(y + \overline{Y}) = \hat{a}\Sigma(x + \overline{X}) + \hat{b}\Sigma(x + \overline{X})^2$$

And since

$$\Sigma x = 0 \qquad \Sigma y = 0$$

the equations are simplified to

$$\overline{Y} = \hat{a} + \hat{b}\overline{X} \tag{4-3a}$$
$$\Sigma xy + n\overline{X}\overline{Y} = \hat{a}n\overline{X} + \hat{b}n\overline{X}^2 + \hat{b}\Sigma x^2 \tag{4-4a}$$

or

$$\Sigma xy = \hat{b}\Sigma x^2$$

Thus

$$\hat{b} = \frac{\Sigma xy}{\Sigma x^2} \tag{4-5}$$

$$\hat{a} = \overline{Y} - \hat{b}\overline{X} \tag{4-6}$$

where $\hat{a}$ and $\hat{b}$ are the least-squares point estimators of a and b. Compare $\hat{b}$ to the linear correlation coefficient r,

$$\hat{b} = \frac{\Sigma xy}{\Sigma x^2} = \frac{\Sigma xy}{nS_x^2} = \frac{\Sigma xy}{nS_x^2} \cdot \frac{S_y}{S_y} = r\frac{S_y}{S_x} \tag{4-7}$$

Also because

$$y = \hat{y} + e$$
$$\begin{aligned}
\Sigma y^2 &= \Sigma\hat{y}^2 + \Sigma e^2 + 2\Sigma\hat{y}e \\
&= \Sigma\hat{y}^2 + \Sigma e^2 + 2\Sigma(\hat{b}x)(y - \hat{b}x) \\
&= \Sigma\hat{y}^2 + \Sigma e^2 + 2\hat{b}\Sigma xy - 2\hat{b}^2\Sigma x^2 \\
&= \Sigma\hat{y}^2 + \Sigma e^2 + 2\hat{b}(\hat{b}\Sigma x^2) - 2\hat{b}^2\Sigma x^2 \\
&= \Sigma\hat{y}^2 + \Sigma e^2
\end{aligned}$$

Therefore

$$r^2 = \hat{b}^2\frac{S_x^2}{S_y^2} = \frac{\hat{b}^2\Sigma x^2}{\Sigma y^2} = \frac{\Sigma\hat{y}^2}{\Sigma y^2}$$

or

$$r^2 = \frac{\Sigma y^2 - \Sigma e^2}{\Sigma y^2} = 1 - \frac{\Sigma e^2}{\Sigma y^2} \tag{4-8}$$

The quantity r^2 is called the *coefficient of determination*. It can be expressed as the ratio of the explained variation and the total variation of Y, or as one minus the ratio of the residual or unexplained variation and the total variation of Y. The maximum value of r^2 is 1 when Σe^2 approaches zero.

In order to make interval estimates of a and b, we need to find the variances of $\hat{a}$ and b. First

$$\hat{b} = \frac{\Sigma xy}{\Sigma x^2} = \frac{\Sigma x(Y - \overline{Y})}{\Sigma x^2}$$

$$= \frac{\Sigma xY}{\Sigma x^2} - \frac{\overline{Y}\Sigma x}{\Sigma x^2} = \frac{\Sigma xY}{\Sigma x^2}$$

$$= \frac{\Sigma x}{\Sigma x^2}(a + bX + u)$$

$$= a\frac{\Sigma x}{\Sigma x^2} + b\frac{\Sigma xX}{\Sigma x^2} + \frac{\Sigma xu}{\Sigma x^2}$$

$$= b\frac{\Sigma x}{\Sigma x^2}(x + \overline{X}) + \frac{\Sigma xu}{\Sigma x^2}$$

$$= b\frac{\Sigma x^2}{\Sigma x^2} + b\overline{X}\frac{\Sigma x}{\Sigma x^2} + \frac{\Sigma xu}{\Sigma x^2}$$

$$= b + \frac{\Sigma xu}{\Sigma x^2}$$

Here we note that

$$E(\hat{b}) = E\left[b + \left(\frac{\Sigma xu}{\Sigma x^2}\right)\right]$$

$$= b + E\left(\frac{\Sigma xu}{\Sigma x^2}\right)$$

When X and u are independent, $\Sigma xu = 0$, then $E(\hat{b}) = b$. The least-squares estimator is unbiased. Also,

$$\hat{b} - b = \frac{\Sigma xu}{\Sigma x^2}$$

$$\text{var}(\hat{b}) = E(\hat{b} - b)^2 = E\left(\frac{\Sigma xu}{\Sigma x^2}\right)^2$$

Assume fixed X values, then Σx^2 is a constant, and

$$\text{var}(\hat{b}) = \frac{1}{(\Sigma x^2)^2} E(x_1^2 u_1^2 + \cdots + x_n^2 u_n^2$$

$$+ 2x_1 x_2 u_1 u_2 + \cdots + 2x_{n-1} x_n u_{n-1} u_n)$$

We further assume that u_i are independent variables with zero mean and constant variance ($E(u_i) = 0$, $E(u_i^2) = \sigma_u^2$ for all i and $E(u_i u_j) = 0$ for $i \neq j$; $i, j = 1, 2, \ldots, n$). Then

$$E(x_i^2 u_i^2) = x_i^2 \sigma_u^2$$

$$\text{var}(\hat{b}) = \frac{\sigma_u^2}{(\Sigma x^2)^2} \Sigma x^2 = \frac{\sigma_u^2}{\Sigma x^2} \tag{4-9}$$

and

$$\hat{a} = \bar{Y} - \hat{b}\bar{X}$$

$$= \frac{\Sigma Y}{n} - \frac{\Sigma xy}{\Sigma x^2} \bar{X}$$

$$= \frac{\Sigma Y}{n} - \bar{X}\left[\frac{\Sigma x(Y - \bar{Y})}{\Sigma x^2}\right]$$

$$= \frac{\Sigma Y}{n} - \bar{X}\frac{\Sigma x Y}{\Sigma x^2}$$

$$= \Sigma\left(\frac{1}{n} - \bar{X}\frac{x}{\Sigma x^2}\right) Y$$

$$= \Sigma\left(\frac{1}{n} - \bar{X}\frac{x}{\Sigma x^2}\right) (a + bX + u)$$

$$= a + b\frac{\Sigma X}{n} - b\bar{X}\frac{\Sigma X^2}{\Sigma x^2} + \Sigma\left(\frac{1}{n} - \bar{X}\frac{x}{\Sigma x^2}\right) u$$

$$= a + \Sigma\left(\frac{1}{n} - \bar{X}\frac{x}{\Sigma x^2}\right) u$$

Thus

$$\hat{a} - a = \Sigma\left(\frac{1}{n} - \bar{X}\frac{x}{\Sigma x^2}\right) u$$

$$\text{var}(\hat{a}) = E(\hat{a} - a)^2$$

$$= E\left[\Sigma\left(\frac{1}{n} - \bar{X}\frac{x}{\Sigma x^2}\right) u\right]^2$$

$$= \left[\frac{n}{n^2} - \frac{2\bar{X}}{n}\left(\frac{\Sigma x}{\Sigma x^2}\right) + \bar{X}^2\frac{\Sigma x^2}{(\Sigma x^2)^2}\right] \sigma_u^2$$

$$= \left(\frac{1}{n} + \frac{\bar{X}^2}{\Sigma x^2}\right) \sigma_u^2$$

$$= \left(\frac{\Sigma x^2 + n\bar{X}^2}{n\Sigma x^2}\right) \sigma_u^2$$

$$= \left(\frac{\Sigma(X - \bar{X})^2 + n\bar{X}^2}{n\Sigma x^2}\right) \sigma_u^2$$

$$= \left(\frac{\Sigma X^2 - 2X\Sigma X + n\overline{X}^2 + n\overline{X}^2}{n\Sigma x^2} \right) \sigma_u^2$$

$$= \frac{\Sigma X^2}{n\Sigma x^2} \sigma_u^2 \qquad (4\text{-}10)$$

Note also

$$E(\hat{a}) = a + E\left(\frac{\Sigma u}{n} - \overline{X} \frac{\Sigma xu}{\Sigma x^2} \right)$$

When we assume $E(u_i) = 0$ and X and u are independent ($\Sigma xu = 0$), $E(\hat{a}) = a$, and $\hat{a}$ is an unbiased estimator of a.

The covariance of $\hat{a}$ and $\hat{b}$ is given by

$$\text{cov}(\hat{a}, \hat{b}) = E(\hat{a} - a)(\hat{b} - b)$$

$$= E\left[\Sigma \left(\frac{1}{n} - \overline{X} \frac{x}{\Sigma x^2} \right) u \frac{\Sigma xu}{\Sigma x^2} \right]$$

$$= E\left[\frac{u(\Sigma xu)}{\Sigma x^2} - \overline{X} \frac{(\Sigma xu)^2}{(\Sigma x^2)^2} \right]$$

$$= E\left[\frac{\Sigma x}{\Sigma x^2} - \overline{X} \frac{1}{\Sigma x^2} \right] u^2$$

$$= - \frac{\overline{X}}{\Sigma x^2} \sigma_u^2 \qquad (4\text{-}11)$$

Using t distribution, the interval estimates of a and b can be expressed as

$$\hat{a} \pm t_{\alpha/2} \cdot \sqrt{\text{var}(\hat{a})} = \hat{a} \pm t_{\alpha/2} \frac{\sqrt{\Sigma X^2}}{\sqrt{n\Sigma x^2}} \sigma_u \qquad (4\text{-}12)^*$$

$$\hat{b} \pm t_{\alpha/2} \cdot \sqrt{\text{var}(\hat{b})} = \hat{b} \pm t_{\alpha/2} \frac{1}{\sqrt{\Sigma x^2}} \sigma_u \qquad (4\text{-}13)^*$$

where $t_{\alpha/2}$ specifies the level of confidence (for sample size larger than 30, standard normal distribution may be used).

The joint distribution for t and X_i is

$$h(t, X_i) = g(t \mid x_i) f(X_i)$$

*The confidence intervals of a and b specified in Eqs. 4-11 and 4-12 involve student's t distribution on the assumption of fixed X_i; that is,

$$P(-t_{\alpha/2} < t < t_{\alpha/2}) = 1 - \alpha$$

where t_i is some function of the observations on X and Y.

where $g(t \mid x_i)$ are the conditional distributions of t given X_i. But

$$1 - \alpha = P(-t_{\alpha/2} < t < t_{\alpha/2})$$

$$= \int_{-t_{\alpha/2}}^{t_{\alpha/2}} g(t \mid X_i)\, dt$$

$$= \int_{-\infty}^{\infty} \cdots \int_{-\infty}^{\infty} \int_{-t_{\alpha/2}}^{t_{\alpha/2}} g(t \mid X_i)\, f(X_i)\, dt\, dX_i$$

Since

$$\int_{-\infty}^{\infty} \cdots \int_{-\infty}^{\infty} f(X_i)\, dX_i = 1$$

$$1 - \alpha = \int_{-\infty}^{\infty} \cdots \int_{-\infty}^{\infty} \int_{-t_{\alpha/2}}^{t_{\alpha/2}} h(t, X_i)\, dt\, dX_i$$

Thus, Eqs. 4-12 and 4-13 are still valid when X_i are random variables, provided that the conditional distribution of Y given X fulfills the assumption of homoscedasticity, ($E(u_i) = 0$, $E(u_i^2) = \sigma_u^2$ for all i and $E(u_i u_j) = 0$ for $i \neq j$; $i, j = 1, 2, \ldots, n$).

Empirically, however, the variance of the disturbance term σ_u^2 is usually unknown and has to be estimated from the sample-error term e. Thus σ_u^2 is replaced by $\hat{\sigma}_u^2$ in the formulas, and $\hat{\sigma}_u^2$ is computed as the following. Since

$$Y_i = a + bX_i + u_i$$

and

$$\overline{Y} = a + b\overline{X} + \overline{u}$$

hence

$$y_i = bx_i + (u_i - \overline{u})$$

Also

$$e_i = y_i - \hat{b}x_i$$

$$= -(\hat{b} - b)x_i + (u_i - \overline{u})$$

$$\Sigma e^2 = (\hat{b} - b)^2 \Sigma x^2 + \Sigma(u - \overline{u})^2 - 2(\hat{b} - b)\Sigma x(u - \overline{u})$$

$$E(\Sigma e^2) = E[(\hat{b} - b)^2 \Sigma x^2 + \Sigma(u - \overline{u})^2 - 2(\hat{b} - b)\Sigma x(u - \overline{u})]$$

Since

$$E[(\hat{b} - b)^2 \Sigma x^2] = \left(\frac{\sigma_u^2}{\Sigma x^2}\right)\Sigma x^2$$

$$= \sigma_u^2$$

$$E[\Sigma(u - \bar{u})^2] = E[\Sigma u^2 + n\bar{u}^2 - 2\bar{u}\Sigma u]$$

$$= E\left(\Sigma u^2 - \frac{(\Sigma u)^2}{n}\right)$$

$$= \frac{n - 1}{n} E(\Sigma u^2)$$

$$= (n - 1)\sigma_u^2$$

$$E[(\hat{b} - b)\Sigma x(u - \bar{u})] = E\left[\left(\frac{\Sigma x_u}{\Sigma x^2}\right)(\Sigma xu - \bar{u}\Sigma x)\right]$$

$$= E\left[\frac{\Sigma x^2 u^2}{\Sigma x^2}\right]$$

$$= \sigma_u^2$$

Thus

$$E(\Sigma e^2) = \sigma_u^2 + (n - 1)\sigma_u^2 - 2\sigma_u^2 = (n - 2)\sigma_u^2$$

An unbiased estimator of σ_u^2 should be

$$\hat{\sigma}_u^2 = \frac{\Sigma e^2}{n - 2} \tag{4-14}$$

Maximum-Likelihood Estimators

The above interval estimates of a and b using the least-squares method are based on the assumption that the X_i values are fixed. In practical applications, however, X_i may also be random variables.

Let $f(X_i), i = 1, 2, \ldots, n$ be the probability distribution of X_i, and assume that the conditional probability distribution of the Y_i given X_i are normal and independent with expected values $(a + bX_i)$ and constant variance σ_u^2. Then the joint distribution of X_i and Y_i can be expressed as

$$L = f(X_i) \cdots f(X_n) \cdots f(Y_1 \mid X_1) \cdots f(Y_n \mid X_n)$$

$$= f(X_1) \cdots f(X_n) \cdot \frac{1}{(2\pi\sigma_u^2)^{n/2}}$$

$$\cdot \exp\left[-\frac{1}{2\sigma_u^2} \Sigma(Y_i - a - bX_i)^2\right] \tag{4-15}$$

Since the logarithm of a function has the maximum point at the respective position as the original function, we take the logarithm of L, which is

$$\log L = \log f(X_1) + \cdots + \log f(X_n) - \left(\frac{n}{2}\right)\log 2\pi$$

$$- \left(\frac{n}{2}\right)\log \sigma_u^2 - \frac{1}{2\sigma_u^2}\Sigma(Y_i - a - bX_i)^2$$

Partially differentiating $\log L$ with respect to a, b, and σ_u^2 gives

$$\frac{\partial \log L}{\partial a} = \frac{1}{\sigma_u^2}\Sigma(Y_i - a - bX_i)$$

$$\frac{\partial \log L}{\partial b} = \frac{1}{\sigma_u^2}\Sigma X_i(Y_i - a - bX_i)$$

$$\frac{\partial \log L}{\partial \sigma_u^2} = -\frac{n}{2\sigma_u^2} + \frac{1}{2\sigma_u^4}\Sigma(Y_i - a - bX_i)^2$$

Equating them to zero, we obtain the maximum-likelihood estimators of a and b:

$$\hat{b} = \frac{n\Sigma XY - (\Sigma X)(\Sigma Y)}{n\Sigma X^2 - (\Sigma X)^2} \quad \text{or} \quad \frac{\Sigma xy}{\Sigma x^2} \qquad (4\text{-}16)$$

$$\hat{a} = \overline{Y} - \hat{b}\overline{X} \qquad (4\text{-}17)$$

$$\hat{\sigma}_u^2 = \frac{1}{n}\Sigma(Y_i - \hat{a} - \hat{b}X_i)^2 \qquad (4\text{-}18)$$

They are the same as the least-squares estimators.

Prediction. Given an X value, X_0, we want to predict the Y value. The starting point would be the point on the regression line:

$$\hat{Y}_0 = \hat{a} + \hat{b}X_0$$

However, prediction involves uncertainty, and we will obtain more information from an interval estimate with a specified level of confidence. Therefore we need to know the variance of $\hat{Y}_0$.

$$\begin{aligned}
\text{var}(\hat{Y}_0) &= E[\hat{Y}_0 - E(\hat{Y}_0 \mid X_0)]^2 \\
&= E[\hat{a} + \hat{b}X_0 - (a + bX_0)]^2 \\
&= E[(\hat{a} - a) + (\hat{b} - b)X_0]^2 \\
&= \text{var}(\hat{a}) + X_0^2\,\text{var}(\hat{b}) + 2X_0\,\text{cov}(\hat{a}, \hat{b}) \\
&= \frac{\Sigma X^2}{n\Sigma x^2}\sigma u^2 + X_0^2\frac{\sigma u^2}{\Sigma x^2} - 2X_0\frac{\overline{X}}{\Sigma x^2}\sigma_u^2
\end{aligned}$$

$$= \sigma_u^2 \left[\frac{\Sigma(x + \overline{X})^2}{n\Sigma x^2} + \frac{X_0^2}{\Sigma x^2} - 2\frac{X_0\overline{X}}{\Sigma x^2} \right]$$

$$= \sigma_u^2 \left[\frac{1}{n} + \frac{\overline{X}^2}{\Sigma x^2} + \frac{X_0^2}{\Sigma x^2} - \frac{2X_0\overline{X}}{\Sigma x^2} \right]$$

$$= \sigma_u^2 \left[\frac{1}{n} + \frac{(X_0 - \overline{X})^2}{\Sigma x^2} \right] \qquad (4\text{-}19)$$

Using t distribution with $n - 2$ degrees of freedom, we have the interval estimate of Y_0, which is

$$(\hat{a} + \hat{b}X_0) \pm t_{\alpha/2}\hat{\sigma}_u \sqrt{\frac{1}{n} + \frac{(X_0 - \overline{X})^2}{\Sigma x^2}} \qquad (4\text{-}20)$$

If we want to predict the actual Y value instead the Y value on the regression line, then the variance of Y_0 will be

$$\begin{aligned} \text{var}(Y_0) &= E(Y_0 - \hat{Y}_0)^2 \\ &= E[(a + bX_0 + u_0) - \hat{a} + \hat{b}X_0)]^2 \\ &= E(u_0^2) + E[(\hat{a} - a) + (\hat{b} - b)X_0]^2 \\ &= \sigma_u^2 \left[1 + \frac{1}{n} + \frac{(X_0 - \overline{X})^2}{\Sigma x^2} \right] \qquad (4\text{-}21) \end{aligned}$$

Thus the interval estimate of Y_0 is

$$(\hat{a} + \hat{b}X_0) \pm t_{\alpha/2}\hat{\sigma}_u \sqrt{1 + \frac{1}{n} + \frac{(X_0 - \overline{X})^2}{\Sigma x^2}} \qquad (4\text{-}22)$$

Three-Variable Linear-Regression Model

Let Y be a variable whose value is determined by two other variables X_2 and X_3. If the relationship can be approximated by a linear plane, it can be expressed by the following equation:

$$\hat{Y} = b_1 + b_2X_2 + b_3X_3$$

where $\hat{Y}$ is used because the true values of X and Y may not lie on the plane. We use Y to denote the true value and write

$$Y = b_1 + b_2X_2 + b_3X_3 + u$$

where u is the difference between Y and $\hat{Y}$.

Now in general we cannot observe all values of X_2, X_3, and Y, but can observe only a finite number of samples. From the sample values we may apply methods such as least squares to estimate the parameters of the equation.

Again, the true sample values of X_2, X_3, and Y may not fall on the estimated regression plane; thus we write

$$Y = \hat{Y} + e$$
$$= \hat{b}_1 + \hat{b}_2 X_2 + \hat{b}_3 X_3 + e$$

where e is the difference between the true sample value of Y and the Y value on the estimated regression plane. If we use the deviations of X_2, X_3, and Y from their respective means, it can be expressed as

$$y = \hat{y} + e$$
$$= \hat{b}_2 x_2 + \hat{b}_3 x_3 + e \qquad (4\text{-}23)$$

The Least-Squares Estimators

Suppose we take n samples of X_2, X_3, and Y and denote them as

$$(X_{21}, X_{31}, Y_1) \cdots (X_{2n}, X_{3n}, Y_n)$$

Then

$$e_i = Y_i - \hat{Y}_i (i = 1, 2, \ldots, n)$$
$$e_i^2 = (Y_i - \hat{Y}_i)^2$$
$$= (Y_i - \hat{b}_1 - \hat{b}_2 X_{2i} - \hat{b}_3 X_{3i})^2$$

The partial derivatives with respect to b_1, b_2, and b_3 are

$$\frac{\partial}{\partial \hat{b}_1} \Sigma e_i^2 = -2\Sigma(Y_i - \hat{b}_1 - \hat{b}_2 X_{2i} - \hat{b}_3 X_{3i})$$

$$\frac{\partial}{\partial \hat{b}_2} \Sigma e_i^2 = -2\Sigma X_{2i}(Y_i - \hat{b}_1 - \hat{b}_2 X_{2i} - \hat{b}_3 X_{3i})$$

$$\frac{\partial}{\partial \hat{b}_3} \Sigma e_i^2 = -2\Sigma X_{3i}(Y_i - \hat{b}_1 - \hat{b}_2 X_{2i} - \hat{b}_3 X_{3i})$$

Equating these to zero and letting $a_{1.23}$, $b_{12.3}$, and $b_{13.2}$ be the least-squares estimates of $\hat{b}_1$, $\hat{b}_2$, and $\hat{b}_3$ respectively, we obtain

$$\Sigma Y_1 = na_{1.23} + b_{12.3}\Sigma X_{2i} + b_{13.2}\Sigma X_{3i}$$

$$\Sigma X_{2i} Y_i = a_{1.23} \Sigma X_{2i} + b_{12.3} \Sigma X_{2i}^2 + b_{13.2} \Sigma X_{2i} X_{3i}$$

$$\Sigma X_{3i} Y_i = a_{1.23} \Sigma X_{3i} + b_{12.3} \Sigma X_{2i} X_{3i} + b_{13.2} \Sigma X_{3i}^2$$

Solving for $b_{12.3}$, $b_{13.2}$, $a_{1.23}$ and using deviation terms of X_2, X_3, and Y,

$$(x_2 = X_2 - \overline{X}_2 \quad x_3 = X_3 - \overline{X}_3 \quad y = Y - \overline{Y})$$

and we obtain

$$b_{12.3} = \frac{(\Sigma x_2 y)(\Sigma x_3^2) - (\Sigma x_3 y)(\Sigma x_2 x_3)}{(\Sigma x_2^2)(\Sigma x_3^2) - (\Sigma x_2 x_3)^2} \qquad (4\text{-}24)$$

$$b_{13.2} = \frac{(\Sigma x_3 y)(\Sigma x_2^2) - (\Sigma x_2 y)(\Sigma x_2 x_3)}{(\Sigma x_2^2)(\Sigma x_3^2) - (\Sigma x_2 x_3)^2} \qquad (4\text{-}25)$$

$$a_{1.23} = \overline{Y} - b_{12.3}\overline{X}_2 - b_{13.2}\overline{X}_3 \qquad (4\text{-}26)$$

Since the formula of simple correlation coefficient between two variables is

$$r = \frac{\Sigma xy}{nS_x S_y}$$

we may write

$$r_{12} = \frac{\Sigma x_2 y}{nS_1 S_2} \qquad r_{13} = \frac{\Sigma x_3 y}{nS_1 S_3} \qquad r_{23} = \frac{\Sigma x_2 x_3}{nS_2 S_3}$$

and Eqs. 4-24 and 4-25 may be written as

$$b_{12.3} = \frac{r_{12} - r_{13} r_{23}}{1 - r_{23}^2} \frac{S_1}{S_2} \qquad (4\text{-}27)$$

$$b_{13.2} = \frac{r_{13} - r_{12} r_{23}}{1 - r_{23}^2} \frac{S_1}{S_3} \qquad (4\text{-}28)$$

The variances of the estimators are

$$\text{var}(b_{12.3}) = \frac{\Sigma x_{1.23}^2}{(n-3) \Sigma x_{23}^2}$$

$$\text{var}(b_{13.2}) = \frac{\Sigma x_{1.23}^2}{(n-3) \Sigma x_{32}^2}$$

where

$$x_{1.23} = y - b_{12.3}x_2 - b_{13.2}x_3$$

$$x_{23} = x_2 - b_{23}x_3$$

and

$$x_{32} = x_3 - b_{32}x_2$$

Test the significance of the relationship between the variables Y, X_2, and X_3.

F test:

Source of Variation	Degrees of Freedom	Mean Square
Explained by X_2 and X_3 $(b_{12.3}\Sigma x_2 y + b_{13.2}\Sigma x_3 y)$	2	$(b_{12.3}\Sigma x_2 y + b_{13.2}\Sigma x_3 y)/2$
Residual or unexplained (Σe^2)	$n-3$	$\Sigma e^2/(n-3)$
Total variation of $Y(\Sigma y^2)$	$n-1$	

The F ratio is

$$F = \frac{(b_{12.3}\Sigma x_2 y + b_{13.2}\Sigma x_3 y)/2}{\Sigma e^2/(n-3)}$$

Compare the F ratio with the critical value found in the F-distribution table. If the F ratio is greater than the critical value, we conclude that a significant relationship exists between the three variables.

Stepwise F tests:

Source of Variation	Degrees of Freedom	Mean Square
Explained by $X_2(\hat{b}_2\Sigma x_2 y)$	1	$\hat{b}_2\Sigma x_2 y[\hat{b}_2 = (\Sigma x_2 y/\Sigma x_2^2)]$
Addition of X_3	1	$(b_{12.3}\Sigma x_2 y + b_{13.2}\Sigma x_3 y) - (\hat{b}_2\Sigma x_2 y)$
Explained by X_2 and X_3 $(b_{12.3}\Sigma x_2 y + b_{13.2}\Sigma x_3 y)$	2	$(b_{12.3}\Sigma x_2 y + b_{13.2}\Sigma x_3 y)/2$
Residual (Σe^2)	$n-3$	$\Sigma e^2/(n-3)$
Total variation of $Y(\Sigma y^2)$	$n-1$	

The significance of the additional X_3 effect is tested by

$$F = \frac{(b_{12.3}\Sigma x_2 y + b_{13.2}\Sigma x_3 y) - (\hat{b}_2\Sigma x_2 y)}{\Sigma e^2/(n-3)}$$

or

Source of Variation	Degrees of Freedom	Mean Square
Explained by X_3 $(\hat{b}_3\Sigma x_3 y)$	1	$\hat{b}_3\Sigma x_3 y[\hat{b}_3 = (\Sigma x_3 y/\Sigma x_3^2)]$
Addition of X_2	1	$(b_{12.3}\Sigma x_2 y + b_{13.2}\Sigma x_3 y) - (\hat{b}_3\Sigma x_3 y)$
Explained by X_2 and X_3 $(b_{12.3}\Sigma x_2 y + b_{13.2}\Sigma x_3 y)$	2	$(b_{12.3}\Sigma x_2 y + b_{13.2}\Sigma x_3 y)/2$
Residual (Σe^2)	$n-3$	$\Sigma e^2/(n-3)$
Total variation of $Y(\Sigma y^2)$	$n-1$	

The significance of the additional X_2 effect is tested by

$$F = \frac{(b_{12.3}\Sigma x_2 y + b_{13.2}\Sigma x_3 y) - (b\Sigma x_3 y)}{\Sigma e^2/(n-3)}$$

t test: The net effect of X_2 and X_3 can also be tested by t values:

$$t_2 = \frac{b_{12.3}}{\sqrt{\dfrac{\Sigma e^2}{n-3}}\,\sqrt{a_{22}}}$$

where $a_{22} = \Sigma x_3^2/[\Sigma x_2^2 \Sigma x_3^2 - (\Sigma x_2 x_3)^2]$, a diagonal element in matrix $(X^T X)^{-1}$.

$$t_3 = \frac{b_{13.2}}{\sqrt{\dfrac{\Sigma e^2}{n-3}}\,\sqrt{a_{33}}}$$

where $a_{33} = \Sigma x_2^2/[\Sigma x_2^2 \Sigma x_3^2 - (\Sigma x_2 x_3)^2]$, a diagonal element in matrix $(X^T X)^{-1}$. If t_2 and t_3 are greater than the respective critical values found in the t-distribution table, the regression coefficients $b_{12.3}$ and $b_{13.2}$ are accepted as significantly different from zero, which indicates significant relationships exist between X_2 and Y, X_3, and Y.

The Coefficient of Multiple Correlation

To measure the linear correlation between X_2, X_3, and Y we use the coefficient of multiple correlation $R_{1.23}$. The square of $R_{1.23}$ is called the *coefficient of determination*, $R_{1.23}^2$. It is the ratio of the explained variation and the total variation of Y.

$$R_{1.23}^2 = \frac{\Sigma \hat{y}^2}{\Sigma y^2}$$

or

$$= 1 - \frac{\Sigma e^2}{\Sigma y^2}$$

Since

$$\Sigma e^2 = \Sigma e(y - \hat{b}_2 x_2 - \hat{b}_3 x_3)$$
$$= \Sigma ey - \hat{b}_2 \Sigma ex_2 - \hat{b}_3 \Sigma ex_3$$

And in the least-squares process,

$$\frac{\partial \Sigma e_i^2}{\partial \hat{b}_2} = -2\Sigma e_i x_2 = 0 \qquad \frac{\partial \Sigma e_i^2}{\partial \hat{b}_3} = -2\Sigma e_i x_3 = 0$$

Thus
$$\Sigma e x_2 = 0 \quad \text{and} \quad \Sigma e x_3 = 0$$

Therefore
$$\Sigma e^2 = \Sigma e y$$
$$= \Sigma(y - b_{12.3} x_2 - b_{13.2} x_3) y$$
$$= \Sigma y^2 - b_{12.3} \Sigma x_2 y - b_{13.2} \Sigma x_3 y$$

We can then write

$$R^2_{1.23} = 1 - \frac{\Sigma e^2}{\Sigma y^2}$$

$$= 1 - \frac{\Sigma y^2 - b_{12.3} \Sigma x_2 y - b_{13.2} \Sigma x_3 y}{\Sigma y^2}$$

$$= \frac{b_{12.3} \Sigma x_2 y + b_{13.2} \Sigma x_3 y}{\Sigma y^2} \tag{4-29}$$

or, using simple correlation coefficients,

$$R^2_{1.23} = \frac{r^2_{12} + r^2_{13} - 2 r_{12} r_{13} r_{23}}{1 - r^2_{23}} \tag{4-30}$$

The significance of $R^2_{1.23}$ may be tested by the following F ratio:

$$F = \frac{R^2_{1.23}(n - m - 2)}{(1 - R^2_{1.23})(m - 1)} \frac{[(m - 1) \text{ degrees of freedom}]}{[(n - m - 2) \text{ degrees of freedom}]}$$

where n is the sample size and m is the number of variables.

Partial-Correlation Coefficients

We may ask whether an observed correlation between Y and X_2 is primarily due to the fact that each is influenced by the third variable X_3, or whether there is a significant net correlation between Y and X_2. Thus, we need to remove the influence of X_3 from both Y and X_2 and see what correlation exists between the residuals. We call this measure the *partial-correlation coefficient* between Y and X_2 with X_3 held constant, and use the symbol $r_{12.3}$. The square of $r_{12.3}$, written as $(r^2_{12.3})$, may be defined as the percent of variation in Y unexplained by X_3 that can be explained by adding X_2 to the model.

Let the linear regression of Y on X_3 be expressed as

$$Y_i = a_{13} + b_{13} X_{3i} + v_i$$

and the linear regression of X_2 or X_3 as

$$X_{2i} = a_{23} + b_{23} X_{3i} + w_i$$

Using deviation terms,

$$v = y - b_{13} X_3$$
$$w = x_2 - b_{23} X_3$$

The partial-correlation between Y and X_2 with X_3 held constant then can be found by the following:

$$r_{12.3} = \frac{\Sigma vw}{\sqrt{\Sigma v^2} \cdot \sqrt{\Sigma w^2}}$$

$$= \frac{\Sigma(y - b_{13}x_3) \cdot (x_2 - b_{23}x_3)}{\sqrt{\Sigma(y - b_{13}x_3)^2} \cdot \sqrt{\Sigma(x_2 - b_{23}x_3)^2}}$$

$$= \Sigma x_2 y - b_{13}\Sigma x_2 \Sigma x_3 - b_{23}\Sigma x_3 y + b_{13}b_{23}\Sigma x_3^2 \Big/$$
$$\sqrt{\Sigma y^2 - 2b_{13}\Sigma x_3 y + b_{13}^2 \Sigma x_3^2}$$
$$\cdot \sqrt{\Sigma x_2^2 - 2b_{23}\Sigma x_2 x_3 + b_{23}^2 \Sigma x_3^2}$$

$$= nS_1 S_2 r_{12} - \left(r_{13}\frac{S_1}{S_3}\right) nS_2 S_3 r_{23} -$$
$$- \left(r_{23}\frac{S_2}{S_3}\right) nS_1 S_3 r_{13} + r_{13}\frac{S_1}{S_3} r_{23}\frac{S_2}{S_3} nS_3^2 \Big/$$
$$\sqrt{nS_1^2 - 2\left(r_{13}\frac{S_1}{S_3}\right) nS_3 S_1 r_{13} + \left(r_{13}\frac{S_1}{S_3}\right)^2 nS_3^2}$$
$$\cdot \sqrt{nS_2^2 - 2\left(r_{23}\frac{S_2}{S_3}\right) nS_2 S_3 r_{23} + \left(r_{23}\frac{S_2}{S_3}\right)^2 nS_3^2}$$

$$= \frac{nS_1 S_2 (r_{12} - r_{13}r_{23})}{nS_1 S_2 \sqrt{1 - r_{13}^2} \cdot \sqrt{1 - r_{23}^2}}$$

$$= \frac{r_{12} - r_{13}r_{23}}{\sqrt{1 - r_{13}^2} \cdot \sqrt{1 - r_{23}^2}} \qquad (4\text{-}31)$$

Similarly,

$$r_{13.2} = \frac{r_{13} - r_{12}r_{23}}{\sqrt{1 - r_{12}^2} \cdot \sqrt{1 - r_{23}^2}} \qquad (4\text{-}32)$$

$$r_{23.1} = \frac{r_{23} - r_{12}r_{13}}{\sqrt{1 - r_{12}^2} \cdot \sqrt{1 - r_{13}^2}} \qquad (4\text{-}33)$$

This three-variable model can be further extended to linear models with more than three variables. However, since the computation will be more complicated when the number of variables increases, use of matrix notations is preferable.

Linear Regression Model in Matrix Form

The normal equations of the three-variable linear model are

$$b_{12.3}\,\Sigma x_2^2 + b_{13.2}\,\Sigma x_2 x_3 = \Sigma x_2 y$$
$$b_{12.3}\,\Sigma x_2 x_3 + b_{13.2}\,\Sigma x_3^2 = \Sigma x_3 y$$

and are expressed in matrix form as

$$\begin{bmatrix} \Sigma x_2^2 & \Sigma x_2 x_3 \\ \Sigma x_2 x_3 & \Sigma x_3^2 \end{bmatrix} \begin{bmatrix} b_{12.3} \\ b_{13.2} \end{bmatrix} = \begin{bmatrix} \Sigma x_2 y \\ \Sigma x_3 y \end{bmatrix}$$

or in general terms as

$$X^T X B = X^T Y$$

where

$$X^T = \begin{bmatrix} x_{21} & x_{22} & \cdots & x_{2n} \\ x_{31} & x_{32} & \cdots & x_{3n} \\ \vdots & & & \\ x_{m1} & x_{m2} & \cdots & x_{mn} \end{bmatrix}$$

$$X = \begin{bmatrix} x_{21} & x_{31} & \cdots & x_{m1} \\ x_{22} & x_{32} & \cdots & x_{m2} \\ \vdots & & & \\ x_{2n} & x_{3n} & \cdots & x_{mn} \end{bmatrix}$$

$$\hat{B} = \begin{bmatrix} b_{12.34\ldots n} \\ b_{13.24\ldots n} \\ \vdots \\ b_{1n.23\ldots(n-1)} \end{bmatrix}$$

and

$$Y = \begin{bmatrix} y_1 \\ y_2 \\ \vdots \\ y_n \end{bmatrix}$$

In the foregoing, n is the number of observations on each variable, and m is the number of explanatory variables. In order to solve the normal equations to obtain estimators of the coefficients, n must be greater than m. Continue with the matrix notation.

$$B = (X^T X)^{-1}(X^T Y) \qquad (4\text{-}34)$$

Now

$$Y = X\hat{B} + e$$

where e is a vector of the error terms:

$$e = Y - X\hat{B}$$
$$e^T e = (Y - X\hat{B})^T (Y - XB)$$
$$= Y^T Y - B^T X^T Y$$

The total variation in Y is $Y^T Y$, and the residual or unexplained variation is

$$e^T e = Y^T Y - B^T X^T Y$$

Thus the variation explained by X_2 and X_3 is $B^T X^T Y$.

Since the coefficient of determination is expressed by the ratio of the explained variation and the total variation, which is

$$R^2 = \frac{B^T X^T Y}{Y^T Y} \qquad (4\text{-}35)$$

Example 11

Sample values of the variables are arbitrary and are only for illustrating the computational procedure:

TWO-VARIABLE LINEAR REGRESSION MODEL

	Y	X	XY	y	x	xy	X^2	y^2	x^2	bx	$(y - \hat{b}x)^2$
1	100	15	1,500	−42.5	−30.5	1,296.25	225	1,806.25	930.25	−51.545	81.812
2	110	27	2,970	−32.5	−18.5	601.25	729	1,056.25	342.25	−31.265	1.525
3	115	32	3,680	−27.5	−13.5	371.25	1,024	756.25	182.25	−22.815	21.949
4	120	35	4,200	−22.5	−10.5	236.25	1,225	506.25	110.25	−17.745	22.610
5	130	40	5,200	−12.5	− 5.5	68.75	1,600	156.25	30.25	− 9.295	10.272
6	145	46	6,670	2.5	0.5	1.25	2,116	6.25	0.25	.845	2.739
7	150	55	8,250	7.5	9.5	71.25	3,025	56.25	90.25	16.055	73.188
8	170	60	10,200	27.5	14.5	348.75	3,600	756.25	210.25	24.505	8.970
9	185	65	12,025	42.5	19.5	828.75	4,225	1,806.25	380.25	32.955	91.107
10	200	80	16,000	57.5	34.5	1,983.75	6,400	3,306.25	1,190.25	58.305	0.648
	ΣY	ΣX	ΣXY			Σxy	ΣX^2	Σy^2	Σx^2		Σe^2
	1,425	455	70,695			5,857.5	24,169	10,212.5	3,466.5		314.82

Solving the normal equations for $\hat{a}$ and $\hat{b}$,

$$\Sigma Y = n\hat{a} + \hat{b}\Sigma X$$
$$\Sigma XY = \hat{a}\Sigma X + \hat{b}\Sigma X^2$$

or

$$\hat{b} = \frac{\Sigma xy}{\Sigma x^2} = \frac{5,857.5}{3,466.5} = 1.69$$
$$\hat{a} = \bar{Y} - \hat{b}\bar{X} = 142.5 - (1.69)(45.5) = 65.61$$

where

$$\bar{Y} = \frac{\Sigma Y}{n} = 142.5$$

$$\bar{X} = \frac{\Sigma X}{n} = 45.5$$

$$x = X - \bar{X}$$

and

$$y = Y - \bar{Y}$$

The equation of the regression line is

$$\hat{Y} = \hat{a} + \hat{b}X$$
$$= 65.61 + 1.69X$$

The correlation coefficient is given by

$$r = \sqrt{1 - \frac{\Sigma e^2}{\Sigma y^2}} = \sqrt{1 - \frac{314.82}{10,212.5}} = .984$$

where

$$e^2 = (y - \hat{b}x)^2$$

or

$$r = \frac{\Sigma xy}{nS_x S_y} = \frac{5,857.5}{10(18.619)(31.957)} = .984$$

where

$$S_x = \sqrt{\frac{\Sigma x^2}{n}} = \sqrt{\frac{3,466.5}{10}} = 18.619$$

$$S_y = \sqrt{\frac{\Sigma y^2}{n}} = \sqrt{\frac{10,212.5}{10}} = 31.957$$

The 95 percent interval estimates of b and a are

$$\hat{b} \pm t_{0.025} \frac{\hat{\sigma}_u}{\sqrt{\Sigma x^2}} = 1.69 \pm 2.3 \frac{(6.273)}{3,466.5} = 1.69 \pm .24495$$

$$\hat{a} \pm t_{0.025} \sqrt{\frac{\Sigma X^2}{n\Sigma x^2}} \; \hat{\sigma}_u$$

$$= 65.61 \pm (2.3) \sqrt{\frac{24,169}{10 \times 3,466.5}} \quad (6.273)$$

$$= 65.61 \pm 12.047$$

where

$$\hat{\sigma}_u = \sqrt{\frac{\Sigma e^2}{n-2}} = \sqrt{\frac{314.82}{8}} = 6.273$$

Given $X_0 = 90$, the predicted value of Y_0 with 95 percent confidence is

$$\hat{Y}_0 = (\hat{a} + \hat{b}X_0) \pm t_{0.025}\hat{\sigma}_u \sqrt{1 + \frac{1}{n} + \frac{(X_0 - \bar{X})^2}{\Sigma x^2}}$$

$$= 65.61 + (1.69)(90)$$

$$\pm (2.3)(6.273) \sqrt{1 + \frac{1}{10} + \frac{(90 - 45.5)^2}{3,466.5}}$$

$$= 217.71 \pm 18.63$$

THREE-VARIABLE LINEAR REGRESSION MODEL

	Y	X_2	X_3	y	x_2	x_3	y^2	x_2^2	x_3^2	$x_2 y$	$x_3 y$	$x_2 x_3$
1	100	15	8	-42.5	-30.5	-21	1,806.25	930.25	441	1,296.25	892.5	640.5
2	110	27	10	-32.5	-18.5	-19	1,056.25	342.25	361	601.25	617.5	351.5
3	115	32	12	-27.5	-13.5	-17	756.25	182.25	289	371.55	467.5	229.5
4	120	35	15	-22.5	-10.5	-14	506.25	110.25	196	236.25	315.0	147.0
5	130	40	20	-12.5	-5.5	-9	156.25	30.25	81	68.75	112.5	49.5
6	145	46	30	2.5	0.5	1	6.25	0.25	1	1.25	2.5	0.5
7	150	55	35	7.5	9.5	6	56.25	90.25	36	71.25	45.0	57.0
8	170	60	48	27.5	14.5	19	756.25	210.25	361	398.75	522.5	275.5
9	185	65	52	42.5	19.5	23	1,806.25	380.25	529	828.75	977.5	448.5
10	200	80	60	57.5	34.5	31	3,306.25	1,190.25	961	1,983.75	1,782.5	1,069.5
	ΣY	ΣX_2	ΣX_3				Σy^2	Σx_2^2	Σx_3^2	$\Sigma x_2 y$	$\Sigma x_3 y$	$\Sigma x_2 x_3$
	1,425	455	290				10,212.5	3,466.5	3,256	5,857.5	5,735.0	3,269.0

Solving the normal equations for $a_{1.23}$, $b_{12.3}$, and $b_{13.2}$,

$$b_{12.3}\Sigma x_2^2 + b_{13.2}\Sigma x_2 x_3 = \Sigma x_2 y$$

$$b_{12.3}\Sigma x_2 x_3 + b_{13.2}\Sigma x_3^2 = \Sigma x_3 y$$

$$(3,466.5)\,b_{12.3} + (3,269)\,b_{13.2} = 5,857.5$$

$$(3,269)\,b_{12.3} + (3,256)\,b_{13.2} = 5,735$$

$$b_{12.3} = 0.54 \qquad b_{13.2} = 1.22$$

and

$$a_{1.23} = \bar{Y} - b_{12.3}\bar{X}_2 - b_{13.2}\bar{X}_3$$

$$= 142.5 - (0.54)(45.5) - (1.22)(29) = 82.55$$

The equation of the regression plane is

$$\hat{Y} = a_{1.23} + b_{12.3}X_2 + b_{13.2}X_3$$
$$= 82.55 + 0.54X_2 + 1.22X_3$$

	Y	$\hat{Y}$	e	e^2
1	100	100.41	−.41	.17
2	110	109.33	.67	.45
3	115	114.47	.53	.28
4	120	119.75	.25	.06
5	130	125.55	1.45	2.10
6	145	143.99	1.01	1.02
7	150	154.95	−4.95	24.50
8	170	173.51	−3.51	12.32
9	185	181.09	3.91	15.29
10	200	198.95	1.05	1.10
				57.59

$$t_2 = \frac{b_{12.3}}{\sqrt{\frac{\Sigma e^2}{n-3}}\sqrt{a_{22}}}$$

$$= \frac{0.54}{\sqrt{\frac{57.29}{7}}\sqrt{\frac{3256}{(3466.5)(3256) - (3269)^2}}} = 2.56$$

$$t_3 = \frac{b_{13.2}}{\sqrt{\frac{\Sigma e^2}{n-3}}\sqrt{a_{33}}}$$

$$= \frac{1.22}{\sqrt{\frac{57.29}{7}}\sqrt{\frac{3466.5}{(3466.5)(3256) - (3269)^2}}} = 5.6$$

Both $b_{12.3}$ and $b_{13.2}$ are significant at 0.05 level ($t_{.025} = 2.365$). The multiple-correlation coefficient is given by

$$R_{1.23} = \sqrt{\frac{b_{12.3}\Sigma x_2 y + b_{13.2}\Sigma x_3 y}{\Sigma y^2}}$$

$$= \sqrt{\frac{0.54(5,857.5) + 1.22(5,735)}{10,212.5}} = .997$$

or

$$R_{1.23} = \sqrt{\frac{r_{12}^2 + r_{13}^2 - 2r_{12}r_{13}r_{23}}{1 - r_{23}^2}}$$

$$= \sqrt{\frac{(.984)^2 + (.995)^2 - 2(.984)(.995)(.973)}{1 - (.973)^2}} = .997$$

where

$$r_{12} = \frac{\Sigma x_2 y}{nS_1 S_2} = \frac{5{,}857.5}{(10)(31.96)(18.62)} = .984$$

$$r_{13} = \frac{\Sigma x_3 y}{nS_1 S_3} = \frac{5{,}735}{(10)(31.96)(18.04)} = .995$$

$$r_{23} = \frac{\Sigma x_2 x_3}{nS_2 S_3} = \frac{3{,}269}{(10)(18.62)(18.04)} = .973$$

and

$$S_1 = \sqrt{\frac{\Sigma y^2}{n}} = \sqrt{\frac{10{,}212.5}{10}} = 31.96$$

$$S_2 = \sqrt{\frac{\Sigma x_2^2}{n}} = \sqrt{\frac{3{,}466.5}{10}} = 18.62$$

$$S_3 = \sqrt{\frac{\Sigma x_3^2}{n}} = \sqrt{\frac{3{,}256}{10}} = 18.04$$

The partial-correlation coefficients are

$$r_{12.3} = \frac{r_{12} - r_{13} r_{23}}{\sqrt{1 - r_{13}^2} \cdot \sqrt{1 - r_{23}^2}}$$

$$= \frac{.984 - (.995)(.973)}{\sqrt{(1 - .995^2)(1 - .973^2)}} = .69$$

$$r_{13.2} = \frac{r_{13} - r_{12} r_{23}}{\sqrt{1 - r_{12}^2} \cdot \sqrt{1 - r_{23}^2}}$$

$$= \frac{.995 - (.984)(.973)}{\sqrt{(1 - .984^2)(1 - .973^2)}} = .92$$

$$r_{23.1} = \frac{r_{23} - r_{12} r_{13}}{\sqrt{1 - r_{12}^2} \cdot \sqrt{1 - r_{13}^2}}$$

$$= \frac{.973 - (.995)(.984)}{\sqrt{(1 - .984^2)(1 - .995^2)}} = -.34$$

Applying the following F test

$$F = \frac{(.997)^2 (10 - 3 - 2)}{(1 - .997^2)(3 - 1)} = 47.8$$

Since

$$F_{0.05}(2.5) = 5.79, \quad F_{0.01}(2.5) = 13.27$$

we may conclude $R_{1.23}$ is significantly different from zero.

Solve the three-variable linear regression model using matrix notation.

For estimating the parameters,

$$X^T X B = X^T Y \qquad \hat{B} = [X^T X]^{-1}[X^T Y]$$

In this case

$$X^T X = \begin{bmatrix} \Sigma x_2^2 & \Sigma x_2 x_3 \\ \Sigma x_2 x_3 & \Sigma x_3^2 \end{bmatrix} = \begin{bmatrix} 3,466.5 & 3,269 \\ 3,269 & 3,256 \end{bmatrix}$$

$$X^T Y = \begin{bmatrix} \Sigma x_2 y \\ \Sigma x_3 y \end{bmatrix} = \begin{bmatrix} 5,857.5 \\ 5,735.0 \end{bmatrix}$$

$$[X^T X]^{-1} = \frac{1}{\det [X^T X]} \text{ adj } [X^T X]$$

$$= \frac{1}{600,563} \begin{bmatrix} 3,256 & -3,269 \\ -3,269 & 3,466.5 \end{bmatrix}$$

$$= \begin{bmatrix} .00542157941 & -.00544322577 \\ -.00544322577 & .00577208386 \end{bmatrix}$$

$$\hat{B} = \begin{bmatrix} b_{12.3} \\ b_{13.2} \end{bmatrix}$$

$$= \begin{bmatrix} .00542157941 & -.00544322577 \\ -.00544322577 & .00577208386 \end{bmatrix} \begin{bmatrix} 5,857.5 \\ 5,735.0 \end{bmatrix}$$

$$= \begin{bmatrix} .54 \\ 1.22 \end{bmatrix}$$

Thus

$$b_{12.3} = .54 \qquad \text{and} \qquad b_{13.2} = 1.22$$

For computing the multiple-correlation coefficient,

$$R^2 = \frac{\hat{B}^T X^T Y}{Y^T Y}$$

In this case

$$R^2 = \frac{[b_{12.3} \quad b_{13.2}] \begin{bmatrix} \Sigma x_2 y \\ \Sigma x_3 y \end{bmatrix}}{[\Sigma y^2]}$$

$$= \frac{[.54 \quad 1.22] \begin{bmatrix} 5,857.5 \\ 5,735.0 \end{bmatrix}}{10,212.5}$$

$$= \frac{10,159.75}{10,212.5} = 0.9948$$

Thus

$$R \cong .997$$

FOURIER SERIES AND SPECTRAL ANALYSIS

In analyzing time series data, linear regression models can only represent the linear trend of the data. However, quite often time series data contain cyclical oscillating properties. For analyzing the frequency and amplitude of the oscillations, one of the analytical methods is spectral analysis, which is based on Fourier theorem. In the following, a basic concept of using Fourier series to analyze time series data is introduced.

Let $F(t)$ be any oscillatory function of time, subject only to the restrictions that the oscillations are the same for each period and that the period T is fixed, then Fourier's theorem shows that $F(t)$ can be represented approximately by the sum of a number of sine and cosine functions.

$$\begin{aligned} F(t) = a_0 &+ (a_1 \cos wt + b_1 \sin wt) \\ &+ (a_2 \cos 2\, wt + b_2 \sin 2\, wt) + \ldots \\ &+ (a_n \cos n\, wt + b_n \sin n\, wt) \ldots \end{aligned}$$

where $a_0, a_1, b_1, a_2, b_2, \ldots, a_n, b_n, \ldots$ are constants. The fixed period T equals to $\frac{2\pi}{w}$ and the fundamental frequency is $\frac{w}{2\pi}$. If the series are convergent, the constants can be found by the following manipulation.

$$\int_0^T F(t) \cos wt\, dt = a_0 \int_0^T \cos wt\, dt$$

$$+ a_1 \int_0^T \cos^2 wt\, dt + b_1 \int_0^T \sin wt \cos wt\, dt$$

$$+ a_2 \int_0^T \cos 2\, wt \cos wt\, dt$$

$$+ b_2 \int_0^T \sin 2\, wt \cos wt\, dt$$

But

$$\int_0^T \cos wt \, dt = \frac{1}{w} \int_0^{\frac{2\pi}{w}} \cos wt \, d \, wt$$

$$= \frac{1}{w} \left[\sin wt \right]_0^{\frac{2\pi}{w}}$$

$$= 0$$

$$\int_0^T \cos^2 wt \, dt = \frac{1}{w} \int_0^{\frac{2\pi}{w}} \cos^2 wt \, d \, wt$$

$$= \frac{1}{w} \int_0^{\frac{2\pi}{w}} (1 - \sin^2 wt) \, d \, wt$$

$$= \frac{1}{w} \int_0^{\frac{2\pi}{w}} d \, wt - \frac{1}{w} \int_0^{\frac{2\pi}{w}} \sin^2 wt \, d \, wt$$

$$= \frac{2\pi}{w} - \frac{1}{w} \int_0^{\frac{2\pi}{w}} \frac{1}{2} (1 - \cos 2 \, wt) \, d \, wt$$

$$= \frac{2\pi}{w} - \frac{1}{w} \left[\frac{1}{2} wt - \frac{1}{4} \sin 2 \, wt \right]_0^{\frac{2\pi}{w}}$$

$$= \frac{2\pi}{w} - \frac{\pi}{w}$$

$$= \frac{\pi}{w}$$

$$\int_0^T \sin wt \cos wt \, dt = \frac{1}{w} \int_0^{\frac{2\pi}{w}} \sin wt \cos wt \, d \, wt$$

$$= \frac{1}{w} \int_0^{\frac{2\pi}{w}} \sin wt \, d \sin wt$$

$$= \frac{1}{w} \left[\frac{1}{2} \sin^2 wt \right]_0^{\frac{2\pi}{w}}$$

$$= 0$$

$$\int_0^T \cos 2 \, wt \cos wt \, dt$$

$$= \frac{1}{w} \int_0^{\frac{2\pi}{w}} (\cos^2 wt - \sin^2 wt) \cos wt \, d \, wt$$

$$= \frac{1}{w} \int_0^{\frac{2\pi}{w}} (1 - 2\sin^2 wt) \, d\sin wt$$

$$= \frac{1}{w} \left[\sin wt - \frac{2}{3} \sin^3 wt \right]_0^{\frac{2\pi}{w}}$$

$$= 0$$

$$\int_0^T \sin 2wt \cos wt \, dt = \frac{1}{w} \int_0^{\frac{2\pi}{w}} (2 \sin wt \cos wt) \cos wt \, dt$$

$$= -\frac{1}{w} \int_0^{\frac{2\pi}{w}} 2 \cos^2 wt \, d\cos wt$$

$$= -\frac{1}{w} \left[\frac{2}{3} \cos^3 wt \right]_0^{\frac{2\pi}{w}}$$

$$= 0$$

Hence

$$\int_0^T F(t) \cos wt \, dt = a_1 \frac{\pi}{w}$$

$$a_1 = \frac{w}{\pi} \int_0^T F(t) \cos wt \, dt$$

Similarly, it can be shown that

$$a_2 = \frac{w}{\pi} \int_0^T F(t) \cos 2wt \, dt, \ldots, a_n = \frac{w}{\pi} \int_0^T F(t) \cos n \, wt \, dt$$

$$b_1 = \frac{w}{\pi} \int_0^T F(t) \sin wt \, dt, \ldots, b_n = \frac{w}{\pi} \int_0^T F(t) \sin n \, wt \, dt$$

The interpretation of Fourier theorem is that any type of oscillation with given period $T \left(\text{frequency } \frac{w}{2\pi} \right)$ can be approximated by the sum of sine and cosine functions which is a Fourier series. The first term of the series represents the oscillation which has the period of $\frac{2\pi}{w}$, the second term $\frac{2\pi}{2w}$, and the nth term $\frac{2\pi}{nw}$ (higher frequency). The constants a_1, b_1, a_2, $b_2, \ldots, a_n$, $b_n, \ldots$ represent the amplitudes of respective oscillations with difference frequencies. The plotting of the constants in rectangular coordinates with the horizontal axis representing frequency and the vertical axis representing amplitude forms the basis of spectral analysis. Attention is brought to those frequencies or cycles which have large peak and trough.

SUMMARY

When we want to describe some characteristic of a population, descriptive statistics provide us with the measures of location, the measures of variation, and the frequency distributions.

When we are unable to observe the entire population, we can take only representative samples from the population, following the sampling theory of randomness. This leads to the development of theories of estimation, testing hypotheses, and analysis of variance. A number of theoretical distributions, both discrete and continuous, have been developed to facilitate the analysis. The estimation procedures not only include the estimation of the mean and proportion of the population but are also applied to the estimation of relationship among variables, which are identified as correlation and regression. And the methods of testing hypotheses are further extended to the analysis of variance.

However, because inductive statistics is based on samples, it cannot insure complete confidence, and the answers are therefore given with specified error probabilities or confidence levels.

PROBLEMS

1. Find the mean and standard deviation of the following variable X

X	Frequency	X	Frequency
10	1	34	15
15	4	36	9
18	7	45	6
25	10	48	3
27	14	52	2

2. Use χ^2 distribution to check whether the above data can be fitted to a binomial distribution with α = .05.

3. A sample of 100 cigarettes of a given brand was tested for nicotine content. The result is that the sample mean $\bar{X}$ = 20 milligrams and the sample variance v = 16 milligrams. Find the confidence limits of the population mean μ with α = .10.

4. A random sample of 500 residents in a community showed that 300 of them favored the Democratic party. Find 90 percent confidence limits for the proportion of population favoring the Democratic party.

5. One hundred students selected at random from a large university showed an average height $\bar{X}$ = 5 ft 8 in. and a sample deviation S = 2 in. If an estimate, accurate to within one inch, is required, how large a sample should be taken?

6. Two sets of 100 students were given a mathematics test. The scores are $\bar{X}_1$ = 90, $\bar{X}_2$ = 85, S_1 = 10, S_2 = 8. Test the hypothesis that the mathematics ability are equal for the two sets of students with α = .10.

7. Find the linear correlation coefficient r for the following data:

X	10	15	18	20	30	28	25	19	17	6
Y	2	4	8	9	7	6	5	3	3	1

Is r significantly different from zero with α = .05?

8. Estimate the parameters of the regression line of Y on X in Prob. 7. Also find the 95 percent confidence intervals of the parameters.

9. In Probs. 7 and 8, if Y equals 10, what will be the estimated value of X. Also find the 95 percent confidence interval which will include the true value of X.

10. The following data represent the number of bushels of wheat produced on three equal-sized lots in the past five years. Test to see whether the productivity of the land is different with α = .05.

	Lot 1	Lot 2	Lot 3
1	40	38	46
2	45	40	39
3	38	31	42
4	43	39	43
5	41	35	38

SELECTED REFERENCES

Hoel, P. G., *Introduction to Mathematical Statistics*. 3d ed. New York: John Wiley & Sons, Inc., 1962.

Li, C. C., *Introduction to Experimental Statistics*. New York: McGraw-Hill Book Company, 1964.

Mood, A. M., and F. A. Graybill, *Introduction to the Theory of Statistics*. 2d ed. New York: McGraw-Hill Book Company, 1963.

Richmond, S. B., *Statistical Analysis*. 2d ed. New York: Ronald Press Company, 1964.

Spiegel, M. R., *Outline of Theory and Problems of Statistics*. New York: Schaum Publishing Company, Inc., 1962.

chapter 5

Statistical Decision Theory

Decisions are based on relevant information obtained on the problem and the value that the decision maker puts on the outcomes. In this section we will discuss decision processes, utility theory, measures of values, and decision rules which lead finally to statistical decision theory.

DECISION PROCESSES

Consumers, businessmen, and government officials all need to make decisions, and are doing it every day. However, decisions can be "good" or "bad." In order to increase the chance of making "good" decisions, we try in this section to describe the decision process in a systematic framework so that the student or reader can check his own decision making to see whether it is rational or has room for improvement.

When a person is required to make a decision, he first needs to know what the alternatives are. If there are no alternatives there are no choices, so no decision is necessary. Secondly, he needs to know what will be the consequences of each alternative. In this respect, there can be two different situations. The first is that the decision maker knows all the consequences with complete certainty prior to making the decision—in other words, the required information is complete and the causes and effects are deterministic. In the other situation, the consequences of each alternative cannot be foreseen with complete certainty. One may only estimate or predict the consequences with a given degree of confidence. In other words, the information is only partial and the causes and effects are probabilistic. Thus there will be risk involved in making a choice, which may not be the "best" one.

Thirdly, the decision maker needs to know exactly what his own objectives are, as well as those of the business firm or the government, so that he can relate the consequences to the objectives. The objectives provide the measure or criteria to check which alternative will be the best to achieve the objectives; the decision maker should choose that alternative as his decision. If the consequences of the choice or decision *do* seem to achieve the objectives as expected, the decision is "good," otherwise it is "bad."

When the objectives are defined, and information about the alternatives and the consequences of each are completely known and certain, the problem may be set up in a special mathematical form called *mathematical programming*, such as linear programming, nonlinear programming, or dynamic programming discussed in Chapters 1 and 2. Here, however, we are concerned with decision processes when the consequence of an action is not completely known. This area of study is referred to as *statistical decision theory*.

We begin with the problem of measurement—that is, how we measure the degree that an outcome satisfies our objectives.

UTILITY THEORY

In a market economy the most common measure is money. However, each individual may have different valuation about money. Also, when a person has accumulated a large sum of money he may value each unit of money less because of the operation of the law of diminishing utility. Thus it is advisable to start with the basic utility theory to explain the measurement of value.

Utility theory generally is based on the following assumptions:

1. *Transitivity.* If an individual is indifferent between two outcomes, A and B and also he is indifferent between outcomes B and C, then he will be indifferent between A and C.

2. *Continuity of Preference.* If an individual prefers outcome A to B and B to C, there exists a probability $P\,(0 < P < 1)$ such that he will be indifferent between B and $[PA + (1 - P)C]$.

3. *Independence.* If an individual is indifferent between outcome A and B, he is also indifferent between outcome C and D, then for any probability $P\ (0 < P < 1)$, he will be indifferent between $PA + (1 - P)C$ and $PB + (1 - P)D$.

4. *Higher Probability of Success Preferable.* If an individual prefers A to B and there are two probabilities P_1 and P_2 such that $P_1 > P_2$, then he will prefer $P_1(A) + (1 - P_1)(B)$ to $P_2(A) + (1 - P_2)(B)$.

5. *Compound Probability.* If P, P_1, and P_2 are three probabilities, and A and B are two outcomes, an individual will be indifferent between $P[P_1A + (1 - P_1)(B)] + (1 - P)[P_2A + (1 - P_2)(B)]$ and $[PP_1 + (1 - P)P_2](A) + [1 - (PP_1 + (1 - P)P_2)](B)$.

With these assumptions of utility, we may proceed to discuss index for measurement of value. The indices may be classified by the amount of information they convey into three classes:

1. *Associative Measures.* The measures are merely numerical identifications of an outcome, similar to the auto tags placed on automobiles—they are merely for identification purpose.

2. *Ordinal Measures.* The measures will rank the outcomes by preference. If outcome A is preferred to B and B to C, then the order should be (i) A (ii) B (iii) C.

3. *Cardinal Measures.* The measures not only will rank the outcomes but give quantitative information telling they are different by how much. For example, A is twice as preferable as B and B is three

times as preferable as C. Since the measure is quantitative, they are additive. Thus if A = 6 utils, B = 3 utils, and C = 1 utils, then $A + B + C$ = 10 utils.

Von Neumann and Morgenstern have proposed an index for predictive purpose. Suppose an event (E) can possibly take two alternative outcomes A and B with the probability of taking A being P and the probability of taking B equal to $(1 - P)$. An individual considers outcome A has utility $U(A)$ and B, $U(B)$, then according to von Neumann and Morgenstern's evaluation, the event has the expected utility

$$U(E) = P \cdot U(A) + (1 - P) U(B)$$

DECISION RULES

As we have defined in the previous section, decisions are required when there are alternatives. And the consequences or outcomes of these alternatives are different with respect to the stated objectives. The utility theory provides a measure to determine which outcome is most favorable to achieve the objectives. In this section we will describe the various strategies that a decision maker may take with different combination of risk and reward.

1. *The Maximin Rule.* This is the most conservative approach. The decision maker expects that the worst outcome will occur whatever alternative he may choose. The rule is to choose among the worst outcomes the one that will do least harm. An example will make this clear.

Outcomes / Alternatives	1	2	3
1	18 utils	9	2
2	3	16	15

The example includes 2 alternatives and 3 different outcomes, with utility of each combination specified in each entry in the table. The combination may be the decision of not bringing a raincoat when later on it rains or the decision of investing a given sum of money when a year later the business venture only breaks even, etc. The quantified utility is a cardinal measure specifying how each situation means to the decision maker. According to the example, if the decision maker chooses the first alternative, the worst outcome will be the third one, and the measure of utility of this particular combination of decision and outcome yields 2 utils. Now, if the decision maker chooses the second alternative, the worst outcome becomes the first one with 3 utils. Following the rule, he should then choose the second alternative because the worst outcome will still yield 3 utils instead of 2 utils. Apparently we can see that this decision rule ignores other information except the information concerning the worst outcome.

2. *Maximax Rule.* This is the most daring approach. The decision maker expects that he always will be lucky, and whatever alternative he chooses the best outcome will occur. So the rule is to choose among the best outcomes the one that will do him most good. In the above example, if the decision maker chooses the first alternative the best outcome will be the first one, which yields 18 utils. And if he chooses the second alternative, the best outcome will be the third one, which yields 15 utils. Therefore, he will choose the first alternative.

This decision rule is similar to the maximin rule that it ignores other information except the one relevant item of information in each row—only their approaches are different, one being conservative and the other daring, willing to take risk.

3. *Weighted Average of Maximum and Minimum Rule.* This approach takes consideration of the most favorable and the most unfavorable outcomes. It may be considered as in between the most conservative and the most daring approach. The

weights assigned to the maximum and minimum utilities may be equal or different according to the decision maker's risk tendency. In the previous example, if equal weights are assigned, for the first alternative, the weighted average is

$$\frac{1}{2} \times 18 + \frac{1}{2} \times 2 = 10 \text{ utils}$$

and the weighted average for the second alternative is

$$\frac{1}{2} \times 15 + \frac{1}{2} \times 3 = 9 \text{ utils}$$

Thus the decision maker should choose the first alternative. With this decision rule, although the two extreme values (the highest and the lowest) are used, there still may be a range of information between the two extreme values that will be ignored.

STATISTICAL DECISION THEORY

The Bayes Rule

In order to utilize all the information provided, there is a procedure derived from probability theory called the Bayes rule which advises that the decision maker should first estimate or assign a priori probabilities to all the outcomes. If historical data are available, the a priori probabilities may be constructed based on the historical data. If no information is available, then equal probabilities may be assigned to all the outcomes. In the above example, for the first alternative the expected utility is then

$$\frac{1}{3} \times 18 + \frac{1}{3} \times 9 + \frac{1}{3} \times 2 = 9\frac{2}{3} \text{ utils}$$

and for the second alternative the expected utility is

$$\frac{1}{3} \times 3 + \frac{1}{3} \times 12 + \frac{1}{3} \times 15 = 10 \text{ utils}$$

The decision maker therefore should choose the second alternative. Since the Bayes rule utilizes all the information, it seems superior than the other decision rules. However, they all use absolute values (in utils) for consideration. The determination of these absolute values is by nature quite difficult; it has been suggested that relative values may be used, since the choice is based on relative merits. Thus if for each outcome we let the value of the least desirable situation (with respect to alternative action) equal zero, and the other values in the column are reduced to the difference between that situation and the least desirable one, we get a table of relative values. Using the previous example, we have

Outcomes / Alternatives	1	2	3
1	0	7	13
2	15	0	0

The relative values are called *regret*. Using the regret table, the decision rule may be to choose the smallest among the greatest regret which may occur in each row—the *minimax rule*: The maximum regret in the first row is 13— that is, if the decision maker chooses the first alternative and the outcome happens to be the third one. Should he choose the second alternative he will gain 13 more utils. In economic terms, his opportunity cost is 13 utils. Similarly, the maximum regret in the second row 15. Comparing these two regrets, 13 is the smaller and thus the decision maker should choose the first alternative.

Another decision rule which may be applied to consecutive decisions is that of *optimum mixed strategy*. Instead of choosing only one alternative the decision rule calls for multiple choice with probabilities assigned to several alternatives, and then finding the probabilities, which will minimize the expected value.

In the previous example, if half the time the decision maker chooses the first alternative and half the time he chooses the second alternative, the expected utility will be as follows.

$$\frac{1}{2} \times 18 + \frac{1}{2} \times 3 = 10\frac{1}{2}$$
$$\frac{1}{2} \times 9 + \frac{1}{2} \times 16 = 12\frac{1}{2}$$
$$\frac{1}{2} \times 2 + \frac{1}{2} \times 15 = 8\frac{1}{2}$$

If equal probability is assigned to the three outcomes, the expected utility is $\frac{1}{3}(10\frac{1}{2} + 12\frac{1}{2} + 8\frac{1}{2}) = 10.5$. Compare to the pure strategy using the Bayes rule, the mixed strategy yields higher expected utility.

More Examples in Statistical Decision Theory

Example 1

A man owns a piece of land in an area where 40 percent of the land has oil deposits underneath, three-fourths of the oil deposits being small wells and one-fourth of them big wells. The feasible alternatives that the man may choose from are: (1) Do not drill. He will bear no cost, but also can expect no gain except by using the land for planting food products; this is the most conservative choice. (2) Drill. In doing so, he will be taking a large risk. If there is no oil deposit underneath, he will lose a great deal of money, equivalent to the cost of the entire operation. However, if there is a large well underneath, he will be a rich man. (3) Subcontract or farm out. This is the middle road; somebody else will bear the drilling cost. If there is no oil well underneath, he loses only one season's crop, the value of which is much smaller than the drilling cost. But if there are oil deposits underneath, he will only receive a portion of the total gain. Assuming that the entire drilling operation will cost $50,000 and that a season's crop will bring approximately $5,000 net profit, a small well is estimated to yield a net return computed in present value terms of $100,000 and a large well $1,000,000. (The drilling cost and the cost of losing crops have already been deducted.) What action should he choose to take?

(a) The possible states of outcome: (1) dry, (2) small well, (3) large well.

(b) The probabilities of the outcomes: (1) dry, .60; (2) small well, .30; (3) large well, .10. This is according to the a priori distribution of oil wells in the area, which is the only information we have. Also, note that the sum of probability is 1, which indicates that all possible outcomes have been included.

(c) The possible sample observations. In this example, we assume no preliminary survey has been performed or is intended.

(d) The available actions: (1) don't drill; (2) drill; (3) farm out.

(e) The available strategies. The strategy that we use here as guidance is to maximize expected gain.

(f) The reward table is as following:

Actions or Events	(A) Dry	(B) Small Well	(C) Large Well
1. Don't drill	5,000	5,000	5,000 (income from crops)
2. Drill	−55,000	100,000	1,000,000
3. Farm out	−5,000	20,000	200,000

(opportunity cost)

The expected gain associated with each action then can be computed by summing the products of probability and net gain associated with each outcome or event.

Action	Expected Gain
1. Don't drill	5,000
2. Drill	$-55,000 \times .6 + 100,000 \times .3$ $+ 1,000,000 \times .1 = 97,000$
3. Farm out	$-5,000 \times .6 + 20,000 \times .3$ $+ 200,000 \times .1 = 23,000$

when "maximize expected gain" strategy is used as guideline, he should choose to drill the land himself.

Example 2

Mr. A is a salesman for a drug manufacturing company. His job requires him to make daily visits to the doctors' offices and hospitals located in the area. In summer the area has storms and heavy showers 60 percent of the time in the afternoon. Every morning in summer before going out on those visits, Mr. A looks at the weather indicator which may show one of three possible observations: (1) fair weather, (2) undetermined weather, (3) stormy weather. Mr. A has three choices: either he wears fair-weather outfit, taking a chance that it won't rain, or brings an umbrella (which is a nuisance to carry if it doesn't rain), or wear boots and raincoat besides carrying an umbrella—which will be even greater a nuisance if it is a fair day. Put Mr. A's problem into a decision-making scheme.

1. The a priori probability distribution of the weather is

Rain	No Rain
.6	.4

2. Assume that the frequency of response of the weather indicator to the weather condition of the day is represented by the following probabilities.

Observations States	Fair	Undetermined	Stormy
Rain	.10	.30	.60
No rain	.40	.40	.20

3. Assume that Mr. A's evaluation of making wrong decisions is represented by the following loss table (on a relative comparison basis).

Actions States	Fair- Weather Outfit	Brings Umbrella	Boots, Raincoat, and Umbrella
Rain	10	3	0
No rain	0	1	8

4. Compute the probability of all the events. For example, the probability of the weather indicator indicating fair in the morning, when actually it rains later in the day, is $.6 \times .1 = .06$.

Observations / States	Fair	Undetermined	Stormy
Rain	.06	.18	.36
No rain	.16	.16	.08
	.22	.34	.44

Note that the sum of all the probabilities is equal to 1.

5. Compute from the conditional probability of having observed that the weather indicator indicating fair, undetermined, or stormy, whether it will actually rain or no rain to obtain the posteriori probabilities of the states.

Observations / States	Fair	Undetermined	Stormy
Rain	$\dfrac{.06}{.22}$	$\dfrac{.18}{.34}$	$\dfrac{.36}{.44}$
No rain	$\dfrac{.16}{.22}$	$\dfrac{.16}{.34}$	$\dfrac{.08}{.44}$
	1.00	1.00	1.00

6. Applying Mr. A's loss table to the conditional probabilities in par. 5, we obtain the expected loss of the different actions that Mr. A may take after observing the weather indicator.

Let a_1 represent Mr. A's choice to wear fair-weather outfit.

Let a_2 represent Mr. A's choice to carry an umbrella.

Let a_3 represent Mr. A's choice to wear boots and raincoat besides carrying an umbrella.

For example, the expected loss resulting from Mr. A's choice of action a_1 when he observes the weather indicator indicating fair is

$$10 \times \frac{.06}{.22} + 0 \times \frac{.16}{.22} = 2.73$$

Observation:	Fair			Undetermined			Stormy		
Action:	a_1	a_2	a_3	a_1	a_2	a_3	a_1	a_2	a_3
Expected loss:	2.73	1.54	5.54	5.29	2.06	3.79	8.18	2.63	1.45

7. If Mr. A adopts the strategy of minimizing the expected loss, his choice of action should be

Observation:	Fair	Undetermined	Stormy
Action:	a_2 (umbrella)	a_2 (umbrella)	a_3 (boots, rai coat, and umbrella)
Expected loss:	1.54	2.06	1.45

8. Some textbooks refer to this as the Bayes rule or strategy, and the weighted average of expected loss may be calculated by multiplying the minimum expected losses to the probabilities of the possible observations:

$$.22 \times 1.54 + .34 \times 2.06 + .44 \times 1.45 = 1.68$$

SUMMARY

We are sometimes required to make decisions in which the outcomes are uncertain. Because of this uncertainty, decision makers may make different decisions based on whether he wants to take greater risk and expect greater reward or to take less risk and expect only moderate reward.

Information is the guidance for better decisions. The more reliable information we get the more confidence we have of reaching a correct decision. Thus statistical theory recommends an adequate number of samples for a given confidence interval, and probability theory indicates that by obtaining increment samples, decision can be improved through conditional probability.

Statistical decision theory provides a framework for choosing decision strategy. The framework usually consists of the following components:

(a) The possible states of outcomes. These indicate what may possibly occur in the future.

(b) The probability distribution of the outcomes. If the past frequency function is used to represent the probability of the occurrences of each state of outcomes, then the distribution is an *a priori probability distribution*. An a priori probability distribution sometimes may be modified to include expectations about future changes.

(c) The possible sample observations. These are the basis on which we may make conjectures about the true state of the outcome with the confidence level specified by probabilities.

(d) The available actions which we may take that will affect the outcome.

(e) The loss table, which indicates the cost associated with each outcome or the reward table which indicates the net gain associated with each outcome.

(f) The available strategies which we may use as guidance in choosing the actions.

PROBLEMS

1. What is the expected utility of the following?

State or outcome:	1	2	3	4	5
Utility:	10	9	8	15	6
Probability:	.1	.3	.3	.1	.2

2. Given the following utility table:

Alternatives \ Outcomes	1	2	3
1	8	2	1
2	7	10	6
3	3	9	14

What is the maximin choice?
What is the maximax choice?

3. If the probabilities of the outcomes in Prob. 2 are all equal, what is the weighted average maximum and minimum choice?

4. A farmer grows three products—potatoes, tomatoes, and watermelons. Every morning he drives to town with a truckload of one product only. If the weather is warm, he should sell tomatoes and if the weather is cool, he should sell potatoes.

His loss table is as follows:

Weather \ Product	Watermelons	Tomatoes	Potatoes
Hot	−20	1	18
Warm	2	−15	9
Cool	16	10	−10

Every evening before he loads the truck he listens to the weather forecast for the next day on the radio. The weather forecast, however, is not always reliable. Its predictability is as follows:

Weather \ Forecast	Hot	Warm	Cool
Hot	.6	.3	.1
Warm	.3	.5	.2
Cool	.2	.3	.5

List every strategy and the average losses. What is the Bayes rule or strategy?

5. A company sells a product with a guarantee for K months. The price is set at $(1,000 + 20K)$ dollars. If the product becomes defective before the K months have expired, the company will refund the purchase price—otherwise no refund. From past records the product life follows an exponential distribution with mean equal to 10 months. What should the company decide on the value of K?

6. A salesman carries three boxes in his car, one containing toys for children under 12 years old, another containing accessories for teenagers, and the other containing items for adults. The houses he visits may (1) have adults, teenagers, and children, θ; (2) have adults and children only, θ_2; (3) have adults and teenagers only, θ_3; (4) have adults only, θ_4. The salesman will choose only one box to bring to the house. The actions are denoted by a_1, bring box for children; a_2, bring box for teenagers; and a_3, bring box for adults. The loss table is

	a_1	a_2	a_3
θ_1	2	3	4
θ_2	1	4	5
θ_3	9	1	3
θ_4	10	8	0

His observation before he makes the choice may have the following different responses:

z_1 = a children's play set in the yard and bicycles in the garage.
z_2 = no play set, only bicycles.
z_3 = no play set or bicycles.

The frequency of response table is

	z_1	z_2	z_3
θ_1	.6	.2	.2
θ_2	.5	.1	.4
θ_3	.2	.5	.3
θ_4	.1	.2	.7

(a) List all the strategies and evaluate their average losses.
(b) Find out the minimax average loss strategy.
(c) If a priori probabilities for θ_1, θ_2, θ_3, and θ_4 and 20, 30, 30, and 20 percent, which is the salesman's best strategy?

SELECTED REFERENCES

Chernoff, H., and L. E. Moses, *Elementary Decision Theory.* New York: John Wiley & Sons, Inc.. 1959.

Davidson, D., P. Suppes, and S. Siegel, *Decision Making: An Experimental Approach.* Stanford, Calif.: Stanford University Press, 1957.

Savage, L. J., *The Foundation of Statistics.* New York: John Wiley & Sons, Inc., 1954.

Schlaifer, R., *Introduction to Statistics for Business Decisions.* New York: McGraw-Hill Book Company, 1961.

Wald, A., *Statistical Decision Functions.* New York: John Wiley & Sons, Inc., 1950.

chapter 6

Elementary Markov Chains

One of the ways to describe the dynamic process of an economic system is to assume that it changes from one state to another with known probabilities. The state which the economic system will be in at any given point of time is dependent on the state which the system was in just previously. The branch of mathematics that deals with this kind of problem is called Markov chain.

Before we discuss the applications of Markov chain in business and economic problems, we first must define some terminology and theorems often used in this kind of analysis.

1. *Stochastic Processes.* Any sequence of experiments that can be subjected to probabilistic analysis is called stochastic processes.
2. *Independent Process.* If an experiment is conducted n times and the probability that the outcome of the nth experiment is independent of the outcomes of the first $(n - 1)$ experiments the process is an independent process.
3. *Markov Chain Process.* When the outcome of a given experiment depends only on the outcome of the immediately preceding experiment and this dependence is the same at all stages, the process is called a *Markov chain process.*
4. *Finite Markov Chain.* There are a given finite set

of states $\{S_1, S_2, \ldots, S_k; k \geq 2\}$, and the process can only be in one and only one of these states.

5. *Initial Starting State.* The initial state the economic or business system is in at the beginning of the process.

6. *Step.* The move from one state to another.

7. *Transition Probability.* The probability that the process moves from one state to another; it depends only on the state that the process occupied before the step. There is a transition probability for every ordered pair of states.

8. *Matrix of Transition Probabilities.* When the transition probability of each ordered pair of states is arranged in matrix form, it becomes a matrix of transition probabilities. All entries must be nonnegative and the sum of the elements in any row must be one. The rows are called *probability vectors.*

Example 1

Assume that the total number of states is three and we have the following transition probability matrix.

	State 1	State 2	State 3
State 1	p_{11}	p_{12}	p_{13}
State 2	p_{21}	p_{22}	p_{23}
State 3	p_{31}	p_{32}	p_{33}

where

$$p_{11} + p_{12} + p_{13} = 1$$
$$p_{21} + p_{22} + p_{23} = 1$$
$$p_{31} + p_{32} + p_{33} = 1$$

which indicates that all the possible transitions are included. Now, at any time period n, the probability that the state of the system be State 1 ($p_1^{(n)}$) may be expressed as the following by the addition and multiplication theorem of probability.

$$p_1^{(n)} = p_1^{(n-1)} p_{11} + p_2^{(n-1)} p_{21} + p_3^{(n-1)} p_{31}$$

Likewise,

$$p_2^{(n)} = p_1^{(n-1)} p_{12} + p_2^{(n-1)} p_{22} + p_3^{(n-1)} p_{32}$$

$$p_3^{(n)} = p_1^{(n-1)} p_{13} + p_2^{(n-1)} p_{23} + p_3^{(n-1)} p_{33}$$

Writing the above in matrix notation,

$$[p_1^{(n)} \ p_2^{(n)} \ p_3^{(n)}] = [p_1^{(n-1)} \ p_2^{(n-1)} \ p_3^{(n-1)}] \begin{bmatrix} p_{11} & p_{12} & p_{13} \\ p_{21} & p_{22} & p_{23} \\ p_{31} & p_{32} & p_{33} \end{bmatrix}$$

or

$$P^{(n)} = P^{(n-1)} P$$

9. *Regular Markov Chain.* If some power of the transition matrix has only positive elements, it is a regular Markov chain. A Markov chain is regular if there is some stage at which the process may be in any of the states regardless of the starting state.

Example 2

$$P = \begin{array}{c|ccc} \text{State} & 1 & 2 & 3 \\ \hline 1 & .5 & .25 & .25 \\ 2 & .5 & 0 & .5 \\ 3 & .25 & .25 & .5 \end{array}$$

Second transition:

$$P^2 = \begin{bmatrix} .5 & .25 & .25 \\ .5 & 0 & .5 \\ .25 & .25 & .5 \end{bmatrix} \begin{bmatrix} .5 & .25 & .25 \\ .5 & 0 & .5 \\ .25 & .25 & .5 \end{bmatrix}$$

$$= \begin{array}{c|ccc} \text{State} & 1 & 2 & 3 \\ \hline 1 & .437 & .187 & .375 \\ 2 & .375 & .25 & .375 \\ 3 & .375 & .187 & .437 \end{array}$$

Theorems

(a) If P is the transition matrix of a regular Markov chain, then P^n approaches a matrix T, which has same probability vector t for each row.

Example 3

State	1	2	3
1	.5	.25	.25
$P =$ 2	.5	0	.5
3	.25	.25	.5

State	1	2	3
1	.437	.187	.375
$P^2 =$ 2	.375	.25	.375
3	.375	.187	.437

State	1	2	3
1	.402	.199	.398
$p^4 =$ 2	.398	.203	.398
3	.398	.199	.402

State	1	2	3
1	.4	.2	.4
$p^8 =$ 2	.4	.2	$.4 \rightarrow T$
3	.4	.2	.4

(b) t is the unique probability vector, such that $tP = t$. All elements of t are positive, and it is called the *fixed point* of the matrix.

Example 4
A 2×2 transition matrix

$$\begin{bmatrix} 1 - x & x \\ y & 1 - y \end{bmatrix}$$

and a probability vector $[1 - z, z]$.

For the vector to be the fixed point of the matrix the following condition must be satisfied:

$$[1 - z, z] \begin{bmatrix} 1 - x & x \\ y & 1 - y \end{bmatrix} = [1 - z, z]$$

$$(1 - z)(1 - x) + zy = (1 - z)$$

$$(1 - z)x + z(1 - y) = z$$

Simplifying the equations, we get

$$z = \frac{x}{x + y}, \qquad 1 - z = \frac{y}{x + y}$$

and the probability vector becomes $\left[\dfrac{y}{x + y}, \dfrac{x}{x + y}\right]$.

When

$$\begin{bmatrix} 1 - x & x \\ y & 1 - y \end{bmatrix} = \begin{bmatrix} .2 & .8 \\ .6 & .4 \end{bmatrix}$$

$$\frac{y}{x + y} = \frac{.6}{.8 + .6} = \frac{3}{7}$$

$$\frac{x}{x + y} = \frac{.8}{.8 + .6} = \frac{4}{7}$$

$$\begin{bmatrix} \frac{3}{7} & \frac{4}{7} \end{bmatrix} \begin{bmatrix} .2 & .8 \\ .6 & .4 \end{bmatrix} = \begin{bmatrix} \frac{.6 + 2.4}{7} & \frac{2.4 + 1.6}{7} \end{bmatrix}$$

$$= \begin{bmatrix} \frac{3}{7} & \frac{4}{7} \end{bmatrix}$$

Example 5

$$t = (.4 \quad .2 \quad .4)$$

$$P = \begin{bmatrix} .5 & .25 & .25 \\ .5 & 0 & .5 \\ .25 & .25 & .5 \end{bmatrix}$$

$$tP = (.4 \quad .2 \quad .4) \begin{bmatrix} .5 & .25 & .25 \\ .5 & 0 & .5 \\ .25 & .25 & .5 \end{bmatrix} = (.4 \quad .2 \quad .4)$$

10. *Ergodic Chain.* When the process is possible to go from every state, to every other state, the Markov chain is called an *ergodic chain*. In an ergodic chain, the average number of times that the process is in a given state i in the first n steps is approximated by t_i.

Example 6

$$
P = \begin{array}{c} \\ 1 \\ 2 \\ 3 \end{array}
\begin{array}{c|ccc}
\text{State} & 1 & 2 & 3 \\
\hline
1 & .5 & .25 & .25 \\
2 & .5 & 0 & .5 \\
3 & .25 & .25 & .5
\end{array}
$$

$$
P^8 \rightarrow T = \begin{array}{c} \\ 1 \\ 2 \\ 3 \end{array}
\begin{array}{c|ccc}
\text{State} & 1 & 2 & 3 \\
\hline
1 & .4 & .2 & .4 \\
2 & .4 & .2 & .4 \\
3 & .4 & .2 & .4
\end{array}
$$

We may predict that in the long run the process will be in state 1,40 percent of the time, in state 2,20 percent of the time, and in state 3,40 percent of the time.

11. *Absorbing Markov Chains.* A state in a Markov chain is an absorbing state if the process is impossible to leave the state. Thus a Markov chain is an absorbing Markov chain if it has at least one absorbing state and from every state, the process is possible to go to an absorbing state. If we put the transition matrix of an absorbing Markov chain in the following form (standard or canonical form):

$$
P = \begin{array}{c} \\ k_1 \\ k_2 \end{array}
\begin{array}{c}
\begin{array}{cc} k_1 & \quad k_2 \end{array} \\
\left(\begin{array}{c|c} I & 0 \\ \hline R & Q \end{array} \right)
\end{array}
$$

in which we have k_1 absorbing states and k_2 nonabsorbing states, where I is a unit matrix and 0 a zero matrix, since the process once reaches any of the absorbing states will stay in it and not go to the nonabsorbing states.

$$
P^2 = \begin{pmatrix} I & 0 \\ R & Q \end{pmatrix} \begin{pmatrix} I & 0 \\ R & Q \end{pmatrix} = \begin{pmatrix} I & 0 \\ R(I + Q) & Q^2 \end{pmatrix}
$$

$$
P^n = \begin{pmatrix} I & 0 \\ R' & Q^n \end{pmatrix}
$$

where R' is a matrix which has no relevance to the discussion here. Q^n represents the probabilities of the process being in each of the nonabsorbing states after n steps for each possible nonabsorbing starting state.

In computing the average number of times in each nonabsorbing state for each possible nonabsorbing starting state, we consider the following series:

$$Q^0 + Q^1 + Q^2 + \cdots + Q^n$$

where Q^0 represents the probabilities of the process being in each of the nonabsorbing states when no step is taken; thus Q^0 must be 1. When n approaches infinity, the probability that the process will be absorbed in one of the absorbing states will be one; thus $Q^n \to 0$, as $n \to \infty$.

The infinite series becomes

$$I + Q + Q^2 + \cdots = (I - Q)^{-1} = S$$

as

$$S = I + Q + Q^2 + \cdots + Q^n$$
$$QS = \quad\ \ Q + Q^2 + \cdots + Q^n + Q^{n+1}$$
$$S(I - Q) = I - Q^{n+1}$$

Since $n \to \infty$, $Q^{n+1} \to 0$,

$$S = (I - Q)^{-1}$$

S is called the fundamental matrix of the absorbing Markov chain.

Theorems

(a) In an absorbing Markov chain the probability that the process will be absorbed is 1.

(b) The entries in the fundamental matrix S give the average number of times the process will be in each nonabsorbing state for each possible nonabsorbing starting state.

(c) In an absorbing Markov chain with k_2 nonabsorbing states, let C be a $k_2 \times 1$ vector with all entries equal to 1. Then the vector SC has as entries the average number of steps the process will be in each absorbing state before being absorbed for each possible nonabsorbing starting state.

(d) Let b_{ij} be the probability that an absorbing Markov chain will be absorbed in state S_j if it starts in non-absorbing state S_i. Let B be the matrix with entries b_{ij}; then

$$b_{ij} = p_{ij} \sum_k p_{ik} b_{kj}$$

where k indicates the number of nonabsorbing states the process goes through before it is absorbed.

$$B = R + QB$$
$$(I - Q)B = R$$
$$B = (I - Q)^{-1}R = SR$$

Example 7

Given the transition matrix as follows:

	State	1	2	3	4	5
	1	1	0	0	0	0
	2	.5	0	.5	0	0
$P =$	3	0	.4	0	.6	0
	4	0	0	.2	0	.8
	5	0	0	0	0	1

States 1 and 5 are absorbing states and states 2, 3, and 4 are nonabsorbing states.

Rearranging the transition matrix in regular form,

	State	1	5	2	3	4
	1	1	0	0	0	0
	5	0	1	0	0	0
$\begin{pmatrix} I & 0 \\ R & Q \end{pmatrix} =$	2	.5	0	0	.5	0
	3	0	0	.4	0	.6
	4	0	.8	0	.2	0

where

	State	2	3	4
	2	0	.5	0
$Q =$	3	.4	0	.6
	4	0	.2	0

and

$$
R = \begin{array}{c} \\ 2 \\ 3 \\ 4 \end{array}
\begin{array}{cc}
\text{State} \quad 1 & 5 \\
\left[\begin{array}{cc}
.5 & 0 \\
0 & 0 \\
0 & .8
\end{array}\right]
\end{array}
$$

The fundamental matrix is then

$$
S = (I - Q)^{-1} = \begin{array}{c} \\ 2 \\ 3 \\ 4 \end{array}
\begin{array}{ccc}
\text{State} \quad 2 & 3 & 4 \\
\left[\begin{array}{ccc}
^{44}\!/_{34} & ^{25}\!/_{34} & ^{15}\!/_{34} \\
^{20}\!/_{34} & ^{50}\!/_{34} & ^{30}\!/_{34} \\
^{4}\!/_{34} & ^{10}\!/_{34} & ^{40}\!/_{34}
\end{array}\right]
\end{array}
$$

Thus, starting from nonabsorbing state 2, the average number of times that the process will be in state 2 is $1^{10}\!/_{34}$, in state 3 is $^{25}\!/_{34}$ and in state 4 is $^{15}\!/_{34}$. If starting from state 3, the average number of times that the process will be in state 2 is $^{20}\!/_{34}$, in state 3 is $1^{16}\!/_{34}$ and in state 4 is $^{30}\!/_{34}$. If starting from state 4, the average number of times that the process will be in state 2 is $^{4}\!/_{34}$, in state 3 is $^{10}\!/_{34}$ and in state 4 is $1^{6}\!/_{34}$.

$$
SC = \begin{bmatrix}
^{44}\!/_{34} & ^{25}\!/_{34} & ^{15}\!/_{34} \\
^{20}\!/_{34} & ^{50}\!/_{34} & ^{30}\!/_{34} \\
^{4}\!/_{34} & ^{10}\!/_{34} & ^{40}\!/_{34}
\end{bmatrix}
\begin{bmatrix}
1 \\ 1 \\ 1
\end{bmatrix}
=
\begin{array}{c}
\text{State} \\
2 \\ 3 \\ 4
\end{array}
\begin{bmatrix}
2^{8}\!/_{17} \\
2^{16}\!/_{17} \\
1^{10}\!/_{17}
\end{bmatrix}
$$

Thus the average number of steps to absorption starting at state 2 is $2^{8}\!/_{17}$, starting at state 3 is $2^{16}\!/_{17}$ and starting at state 4 is $1^{10}\!/_{17}$.

The B matrix is

$$
B = SR = \begin{bmatrix}
^{44}\!/_{34} & ^{25}\!/_{34} & ^{15}\!/_{34} \\
^{20}\!/_{34} & ^{50}\!/_{34} & ^{30}\!/_{34} \\
^{4}\!/_{34} & ^{10}\!/_{34} & ^{40}\!/_{34}
\end{bmatrix}
\begin{bmatrix}
.5 & 0 \\
0 & 0 \\
0 & .8
\end{bmatrix}
$$

$$
= \begin{array}{c} \\ 2 \\ 3 \\ 4 \end{array}
\begin{array}{cc}
\text{State} \quad 1 & 5 \\
\left[\begin{array}{cc}
^{11}\!/_{17} & ^{6}\!/_{17} \\
^{5}\!/_{17} & ^{12}\!/_{17} \\
^{1}\!/_{17} & ^{16}\!/_{17}
\end{array}\right]
\end{array}
$$

Thus, starting from nonabsorbing state 2, the probability of being absorbed in state 1 is $^{11}/_{17}$ and in state 5 is $^6/_{17}$. If starting from state 3, the probability of being absorbed in state 1 is $^5/_{17}$ and in state 5 is $^{12}/_{17}$. If starting from state 4, the probability of being absorbed in state 1 is $^1/_{17}$ and in state 5 is $^{16}/_{17}$.

AN INVESTMENT DECISION MODEL

A family lives in an apartment on which the monthly rental is $100. They consider buying a house in four years, preferably near Christmas. They estimate that they will need to borrow $10,000. The current interest rate is 7 percent per annum. In the next three years, the rate may go down to 6.5 or 6 percent. The probability that the interest rate will change from one state to another in each subsequent year is described by the following transition matrix.

State	.07	.065	.06
.07	.5	.4	.1
.065	.2	.6	.2
.06	.1	.4	.5

If the family waits until the interest rate has gone down before buying a house, a substantial amount of payment may be saved. Assume that the interest rate will go down to 6.5 percent and the estimated net savings (compared to buying the house on the first Christmas at 7 percent interest rate) are as follows:

Period	Net Savings
First year	$1000
Second year	800
Third year	600

If the interest rate goes down to 6 percent, the net savings are estimated as follows:

Period	Net Savings
First year	$1,500
Second year	1,000
Third year	800

Using the Markov chain, we may evaluate the decision rule as follows.

1. If they buy a house on the first Christmas when the interest rate is 7 percent, the net savings will be zero.
2. If they wait until the interest rate goes down to 6.5 percent or less, the transition matrix becomes

State	.07	.065	.06
.07	.5	.4	.1
.065	0	1	0
.06	0	0	1

As both states .065 and .06 will be absorbing, the initial state vector is

$$[1, \quad 0, \quad 0]$$

The first-year state vector is

$$[1, \quad 0, \quad 0] \begin{bmatrix} .5 & .4 & .1 \\ 0 & 1 & 0 \\ 0 & 0 & 1 \end{bmatrix} = [.5 \quad .4 \quad .1]$$

The second-year state vector is

$$[.5 \quad .4 \quad .1] \begin{bmatrix} .5 & .4 & .1 \\ 0 & 1 & 0 \\ 0 & 0 & 1 \end{bmatrix} = [.25 \quad .6 \quad .15]$$

The third-year state vector is

$$[.25 \quad .6 \quad .15] \begin{bmatrix} .5 & .4 & .1 \\ 0 & 1 & 0 \\ 0 & 0 & 1 \end{bmatrix} = [.125 \quad .7 \quad .175]$$

Thus

Period	Probability of 6.5% or Less	Change of Probability	Net Savings	Expected Net Savings
First year	.4	.4	$1,000	$400
Second year	.6	.2	800	160
Third year	.7	.1	600	60
		.7		$620

3. If they wait until the interest rate goes down to 6 percent, the transition matrix becomes

State	.07	.065	.06
.07	.5	.4	.1
.065	.2	.6	.2
.06	0	0	1

As only state .06 is absorbing, the initial state vector is still

$$[1, \quad 0, \quad 0]$$

The first-year state vector is

$$[1, \quad 0, \quad 0] \begin{bmatrix} .5 & .4 & .1 \\ .2 & .6 & .2 \\ 0 & 0 & 1 \end{bmatrix} = [.5 \quad .4 \quad .1]$$

The second-year state vector is

$$[.5 \quad .4 \quad .1] \begin{bmatrix} .5 & .4 & .1 \\ .2 & .6 & .2 \\ 0 & 0 & 1 \end{bmatrix} = [.33 \quad .44 \quad .23]$$

The third-year state vector is

$$[.33 \quad .44 \quad .23] \begin{bmatrix} .5 & .4 & .1 \\ .2 & .6 & .2 \\ 0 & 0 & 1 \end{bmatrix} = [.253 \quad .396 \quad .351]$$

Thus

Period	Probability of 6%	Change of Probability	Net Savings	Expected Net Savings
First year	.1	.1	$1,500	$150
Second year	.23	.13	1,000	130
Third year	.351	.121	800	96.8
		.351		$376.8

In view of the above analysis, the largest expected net savings is $620, and the family should buy a house at or near the Christmas when the interest rate goes down to 6.5 percent or less for the first time.

A REPLACEMENT MODEL

A firm wishes to compare two policies of replacing its automobiles. One is to replace a car when the maintenance and operation cost exceeds $500 but less than $1,000 a year. The other is to replace the car only when the maintenance and operation cost amounts to $1,000 a year. Suppose we define four different states: (1) new car, (2) car in operation with maintenance and operation cost less than $500 a year, (3) car in operation, with maintenance and operation cost between $500 and $1,000, or average of $750 a year. (4) The maintenance and operation costs add up to $1,000 a year, and we find the transition matrix in the period of one year is as follows:

State	(1)	(2)	(3)	(4)
(1)	0	$9/10$	$1/10$	0
(2)	0	$3/5$	$2/5$	0
(3)	0	0	$1/2$	$1/2$
(4)	1	0	0	0

Consider the second alternative. Given

$$P = \begin{matrix} & 1 & 2 & 3 & 4 \\ 1 & \begin{bmatrix} 0 & 9/10 & 1/10 & 0 \\ 2 & 0 & 3/5 & 2/5 & 0 \\ 3 & 0 & 0 & 1/2 & 1/2 \\ 4 & 1 & 0 & 0 & 0 \end{bmatrix} \end{matrix}$$

We may compute the fixed point t of the matrix by the following computation:

$$t_1 = t_4$$
$$t_2 = \tfrac{9}{10}t_1 + \tfrac{3}{5}t_2$$
$$t_3 = \tfrac{1}{10}t_1 + \tfrac{2}{5}t_2 + \tfrac{1}{2}t_3$$
$$t_4 = \tfrac{1}{2}t_3$$
$$t_1 + t_2 + t_3 + t_4 = 1$$

The simultaneous solution is

$$t_1 = \tfrac{4}{25}$$

$$t_2 = \frac{9}{25}$$
$$t_3 = \frac{8}{25}$$
$$t_4 = \frac{4}{25}$$

Thus if the firm adopts the second policy the expected average cost per car per year is

$$1,000t_4 = 1,000\frac{4}{25} = \$160$$

Now consider the first alternative, since state (4) will never be reached, the transition matrix becomes

$$P = \begin{array}{c} \\ 1 \\ 2 \\ 3 \end{array} \begin{array}{ccc} 1 & 2 & 3 \\ \hline 0 & \frac{9}{10} & \frac{1}{10} \\ 0 & \frac{3}{5} & \frac{2}{5} \\ 1 & 0 & 0 \end{array}$$

The fixed point t of the matrix may be computed by the following simultaneous equations:

$$t_1 = t_3$$
$$t_2 = \frac{9}{10}t_1 + \frac{3}{5}t_2$$
$$t_3 = \frac{1}{10}t_1 + \frac{2}{5}t_2$$
$$t_1 + t_2 + t_3 = 1$$

The solution is

$$t_1 = \frac{4}{17}$$
$$t_2 = \frac{9}{17}$$
$$t_3 = \frac{4}{17}$$

Thus if the firm adopts the first policy the expected average cost per car per year is

$$750t_3 = 750 \times \frac{4}{17} = \$176\frac{8}{17}$$

Therefore the second policy is preferable.

SUMMARY

Markov chain or process utilizes probability transition matrix to describe the transition among a finite number of states. Some states in a Markov chain may be absorbing states, that is, once the process reaches any of those states it is impossible for the process to go to another state. If a Markov chain has one or more absorbing states it is an absorbing Markov chain and the probability that the process will be eventually absorbed is 1. Analytical methods are available to calculate the expected number of times that the process will go through a nonabsorbing state when started at another nonabsorbing state and the expected number of steps the process will take from a nonabsorbing state to an absorbing state. This is one area of Markov chain that finds many applications in business and economic analysis.

When the study of Markov chain goes further to allow the probabilities in the transition matrix to change, the analysis immediately becomes very complex. Computer simulation methods may then be used to deal with the situation.

PROBLEMS

1. Will the following probability transition matrix form a regular Markov chain?

State	1	2	3
1	.3	.3	.4
$P =$ 2	.1	.2	.7
3	.5	.2	.3

If so, find the fixed point of the matrix.

2. Given the following probability transition matrix:

State	1	2	3	4
1	0	0	0	1
2	.3	.5	.1	.1
$P =$ 3	0	0	1	0
4	.2	.2	.2	.4

Which state is the absorbing state? Starting from state 2, what is the average number of steps to absorption?

3. The possible states of the weather are classified as fair, cloudy,

and foul, and the probability transition matrix of the day-to-day weather is as follows:

	Fair	Cloudy	Foul
Fair	.5	.5	0
Cloudy	.25	.25	.5
Foul	.25	.5	.25

Starting from a fair day, what is the probability that it will rain three days later? What is the probability that it will be cloudy three days later? What is the probability that it will still be fair three days later?

4. A chute is separated by doors to form three compartments as shown:

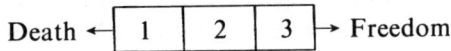

Death ←| 1 | 2 | 3 |→ Freedom

A mouse is put in one of the compartments. The probability of its going through the right-hand door is $2/3$ and the probability of it going through the left-hand door is $1/3$. Starting from compartment 2, what is the probability that the mouse will find freedom, and what is the probability that the mouse will face death?

5. A foundation's money is granted to research areas classified as natural science, social science, engineering, and business. The area to which the money is given changes every year. (1) Assume that if the money is initially granted to natural science, then in the subsequent year there is 10 percent probability that it will still be given to natural science, 50 percent probability it will be given to social science, 20 percent to engineering, and 20 percent to business. (2) Assume that if the money is initially granted to social science, then in the subsequent year there is 10 percent probability that the money will still be given to social science, 60 percent probability it will be given to natural science, 10 percent to business, and 20 percent go to engineering. (3) Assume that if in the initial year the money is granted to engineering, then in the subsequent year there is 20 percent probability it will still be given to engineering, 40 percent to natural science, 10 percent to social science, and 30 percent to business. (4) Assume that if the money is initially granted to business, then in the subsequent year there is 30 percent probability it will still be given to business, 30 percent

to engineering, 30 percent to social science, and 10 percent to natural science. Assume the transition probabilities remain the same through the years. Find the probability that in the first year the money is granted to engineering research but in the fifth year the money will be given to business research.

SELECTED REFERENCES

Bharucha-Reid, A. T., *Elements of the Theory of Markov Processes and Their Applications.* New York: McGraw-Hill Book Company, 1960.

Howard, R. A., *Dynamic Programming and Markov Processes.* New York: John Wiley & Sons, Inc., 1960.

Kemeny, J. G., and J. L. Snell, *Finite Markov Chains.* Princeton, N.J.: D. Van Nostrand Company, Inc., 1959.

Kemeny, J. G., H. Mirkil, J. L. Snell, and G. L. Thompson, *Finite Mathematical Structure.* Englewood Cliffs, N.J.: Prentice-Hall, Inc., 1959, Chap. 6.

chapter 7

Elementary Waiting-Line or Queuing Models

In any organization there always exist problems of waiting lines. For example, the checkout lines in a super-market, the flow of parts and materials on an assembly line, the inquiries sent into a central information bank of a computer system. If waiting time is too long, the completion date of a job may be delayed, increasing the operating cost or losing customers. On the other hand, too many facilities may result in a large amount of idle time, which is an economic waste. Thus we need to find the proper balance between the required work load or service and the available personnel and facilities.

A SINGLE-STATION MODEL

The simplest waiting-line model is a single-station model in which inputs arrive at the station, the time intervals between consecutive arrivals are expressed by a probability distribution, and the service time intervals required to complete each job or service are expressed by another probability distribution. One of the models which has analytical solution assumes that both the interarrival time and the service time are exponentially distributed.

Conventionally, however, we count the number of arrivals and departures in a unit time interval, so that they become discrete distributions. The equivalent of exponential distribution in discrete form is called a *Poisson distribution*. Let us assume that the mean of the arrival rate is λ and the mean service or departure rate equals μ. The probability that there are n units in the station at time $(t + \Delta t)$ may be expressed by

$$P_n(t + \Delta t) = P_n(t)(1 - \lambda \Delta t)(1 - \mu \Delta t)$$
$$+ P_{n-1}(t) \lambda \Delta t(1 - \mu \Delta t) + P_{n+1}(t) \mu \Delta t(1 - \lambda \Delta t)$$

where $(\lambda \Delta t)$ is the probability of an arrival in a small time interval Δt and $(\mu \Delta t)$ the probability of a departure in Δt. The first term indicates the probability that there will be n units in the station, that none of them will leave, and that no input will arrive in a short time interval Δt. The second term indicates the probability that $n - 1$ units are in the station, that none of them will leave, but that a new input will arrive in Δt. The third term indicates the probability that $n + 1$ units are in the station, that there are no new arrivals, but that one will leave the station in Δt. These three terms include all possibilities that will result in having n units in the station at time $(t + \Delta t)$. Δt is chosen so small that the probability of having either two units arrive at the station or two units leave the station in Δt is zero.

Since Δt is very small, say .00001, we may assume $(\Delta t)^2$ approaches zero. Thus

$$P_n(t + \Delta t) = P_n(t) - P_n(t) \lambda \Delta t - P_n(t) \mu \Delta t$$
$$+ P_{n-1}(t) \lambda \Delta t + P_{n+1}(t) \mu \Delta t$$

$$\frac{P_n(t + \Delta t) - P_n(t)}{\Delta t} = -P_n(t)(\lambda + \mu) + P_{n-1}(t) \lambda + P_{n+1}(t) \mu$$

When $\Delta t \to 0$,

$$\frac{dP_n(t)}{dt} = -P_n(t)(\lambda + \mu) + P_{n-1}(t) \lambda + P_{n+1}(t) \mu$$

In a steady-state waiting line,

$$\frac{dP_n(t)}{dt} = 0$$

and

$$-P_n \cdot (\lambda + \mu) + P_{n-1} \cdot \lambda + P_{n+1} \cdot \mu = 0$$

In the case of $n = 0$, no departure is possible and $(n - 1)$ does not exist.

$$-P_0\lambda + P_1\mu = 0$$

$$P_1 = \frac{\lambda}{\mu} P_0$$

In the case of $n = 1$,

$$-P_1(\lambda + \mu) + P_0\lambda + P_2\mu = 0$$

$$\begin{aligned} P_2 &= P_1 \frac{\lambda + \mu}{\mu} - P_0 \frac{\lambda}{\mu} \\ &= P_0 \frac{\lambda}{\mu} \frac{\lambda + \mu}{\mu} - P_0 \frac{\lambda}{\mu} \\ &= \frac{\lambda}{\mu}^2 P_0 \end{aligned}$$

Similarly,

$$P_n = \left(\frac{\lambda}{\mu}\right)^n P_0 \quad \text{for } n \geq 0$$

Since the sum of all probabilities $\displaystyle\sum_{n=0}^{\infty} P_n = 1$,

$$P_0 + \left(\frac{\lambda}{\mu}\right) P_0 + \left(\frac{\lambda}{\mu}\right)^2 P_0 + \cdots + \left(\frac{\lambda}{\mu}\right)^n P_0 = 1$$

$$\left[1 + \left(\frac{\lambda}{\mu}\right) + \left(\frac{\lambda}{\mu}\right)^2 + \cdots + \left(\frac{\lambda}{\mu}\right)^n\right] P_0 = 1$$

According to formula, the sum of a geometric series

$$\left[\frac{1 - (\lambda/\mu)^{n+1}}{1 - (\lambda/\mu)}\right] P_0 = 1$$

However, the mean service rate μ has to be greater than the mean arrival rate λ, otherwise we will have an infinite waiting line (since the interarrival and service time are not constant). Thus when n approaches infinity, $(\lambda/\mu)^{n+1}$ approaches zero:

$$P_0 = 1 - \frac{\lambda}{\mu}$$

and

$$P_n = \left(1 - \frac{\lambda}{\mu}\right)\left(\frac{\lambda}{\mu}\right)^n$$

Example 1

The customers arrive at a service station in Poisson distribution, with the mean arrival rate of 10 per hr. The service-station attendant performs the service in lengths of time exponentially distributed, with a mean service rate of 20 per hr (or 3 min per service). What is the probability of having 3 customers in the station, one being serviced and two waiting to be serviced?

$$\lambda = 10 \qquad \text{and} \qquad \mu = 20$$

$$P_3 = \left(1 - \frac{10}{20}\right)\left(\frac{10}{20}\right)^3$$

$$= .0625 \text{ or } 6.25 \text{ percent of the time}$$

The expected number of units in the station may be computed as follows:

$$E(n) = \sum_{n=0}^{\infty} nP_n = \sum_{n=0}^{\infty} n\left(1 - \frac{\lambda}{\mu}\right)\left(\frac{\lambda}{\mu}\right)^n$$

$$= \left(1 - \frac{\lambda}{\mu}\right)\sum_{n=0}^{\infty} n\left(\frac{\lambda}{\mu}\right)^n$$

$$= \left(1 - \frac{\lambda}{\mu}\right)\left[\frac{\lambda}{\mu} + 2\left(\frac{\lambda}{\mu}\right)^2 + 3\left(\frac{\lambda}{\mu}\right)^3 + \cdots\right]$$

$$= \left(1 - \frac{\lambda}{\mu}\right)\left(\frac{\lambda}{\mu}\right)1 + 2\left(\frac{\lambda}{\mu}\right) + 3\left(\frac{\lambda}{\mu}\right)^2 + \cdots\right]$$

$$= \left(1 - \frac{\lambda}{\mu}\right)\left(\frac{\lambda}{\mu}\right)\frac{1}{[1 - (\lambda/\mu)]^2}$$

$$= \frac{\lambda/\mu}{1 - (\lambda/\mu)}$$

$$= \frac{\lambda}{\mu - \lambda}$$

Since λ is the mean arrival rate, $1/\lambda$ is the time between arrivals. Let $E(T)$ be the expected time an arrival spends in the station. Then the product of the average number of units in the system and the average interarrival time is the average time an arrival spends in the system or, in other words, the number of units divided by the time is the rate.

$$E(T) = E(n) \cdot \frac{1}{\lambda}$$

$$= \left(\frac{\lambda}{\mu - \lambda}\right)\left(\frac{1}{\lambda}\right)$$

$$= \frac{1}{\mu - \lambda}$$

Since μ is the mean service rate, $1/\mu$ is the mean service-time interval. Let $E(W)$ be the expected waiting time of an arrival, then the average waiting time is the difference between the average time an arrival spends in the system and the average service time:

$$E(W) = E(T) - \frac{1}{\mu}$$

$$= \frac{1}{\mu - \lambda} - \frac{1}{\mu}$$

$$= \frac{\lambda}{\mu(\mu - \lambda)}$$

Thus

$$E(n) = \frac{10}{20 - 10} = 1 \text{ unit}$$

$$E(T) = \frac{1}{10} \text{ hr or 6 min}$$

$$E(W) = \frac{10}{20(20 - 10)} = \frac{1}{20} \text{ hr or 3 min}$$

A MULTISTATION MODEL

In this model we assume that there are m identical service stations, each with mean service rate μ. Arrivals come with mean arrival rate λ and form a single waiting line. The waiting-line discipline is first-come, first-served, with a unit going into service at the moment a station becomes empty.

When the number of units arrived (n) is less than the

number of service stations (m), the probability of having n units in the system is*

$$P_n = \frac{1}{n!}\left(\frac{\lambda}{\mu}\right)^n P_0 \qquad n = 0, 1, 2, \ldots, m - 1$$

When the number of units arrived equals or exceeds the number of service stations, the probability becomes

$$P'_n = \frac{1}{m!\,m^{n-m}}\left(\frac{\lambda}{\mu}\right)^n P_0 \qquad n \geq m$$

where P_0 is the probability of no units in the system.
    Since

$$\sum_{n=0}^{m-1} P_n + \sum_{n=m}^{\infty} P'_n = 1$$

or

$$\sum_{n=0}^{m-1} \frac{1}{n!}\left(\frac{\lambda}{\mu}\right)^n P_0 + \sum_{n=m}^{\infty} \frac{1}{m!\,m^{n-m}}\left(\frac{\lambda}{\mu}\right)^n P_0 = 1$$

*With this multistation model,

$$P_n(t + \Delta t) = P_n(t)(1 - \lambda\Delta t)(1 - n\mu\Delta t)$$
$$+ P_{n-1}(t)\lambda\Delta t[1 - (n - 1)\mu\Delta t]$$
$$+ P_{n+1}(t)(n + 1)\mu\Delta t(1 - \lambda\Delta t)$$

$$\frac{dP_n(t)}{dt} = \lim_{\Delta t \to 0} \frac{P_n(t + \Delta t) - P_n(t)}{\Delta t}$$
$$= -(\lambda + n\mu)P_n(t) + \lambda P_{n-1}(t) + (n + 1)\mu P_{n+1}(t)$$

At stable conditions,

$$\frac{dP_n}{dt} = 0$$

and

$$-(\lambda + n\mu)P_n + \lambda P_{n-1} + (n + 1)\mu P_{n+1} = 0$$

When $n = 0$,

$$-\lambda P_0 + \mu P_1 = 0; \quad P_1 = \left(\frac{\lambda}{\mu}\right)P_0$$

When $n = 1$,

$$-(\lambda + \mu)P_1 + \lambda P_0 + 2\mu P_2 = 0; \quad P_2 = \frac{1}{2}\left(\frac{\lambda}{\mu}\right)^2 P_0$$

When $n = 2$,

$$-(\lambda + 2\mu)P_2 + \lambda P_1 + 3\mu P_3 = 0; \quad P_3 = \frac{1}{3.2}\left(\frac{\lambda}{\mu}\right)^3 P_0$$

Then

$$P_0 = \cfrac{1}{\displaystyle\sum_{n=0}^{m-1} \frac{1}{n!}\left(\frac{\lambda}{\mu}\right)^n + \sum_{n=m}^{\infty} \frac{1}{m!\,m^{n-m}}\left(\frac{\lambda}{\mu}\right)^n}$$

$$= \cfrac{1}{\displaystyle\sum_{n=0}^{m-1} \frac{1}{n!}\left(\frac{\lambda}{\mu}\right)^n + \frac{1}{m!}\left[\left(\frac{\lambda}{\mu}\right)^m + \frac{1}{m}\left(\frac{\lambda}{\mu}\right)^{m+1} + \frac{1}{m^2}\left(\frac{\lambda}{\mu}\right)^{m+2} + \cdots\right]}$$

$$= \cfrac{1}{\displaystyle\sum_{n=0}^{m-1} \frac{1}{n!}\left(\frac{\lambda}{\mu}\right)^n + \frac{1}{m!}\left(\frac{\lambda}{\mu}\right)^m\left(1 + \frac{\lambda}{m\mu} + \frac{\lambda}{m\mu}^2 + \cdots\right)}$$

$$= \cfrac{1}{\displaystyle\sum_{n=0}^{m-1} \frac{1}{n!}\left(\frac{\lambda}{\mu}\right)^n + \frac{1}{m!}\left(\frac{\lambda}{\mu}\right)^m\left(\frac{1}{1 - (\lambda/m\mu)}\right)}$$

$$= \cfrac{1}{\displaystyle\sum_{n=0}^{m-1} \frac{1}{n!}\left(\frac{\lambda}{\mu}\right)^n + \frac{1}{m!}\left(\frac{\lambda}{\mu}\right)^m\left(\frac{m\mu}{m\mu - \lambda}\right)}$$

The formula is valid when $m\mu > \lambda$. If $m\mu \leq \lambda$, the waiting line will build up infinitely.

The expected number of units in the system can be computed by the following formula:

$$E(n) = \sum_{n=0}^{m-1} n\left(\frac{1}{n!}\right)\left(\frac{\lambda}{\mu}\right)^n P_0 + \sum_{n=m}^{\infty} n\,\frac{1}{m!\,m^{n-m}}\left(\frac{\lambda}{\mu}\right)^n P_0$$

$$= \frac{\lambda\mu(\lambda/\mu)^m}{(m-1)!(m\mu - \lambda)^2} P_0 + \frac{\lambda}{\mu}$$

The expected time that an arrival spends in the system can be computed by

$$E(T) = E(n)\cdot\frac{1}{\lambda} = \frac{\mu(\lambda/\mu)^m}{(m-1)!(m\mu - \lambda)^2} P_0 + \frac{1}{\mu}$$

And the expected waiting time of an arrival can be computed by

$$E(W) = E(T) - \frac{1}{\mu} = \frac{\mu(\lambda/\mu)^m}{(m-1)!(m\mu - \lambda)^2} P_0$$

Example 2

Customers arrive at a barbershop in Poisson fashion at an average rate of 10 per hr. There are three barbers in the shop who are equally efficient, and the service time is exponentially distributed, with the mean equal to 10 min per customer. Find (1) the average number of customers in the barbershop, (2) the average time a customer spends in the barbershop, (3) the average time the customer has to wait, and (4) the average number of idle barbers at any specified instant. The mean arrival rate is

$$\lambda = 10 \text{ customers per hr}$$

The mean service rate is

$$\mu = {}^{60}\!/_{10} = 6 \text{ customers per hr}$$

The number of barbers is

$$m = 3$$

$m\mu = 18$ which is greater than 10, the waiting line is finite:

$$P_0 = \frac{1}{1 + ({}^{10}\!/_6) + ({}^1\!/_2)({}^{10}\!/_6)^2\,{}^1\!/_6({}^{10}\!/_6)^3({}^{18}\!/_8)}$$

$$= \frac{72}{417} = .17$$

1. The average number of customers in the barbershop is

$$E(n) = \frac{10 \times 6 \times ({}^{10}\!/_6)^3}{2!(18 - 10)^2}\left(\frac{72}{417}\right) + \frac{10}{6}$$

$$= 2.03 \text{ customers}$$

2. The average time a customer spends in the barbershop is

$$E(T) = E(n) \cdot \frac{1}{\lambda} = 2.03\,\frac{1}{10} = .203 \text{ hr or } 12.18 \text{ min}$$

3. The average time a customer has to wait is

$$E(W) = E(T) - \frac{1}{\mu} = .203 - \frac{1}{6} = .0365 \text{ hr or } 2.18 \text{ min}$$

4. The average number of idle barbers is

$$3P_0 + 2P_1 + 1P_2 = 3\left(\frac{72}{417}\right) + 2\left(\frac{10}{6}\right)\left(\frac{72}{417}\right) + \left(\frac{10}{6}\right)^2\left(\frac{1}{2!}\right)\left(\frac{72}{417}\right)$$

$$= \frac{556}{417} = 1.3 \text{ barbers}$$

The simple waiting-line models may be developed into more complicated models with the stations both arranged serially and in parallel, and with the distributions of the random interarrival time and service time changed into other distributions beside Poisson and exponential. However, the analytical method becomes insufficient to solve those complicated situations. Recently computer simulation methods have been extensively used to experiment with these models, the techniques of which are discussed in a later chapter.

SUMMARY

Time is of the essence. In any organization or system, efficiency can be obtained if we can reduce waiting time and make better use of idle facilities. In order to facilitate the analysis, waiting-line models are built. The simplest model is a single-station model with the assumption that the input units arrive in Poisson distribution, the waiting line discipline is first-come, first-served, and the service times are in exponential distribution. Another simple model is the multistation model, in which the input units are still assumed to arrive in Poisson fashion and form one waiting line, with a unit going into service the moment a station becomes empty. The service time at each station is assumed to be exponentially distributed with equal parameters. Analytical methods give simple formulas to compute the average waiting time of an arrival, average time an arrival spends in the system, and average number of units in the system for these models.

More complicated waiting-line models in which the service stations are arranged in series or in parallel, with service times at different stations in different distributions, are more difficult of solution by analytical methods. In Chapter 9, computer-simulation methods are introduced to help analyze different designs of station arrangement with different assumptions of interarrival and service-time distributions.

PROBLEMS

1. Arrivals at a gasoline station are considered to be Poisson. The average interarrival time is 15 min. The service time is considered as exponentially distributed with mean equals 10 min. What is the expected waiting time for each arrival and the expected time each arrival spends in the system? What is the average number of cars in the station?

2. A barbershop has three chairs and three barbers. The three barbers are equally efficient. The time that each barber takes to serve one customer is considered as exponentially distributed with mean equals 15 min. The customers enter the barbershop in Poisson distribution average 10 customers per hr. What is the expected waiting time and the average number of customers in the barbershop?

3. In Prob. 1, if waiting time needs to be reduced to half, what should be the mean service time?

4. In Prob. 2, if one more chair and one more equally efficient barber is added in the barbershop, how will this affect the average waiting time and the average number of customers in the barbershop?

5. Patients arrive at a doctor's office in Poisson distribution with an average rate of four per hour. The doctor examines them in two phases, with the average time of the first phase two minutes and the second phase five minutes, the distribution of time spent on each phase being exponentially distributed. What is the average time the patients spend in waiting? What is the average time they spend in examination? What is the average time the patients stay in the doctor's office?

6. Inputs arrive at a service station at a rate of one unit every 10 min. The waiting cost is a dollar per unit per min, and the cost of serving one unit is $5. Define the cost as a function of the service interval, and find the minimum cost service interval.

7. A company owns 100 processing machines. Each machine needs maintenance service in an average interval of one hr. The mean service time is 10 min. Both between maintenance and service time intervals are approximately exponentially distributed. Each minute a machine is due for maintenance and none of the maintenance men is available will cost $0.1. Maintenance men's wage rate is $15 per hr, including overhead. How many maintenance men should the company hire to minimize cost? What is the minimum cost of maintenance men's wage and the cost of the machines in idle?

8. A company owns 10 trucks to ship materials from warehouse to factory. Each truck goes to the warehouse for reloading at an average interval of 2 hr. It takes an average of 30 min to load a truck by a driver and one helper at the warehouse. The two time intervals are approximately exponentially distributed. If every helper at the warehouse is busy in loading trucks, a truck arriving at the warehouse has to wait in queue. The cost of waiting is estimated to be $10 per truck per hr and the wage rate of the helpers at the warehouse is $2 per hr. How many helpers should the company have at the warehouse? What is the minimum cost of waiting plus the cost of the helpers?

SELECTED REFERENCES

Churchman, C. W., R. L. Ackoff, and E. L. Arnoff, *Introduction to Operations Research.* New York: John Wiley & Sons, Inc., 1957.

Cox, D. R., and W. L. Smith, *Queues.* New York: John Wiley & Sons, Inc., 1961.

Morse, P. M., *Queues, Inventories, and Maintenance.* New York: John Wiley & Sons, Inc., 1958.

Saaty, T. L., *Elements of Queuing Theory.* New York: McGraw-Hill Book Company, 1961.

Sasieni, M., A. Yaspan, and L. Friedman, *Operations Research.* New York: John Wiley & Sons, Inc., 1959.

Takacs, L., *Introduction to the Theory of Queues.* New York: Oxford University Press, 1962.

chapter **8**

Elementary Inventory Models

Economists consider that businessmen follow the practice of holding inventory because of the following reasons:

1. *Transactionary Purpose.* Since most of the goods and services are not manufactured or sold to customers on a while-you-wait basis, the materials used in producing the goods or providing the services cannot be acquired immediately unless there is inventory on hand.

2. *Precautionary Purpose.* Since certain economic goods are scarce, they can be in short supply at times. Businessmen expecting these shortages may obtain more of such goods than the current demand requires, thus creating inventory.

3. *Speculationary Purpose.* Since supply and demand are not constant all the time, the prices of economic goods will fluctuate. Businessmen because of their profit-seeking motive want to buy when price is low and sell when price is high. These speculative transactions create inventory at some time periods.

However, storing goods costs money. Decision making rules thus have to be developed with respect to how much and when to purchase or produce for inventory. In this section, several simple inventory models are introduced with the objective of minimizing the total cost.

1. Constant-demand, no-shortage-allowed inventory model.

Let c_1 = the inventory cost for carrying one unit of item for a unit of time

c_2 = the setup cost per production run or per order

In the model shown in Fig. 8-1 the assumptions are the following.

1. The demand is constant (linear slope).
2. No shortage is allowed.
3. No time lag is allowed for production or order, and each time a fixed amount of q is produced or ordered which will last a constant time period t.

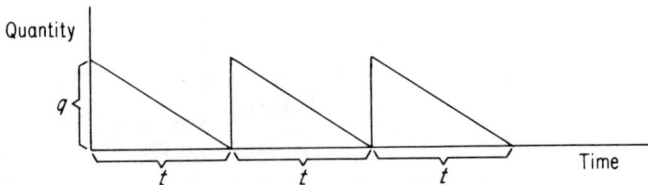

Fig. 8-1

Since the average inventory for this model is $q/2$ units, the inventory cost for $q/2$ units per unit time is

$$c_1 \times \frac{q}{2}$$

Also, let the demand or output rate be r, which is assumed to be constant

$$q = rt$$

or

$$t = \frac{q}{r}$$

The setup cost per unit time is

$$\frac{c_2}{t} = c_2 \frac{r}{q}$$

Therefore the total cost per unit time is

$$C = c_1 \frac{q}{2} + c_2 \frac{r}{q}$$

In searching for the minimum total cost, we set the first derivative of C with respect to q equal to zero:

$$\frac{dC}{dq} = \frac{c_1}{2} - \frac{c_2 r}{q^2} = 0$$

$$q_0 = \sqrt{\frac{2 c_2 r}{c_1}}$$

which gives the quantity that the firm should order or produce each time, and

$$t_0 = \frac{q_0}{r} = \sqrt{\frac{2 c_2}{c_1 r}}$$

which gives the time interval between orders or production runs. The minimum total cost per unit time is therefore

$$C_0 = c_1 \frac{q_0}{2} + c_2 \frac{r}{q_0}$$

$$= \sqrt{\frac{c_1 c_2 r}{2}} + c_2 r \sqrt{\frac{c_1}{2 c_2 r}}$$

$$= \sqrt{2 c_1 c_2 r}$$

The quantity q_0 is sometimes called *economic lot size.*

2. Constant-demand, shortage-allowed inventory model.

Let $c_3 = $ the shortage cost per unit of item for a unit of time. In the model shown in Fig. 8-2 it is assumed

1. The demand is still constant (demand rate is r).
2. Shortage is allowed, however a cost will incur.
3. No production (or order) time lag.

According to the figure, in each cycle t, the inventory will last t_1 time units and shortage will occur in the

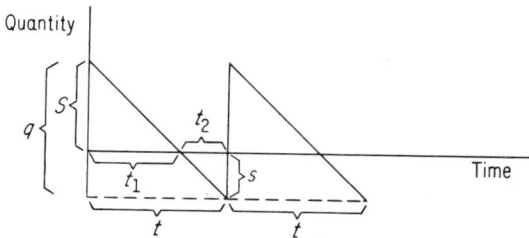

Fig. 8-2

remaining t_2 time units. Let q be the quantity produced or ordered each time, S be the highest inventory level, and s be the lowest shortage level. The inventory cost per unit time is

$$c_1 \left(\frac{S}{2}\right)\left(\frac{t_1}{t}\right) = c_1 \left(\frac{S}{2}\right)\left(\frac{S}{q}\right) = \frac{c_1}{2}\frac{S^2}{q}$$

The setup cost per unit time is still $c_2(r/q)$. The shortage cost per unit time is

$$c_3\left(\frac{s}{2}\right)\left(\frac{t_2}{t}\right) = c_3\left(\frac{s}{2}\right)\left(\frac{s}{q}\right) = \frac{c_3}{2}\frac{s^2}{q}$$
$$= \frac{c_3}{2}\frac{(q - S)^2}{q}$$

Therefore the total cost per unit time is

$$C = \frac{c_1}{2}\frac{S^2}{q} + c_2\frac{r}{q} + \frac{c_3}{2}\frac{(q - S)^2}{q}$$

In order to find the minimum total cost condition, we take first derivatives with respect to S and q:

$$\frac{\partial C}{\partial s} = \frac{S}{q}c_1 - \frac{c_3}{q}(q - S) = 0 \qquad S_0 = \left(\frac{c_3}{c_1 + c_3}\right)q_0$$

$$\frac{\partial C}{\partial q} = -\frac{c_1 S^2}{2q^2} - \frac{c_2 r}{q^2} + \frac{c_3}{2}\left(\frac{2q(q - S) - (q - S)^2}{q^2}\right) = 0$$

$$c_3 q_0^2 = (c_1 + c_3)S_0^2 + 2c_2 r$$

$$= (c_1 + c_3)\left(\frac{c_3}{c_1 + c_3}\right)^2 q_0^2 + 2c_2 r$$

$$q_0 = \sqrt{\frac{2c_2(c_1 + c_3)r}{c_1 c_3}}$$

which gives the quantity which will minimize the total cost, and

$$t_0 = \frac{q_0}{r} = \sqrt{\frac{2c_2(c_1 + c_3)}{c_1 c_3 r}}$$

which is the time interval between production runs or orders.

The optimum inventory level (highest) should be

$$S_0 = \left(\frac{c_3}{c_1 + c_3}\right)q_0$$

$$= \sqrt{\frac{2c_2 c_3 r}{c_1(c_1 + c_3)}}$$

and the minimum total cost per unit time is therefore,

$$C = \frac{c_1}{2}\left(\frac{c_3}{c_1 + c_3}\right)\sqrt{\frac{2c_2(c_1 + c_3)r}{c_1 c_3}} + c_2\sqrt{\frac{c_1 c_3 r}{2c_2(c_1 + c_3)}}$$

$$+ \frac{c_3}{2}\left(\frac{c_1}{c_1 + c_3}\right)^2 \sqrt{\frac{2c_2(c_1 + c_3)r}{c_1 c_3}}$$

$$= \sqrt{\frac{2c_1 c_2 c_3 r}{c_1 + c_3}} + \left(\frac{c_1}{c_1 + c_3}\right)\sqrt{\frac{c_1 c_2 c_3 r}{2(c_1 + c_3)}}$$

$$= \left(\frac{3c_1}{c_1 + c_3}\right)\sqrt{\frac{c_1 c_2 c_3 r}{2(c_1 + c_3)}}$$

3. Uncertain demand inventory model (for simplicity, assume setup cost is negligible, or $c_2 = 0$). The rate of demand may be different from period to period.

Let x be the demand in period t.

When no shortage occurs, the results are as shown in Fig. 8-3. According to the figure, the average inventory

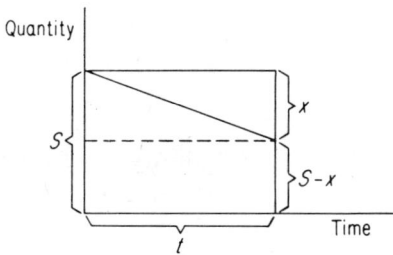

Fig. 8-3

level is

$$I = (S - x) + \frac{x}{2}$$

$$= S - \frac{x}{2}$$

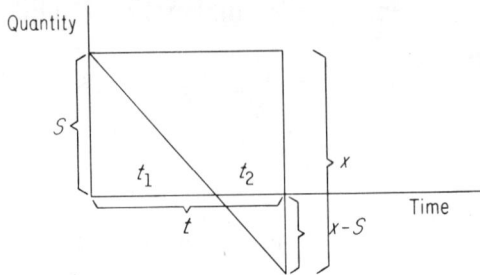

Fig. 8-4

When shortage occurs, the results are as shown in Fig. 8-4. The average inventory level is

$$I_1 = \left(\frac{S}{2}\right)\left(\frac{t_1}{t}\right)$$

$$= \left(\frac{S}{2}\right)\left(\frac{S}{x}\right)$$

$$= \frac{S^2}{2x}$$

The average shortage level is

$$I_2 = \left(\frac{x - S}{2}\right)\left(\frac{t_2}{t}\right)$$

$$= \left(\frac{x - S}{2}\right)\left(\frac{x - S}{x}\right)$$

$$= \frac{(x - S)^2}{2x}$$

Let $f(x)$ be the probability distribution of demand x; then the total expected cost per unit time for this model is

$$EC(S) = \int_0^S c_1\left(S - \frac{x}{2}\right)f(x)\,dx$$

$$+ \int_S^\infty \left(c_1\frac{S^2}{2x} + c_3\frac{(x - S)^2}{2x}\right)f(x)\,dx$$

In order to find the optimum inventory level S_o, the

calculus of variation method has to be used. The formula is

For

$$f(x) = \int_{h(x)}^{k(x)} g(x,y)\, dy$$

$$\frac{\partial f(x)}{\partial x} = \int_{h(x)}^{k(x)} \frac{\partial q(x,y)}{\partial x}\, dy$$

$$+ \left[\frac{dk(x)}{dx} g(x,k(x)) - \frac{dh(x)}{dx} g(x,h(x)) \right]$$

In this case,

$$\frac{EC(S)}{S} = c_1 \int_0^S f(x)\, dx + c_1 \frac{S}{2} f(x) + \int_S^\infty c_1 \frac{S}{x} f(x)\, dx$$

$$- \int_S^\infty c_3 \frac{x - S}{x} f(x)\, dx - c_1 \frac{S}{2} f(x)$$

$$= c_1 \int_0^S f(x)\, dx - c_3 \int_S^\infty f(x)\, dx$$

$$+ (c_1 + c_3) \int_S^\infty \frac{S}{x} f(x)\, dx$$

$$= c_1 \int_0^S f(x)\, dx - c_3 \left[1 - \int_0^S f(x)\, dx \right]$$

$$+ (c_1 + c_3) \int_S^\infty \frac{S}{x} f(x)\, dx$$

Setting the derivative equal to zero,

$$c_3 = (c_1 + c_3) \left[\int_0^S f(x)\, dx + \int_S^\infty \frac{S}{x} f(x)\, dx \right]$$

or

$$\frac{c_3}{c_1 + c_3} = \int_0^S f(x)\, dx + \int_S^\infty \frac{S}{x} f(x)\, dx = L(S)$$

Thus we should find a value of S, (S_o), which, when S_o is substituted in $L(S)$, will make $L(S_o)$ equate to $c_3/(c_1 + c_3)$. Therefore

$$L(S) = \frac{c_3}{c_1 + c_3}$$

is the condition for the optimum level of inventory.

4. Stochastic demand model.

In this model, demand is assumed to be a continuous random variable but with its probability function known. Let

(a) x = demand during a given period and the probability function of the demand be $f(x)$
(b) y = quantity to be produced (or purchased) at the beginning of the period
(c) c = production cost per unit of item
(d) c_1 = holding cost per unit of item per unit time
(e) c_3 = shortage cost per unit of item

Then, when demand is below or equal to y, the amount sold will by x, but when demand is above y the amount sold will be y, since more units are not available. The total direct production cost for the period is cy, and the total holding cost for the period is

$$c_1 \int_0^y (y - x) f(x) \, dx$$

and the total shortage cost for the period is

$$c_3 \int_y^\infty (x - y) f(x) \, dx$$

Adding the three terms together to get the total cost function,

$$g(y) = cy + c_1 \int_0^y (y - x) f(x) \, dx$$
$$+ \; c_3 \int_y^\infty (x - y) f(x) \, dx$$

In order to obtain the optimum solution, set the first derivative of the function equal to zero:

$$\frac{dg(y)}{dy} = c + c_1 \int_0^y f(x) \, dx - c_3 \int_y^\infty f(x) \, dx = 0$$

Since $\int_0^\infty f(x)\,dx$ must'equal to one:

$$c + c_1 \int_0^y f(x)\,dx - c_3 \int_y^\infty f(x)\,dx$$

$$= c + c_1 \int_0^y f(x)\,dx - c_3\left[1 - \int_0^y f(x)\,dx\right]$$

$$= c - c_3 + (c_1 + c_3)\int_0^y f(x)\,dx$$

$$= 0$$

The second derivative of $g(y)$ is

$$\frac{d^2 g(y)}{dy^2} = (c_1 + c_3)f(x) > 0 \qquad (c_1, c_3, f(x) \text{ all positive})$$

Thus the condition for minimum total cost is

$$\int_0^{y^0} f(x)\,dx = \frac{c_3 - c}{c_1 + c_3}$$

Example 1

The demand for a product in a given season is exponentially distributed in the form

$$f(x) = \frac{1}{100} e^{-x/100}$$

The production cost of the product is $10 per item, the holding cost is $1 per item for the period, and the shortage cost is estimated to be $100 per item. To find the optimum quantity to produce at the beginning of the period, the following is computed:

$$\int_0^y f(x)\,dx = \int_0^y \frac{1}{100} e^{-x/100}\,dx = 1 - e^{-y/100}$$

and

$$\frac{c_3 - c}{c_1 + c_3} = \frac{100 - 10}{100 + 1} = \frac{90}{101}$$

Equating the above,

$$1 - e^{-y^0/100} = \frac{90}{101}$$

$$e^{-y^0/100} = \frac{11}{101}, \quad -\frac{y^0}{100} = \log \frac{11}{101}$$

$$y^0 = 100 \log \frac{101}{11} = 222 \text{ items}$$

SUMMARY

Business firms and other organizations are concerned about reducing cost. Besides the cost factors, such as labor, raw material, machinery and equipment, etc., a very important cost item is the inventory cost. In order to facilitate the analysis, inventory models are built. Most of the inventory models are concerned with the inventory carrying cost, the setup or ordering cost, and the shortage cost. Demand is assumed either to be fixed or to change randomly according to a given probability distribution. Optimization techniques are then applied to the models to find the optimum operational policy which will minimize the total cost. For more complicated models, when analytical methods fail to find the optimum operational policy, Monte Carlo or other computer-simulation methods (discussed in Chapter 9) may be used to compare the advantages and disadvantages of alternative policies or procedures.

PROBLEMS

1. A newspaper boy buys papers for 5 cents each and sells them for 10 cents. He cannot return unsold papers. From previous experience, daily demand shows the following distribution:

Number of papers sold	90	91	92	93	94	95	96	97	98	99	100
Frequency	2	7	12	19	18	16	13	8	5	5	4

In order to maximize daily profit, how many papers should be buy each day?

2. A producer has to supply a retail outlet 10,000 units of product per day. When he starts a production run he can produce 30,000 units per day. The storage cost of one unit of product is 1 cent per week, and the setup cost per each production run is $50. How frequently should production run be made?

3. Firm A produces parts for another firm B. The contract between these two firms states that firm A should supply firm B 100 units per day. The penalty for missing the scheduled delivery date is $10 per unit per day. Firm A makes one production run at the beginning of each week and the inventory storage cost is $1 per unit per day. How many units should A produce each week?

4. In Prob. 3, if firm A can make production run any number of times each week and the setup cost is $100 per run, how often should firm A make production runs, and how many units should be produced each time?

5. The weekly demand for a product is normally distributed in the form

$$f(x) = \frac{1}{\sqrt{2\pi}} e^{-1/2(x-100)^2}$$

The production cost is $5 per unit, the storage cost of one unit of product is $1 per week, and the shortage cost is estimated to be $10 per item per week due to loss of sales. Assuming that one production is made each week, how many units should be produced per each run in order to minimize the total cost?

6. A manufacturer purchases 1,000 parts every year for his factory production. Each time he makes a purchase the procurement costs him $100 and the price of the parts; the first 100 costs him $10 per unit, and beyond that quantity the supplier gives him a discount and charges him only $9 per unit. The monthly storage cost is estimated to be 25 cents per part. What is the optimum purchase quantity, and how often will the manufacturer make purchase?

7. A manufacturer requires 100 units of certain parts in his daily manufacturing process. If he produces these parts by himself, the setup cost is $500 and in each run he can produce 1,000 units. The manufacturing cost is $50 per part and the holding cost is $0.5 per part per day. Find the minimum cost production quantity per run. What is the minimum daily cost for these parts?

8. The demand for an item is 50 units per day. Procurement lead time is 10 days, holding cost is $0.1 per unit per day, and shortage cost is $1 per unit per day. Find the minimum cost procurement quantity and how frequent the items should be procured.

9. In Prob. 8, assume that the item also can be produced by the manufacturer himself at $5 per unit, $100 for each setup and a production lead time of 7 days. Compare to procurement, which will cost $8 per unit and a procurement cost of $10, what will be the most economic policy?

10. A company produces two products, A and B. Monthly demand for A is 500 units and for B is 1,000 units. Production setup cost for A is $100, for B is $50. Direct cost, which includes raw material and labor, for A is $20 per unit and for B is $10 per unit. Storage cost is 10 cents per month for A and 5 cents per month for B. How often should the company set up to produce A and B, and what are the optimum production quantities?

SELECTED REFERENCES

Brown, R. G., *Decision Rules for Inventory Management.* New York: Holt, Rinehart and Winston, Inc., 1967.

Buchan, J., and E. Koenigsberg, *Scientific Inventory Management.* Englewood Cliffs, N.J.: Prentice-Hall, Inc., 1963.

Fetter, R. B., and W. C. Dalleck, *Decision Models for Inventory Management.* Homewood, Ill.: Richard D. Irwin, 1961.

Hadley, G., and T. M. Whitin, *Analysis of Inventory Systems.* Englewood Cliffs, N.J.: Prentice-Hall, Inc., 1963.

Hanssmann, F., *Operations Research in Production and Inventory Control.* New York: John Wiley & Sons, Inc., 1962.

Magee, J. F., and D. M. Boodman, *Production Planning and Inventory Control.* 2d ed. New York: McGraw-Hill Book Company, 1967.

Naddor, E., *Inventory Systems.* New York: John Wiley & Sons, 1966.

Starr, M. K., and D. W. Miller, *Inventory Control: Theory and Practice.* Englewood Cliffs, N.J.: Prentice-Hall, Inc., 1962.

chapter 9

Computerized
Information System and
Computer Simulation

MANAGEMENT INFORMATION SYSTEMS

The manager of a firm needs information in order to make "good" decisions. The information relevant to a decision has to be accurate and must reach the manager in time —that is, it must be at his command before he is required to make the decision. Since the advent of the computer, much more information may be continuously stored in and generated from the computer system with great speed. However, the tendency of some of the firms to grow bigger and bigger and for modern business to become more and more complicated each day creates new problems. One, the manager is sometimes buried in an overabundance of irrelevant information. It is time-consuming if not impossible to eliminate the irrelevant from the relevant. Two, the business becomes so complicated that the manager sometimes doesn't know what information is relevant to a decision because of the indirect relationship of some information to the issues in question; or he does not know all the norms to be used as standards for comparing with current performance. Three, the decision rules of second- or third-level managers may be based on objectives of their own departments, which may differ or even conflict with each other. For instance, the marketing research group of a firm, after gathering data about the marketing potential of a product, submits a report which contains the most likely estimate, the more optimistic estimate, and the more pessimistic estimate of the sales of the product. The report is distributed to both the sales department and the purchasing department. The sales manager, trying to minimize the chances of running short on the product (which will hurt his performance) may quite naturally request the purchasing manager to make available the amount suggested by the more optimistic estimate. However, the purchasing manager also sees the report and, knowing that the sales manager always uses the more optimistic estimate, doesn't want to be responsible for the high inventory cost and thus he may decide to adjust the purchasing amount down to the most likely estimate. Therefore, conflict may result because information flow causes clear confrontation of different points of view.

To solve the above-mentioned problems and to have an information system that will help the managers to make good decisions, the following steps are suggested:

1. *A complete analysis of the decision system of the organization.* A complete flow chart of the decision-making processes is most useful. It will indicate when, where, and by whom in the organization decisions are made. Comparing the chart with the overall objectives of the organization may reveal that in some areas decisions are being made by the wrong person or at the wrong time; or that in other areas decisions on the same matter are being made by several different persons, thus creating continuous conflict. It may suggest a revision of the organization structure, the managerial responsibility, the measure of performance, and the reporting system.

2. *An analysis of information requirement.* Rational decision making requires information. Thus after we have analyzed the decision system we have to review the information network and to analyze the

content of information that should flow through each channel, and the timeliness of this information in reaching the proper hands. Irrelevant information should not be allowed to pass, priorities should be established among the relevant information, and the load of each information channel should be examined. Queuing theories may be used in the analysis, and alterations of the system may be made in order to even out the load distribution in all the channels.

3. *Design of a computer information-processing system.* This may involve the study of the optimum utilization of the existing computer facilities, or the acquisition of new computer facilities which will be most suitable to implement the information system we have discussed in (1) and (2)—which includes collecting, processing, storing, retrieving, and disseminating all relevant information.

4. *Design of the controls of the information system.* As mentioned earlier, a manager does not always recognize the relevance of certain information to a decision. The information system should be designed in such a way that if any exceptional event occurs—that is, any event which deviates from the norm—the information should immediately catch the attention of the decision maker, so that proper adjustment action may be taken in time to correct it. For example, the system should constantly scan the near shortage of some important items needed in an assembly line or the overstock of some valuable parts which not only will increase the inventory cost but also will tie down a substantial amount of working capital. When such events occur, a warning signal will be given so that actions can be taken before the damage is done. A good information system should also have adequate flexibility. The more adaptive information system is a man-machine system. A decision maker should be allowed to make inquiries about certain information deemed necessary at the time, and what is originally pro-

grammed in the computer should be modified when empirical evidence indicates the existence of error or inefficiency. After all, no system is perfect—it needs constant analysis and adjustment.

Figure 9-1 is a simple system model illustrating the essential parts of such a design. Block I represents a com-

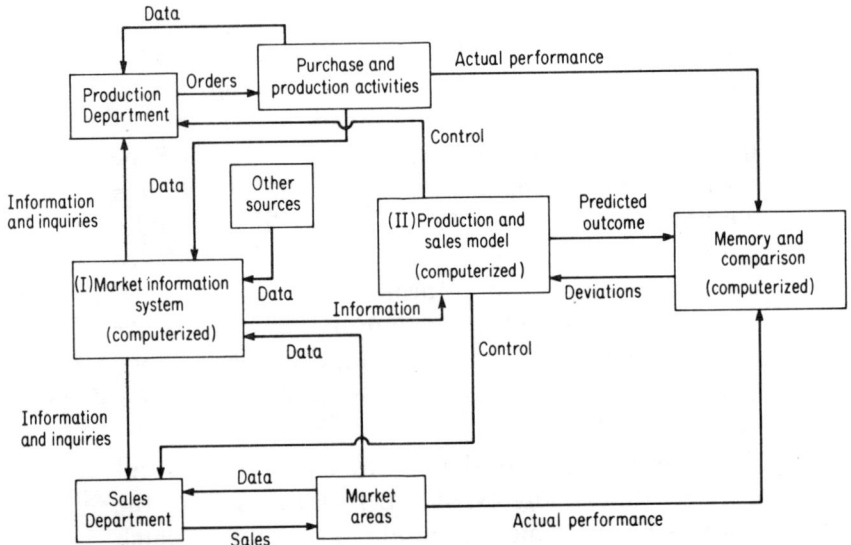

Fig. 9-1.   Flow diagram of a management information system model.

puterized market information system. It receives data from different market areas about the sales of the various products produced by the firm. At the same time, it receives data from the production department of the firm concerning the quantities and qualities of labor and of raw materials and products both in stock and in process. It also collects information from industry and government about modern production technologies, market trends etc., relating to the products. All the information is classified and analyzed, and the result is stored in proper orders on magnetic tapes or disks. The system can then answer inquiries from the sales department about the predicted market trends or potentials, and may give recommendations about which areas sales promotion efforts should be directed to and which products should be pushed. Or it may send information to the production department concerning which production lines should be stopped and which lines extended or accelerated, or which technology should be adopted and which specifications of a product should be respecified in order to meet changing consumer tastes.

Block II is a production and sales model. It is programmed in computer language and encompasses the objectives, both short-range and long-range, of the firm and its constraints and capabilities. Through computer networks, the model controls the routine operations of the production and sales departments. It receives information from the market-information system and computes deviations between the computer-projected results and the actual performance of the production and sales departments. Its decisions are made in accordance with the decision rules programmed into it. The head of sales department may, by analyzing the information coming from the market areas and the market information system, decide to modify the decisions. Similarly, the head of the production department may, by analyzing the information coming from actual purchase (labor and raw materials) and production activities, decide to modify the orders issued by the production and sales model.

What this example illustrates is that the firm uses a computerized information system to connect all relevant functions together. The computer collects, processes, and analyzes information. And it makes decisions which control the operation of the firm under normal and routine conditions. But experienced managers at all levels still closely supervise the operation. If situations arise that warrant human intervention, the manager may modify the decision through some computer input device. And the expected or projected results are continuously compared with the actual performances, so that any errors in decision making may be corrected or adjusted at an early stage.

COMPUTER SIMULATION[1]

Introduction

In studying any business or economic system, one would like generally to be able to describe the system, to identify and relate its elementary parts, and once given the system's input, to predict its output. The description can be either verbal or mathematical. But, on the one hand, verbal description is not exact and often needs quantification, and on the other, it may be impossible to describe by mathematical equations the complicated and dynamic relationships between the parts of the system. Moreover, assuming the equation set is adequate for the purpose, a solution of the equations may not exist. Since the invention of the electronic computer, however, a research technique new to the social science, called *simulation*, has been developed to aid in explaining and predicting the behavior of complex economic systems.

The term simulation as used here is in accordance with John Harling's definition.[2]

By simulation is meant the technique of setting up a stochastic model of a real situation, and then performing sampling experiments upon the model. The feature which distinguishes a simulation from a mere sampling experiment in the classical sense is that of the stochastic model. Whereas a classical sampling experiment in statistics is most often performed directly upon raw data, a simulation entails first of all the construction of an 'abstract model of the system to be studied.

Early use of simulation involved experimenting with models given a physical embodiment.[3] For example, a sand table was used by the military to represent a small-scale

---

[1] The material contained in this section is originally included in the author's dissertation, "*Computer Simulation of Certain Stochastic Relationships in Micro-Economic Systems,*" Tulane University, New Orleans, La., 1964.

[2] John Harling, "Simulation Techniques in Operations Research— A Review," *Operation Research,* Vol. VI (May–June 1958), p. 307.

[3] G. H. Orcutt, "Simulation of Economic Systems," *American Economic Review,* Vol. D (December 1960), p. 895.

model of actual geographical terrain. Social phenomena, however, are not easily given simple physical embodiment, thus limiting the use of this type of simulation approach in the field of economics. In fact, only few attempts have met with any success, a famous example being the hydraulic model built by Irving Fisher[4] at the London School of Economics to help explain the circular flows of money and commodities in a macroeconomic system.

The advent of the electronic digital computer opens a new way for simulating economic systems without relying on a physical embodiment. In essence, the complicated relationships of an economic system are simulated through the use of the logic-arithmetic device of the computer.

Procedure

1. Formulation of the Problem. The problem to be explored and the questions to be answered must be determined and clearly defined at the start. In microeconomics, the basic problem is the optimum allocation of scarce and finite resources among competing entrepreneurial goals. The following questions are some that must be answered preparatory to formulating a model depicting a microeconomic system: How is the system presently organized? What are the flows of traffic in the system? Are there any bottlenecks or areas of traffic congestion in the system? If bottlenecks or areas of traffic congestion exist, where are they and what is their effect on costs and profit? Are there any idle facilities in the system? If so, where are they, how many are they, and what are their costs? Where are the information feedback cycles and what are the decision-making processes at each level of the system? etc.

2. Construction of the Model. Before a model can be constructed, which is to represent certain aspects of a microeconomic system, relevant information regarding the system must be gathered. Possible kinds and sources of information include the following:

1. Verbal descriptions of the activities of each ele-

---

[4]I. Fisher, *Mathematical Investigations in the Theory of Value and Prices* (New Haven: Yale University Press, 1925), p. 44. This model was built basically as a teaching device.

mentary part of the system and the arrangement of these elementary parts inside the system and their interrelationships are obtainable from either the management or operating personnel.

2. The values of the parameters in the simulation model, such as the means and the variances of the assumed probability distributions of the variables, may be estimated from information obtained by sampling different system processes.

3. Analytical solutions of the behavior of some elementary parts of the system, which have already been theoretically or empirically verified and proved, can be adopted and integrated into the main simulation program.

When enough information relevant to the purpose of the study has been collected and analyzed, a block diagram embodying the logic and action of the model is produced. This diagram will indicate the physical flows of the input units and the flows of information in the system. When a block diagram is drawn, the model is considered as having been built.

It should be made clear that a simulation model of a microeconomic system is not an exact replica of the real environment. Only certain aspects of the system relevant to the problem under consideration are simulated. The reason, besides the financial one, is to keep the researcher from being overburdened with facts; otherwise the points which need to be illustrated might become obscured.

John Harling, in the paper[5] previously cited, made the following comment: ". . . The construction of a model of the real system should neither oversimplify the system to the point where the model becomes trivial, nor carry over so many features from the real system that the model becomes intractable and prohibitively clumsy. . . ." Computer simulation model can be a static one which is mainly to describe the structure of a system, or a stochastic one which includes random fluctuating events, or a dynamic one which simulates the time-dependent causal relationship among the

[5]Harling, op.cit.

variables. Most of the models, however, are both stochastic and dynamic.

3. Formation of a Computer Program. After a block diagram is drawn, the model is then described through a well-defined computer language, thus becoming a computer program. [In the following, we choose to illustrate the procedure of computer simulation with (a) FORTRAN language, because it is a well-known computer language, and (b) waiting-line problems, because they exist in almost every microeconomic model.] The activities of each elementary part of the model will be described by an individual subprogram which becomes an entity and which can be modified as the situation warrants. These subprograms can be considered as the building blocks of the main program, the whole of which describes the model representing the system. While integrating the subprograms into one main program, emphasis will be placed on queues, or waiting lines, the arrangement of service stations or facilities, information feedback loops, and decision-making processes which affect and are affected by environment.

The information on which the simulation is based may change quite often; the input rate may change due to the change of the demand, and the service rate may change due to the improvement of technology. This problem, however, can be easily handled, since the number of subprograms can be altered and parameters modified prior to any computer run. Thus, the building-block method of program construction provides adequate flexibility.

4. Design of Experiments. The system being simulated is described by the simulation model in terms of components, variables, parameters, and relationships. Some of the variables are assumed to be endogenous to the system and some of them exogenous to the system. Some of the variables are considered as decision variables by the management, and some represent the objectives or measures of performance of the system. In designing simulation experiments, the problems requiring solution or the hypotheses requiring testing have to be defined, and the measurement of objective variables have to be established. Also, the levels of each decision variables have to be chosen in such a way that they are both efficient and realistic. Data about the variables have to be collected, wherever and whenever appropriate, from the records of the real system. In general, statistical theories are extensively relied on in the design of experiments, so that the causes and effects or the factors and responses can be shown with high degree of confidence.

5. *Analysis of Simulation Data.* When simulation experiments on the model have been completed, the simulation data have to be properly analyzed in order to obtain solutions to the problems or to verify the correct hypothesis. In organizing the data, care has to be taken to distinguish data obtained when the model is in transient state from data obtained when the model is in steady state. If we are interested in the long-run behavior of the model, then we should analyze data obtained when the model has already passed the transient state and has reached the steady state. For example, when we are simulating the waiting lines at the checkout points in a supermarket, we cannot use only the data obtained in the first half-hour for analysis, because the customers might be still choosing products and very few of them may be ready for checkout. The steady state might not be reached until two hours after the opening of the market. The general methods used in the analysis of the simulation data include correlation and regression, factor analysis, analysis of variance, multiple ranking, etc. For analyzing time-dependent processes, there are autocorrelation and autoregression, spectral analysis, and other related techniques.

6. *Evaluation of the System.* After examining the results obtained from simulation runs[6] with the computer program we will be able to evaluate the system which we have modeled. In the case of a waiting-line model of a firm, the following are some of the important items we may examine. First, the area or areas where the flow of traffic is

[6]"Simulation run" is defined by Guy H. Orcutt as "an individual simulation run may be thought of as an experiment performed upon a model. . . . Given completely specified initial conditions, parameters and exogenous variables, a single simulation run yields a single set of time paths of the endogenous variables." See G. H. Orcutt. "Simulation of Economic Systems," *American Economic Review,* Vol. 50 (December 1960), p. 893.

delayed or where capacity becomes idle can be determined. Second, if the unit cost of idle time and waiting time can be ascertained, the profit significance of the system's behavior can be assessed. Third, experimentation with the model will expose the interrelationship between components of the system and thus may indicate alternative ways of organization —and may, additionally, generate new ideas to improve the system. Fourth, by evaluating the relative risks of both bold and conservative courses of action, the user of the program may gain a greater appreciation of the risk involved in each alternative decision.

There is one word of warning, however. Periodic re-examination of the parameter values and the basic assumptions involved in the simulation model and comparing the simulation results against empirical data whenever they become available are very important in keeping the program useful and current.

7. *Suggestions Regarding the Improvement of an Existing System or the Design of a New System.* After system evaluation, the user of the program can then proceed to find ways of bringing into optimum balance the many diverse objectives involved. For example, the objective may be to minimize cost; then if the relationship of cost to time were known, several adjustments might be made to improve the efficiency of an existing system. For example, the simulation runs will indicate the areas where facilities are often lying idle and where the flow of traffic is frequently interrupted because of a shortage of facilities. By internal rearrangement of these facilities—the movement of facilities from slack areas to congestion areas or the change of some series arrangement of facilities to parallel arrangement—the individual waiting time and the idle time may be reduced, thereby reducing the total cost of waiting time and idle time.

In addition, the simulation runs will show whether the congestion areas are causing other parts of the system to become idle, thus prolonging the total service time and causing fluctuation in the rate of the traffic flow, thereby increasing total cost. In some cases it may be the cause of losing a part of the effective demand. Therefore, evaluation should be made to see whether it would be more profitable to hire additional resources from outside the system and apply them to the more sensitive areas in the system.

A further example of model evaluation can be seen in the following: If internal rearrangement of facilities and hiring additional resources from outside are impractical due to other considerations, the results of simulation runs will at least indicate where effort should be directed to finding ways of speeding up the service rate, information relays, and decision-making processes.

In designing a new system it would be advisable to build a simulation model first. The simulation runs will show the behavior and characteristics of the new design which otherwise may not be determined until the system is actually organized and in operation. With repeated simulation runs and modifications of the design completed by the time the real system is organized and constructed, many of the flaws of the original design may already have been corrected. Thus the simulation model will provide the user with a working analogy to test the implication of new plans, new schemes, and new ideas in compressed time. Because the simulation runs reveal the interrelationships between all the elementary parts and the subsystems in a microeconomic system, management control can be designed and established to check the actual output at each step against the desired output, and control devices can be installed to hold the operational variables within desired limits.

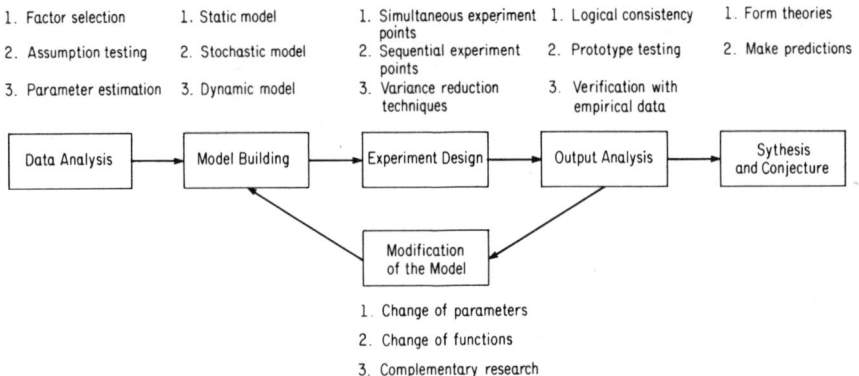

1. Factor selection	1. Static model	1. Simultaneous experiment points	1. Logical consistency	1. Form theories
2. Assumption testing	2. Stochastic model	2. Sequential experiment points	2. Prototype testing	2. Make predictions
3. Parameter estimation	3. Dynamic model	3. Variance reduction techniques	3. Verification with empirical data	

Data Analysis → Model Building → Experiment Design → Output Analysis → Sythesis and Conjecture

Modification of the Model

1. Change of parameters
2. Change of functions
3. Complementary research

Fig. 9-2.   Flow diagram of a computer-simulation process.

In summary, the entire computer-simulation process may be described by the flow diagram in Fig. 9-2.

MODEL CONSTRUCTION

The purpose of this section is to set forth the procedures for constructing a simulation model of a microeconomic system. FORTRAN language is used as a vehicle for illustration. The presentation consists of a detailed discussion of the use of subprograms to simulate the behavior of the elementary parts of the system and a main program to link the parts together and simulate the behavior of the whole system. Using information obtained from an existing system or assumptions made regarding a hypothetical or a new design of a system, a block or flow diagram is prepared which will indicate the structure of the system and the interrelationships among its parts.

If the quantities which measure the behavior of the elementary parts of the system (such as the interarrival-time intervals and the service-time intervals at each service point in the system, or weights or volumes of the input raw materials and output products) are stochastic in nature, computer programs can be written to simulate these stochastic relationships. A main program, utilizing the subprograms at appropriate places, can then be written to simulate the whole system.

Once the main program is completed, experimentation with the model is accomplished by varying the parameters of the system, typical parameters being the means and variances of input and service rates, or the means and variances of the conversion rates of raw materials to finished products. The computer will then, for each set of parameter values, go through the step-by-step procedure specified by the simulation programs.

Subprograms

Subprograms are written to simulate the activities in each elementary part of the microeconomic system. As an illustration, the time interval between arrivals and the time interval that each unit stays in each station of the system are simulated. The technique of simulating these time intervals is as follows.

Sample observations of the time intervals t actually occurring in the real system are made and then organized in a frequency distribution. A theoretical probability distribution such as a normal, exponential, or gamma distribution is selected and compared with the empirical distribution. Goodness-of-fit testing may be used to determine whether any of the theoretical distributions can be accepted as representing the population distribution. If none of the theoretical distributions can be fitted to the empirical distribution, least-squares or other estimation methods as described in Chapter 4 may be used to find the curve which best approximates the frequency distribution of the sample observations. The procedure of using the least-squares method to find the curve is sometimes referred to as "the polynomial approximation to the distribution."[7] The curve thus obtained may be considered as an approximate representation of the population distribution. Having then a suitable representative distribution, the Monte Carlo method of sampling[8] may be used to generate the appropriate random variate.

GENERATION OF RANDOM NUMBERS

In order to generate a random variate it is first necessary to generate a sequence of random numbers. Of course the easiest way of accomplishing this is to utilize a random-number table. However, when a computer is used, storage restrictions often rule out the possibility of maintaining an adequate-sized table. The alternative is to generate the

[7]John Harling, "Simulation Techniques in Operations Research—A Review," *Operations Research,* Vol. VI (May–June 1958), p. 307.
[8]The range of the cumulative probability function for any probability distribution is from 0 to 1. The Monte Carlo method of sampling is to generate a random number in the range of 0 to 1, representing the cumulative probability function, and the corresponding value of the variable is a sample value. See Maurice Sasieni, Arthur Yaspan, and Lawrence Friedman, *Operations Research—Methods and Problems* (New York: John Wiley & Sons, Inc., 1959), p. 58.

random numbers in the computer. This latter process has one obvious advantage—the properties of the sequence of the random numbers generated are known prior to using the numbers in a particular problem. The methods of generating pseudorandom numbers may be additive, mid-square, multiplicative or mixed, etc. The IBM reference manual, "Random Number Generation and Testing,"[9] proposes a procedure for generating pseudorandom numbers by multiplicative method, and the results have passed various statistical tests. The procedure is as follows:

Let d be the number of digits contained in the random-number variate, N, the starting value of a random number sequence, an integer not divisible by 2 or 5. M, the constant multiplier, equals to $200 K + r$, where K is an integer, and r any of the following values: 3, 11, 13, 19, 21, 27, 29, 37, 53, 59, 61, 67, 69, 77, 83, 91 (a value of M close to $10^{d/2}$ is a good choice).

The product of N and M is a 2 d-digit number. The higher-order d-digits are discarded and the lower-order d-digits are the value of the next random number. Each successive random number is then obtained from the lower-order d-digits of the product ($N_i \times M$), N_i being the preceding random number. The procedure will produce $5 \times 10^{d-2}$ pseudorandom numbers[10] before repeating for d greater than 3.

GENERATION OF RANDOM VARIATES[11]

Since the range of the cumulative probability function of any probability distribution of a variable is from 0 to 1, random numbers ranging over this interval may be generated to represent a set of cumulative probabilities. The values of the variable corresponding to the cumulative probabilities therefore may be considered as the random variate taken from a particular distribution. This method

[9] IBM Reference Manual, "Random Number Generation and Testing," 1959.

[10] This process is known as the *generation of pseudorandom digits by determinate sequences.*

[11] Each occurrence of the variable is called a *variate.*

of sampling is called the *Monte Carlo method*. The cumulative probability function may also be stored in the memory of a computer and the random number may be used as the argument in a "table look-up" routine[12] to find the corresponding random variate. However, if the memory space of the computer imposes a limitation, then the Monte Carlo method of sampling is usually preferred.

In some cases the method for generating random variates for a given distribution may depend on the particular feature of the distribution and the way in which it is related to other distributions. The following are methods for generating the random variates of some of the theoretical and nontheoretical distributions used in the examples of this text. Other methods of generating the same variates, or variates of other probability distributions, may be found in the texts listed in the bibliography at the end of this chapter.

1. Generation of a Uniformly Distributed Variate

The density function of a uniform distribution is

$$f(x) = \frac{1}{B - A}$$

where A is the lower limit and B is the upper limit of the variable x. The mean and variance of x are $\frac{B - A}{2}$ and $\frac{(B - A)^2}{12}$ respectively. The distribution implies that x can be any of the values included in the interval specified by A and B with equal probability.

Given A and B as the lower and upper limit, and R a random number ranging from 0 to 1, the uniformly distributed variate x may be generated by the following formula:

$$x = A + (B - A) \cdot R; 0 \leq R \leq 1$$

---

[12] A *table look-up routine* means comparing a single number with a list of numbers arranged in either ascending or descending order; when the number of the list equals to this single number, the comparison stops and the respective position of this single number on the list is found.

2. Generation of Exponentially Distributed Variate

The density function of an exponential distribution is $f(x) = Ae^{-Ax}$, where A is a positive constant and where the range of the variable x is from 0 to infinity.

The mean of x is $1/A$ and its variance is $1/A^2$. The cumulative probability function of x is $P(x) = 1 - e^{-Ax}$. Since the range of the cumulative probability function is from 0 to 1, the value of $(1 - e^{-Ax})$ will increase from 0 to 1 as x starts at zero and goes to infinity, or the value of e^{-Ax} will decrease from 1 to 0 as x starts at 0 and goes to infinity.

Consider the following: Let $R = e^{-Ax}$, where R is a random number in the unit interval. Then $\log R = \log e^{-Ax} = -Ax$. Thus the variate x of the exponential distribution, with mean and standard deviation both equal to T, can therefore be generated by the following formula:

$$x = \frac{-1}{A} \log R = -T \log R$$

3. Generation of the Variate of a kth Erlang Gamma Distribution

The density function of an Erlang gamma distribution is

$$f(x) = \frac{A^k}{(k-1)!} x^{k-1} e^{-Ax},$$

where A is a constant and k is an integer. The range of x is from zero to infinity. If there are k random variables, namely $t_1, t_2, \ldots, t_k$, which are independent and with a common exponential distribution with mean equal to $1/A$ and variance equal to $1/A^2$ then the random variable $(t_1 + t_2 + \cdots + t_k)$ follows the kth Erlang distribution with mean equal to k/A and variance equal to k/A^2.

Thus the variate of a kth Erlang gamma distribution may be generated by the formula

$$x = \sum_{i=1}^{k} t_i = -\sum_{i=1}^{k} \frac{1}{A} \log R_i$$

where the R_i are random numbers ranging from 0 to 1.

4. Generation of a Normally Distributed Variate [13]

The density function of a normal distribution is

$$f(x) = \frac{1}{\sqrt{2\pi}\,\sigma}\, e^{-\left(\frac{x-\mu}{\sigma}\right)^2}$$

where μ and σ^2 are, respectively, the mean and variance. The range of the variable x is from $-\infty$ to $+\infty$.

A normally distributed variate may be generated by summing short sequences of uniformly distributed variables.[14] For the sake of simplifying the calculation, a uniform distribution with its variable y ranging from 0 to 12 is chosen. The mean μ_y and variance σ_y^2 are 6 and 12. Samples of 12 observations (N) each are taken from the distribution. The standardized normal variate of the distribution of the sample means is therefore

$$z = \frac{\bar{y} - \mu_{\bar{y}}}{\sigma_{\bar{y}}} = \sum_{i=1}^{12} R_i - 6; 0 \leq R_i \leq 1$$

where

$$\mu_{\bar{y}} = \mu_y = 6 \qquad \text{and} \qquad \sigma_{\bar{y}} = \frac{\sigma_y}{\sqrt{N}} = \frac{\sqrt{12}}{\sqrt{12}} = 1$$

Let μ and σ be the mean and standard deviation of a normal distribution, then the variate of the distribution may be generated by the formula

$$x = \mu + \sigma \cdot z$$

where z is the standardized normal variate generated by the preceding formula.

5. Generation of a Log-Normally Distributed Variate

The density function of a log-normal distribution is

$$f(x) = \frac{1}{\sqrt{2\pi}\,\sigma}\, e^{-\frac{1}{2}\left(\frac{\log x - \mu}{\sigma}\right)^2}$$

[13] A normal distribution is a symmetric distribution which usually has smaller variance than an exponential distribution of the same mean.

[14] The central limit theorem states that the distribution of the sample means is a normal distribution.

where

$$\mu = \frac{\sum\limits_{i=1}^{N} \log x_i}{N}$$

$$\sigma^2 = \frac{\sum\limits_{i=1}^{N} (\log x_i - \mu)^2}{N}$$

and

$$0 \le x \le \infty$$

A log-normal distribution will become a normal distribution, if the abscissa scale is logarithmic. Therefore the relationship between the mean μ and variance σ^2 of a log-normal distribution and the mean μ_y and variance σ_y^2 of the normal distribution can be expressed by

$$\mu_y = \log \mu - \frac{1}{2} \log\left(\frac{\sigma^2}{\mu^2} + 1\right)$$

$$\sigma_y^2 = \log\left(\frac{\sigma^2}{\mu^2} + 1\right)$$

Thus a log-normally distributed variate x may be generated by the formula

$$x = e^{\mu_y + \sigma_y \cdot z}$$

where z is the standard normal variate.

6. Generation of Variate of a Sinusoidal Function

If the mean of a probability distribution does not remain constant during the passage of time but instead fluctuates according to some trignometric function, with constant period, then the mean μ of this function can be determined at any particular point of time T by

$$\mu = \mu_0 + A \cdot (\sin \theta), \quad \theta = \frac{T}{P} \cdot 2\pi$$

Here, μ_0 is the initial value of the mean, A the amplitude, and P the period of the cycle. T varies from 0 to P, θ therefore will take on values ranging from 0 to 2π.

A more complex situation is one in which the value of the mean oscillates according to more than one trignometric functions, each with different periods and amplitudes. One such situation can be represented by:

$$\mu = \mu_0 + \left[A \sin\left(\frac{\theta}{w_1}\right) + A_2 \cos\left(\frac{\theta}{w_2}\right)\right]$$

where w_1 and w_2 are the different angular velocities.

7. Generation of the Variate of a Nontheoretical Distribution

There are many other methods of generating variates of known theoretical distributions, which are either introduced or left out in this section. Interested readers may check some of the references listed in the end of this chapter. However, when none of the known theoretical distributions can be accepted as a close approximation of the empirical distribution obtained from random sample observations, numerical integration may be used to generate the random variate of the distribution.

Consider Fig. 9-3, where A is the lower and B the upper

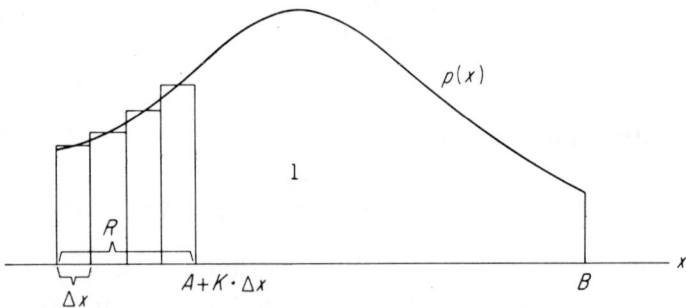

Fig. 9-3.   Diagram of the numerical integration of a probability function.

limit of the range of the variable x. Call $p(x)$ the probability distribution of x obtained by polynomial approximations of empirical observations. Then the following is known:

$$\int_{-\infty}^{A} p(x)\,dx = 0 \qquad \int_{A}^{B} p(x)\,dx = 1 \qquad \int_{B}^{+\infty} p(x)\,dx = 0$$

To generate a sample value of x, a random number R with values ranging from 0 to 1 is first generated. Then a numerical integration method, such as the trapezoidal rule,[15] may be used to integrate the area under the curve $p(x)$ starting from A. When it reaches a point where the area under the curve is equal to the random number, the corresponding value on the abscissa is a sample value of the variate.

When sample values of a distribution have been generated by using the methods described above, their acceptability has to be examined. One way is by looking at the moments of the sample distribution, such as the sample mean and the sample variance.

The theory underlying the testing whether a sample of size n can be accepted as being taken from a given distribution is that if the sample is randomly drawn from a known distribution with mean equal to μ and standard deviation equal to σ, then the sample mean $\bar{x}$ will be included in the interval $\mu + z \dfrac{\sigma}{\sqrt{n}}$ where $\dfrac{\sigma}{\sqrt{n}}$ is the standard error of the mean, with a probability set by the value of z. For example, to establish a 95 percent confidence interval, z is set to be 1.96. Also, when the sample size exceeds 30, the sample standard deviation σ' can be assumed to be normally distributed about σ with standard error equal to $\dfrac{\sigma}{\sqrt{2n}}$.

Thus σ' will be included in the interval $\sigma \pm z \dfrac{\sigma}{\sqrt{2n}}$ with a probability set by the value of z. Once the standard errors are determined, the required sample size can be calculated. If it is decided that the sample mean $\bar{x}$ should fall inside the interval[16] $\mu \pm A$ with a probability of .95, then the required sample size n should be set approximately equal to $\left(\dfrac{z\sigma}{A}\right)^2$, and if it is decided that the sample standard deviation should fall inside the interval $\sigma \pm B$ with a probability of

[15] See any textbook on numerical methods, such as M. G. Salvadori and M. L. Baron, *Numerical Methods in Engineering* (Englewood Cliffs, N.J.: Prentice-Hall, Inc., 1961), p. 89.

[16] Sometimes A is expressed as a percentage of μ, for example, $A = 0.1\,\mu$.

.95, then the required sample size n should be set approximately equal to $\left(\dfrac{z\sigma}{\sqrt{2}B}\right)^2$, where z is set[17] to be 1.96.

VARIANCE-REDUCING TECHNIQUE

Using the Monte Carlo method of sampling from a given cumulative distribution function, we first generate random numbers uniformly distributed between zero and one and then map it on the cumulative distribution function to obtain the respective value of the variable. However, if the distribution of the variable has long tails, then large number of samples have to be generated in order to produce extreme values of the variable. For example, the exponential distribution in Fig. 9-4a has a long right tail, and its cumulative distribution will be like in Fig. 9-4b.

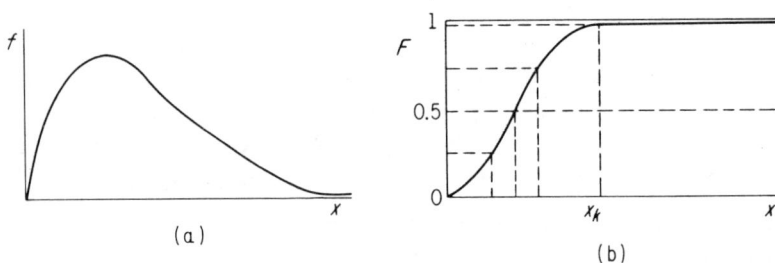

(a)

(b)

Fig. 9-4

It can be seen that the probability of getting a value greater than x_k is very small. Nevertheless, those extreme values may be crucial to our analysis. In order to have adequate number of extreme values included in the sample and at the same time not to increase the sample size, the following variance-reducing technique may be used.

Stratified Sampling

First we specify the strata in terms of the cumulative distribution—that is, first stratum, from $F(x) = 0$ to $F(x) = K_1$; second stratum, from $F(x) = K_1$ to $F(x) =$

---

[17] See any textbook on statistics and quality control, such as A. J. Duncan, *Quality Control and Industrial Statistics* (Homewood, Ill.: Richard D. Irwin, Inc., 1959), p. 49.

$K_2 \ldots$; and last or the nth stratum, from $F(x) = K_{n-1}$ to $F(x) = 1$. Where K_1, $K_2, \ldots, K_{n-1}$ are constants between 0 and 1. Next, specify the number of samples to be drawn from each stratum. Generally they are set to be equal to the probability of a random sample falling in the stratum multiplied by the standard deviation within the stratum. In sampling a variate in the jth stratum we generate a random number R_i in the unit interval and transform R_i to R_i' by the formula

$$R_i' = K_{j-1} + (K_j - K_{j-1}) R_i$$

We then map R_i' to the cumulative distribution function to obtain the respective value of the variable. In estimating the mean value of the distribution, the sample values have to be weighted by the following weight before averaging:

$$w_i = \frac{n_j/n}{K_j - K_{j-1}}$$

where n is the total sample size and n_j the sample size for the jth stratum.

There are other similar methods of reducing the variance of the output variables such as regression sampling, which uses positively correlated random number sequences; antithetic variate sampling, which uses negatively correlated or complementary random number sequences; and importance sampling or control variate, which assume that the weight w_i follows either the quotient or difference of some probability distributions instead of being a constant.

Subprograms, beside used in generating sample variates of various probability distribution, may also be written to describe a component or subsystem of the total system.

Main Program

The main program is written to simulate the structure and activities of the entire system. This structure depicts how the various elementary parts are arranged and connected to each other. Additionally, the main program will contain "call" statements which will call the respective subprograms at those places where the activities or interactions of the elementary parts are to be simulated. Thus subprograms are the building blocks of the main program.

The activities of the microeconomic system simulated in the examples included in this Section are the time-dimensional flows of the input units through the entire system, whether waiting to be admitted or being served in the elementary parts of the system. A flow starts when a unit arrives at the system and ends when the unit leaves the system. The congestion or discontinuity of the flows and the rates of the flows or the length of the time intervals that the input units spend in each elementary part of the system will be recorded. In addition, the waiting time of the input units and the idle time of each elementary part will be calculated and analyzed.

The entire procedure of the computer simulation is reviewed and illustrated in Fig. 9-5.

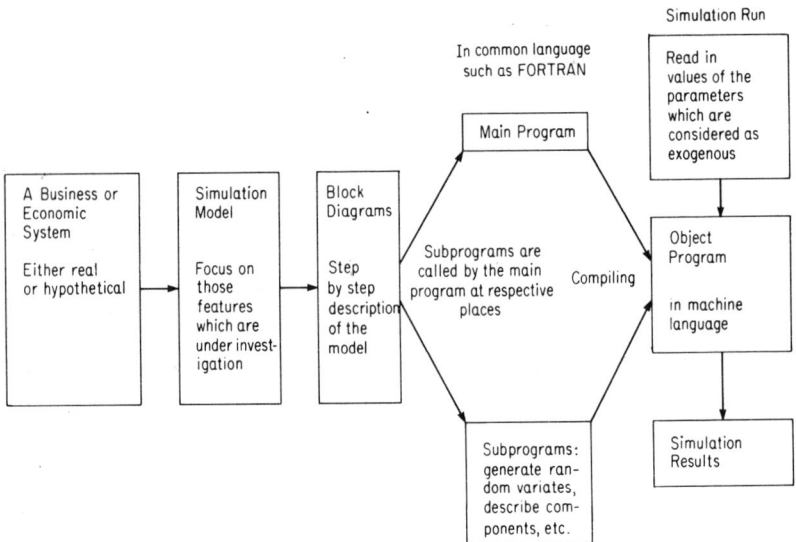

Fig. 9-5.   Flow diagram of the procedure of computer simulation.

METHODS OF SIMULATING TIME FLOW[18]

Two different methods of computer simulation are generally used to simulate the time flow inside the micro-

[18]The material contained in this section was rewritten and published by Kong Chu and Thomas H. Naylor "Two Alternative Methods for Simulating Waiting Line Models," *Journal of Industrial Engineering* (November–December 1965) and included in T. H. Naylor et al., *Computer Simulation Techniques* (New York: John Wiley & Sons, Inc., 1966).

economic system. The first method can best be described by the block diagram in Fig. 9-6.

AT = Interarrival-time interval
ST = Service-time interval
WL = Number in waiting line
WT = Waiting time
IDT = Idle time

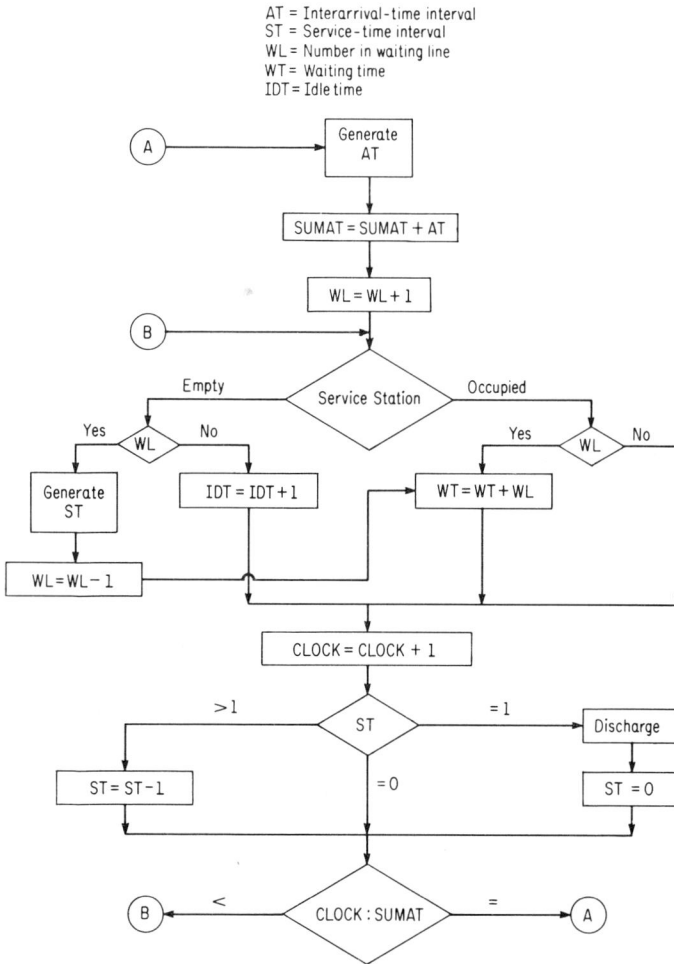

Fig. 9-6. **Block diagram of simulation method 1 of time flow.**

The diagram shows that an interarrival-time interval is first generated[19] and recorded and the arrived unit is put in the waiting line. Next, a check is made to determine whether the service station is occupied or empty at the

[19]Time intervals are generated by the computer subprograms presented earlier in the section.

moment. If the service station is empty, a test is made to ascertain if a unit is now waiting to enter the service station; if there is none, a unit of idle time is recorded. If a unit is waiting, it enters into the service station and a service time interval is generated, while simultaneously the waiting line is reduced by one. If more units are waiting, each unit causes the total waiting time to be increased by one.

On the other hand, if the service station is occupied, a test is also made to determine whether there is any unit waiting. If no unit is waiting, no waiting time is recorded; if there are units waiting, each unit in the waiting line causes the total waiting time to be increased by one time unit.

The next step is to advance the clock by one time unit and check the service-time interval. If the interval equals one, then the service on that particular unit is completed, a discharge is therefore recorded, and the service interval is reduced to zero. If the interval is equal to zero, indicating that the station is empty, no action is taken. If the interval is greater than one, it is decreased by one time unit.

The next step is to compare the clock time with the interarrival time. If they are equal, indicating that the next unit has just arrived at the service station, another inter-arrival-time interval is generated and the new arrived unit is put in the waiting line. If the clock time is shorter than the next arrival time, the process is to go back to check the service station again. This process is carried on until the last input unit has arrived and been served.[20]

The second method is described by the block diagram in Fig. 9-7.

According to the diagram, the first arrival unit does not wait for service (waiting time is zero), and required service time is generated for this unit. Then an interarrival time interval is generated to indicate the arrival time of the next input unit. Comparing the service-time interval with the interarrival-time interval, if the service-time interval is longer, then waiting time has occurred and the absolute

[20]This method may be called the *fixed time increment method* and presupposes discrete or rounded service and interarrival time distributions.

AT = Interarrival-time interval
ST = Service-time interval
WT = Waiting time
IDT = Idle time

```
                    ┌─────────────┐
                    │   WT = 0    │
                    └──────┬──────┘
                           │
        ┌───┐       ┌─────────────┐
        │ A │──────▶│  Generate   │
        └───┘       │     ST      │
                    └──────┬──────┘
                           │
                    ┌─────────────┐
                    │  Generate   │
                    │     AT      │
                    └──────┬──────┘
                           │
                    ┌─────────────┐
                    │ AT = AT-WT  │
                    └──────┬──────┘
                           │
    >              ◇ ST : AT ◇              <
 ┌────────────────╱                ╲────────────────┐
 │                       =                          │
 │                       │                          │
┌──────────────┐  ┌──────────────┐  ┌──────────────┐
│ WT = ST-AT   │  │   WT = 0     │  │   WT = 0     │
│ IDT = 0      │  │   IDT = 0    │  │ IDT = AT-ST  │
└──────┬───────┘  └──────┬───────┘  └──────┬───────┘
       │                 │                 │
       └─────────────────┼─────────────────┘
                         │
                       ┌───┐
                       │ A │
                       └───┘
```

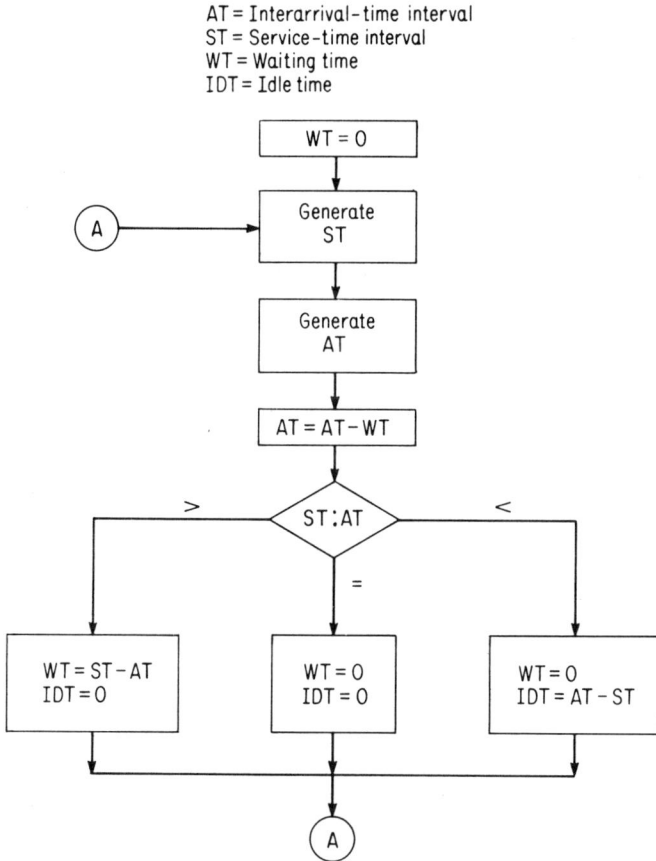

Fig. 9-7. Block diagram of simulation method 2 of time flow.

difference of the two intervals is the length of the waiting time. If the interarrival-time interval is longer, then idle time has occurred and the absolute difference of the two intervals is the length of the idle time.   If the two intervals are equal, neither waiting time nor idle time has occurred.

The next step is to go back to generate another set of service-time intervals and interarrival-time intervals. However, before comparing the two time intervals, the waiting time of the preceding unit, if any, has to be deducted from the interarrival time to make the computation valid (see Fig. 9-8 for explanation). This process is carried on until

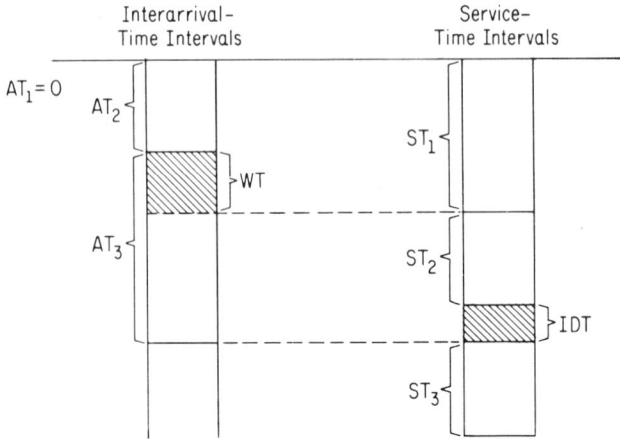

Fig. 9-8. Subsidiary diagram of simulation method 2 of time flow.

all the input units have arrived at the service station and been served.[21]

All the information about the behavior of the flows is stored in the memory of the computer and is retrievable at the end of each simulation run.

Figure 9-8 gives another illustration of the method. Using the same abbreviation, AT_1 is the interarrival-time interval between input unit 1 and 2, and ST_1 is the service time required for unit 1. Since ST_1 is longer than AT_1, waiting time occurs, and WT_2 indicates the length of the waiting time. AT_2 is the interarrival interval between unit 2 and 3 and ST_2 is the service time required for unit 2. As ST_2 is shorter than AT_2, idle time occurs, and IDT is the length of the idle time.

When the first method was used in constructing a waiting-line model, even though the concept is easier to comprehend, the time necessary for a simulation run was usually longer than that for the second method because the "clock" advances only one discrete time unit at each step. Therefore, the second method, which may be called the *variable time increment method*, is used in the construction

---

[21]This method may be called the *variable time increment method*. The process moves from one event (for example, a unit arrives) to the next event (for example, a service completed).

of all the illustrative simulation models presented in the following sections.

Simulation Results and Analytical Solutions

The purpose of this section is to test the accuracy of the simulation method presented in the previous section. This will be accomplished by selecting two basic waiting-line models for which, in addition to the results obtained from the simulation runs, analytical solutions can also be found. By comparing the simulation results with the analytical solutions, it can be determined whether any statistically significant difference exists between the two.

Model 1

The first model is a single-channel model which depicts a situation in which all the service stations in a micro-economic system are arranged in series. The input units pass through these service stations, one by one, in a given order. It is described by Fig. 9-9 and equations.

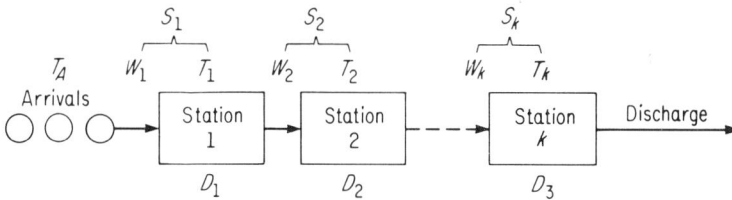

Fig. 9-9.   Diagram of a single-channel model.

In Fig. 9-9, T_A represents the interarrival-time intervals of the input units, W_i ($i = 1, 2, \ldots, k$) are the waiting-time intervals, T_i ($i = 1, 2, \ldots, k$) are the service-time intervals, D_i ($i = 1, 2, \ldots, k$) are the idle-time intervals, S_i ($i = 1, 2, \ldots, k$) are the sums of W_i and T_i, and k is the total number of service stations in the system.

For the first arrival of the input units, the following equations are applicable: (input unit $n = 1$).

$$(T_A)_1 = 0$$
$$(W_1)_1 = 0, (W_2)_1 = 0, \ldots, (W_k)_1 = 0$$

$$(D_1)_1 = 0, (D_2)_1 = (T_1)_1, \ldots, (D_k)_1 = \sum_{j=1}^{k-1} (T_j)_1$$

$$(S_1)_1 = (T_1)_1, (S_2)_1 = (T_2)_1, \ldots, (S_k)_1 = (T_k)_1$$

For subsequent arrivals, the equations are changed to the following, $n = 2, 3, \ldots, N$, where N is the total number of the input units:

$$(S_1)_n = (W_1 + T_1)_n$$
$$(S_2)_n = (W_2 + T_2)_n$$
$$\vdots$$
$$(S_k)_n = (W_k + T_k)_n$$

Whether waiting time or idle time will occur depends on the differences between $(S_1)_{n-1}, (S_1 + S_2)_{n-1}, \ldots, (S_1 + S_2 + \cdots + S_k)_{n-1}$ and $(T_A)_n, (T_A + W_1 + T_1)_n, \ldots, (T_A + W_1 + T_1 + \cdots + W_{k-1} + T_{k-1})_n$. If the differences are positive, idle time will be zero, and waiting time can be calculated by

$$(W_1)_n = (S_1)_{n-1} - (T_A)_n$$
$$(W_2)_n = (S_1 + S_2)_{n-1} - (T_A + W_1 + T_1)_n$$
$$\vdots$$
$$(W_k)_n = (S_1 + S_2 + \cdots + S_k)_{n-1}$$
$$\quad - (T_A + W_1 + T_1 + \cdots + W_{k-1} + T_{k-1})_n$$

If the differences are negative, waiting time will be zero, and idle time can be calculated by

$$(D_1)_n = (T_A)_n - (S_1)_{n-1}$$
$$(D_2)_n = (T_A + W_1 + T_1)_n - (S_1 + S_2)_{n-1}$$
$$\vdots$$
$$(D_k)_n = (T_A + W_1 + T_1 + \cdots + W_{k-1} + T_{k-1})_n$$
$$\quad - (S_1 + S_2 + \cdots + S_k)_{n-1}$$

If these differences are zero, both waiting time and idle time will be zero.

In waiting-line problems, if the input units arrive at a service station in a random and independent fashion, they may be described by a Poisson distribution with parameter λt, where λ is the average arrival rate and t is a time interval of fixed length. In other words, the distribution indicates the variation of the number of arrivals occurring in time intervals of specified length. However, if the time intervals between each two consecutive arrivals, rather than the number of arrivals within an interval, are under investigation, the appropriate distribution is a negative exponential distribution with mean equal to $1/\lambda$ and variance equal to $1/\lambda^2$. In contrast, then, this distribution describes the variation in length of the interarrival intervals. This latter distribution is also used to describe the variation in service time required to complete a service, provided that the service time is a random and independently distributed variable.

In order to derive an analytical solution to the model, it is assumed that there is only one service station; in other words, k equals 1. It is further assumed that (1) input units arrive at the service station in a Poisson fashion with mean arrival rate λ equal to $\frac{1}{6}$, and (2) the service times follow an exponential distribution, with mean service rate μ equal to $\frac{1}{5}$. Since the mean of the service rate μ is greater than the mean of the arrival rate λ, the expected waiting time for the input units can be found analytically by the following well-known formula, where $E(w)$ is the expected value of waiting time for the model.[22]

$$E(w) = \frac{\lambda}{\mu(\mu - \lambda)} = 25 \text{ time units}$$

A total[23] of 4,900 input units were simulated to pass through the system on the computer run of this single-channel model. The simulation results showed that the

[22]See Chapter 7, "Elementary Waiting-Line Models."
[23]Trial runs show that for generating variates of the following probability distributions, a sample of 100 input units already give high precision. The results are listed below.

	True Mean	True S.D.	Sample Mean ($N = 100$)	Sample S.D. ($N = 100$)	z
Exponential	20	20	20.37	19.66	.19
Normal	20	5	19.92	5.49	−.14
Log-normal	20	5	20.01	5.18	.02

Here, a large sample of 4,900 input units was used in order to assure greater precision.

mean and standard deviation of the waiting time for these input units were 25.09 and 29.82 respectively. The standard error[24] is therefore .42. The difference between the simulation result and the analytical solution is .09. The null hypothesis that this difference is statistically significant was rejected at the .05 level. Thus it is interpreted that the difference is due to random perturbation.

Model 2

The second model, Fig. 9-10, is a multichannel model as in the diagram which depicts a situation in which the

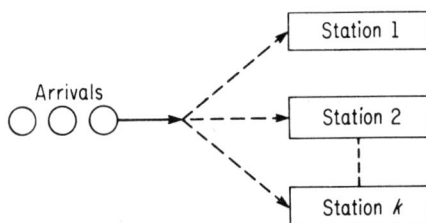

Fig. 9-10.   Diagram of a multi-channel model.

service stations in a microeconomic system are arranged in parallel, such as in a barbershop.

Here each input unit may pass through any one of the service stations, provided that the service station is empty at the moment. In the simulation program, the number of channels is a parameter which is set by the user at the beginning of each simulation run. A graphical representation of the simulation procedure is illustrated in Fig. 9-11, using a three-channel model as an example.[25]

The diagram represents a three-channel model with one waiting line and an admission policy of first-come,

[24]Standard error:

$$\frac{\sigma}{\sqrt{n}} = \frac{29.82}{4,900} = .42$$

$$z = \frac{25.09 - 25}{.42} = .21$$

[25]The same logic applies to any number of channels.

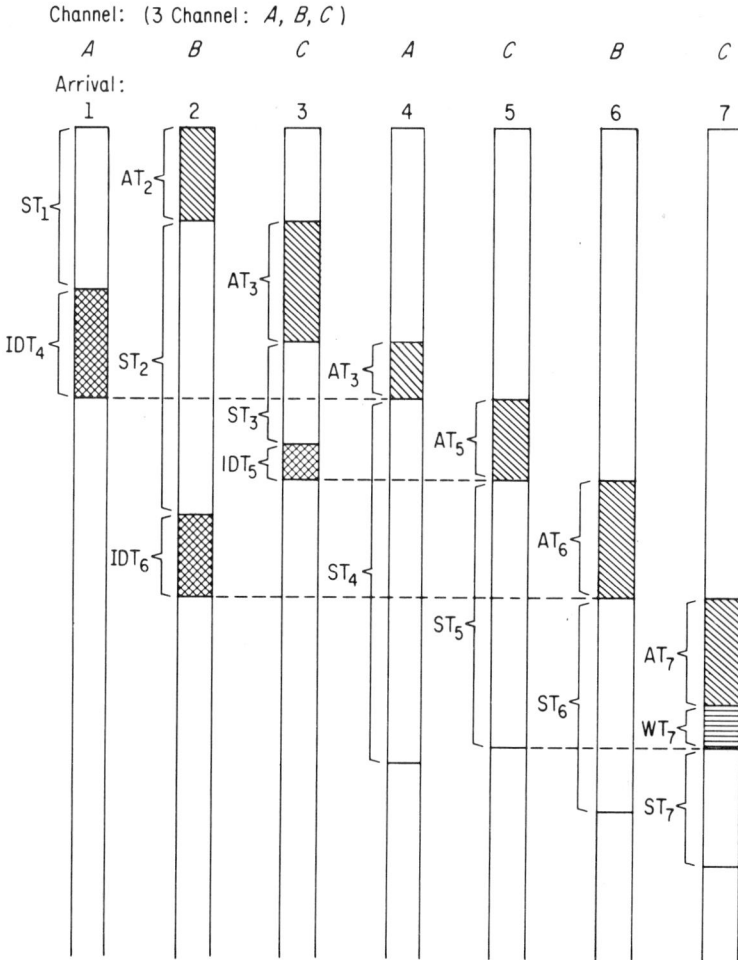

Fig. 9-11. Graphical representation of the simulation procedure of a multichannel model.

first-served. With N being the sample size, AT_i ($i = 1, 2, \ldots, N$) are the interarrival intervals, ST_i ($k = 1, 2, \ldots, N$) the service-time intervals, IDT_i ($i = 1, 2, \ldots, N$) the idle-time intervals, and WT_i ($i = 1, 2, \ldots, N$) the waiting-time intervals. As a unit arrives at the system, the service channels are checked to determine whether any one of them is unoccupied at the moment. If all three are occupied, waiting time occurs until one channel becomes vacant. When a channel becomes vacant before another unit arrives, idle time occurs until a unit arrives and enters the channel. Thus in Fig. 9-11, WT_7 is a waiting-time interval and IDT_4, IDT_5, and IDT_6 are idle-time intervals.

The analytical solution of the model is based on the following assumptions. First, there are k service stations in the system. Second, the input units arrive at the system in a Poisson fashion with mean arrival rate μ equal to $\frac{1}{5}$. And third, the service-time intervals at each station are exponentially distributed with a mean service rate λ equal to $\frac{1}{20}$. The analytical solution can be found by the following formula, where $E(w)$ is the expected waiting time:[26]

$$E(w) = \frac{\mu(\lambda/\mu)^k}{(k-1)!(k\mu - \lambda)^2}$$

$$= \frac{1}{\sum\limits_{n=0}^{k-1} \frac{1}{n!}\left(\frac{\lambda}{\mu}\right)^n + \frac{1}{k!}\left(\frac{\lambda}{\mu}\right)^k \left(\frac{k\mu}{k\mu - \lambda}\right)}$$

Again, 4,900 input units were stimulated to pass through the system. However, for this model several runs were made, each with a different value for k. The simulation results and the corresponding analytical solutions for the runs are listed in Table 9-1.

TABLE 9-1

VALUES OF THE EXPECTED WAITING TIME OF A
MULTICHANNEL MODEL OBTAINED BOTH FROM
ANALYTICAL SOLUTIONS AND SIMULATION RUNS

Number of Channels	Analytical Solutions	Simulation Results	z Values
4	∞	Storage Overflow	—
5	11.081	11.07	0.41
6	3.632	3.75	0.94
7	1.159	1.09	1.32
8	0.398	0.39	0.30
9	0.124	0.12	0.31
10	0.038	0.03	1.30

In Table 9-1, the storage overflow indicates that the value became very large and was assumed to be approach-

[26]See Chapter 7, "Elementary Waiting-Line Models."

ing infinity. The z values are calculated by the formula

$$z = \frac{\beta' - \beta}{\sigma_\beta}$$

where β' is the analytical solution, β is the simulation result, and σ_β is the standard error of β. A test of the tabulated values of z indicate that the analytical solutions and the simulation results have no significant differences at the .05 probability level.

The results of these simulations would seem to indicate that the method selected for use is quite appropriate for time-flow analysis.

This also leads to the suggestion that simulation methods and analytical methods should be used complementary in experiments. Computer simulation is used to reveal or discover more information about the interrelationship among the components of the system. And once we have reached a better understanding of the operational and behavioral characteristics of the system, we may formulate them into mathematical equations and attempt to solve the equations analytically. Then again we use simulation methods to do more experiments and to search for more information so that better analytical structures of the system can be developed.

SIMULATION OF WAITING LINES

In this section, four simulation models are presented, each embodying some of the features that may be conceived to exist in a microeconomic system. Those features either indicate that the distributions of the interarrival- and service-time intervals do not follow simple theoretical distributions or that they are dependently related to each other.

Simulation runs of these four models are made with arbitrary parameter values to illustrate the kinds of information that can be obtained from the simulation results. Also, the method of determining the validity of these or similar simulation results are discussed at the end of this section.

Model A

The flow diagram of this model is given in Fig. 9-12. Model A is a single-channel model with three service stations. The interarrival-time intervals of the input units are assumed to follow an exponential distribution. The distributions of service-time intervals for the three service stations, however, are assumed to be all different. These distributions are assumed as follows: station 1, normal distribution; station 2, exponential distribution; and station 3, log-normal distribution. Further, the mean of the arrival rate of the input units is assuming to vary depending upon the length of the time interval the previous unit stays in the system. If this time interval is longer than a specified period, the arrival rate will be decreased and conversely. This is one case of output-input feedback, in that the input rate is affected by the output rate of the system. The model can be modified by changing one or all of the following: the number of stations in the system, the probability distributions of the interarrival intervals and/or service-time intervals, and the nature of the output-input feedbacks.

A simulation run with the following values for the parameters was performed to investigate the behavior of this hypothetical model of a microeconomic system. (1) The mean of the distribution of the service time intervals (i.e., normal distribution) at station 1 is set equal to 10 min, and the standard deviation of the distribution is assumed to equal to 2 min. (2) The mean and standard deviation of the distribution of the service-time intervals (i.e., exponential) at station 2 are both set equal to 15 min. (3) The mean of the distribution of the service-time intervals (i.e., lognormal) at station 3 is assumed to be equal to 20 min, and the standard deviation of the distribution is assumed to be 5 min. (4) It is assumed that if the total time that an input unit stays in the system is less than 50 min, the mean of the distribution of the interarrival intervals of the following units will be 10 min. However, if the total time that an input unit stays in the system exceeds 50 min, the mean of the distribution of the interarrival intervals of the subsequent units will be increased to 20 min. In other words, the arrival rate changes from $\frac{1}{10}$ unit per min to

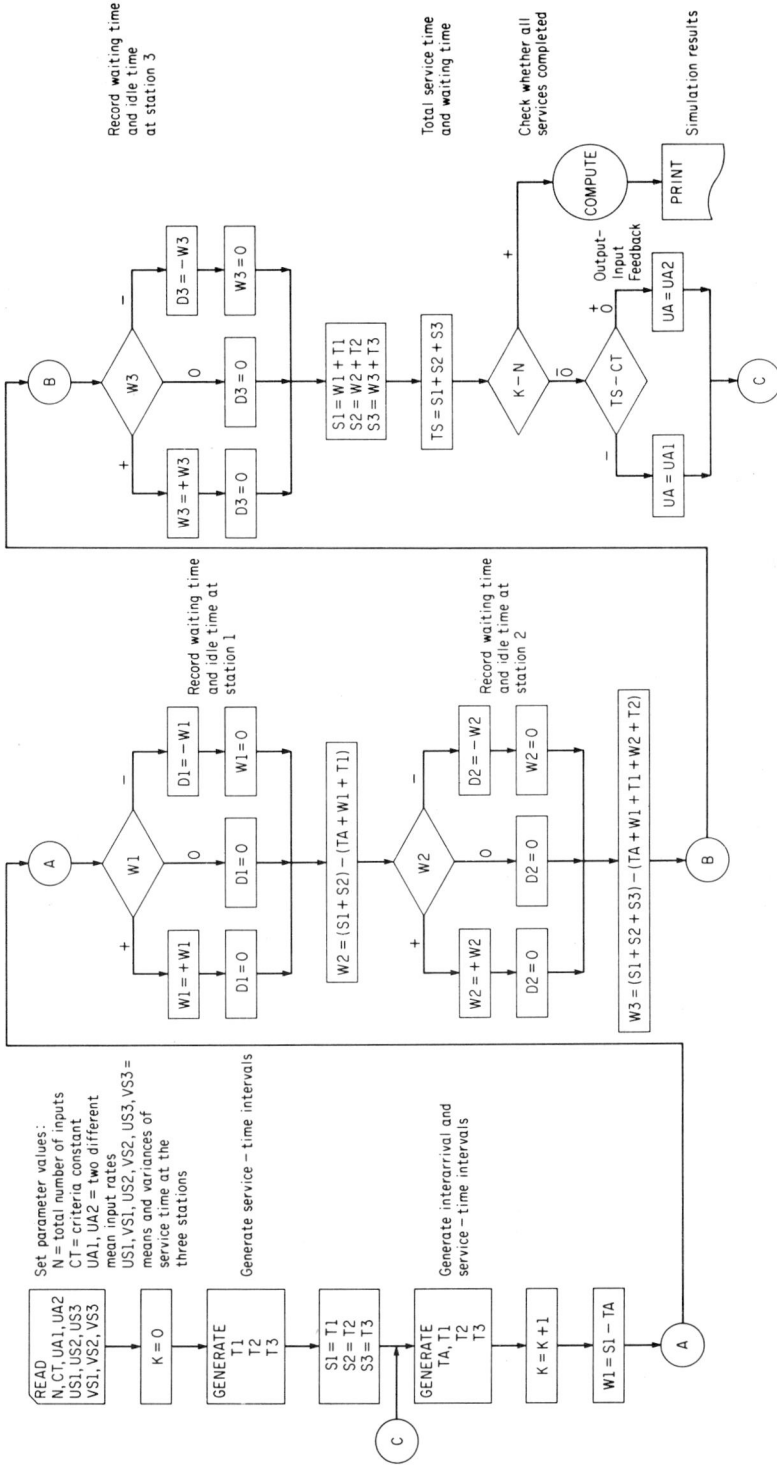

Fig. 9-12. Flow diagram of Model A, a single-channel, three-station model with output-input feedbacks.

$1/20$ unit per min, when it takes more than 50 min to complete the service on one unit.

The result of the simulation run shows that it will require 13,764 min to complete services on 100 input units. The average waiting time at station 1 is 6.52 min, at station 2, it is 18.94 min, and at station 3, it is 67.50 min. The total idle time at station 1 is 1,059 min, at station 2 it is 625 min, and at station 3, 87 min. Station 1 is engaged in service 48 percent of the time, station 2, 70 percent of the time, and station 3, 95 percent of the time. These percentages show that the work load is not evenly distributed at the three stations; for example, station 1 is idle more than half of the time and station 3 is busy almost constantly.

An attempt was then made to find a more efficiently operating system by performing another simulation run with all assumptions remaining the same but with the following parameter changes: (1) the mean of the distribution of the service-time intervals at station 1 is increased to 15 min, and (2) the mean of the distribution of the service-time intervals at station 3 is decreased to 16 min. The assumption here is that by moving some of the facilities from station 1 to station 3, the service rate at station 3 will increase and the service rate at station 1 will decrease. The result of this second simulation run shows that it now takes only 10,094 min instead of 13,764 min to complete the services on the 100 input units and the work load is more evenly distributed, with station 1 engaged in service 74 percent of the time, station 2, 71 percent of the time and station 3, 78 percent of the time.

The above illustration shows that by moving facilities from the slack area to the congested area in a system, the total service time can be reduced, thus possibly decreasing the total cost of the services. The optimum distribution of the facilities among the various service stations in a system may be found by repeated simulation runs with different parameter values.

Model B

Model B (Fig. 9-13) is a multichannel model with N service stations in parallel arrangement. The mean arrival

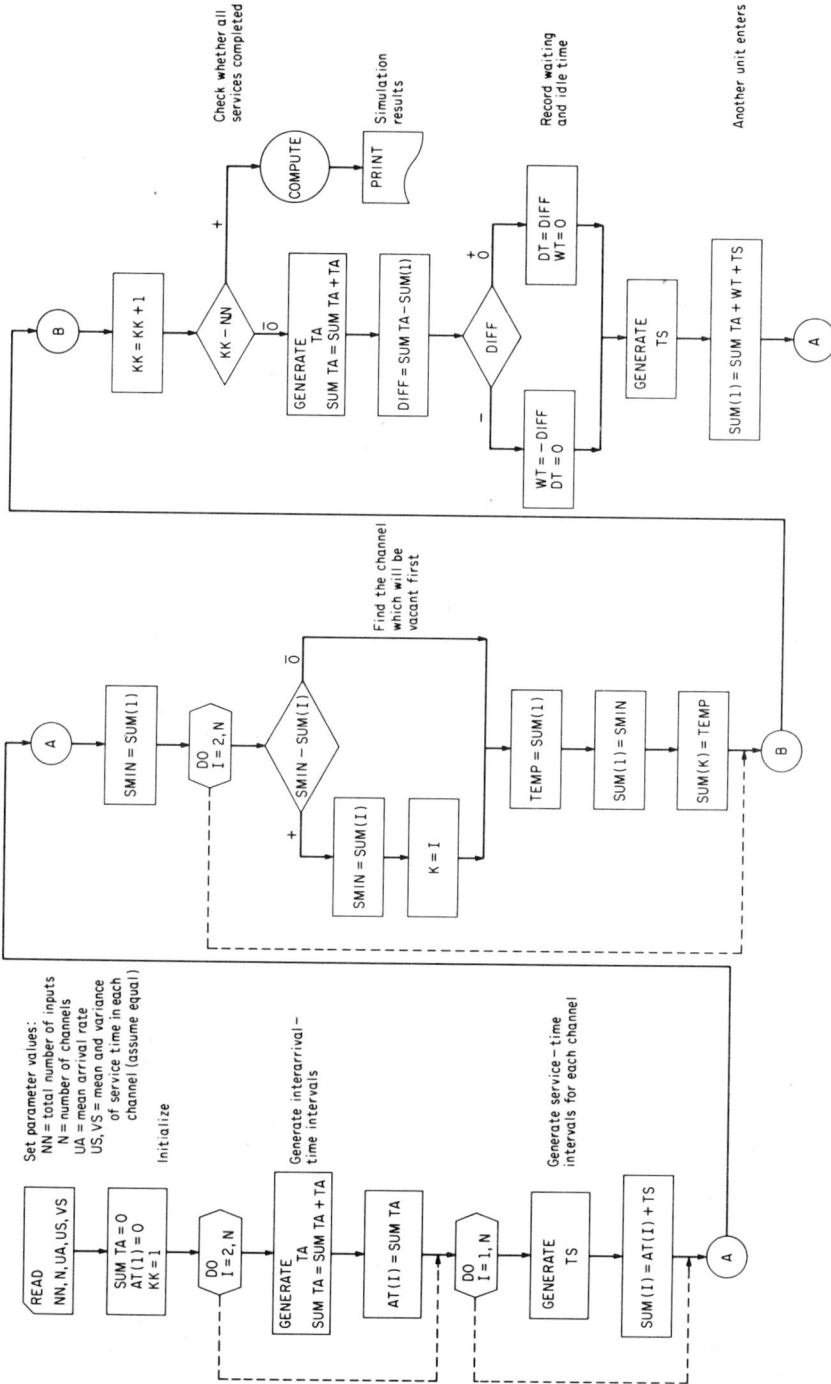

Fig. 9-13. Flow diagram of Model B, a multichannel model with fluctuating input rate.

rate is assumed to be fluctuating according to a trigono-metric function with its period equal to a specified interval. The admission policy is assumed to be first-come, first-served, and the service-time intervals at each station are assumed to be exponentially distributed. This model may be modified by altering the admission policy and the dis-tribution of the service-time intervals at each station, and may be further modified by assuming other kinds of cyclical curves that may trace out the change of the arrival rate. Also, Model A and Model B can be combined together to form a model with service stations arranged in both series and parallel.

A simulation run was made with the interarrival-time intervals equal initially to 20 min. These intervals then fluc-tuated according to a trigonometric function, with the period of each cycle equal to approximately 12 hr. At the peak of the cycle the interval is 30 min and at the trough it equals 10 min. In other words, the amplitude of the fluctu-ation is 10 min both ways. The model is assumed to have five service stations arranged in parallel, with the mean of the distribution of the service-time intervals of each station (i.e., exponential) assumed to equal 80 min. The results of the simulation run showed that about 8,187 min were re-quired to complete services on the 100 input units. The average waiting time of the input units was 64.92 min, the average idle time for the five service stations was 295 min, and each station was engaged in service an average of 85 percent of the time.

Now suppose the management of this microeconomic system decides to open an additional service station. An-other simulation run is made, but on this run there are six instead of five service stations arranged in parallel. The results showed that now only 2,816 min are required to complete servicing the 100 input units. This resulted from drastic reduction of average waiting time from 64.92 to 14.03 min per input unit. However, the average idle time for each of the six service stations increased to 549 min, and each station is engaged in service an average of only 72 per-cent of the time.

The above illustration shows that by increasing the

number of service channels in a system the total waiting time will be reduced while the total idle time will be increased. Given the unit cost of waiting time and idle time, the optimum number of service channels may be found by simulation runs with different numbers of channels.

Model C

Model C (Fig. 9-14) has N main service stations arranged in parallel and an extra ancillary service station. The input units arrive at the system in a Poisson fashion and are admitted to the N main service stations whenever there is a vacancy. While occupying one of the main service stations, the unit first waits for the services of the ancillary service station. The length of the service-time intervals at the ancillary service station follows an Erlang gamma distribution with the parameter K determined by the length of the waiting time of the preceding unit waiting to be served by the ancillary service station. If the waiting time of the preceding unit is longer than a specified interval, then K is reduced, and conversely. After being served by the ancillary service station, the unit remains in the main service station for a certain period of time, this latter period being assumed to follow a log-normal distribution. This model may be modified by changing the admission policies of both the main service stations and the ancillary service station, and by assuming alternative probability distributions for the interarrival intervals and the service-time intervals both at the main service stations and at the ancillary service station.

Suppose, for example, the model is a simulation of a simple school medical clinic which consists of a five-bed ward and a laboratory for testing. Assume further that (1) the time intervals between arrivals of the patients are exponentially distributed with mean and standard deviation equal to 22, (2) the time intervals required to complete a laboratory test are also exponentially distributed, but with mean and standard deviation equal to 3 hr, and (3) the periods that the patients stay in the ward after having taken the tests follow a log-normal distribution with mean equal to

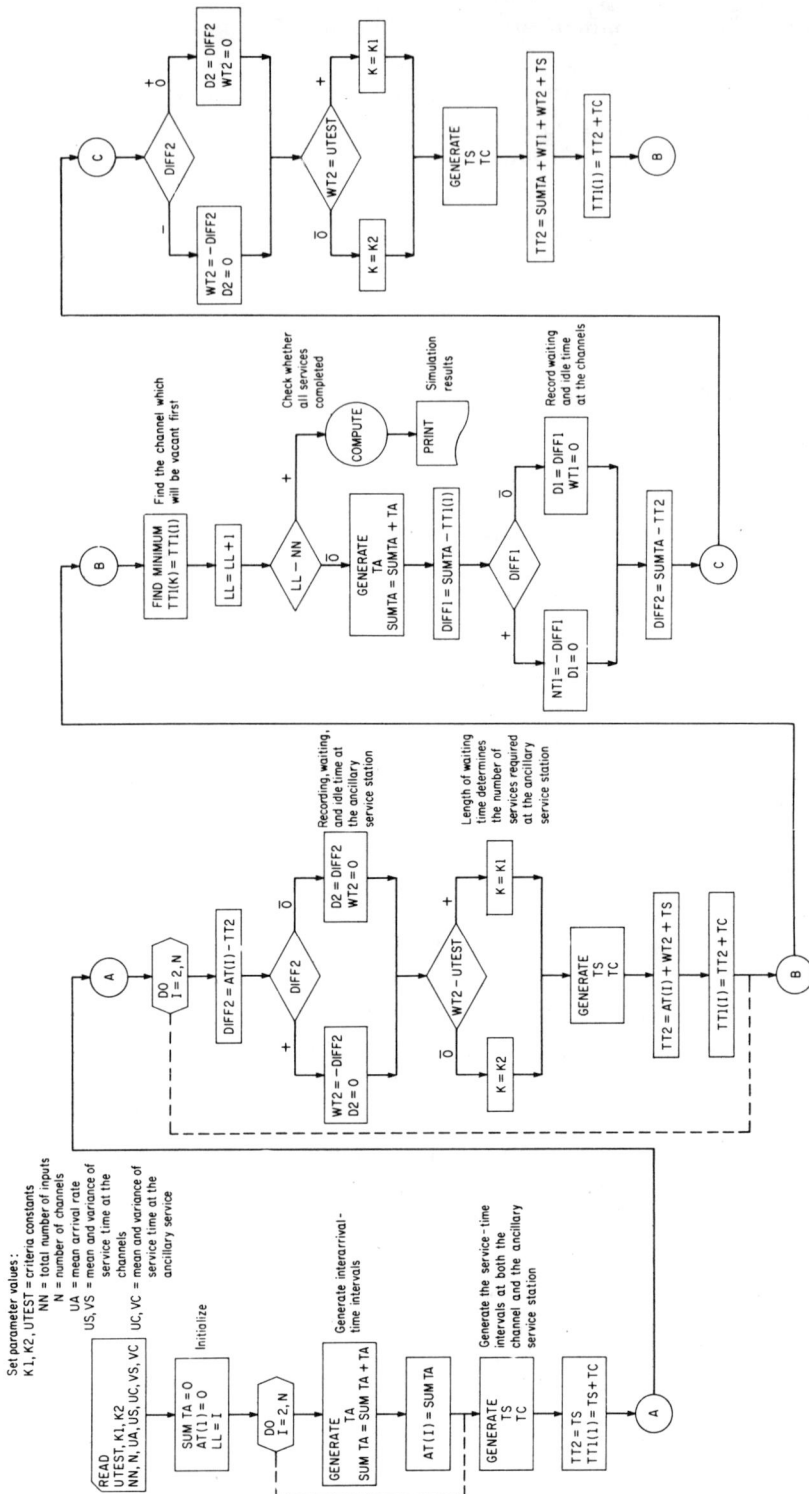

Fig. 9-14 Flow diagram of Model C, a multichannel model with an attached ancillary service station. (Number of services performed on each unit at the ancillary service station is dependent on the length of the waiting time.)

2 hr and standard deviation equal to 4 hr. Consider that a physician generally orders six tests per patient; however, when the waiting time between the ordering of a test and its execution exceeds 20 hr, the physician orders only four tests per patient.

A simulation run with a sample of 100 patients passing through the ward gives the following results. The average waiting time of the patients to be accepted into the ward is 1.61 hr, the average waiting time between a test ordered and performed is 18.73 hr, and each bed in the ward is occupied an average of 46 percent of the time and the laboratory is busy 69 percent of the time.

Now, consider the following situation. The school authorities, in anticipation of a mild epidemic on the campus, desire to know how many patients this small clinic can service, knowing that the beds in the ward may be fully occupied all the time, and that the laboratory must be allowed some leisure time in order to prevent the technician from giving erroneous tests or inaccurate reports. Thus another simulation run is made with the mean and standard deviation of the distribution of the interarrival intervals decreased to 20 hr, and the number of tests performed on each patient limited to the essential four. The result shows that the laboratory now is engaged in work 86 percent of the time, and each bed in the ward is occupied an average of 99 percent of the time. These results also indicate that with the capacity of the clinic and the service rate remaining the same, any further increase in the arrival rate will form a waiting line infinitely long, the consequence of which is that some of the patients have to be sent somewhere else for treatment.

The above illustration shows that the acceleration of the input rate to a system will increase its work load and thus may increase the total waiting time. One way to ease the situation is to reduce the number of services performed on each unit at the most congested point in the system. As with the preceding models, the optimum input rate in a particular situation may be found by repeated simulation runs with varying parameters.

Model D

Model D (Fig. 9-15) is also a multichannel model with input units arriving at the system in a Poisson process. However, in this model when the unit is admitted into the system, the service-time interval is composed of two parts. The first part is assumed to be in Erlang gamma distribution with the value of the parameter K varying according to a known probability distribution, and the second part is assumed to be log-normally distributed with mean and standard deviation functionally related to the length of the time interval of the first part. If the first part of the interval is longer than a given length, then the mean and standard deviation of the distribution of the second part of the interval will be longer, and conversely. Model modification may be achieved by altering the distribution of the interarrival intervals, the distributions of the two parts of the service-time intervals, and the functional relationship between the first part and the second part of the interval.

This model may also be considered as a simple hospital model. The period during which the patients stay in the ward may be broken into two intervals; the first interval is the diagnostic period, the second interval the convalescent period. Assume that there are five beds in the ward, and that the patients arrive at the ward in intervals with a mean and a standard deviation both equal to 20 hr. Further, assume that 60 percent of the patients need to take six different laboratory tests or preliminary examinations before the completion of the diagnostic period, and the other 40 percent need take only three. If the diagnostic period is longer than 100 hr, then the convalescent period of the patient will be a variate of a log-normal distribution with mean equal to 100 hours and standard deviation equal to 20 hr. Otherwise, the mean and standard deviation are equal to 50 and 10 hours.

The results of a simulation run with a sample of 100 patients passing through the ward of this model show that the average waiting time of the patients to get into the ward is 5.11 hr, and the average time interval that each patient stays in the ward is 66.33 hr. Also, each bed in the ward is occupied an average of 63 percent of the time.

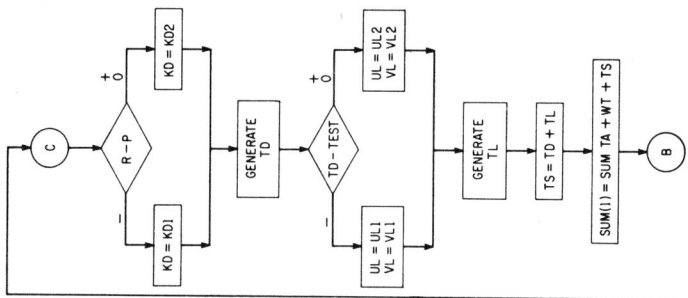

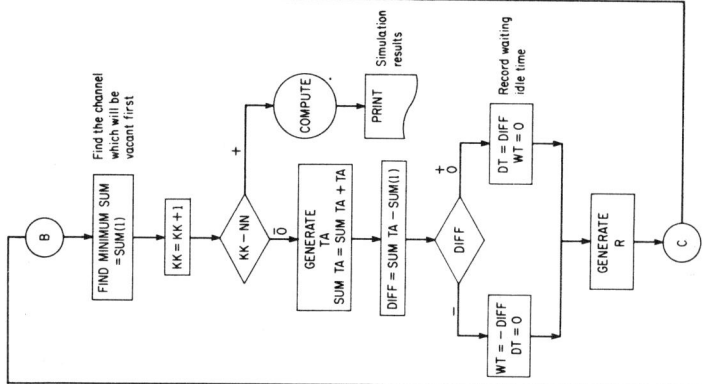

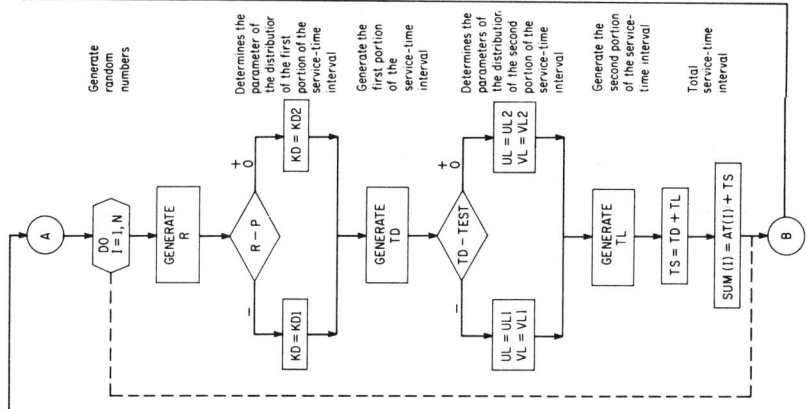

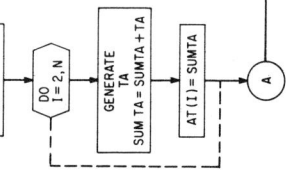

Fig. 9-15. Flow diagram of Model D, a multichannel model with two intervals of service time. (The length of the second interval is dependent on the length of the first.)

Now suppose the community which the hospital serves is growing, and the absolute number of patients increases with the increase of the population. The model can be altered to account for this increase in the number of patients by decreasing the mean and standard deviation of the distribution of the interarrival intervals to 15 hr. A question is raised as to how the situation can be met without increasing the existing facilities of the hospital. One solution is to shorten the convalescent periods of the patients staying in the hospital. To examine this possibility, another simulation run is made with the mean of the distribution of the convalescent periods reduced to eighty hours for those whose diagnostic periods exceeded 100 hr, and 40 hr for those whose diagnostic period did not exceed 100 hr. The results show that the average waiting time is now 6.93 hr, the average time that each patient stays in the ward, 56.05 hr, and the beds in the ward are occupied by the patients 71 percent of the time.

The results of these simulation runs clearly show that the increase of the work load due to the increase of the input rate to a system may be balanced by shortening the length of the service time spent on each unit. The optimum balance of the input rate and the service rate of a particular system may be found for this model by simulation runs with different sets of input rates and service rates.

The models presented above are only intended as illustrations. Model A indicates the effect of rearranging facilities within a system. In Model B the effect of changing the number of parallel arranged service stations is illustrated. In Model C the effect of altering the decision rules regarding admission policy and requests for laboratory services in a hypothetical school clinic is evaluated, and in Model D the effect of changing the discharge policy in a simple hospital system to meet the changing demand is studied. There is other information that can be obtained by experimenting with the models. For example, the distribution of the waiting time or idle time may be approximated by smoothing the histograms generated from information printed out by the computer for each individual input unit. The application of the technique in a real world research problem, however, depends on the purposed and imagination of the person who undertakes the research.

Validation of Simulation Results

After a simulation model has been constructed and the simulation runs have been made, a question immediately arises: how valid are these simulation results?

If a computer simulation is made of an existing system for the purpose of explaining and predicting the behavior of that system, the results of the simulation runs can be compared continuously to sample observations made on the existing system, thus insuring the validity of the simulation model. But if the computer simulation is for the purpose of helping design a new system and actual observations cannot be made, then the validity of the model will have to depend on how realistic the basic assumptions are, and whether the relationships derived from these basic assumptions have been logically deduced.

A simulation model of a microeconomic system when first programmed may be too simple an extraction from reality or may have errors in its basic assumptions. For example, a common error occurs when an interdependent scheduling process is applied to the system—that is, when the arrivals are scheduled in such a way that the interarrival-time intervals fluctuate in phase with the fluctuations of the service-time intervals. When the service time becomes longer, the arrivals will be scheduled to arrive at the system in longer time intervals, and when the service time becomes shorter the arrivals will be scheduled to arrive at the system more frequently. If this kind of interdependence between the time variates does exist in a real situation but is not considered while constructing the simulation model, then even though the distributions of both the interarrival time intervals and the service time intervals are correctly described by the simulation model, a large discrepancy may occur between the observed waiting-time–idle-time of the real situation as compared to the result of the simulation runs. But as the subprograms and the main program can be modified easily, and the parameters such as the means and variances of the distributions of the variables are set for each simulation run, it is possible to constantly review and improve the simulation model and keep it from deviating from reality.

SIMULATION OF MARKOV CHAINS

Markov-chain theory assumes known transition probabilities between different states in a given period of time. Since we can generate pseudorandom numbers very rapidly in the computer, we can also simulate the Markov chain process going from one state to another by using random numbers in a unit interval ($0 \leq R \leq 1$) to determine which state the process will be in during the subsequent period. If the process is finally absorbed in an absorbing state, we may find out how many iterations it takes, which may also be translated into a time dimension. If the process goes on indefinitely, we may find out what proportions of time it stays in each different state. The flow diagram of Fig. 9-16 describes such a computer simulation model.

The Markov-chain model can become very complicated when the transition probability matrix is not fixed, but varies among several different probability matrices according to a given probability distribution. If such is the case, analytical solutions such as these given in Chapter 6 will be difficult or even impossible to find. However, computer programming, following the same procedure, may be used to simulate all different situations without much difficulty.

SIMULATION OF INVENTORY SYSTEM

In a realistic business operation, demand is stochastic, production time may be delayed because of late arrival of materials, machine breakdowns, etc. When these complications exist, we may not have ready analytical solutions such as described in Chapter 8. However, we may rely on computer simulation to describe the complicated situation and to try out alternative inventory policies for comparing their

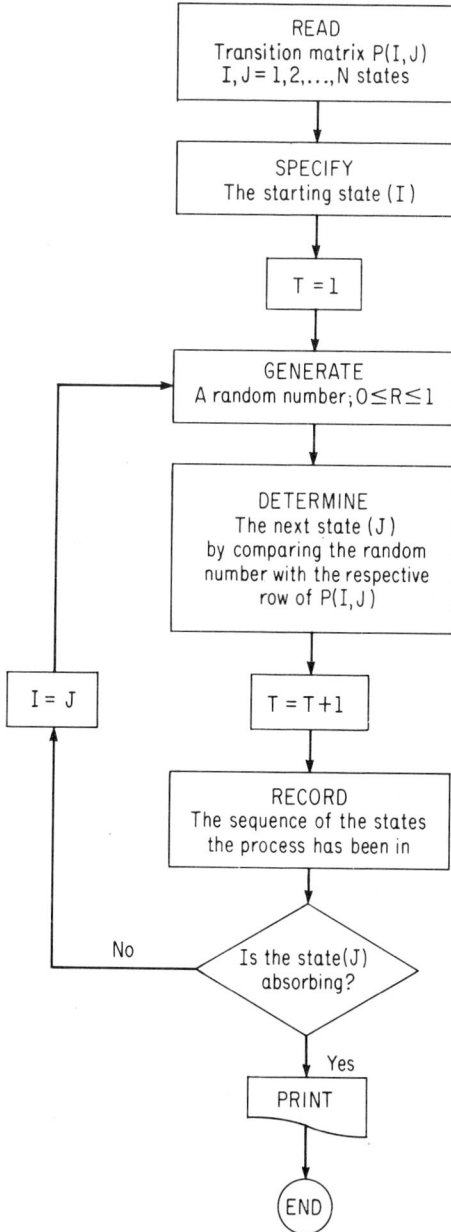

Fig. 9-16. A Markov-chain simulation model.

merits. And then we can make a choice of the policy which will most likely satisfy our objectives. The flow diagram (Fig. 9-17) depicts an inventory model which simulates the

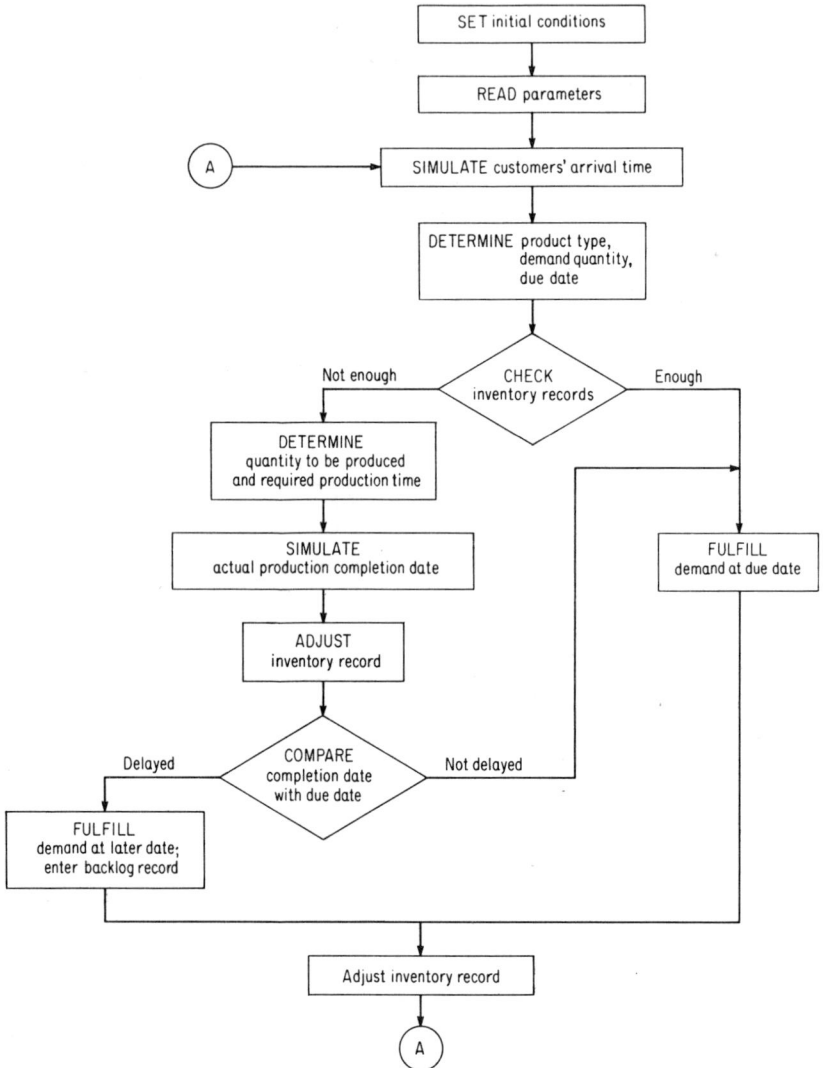

Fig. 9-17.   Flow diagram of an inventory simulation model.

arrivals of customers, the type of product they demand, and the quantity they order according to given probability distributions. The computer program then checks the inventory record to determine whether the available stock is enough to meet the demand. If enough, no production is ordered. If not enough, a production order of a particular lot size is issued according to a given inventory policy. Simulation is then made on the production process and the production completion date. When the date to fulfill the demand is due, a check is again made on the inventory record to determine whether the demand can be fulfilled. If the demand can and is fulfilled, the inventory record is duly adjusted. If the demand cannot be fulfilled, a backlog is noted, which will be cleared when the production order is executed and completed. The simulation usually goes on for a lengthy period of time and the results are examined to check the merits or desirability of the inventory policy.

SIMULATION OF A FIRM

The operation of a firm is divided into three major areas. One area is the factors markets, from which the firm draws the factors of production (intermediate products may be included) essential to its production. The prices and available quantities of the factors are given in functional forms similar to the supply curves discussed in economic theories. The firm examines the quantities it requires, the prices it has to pay, and the amount it can obtain and then make purchase or employment decisions according to some predetermined rules. (The business games are different from the simulating models introduced here in that they involve human decisions in the simulation process and have different teams representing different firms competing with each other in an oligopolistic environment.)

The second area is the production activities inside the firm. The model simulates the transformation of the factors or production (intermediate products may be included) into final products. The quantities of the factors of production used to produce a given amount of finished product and the time elapsed during the production process usually are stochastic measurements. Thus queueing theories and probability distributions may be applied in this part of the simulation.

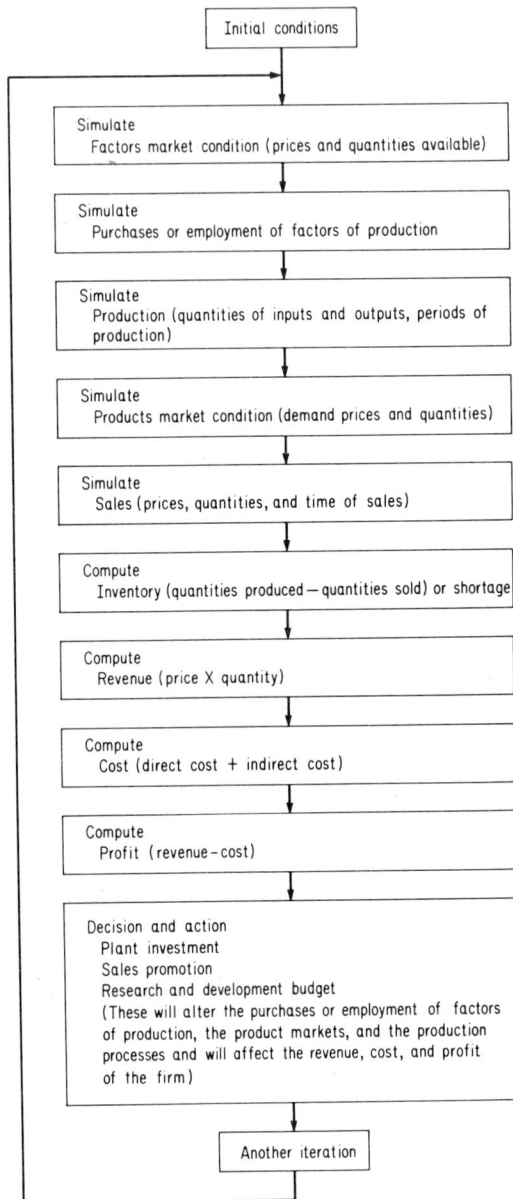

```
                    ┌─────────────────────┐
                    │  Initial conditions │
                    └─────────────────────┘
                              │
    ┌──────────────────────────────────────────────────┐
    │  Simulate                                          │
    │    Factors market condition (prices and quantities available)
    └──────────────────────────────────────────────────┘
                              │
    ┌──────────────────────────────────────────────────┐
    │  Simulate                                          │
    │    Purchases or employment of factors of production
    └──────────────────────────────────────────────────┘
                              │
    ┌──────────────────────────────────────────────────┐
    │  Simulate                                          │
    │    Production (quantities of inputs and outputs, periods of
    │    production)                                      │
    └──────────────────────────────────────────────────┘
                              │
    ┌──────────────────────────────────────────────────┐
    │  Simulate                                          │
    │    Products market condition (demand prices and quantities)
    └──────────────────────────────────────────────────┘
                              │
    ┌──────────────────────────────────────────────────┐
    │  Simulate                                          │
    │    Sales (prices, quantities, and time of sales)   │
    └──────────────────────────────────────────────────┘
                              │
    ┌──────────────────────────────────────────────────┐
    │  Compute                                           │
    │    Inventory (quantities produced — quantities sold) or shortage
    └──────────────────────────────────────────────────┘
                              │
    ┌──────────────────────────────────────────────────┐
    │  Compute                                           │
    │    Revenue (price X quantity)                      │
    └──────────────────────────────────────────────────┘
                              │
    ┌──────────────────────────────────────────────────┐
    │  Compute                                           │
    │    Cost (direct cost + indirect cost)              │
    └──────────────────────────────────────────────────┘
                              │
    ┌──────────────────────────────────────────────────┐
    │  Compute                                           │
    │    Profit (revenue − cost)                         │
    └──────────────────────────────────────────────────┘
                              │
    ┌──────────────────────────────────────────────────┐
    │  Decision and action                               │
    │    Plant investment                                │
    │    Sales promotion                                 │
    │    Research and development budget                 │
    │    (These will alter the purchases or employment of factors
    │    of production, the product markets, and the production
    │    processes and will affect the revenue, cost, and profit
    │    of the firm)                                    │
    └──────────────────────────────────────────────────┘
                              │
                    ┌─────────────────────┐
                    │  Another iteration  │
                    └─────────────────────┘
```

Fig. 9-18.   Model of a firm.

The third area is the products markets. We assume a pure competition situation. The firm has no control over the prices of the products; it can only sell its products at the current market prices. However, the demand for its products is simulated according to some given probability distributions. The comparison of the demand and production rates will give inventory quantities and shortage frequencies of the products of the firm.

Finally, at some fixed time interval the total revenue and cost are computed and the total profit of the firm is evaluated.

At the end of each simulation run the user of the model may review the results and revise the decision rules and start another run.

The flow chart of this model is given in Fig. 9-18.

SIMULATION OF GAMES

As mentioned in Chapter 3, games sometimes can be very complicated; there may be so many alternatives or combinations of alternatives for the players that the optimum strategy for each is difficult if not impossible to determine by analytical methods. However, we may program the computer to play the games. The procedure is generally to let the computer examine the results at each subsequent stage of the game and make a choice for each player based on a given set of decision rules. The rules may be fixed during the entire game or may themselves be random-based on some given probability distributions. When numerous plays are made, the results will indicate an approximately optimum strategy for each player.

Following is a simple illustration of a game played by two players, each with three alternatives. The payoff matrix of the first player A is given. The rule is that the first player A attempts to maximize the payoff and the second player B attempts to minimize the payoff. Ten plays made by each player are listed below. (With the computer, thousands of plays can be done within minutes. The flow diagram of the computer program is given in Fig. 9-19.) The result indi-

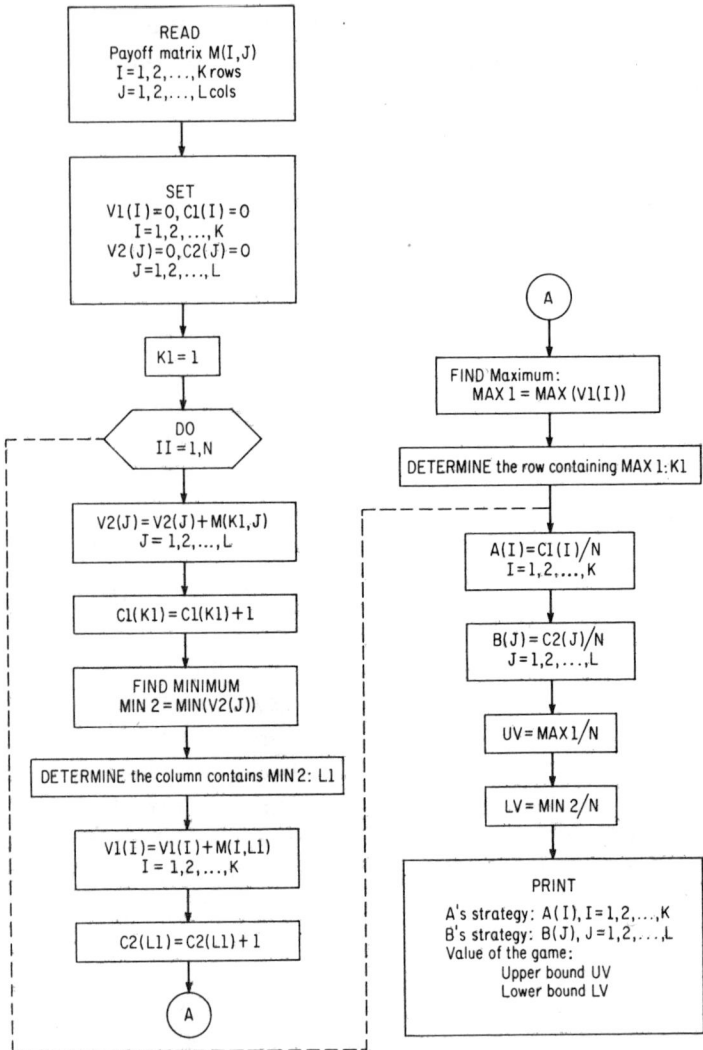

Fig. 9-19. Flow diagram of solving a game by computer simulation.

cates that *A* played once the first alternative, three times the second alternative and six times the third alternative, giving an upperbound of the expected value of the game of $^{21}/_{10}$. *B* played three times the first alternative, four times the second alternatives and three times the third alternative, giving a lower bound of the expected value of the game of $^{19}/_{10}$. Comparing this with the analytical solution of *A*'s optimum strategy $\left(\frac{1}{4}, \frac{1}{4}, \frac{2}{4}\right)$, B's optimum strategy $\left(\frac{1}{3}, \frac{1}{3}, \frac{1}{3}\right)$ and the expected value of the game of 2, we see that they are quite close.

The similar simulation procedure may be applied to games with more players and/or different decision rules. With large number of plays, we may examine the results to find approximate optimum strategy for each player.

		B			B's choice (minimum payoff)										A's strategy
		1	2	3	(2)	(4)	(6)	(8)	(10)	(12)	(14)	(16)	(18)	(20)	
A	1	2	1	3	1	3	4	7	9	⑫ *	13	15	16	19	$\frac{1}{10}$
	2	4	1	1	1	⑤	6	7	⑪	12	13	⑰	18	19	$\frac{3}{10}$
	3	1	3	2	③	4	⑦	⑨	10	12	⑮	16	⑲	㉑	$\frac{6}{10}$

A's choice (maximum payoff)

(1)	2	①	3
(3)	③	4	5
(5)	7	⑤	6
(7)	8	8	⑧*
(9)	⑨	11	10
(11)	13	12	⑪
(13)	15	⑬	14
(15)	⑯	16	16
(17)	20	⑰	17
(19)	21	20	⑲

B's strategy

$\frac{3}{10}$ $\frac{4}{10}$ $\frac{3}{10}$

*When the values are equal, use a random number to make the choice.

Expected value:

Upper bound: $\frac{21}{10}$

Lower bound: $\frac{19}{10}$

If we run the experiment for many iterations, the result will come out as the following:

A's strategy: $\left(\dfrac{1}{4}, \dfrac{1}{4}, \dfrac{2}{4}\right)$

B's strategy: $\left(\dfrac{1}{3}, \dfrac{1}{3}, \dfrac{1}{3}\right)$

Expected value: $\frac{1}{4} \times 2 + \frac{1}{4} \times 4 + \frac{2}{4} \times 1 = 2$

or $\qquad\qquad\quad \frac{1}{3} \times 2 + \frac{1}{3} \times 1 + \frac{1}{3} \times 3 = 2$

Computer simulation is also used to help analyze business strategies through the play of a business game. Usually the game describes several oligopolistic firms in the same industry competing for the market by manipulating the price, output, and investment. Figure 9-20 is a flow diagram describing how generally such a game is structured. First, the parameters of the general economic conditions and trends are estimated and read into the computer. Second, the initial history of each firm, which includes production capacity, inventory, market share, etc., is read into the machine. Then the players, who represent each firm, put in their decisions for the period. The decisions may include prices, product type, production quantities, marketing expenditure, capital investment, research and development expenditure, and the like. After that the computer takes over; it simulates and computes the operation results of the firms during the period, such as new plant capacity, production cost, market share, inventory cost, actual sales, total revenue, administrative expenses, and total profit, according to several preprogrammed rules and equations, including random disturbances. The results are printed out and distributed to the players. The players study the results and make new decisions for the next period. This process continues for several periods. The exercise is useful both for students who are trained to be managers (for it provides them with decision-making experience) and for business managers who may need some a priori knowledge of the quantitative relationship of some of the important economic factors, such as, how the sales and profit of the firm change when price is increased 10 percent at the same time marketing expenditure is increased by $1 million.

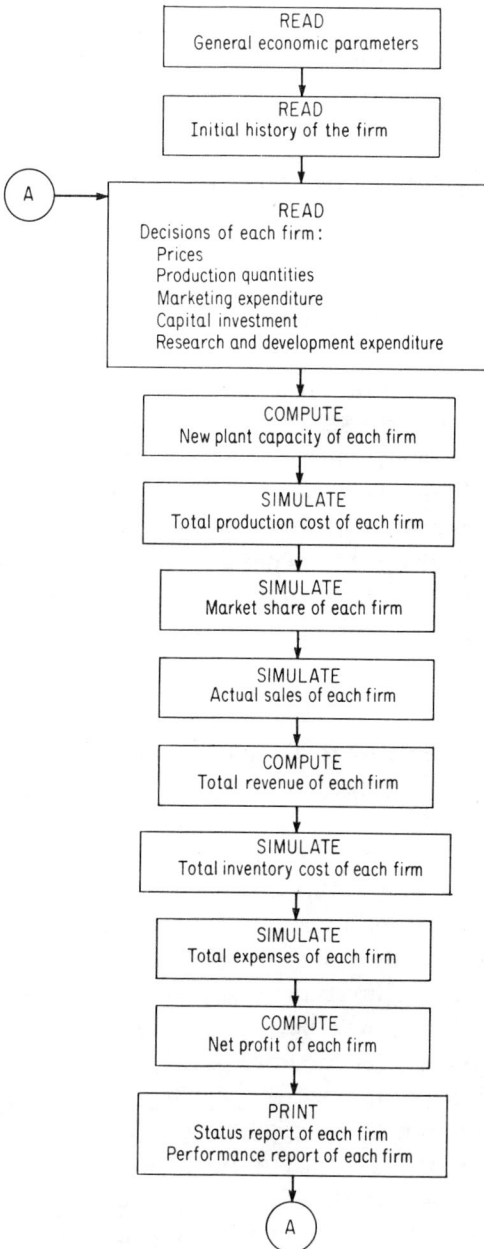

Fig. 9-20.   Flow diagram of a business
game model.

Simulation of this kind is not limited to business competition. It is also applied to military confrontation, international trade conflicts, and many other situations of similar nature.

ANOTHER APPROACH OF SIMULATING ECONOMIC SYSTEMS

In this Section a different approach in simulating a general economic system is introduced. It is based on mathematical economic theories. The relationships among the components or variables of an economic system is first formulated into a set of simultaneous difference equations. Then econometric method is applied to estimate the values of the parameters of the equations from sample data. Finally, computer-simulation methods are used to generate the time paths of the dependent or endogenous variables of the system by supplying the random-disturbance terms. The following is an illustration of the procedure.

The Problem

Economists are primarily interested in the optimum allocation of scarce resources. In any community, the social demands are various and unlimited, but the resources available to satisfy these demands are always limited. Facing the administrator or the management is the important question: which is the best way to allocate these limited resources? For an economic region, many of the commitments or projects necessarily have to be long-range. It will be costly or sometimes impossible to change them after they are initiated or implemented. Since the welfare of many employees is involved, extreme caution must be taken at the beginning to decide which set of economic programs, once implemented, will yield the maximum benefit for all. Social science is said to be different from natural science in that the latter can be controlled and experimented with in a laboratory but the former cannot. However, with the invention and improvement of the electronic digital computer we may utilize its fast and accurate computational capability to do some pseudocontrol experiments in the area of social science. Here a computer model for evaluating regional development programs is introduced to illustrate the concept and methodology of using computer-simulation techniques for describing and projecting the intricate dynamic economic relationship among components of a macroeconomy involving a set of economic development programs without actually implementing these programs.

The Model

A model is an abstraction of the real system. With different viewpoints or approaches, different models may be constructed as representations of the same system. The approach suggested here is first constructing a very simplified model to give a rough overall representation of the system so that the general framework will be set. Later on, more detailed descriptions of the components and relationships may be added to make the model more representative and more capable of yielding answers to various questions.

From an economist's point of view, a macroeconomy may be represented by the diagram in Fig. 9-21.

In the model, the assumptions are that the scale of production is affected by the interest rate and the feedback of

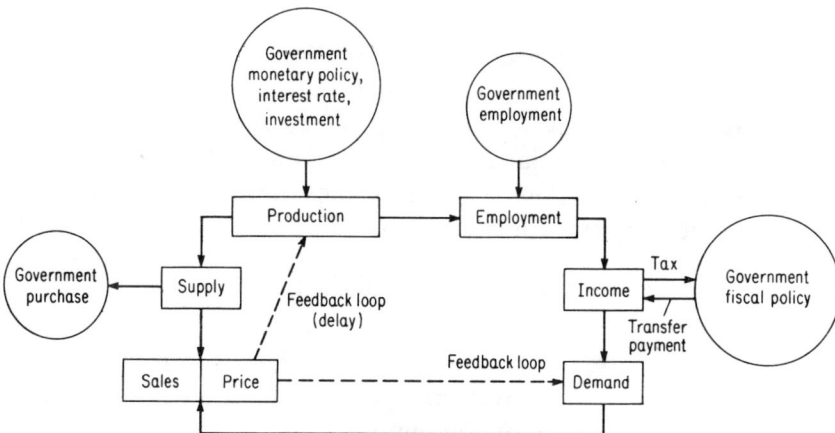

Fig. 9-21

the prices of the transactions made. Employment is contributed by the production sector of the economy and the government's employment. Employment generates income, and total income is reduced by tax and increased by government's transfer payments to arrive at the total amount of disposable income. Demand is a function of income representing the consumers' behavior. Economists refer to this as *income elasticity of demand*. Demand is also affected by the market prices of the goods and services. On the supply side, production generates goods and services. A portion of the goods and services will be siphoned out of the consumer's market by government purchases. The remaining portion goes to the market. The market-clearing condition determines the final sales volume. And thus the economic cycle is completed.

In Fig. 9-21 the rectangular boxes represent variables endogenous to the model, with employment, income, and price as the target variables. In the circles are the exogenous variables, which affect the endogenous variables but are not affected by them. Their values are determined outside of the model, and they are identified as the control variables through which the government is trying to steer the economy to the desirable objectives—full employment, steady growth of income, stable prices, or a mixture of all. The dotted lines are the feedback loops. The market prices of goods and services will affect the demand. Economists describe this behavior relationship as the *price elasticity of demand*. The market prices also will affect the producers' behavior, which the economists call the *price elasticity of supply*. However, because production usually requires a lead time, this relationship is a lagged relationship, or a *delayed relationship*. The variables and equations of the model may be expressed as follows.

Control variables exogenous to the model

1.	Tax rate	Tr
2.	Transfer payments	Tp
3.	Government employment	Ge
4.	Government purchase	Gp
5.	Interest rate	I

Target variables endogenous to the model

      1. Employment E

      2. Income—disposable Y

      3. Price P

Other endogenous variables

      1. Production Pd

      2. Demand D

      3. Supply S

      4. Tax T

Initial condition

$$P_0$$

The Model

1. $(Pd)_t = aP_{t-1} + \dfrac{b}{I_t} + u_t$ Producers' behavior

2. $S_t = (Pd)_t - (Gp)_t$

3. $E_t = c(Pd)_t + (Ge)_t$

4. $T_t = (T_r)_t(dE_t)$

5. $Y_t = dE_t - T_t + (Tp)_t$

6. $D_t = eY_t + \dfrac{g}{P_t} + v_t$ Consumers' behavior

7. $D_t = S_t + w_t$ Market-clearing condition

Where a, b, c, d, e, and g are the parameters, their values may be estimated from empirical data by some econometrics method, such as the least-squares and maximum-likelihood methods. The symbols u, v, and w represent random errors, and may be assumed to be normally distributed with zero means and constant variances.

From Eq. 7,

$$D_t = S_t + w_t$$

$$eY_t + \frac{g}{P_t} + v_t = (Pd)_t - (Gp)_t + w_t$$

$$= aP_{t-1} + \frac{b}{I_t} - (Gp)_t + u_t + w_t$$

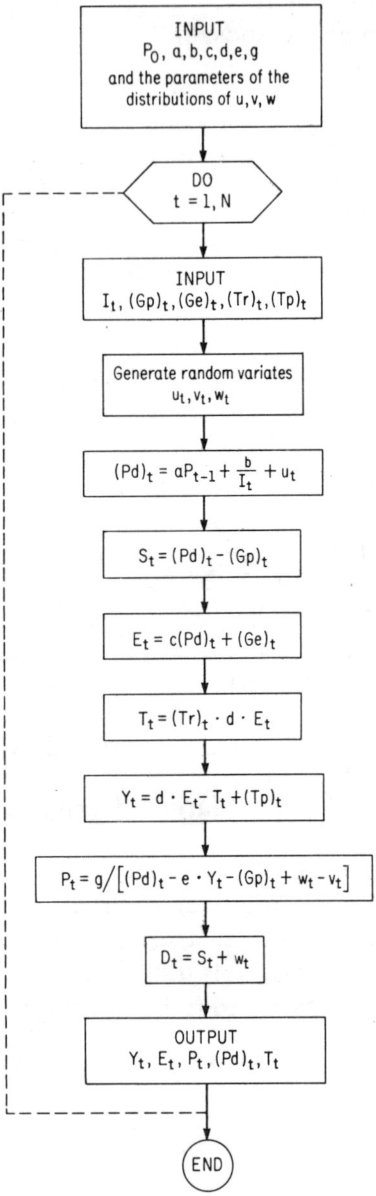
INPUT
P0, a, b, c, d, e, g
and the parameters of the distributions of u, v, w
DO
t = 1, N
INPUT
It, (Gp)t, (Ge)t, (Tr)t, (Tp)t
Generate random variates
ut, vt, wt
(Pd)t = aPt-1 + b/It + ut
St = (Pd)t - (Gp)t
Et = c(Pd)t + (Ge)t
Tt = (Tr)t · d · Et
Yt = d · Et - Tt + (Tp)t
Pt = g/[(Pd)t - e · Yt - (Gp)t + wt - vt]
Dt = St + wt
OUTPUT
Yt, Et, Pt, (Pd)t, Tt
END

Fig. 9-22

Simplifying, we get

$$P_t = \frac{g}{aP_{t-1} + \dfrac{b}{I_t} - eY_t - (Gp)_t + u_t + w_t - v_t}$$

Computer Simulation

The model then can be expressed by the block diagram of Fig. 9-22. First, the initial price and the parameters of all the equations and the probability distribution of the error terms are read into the computer. Then, for every iteration, which indicates one time period, a set of values of the control variables representing the suggested package of economic program is read in. After that, the simulation process starts by first generating sample values of the random errors and then tracing out the time paths of all the endogenous variables. By checking the output values of the target variables such as income, employment, and price in several consecutive periods, the decision maker can decide the desirability or acceptability of a given package of economic programs.

Further Extension of the Model

Computer-simulation models may be used to evaluate economic programs as illustrated by the simplified model above. They may provide knowledge of economic relationship between government-initiated programs and the activities of a market economy similar to the laboratory research experiments of natural science. The model may be designed in such a way to answer the particular questions that an economist wants to ask. A simple model of general description may have particular details added to suit particular purposes. For example, production and employment may be classified into various industrial sectors of the region. Taxes may be divided into business income tax and personal income tax, and demand may be specified as demand for different industrial products or services. The model may be opened up by including export and import sectors in it. Thus computer simulation may well be an effective tool for evaluating economic programs and planning economic development.

DIFFERENCE BETWEEN THE INDUSTRIAL SIMULATION MODELS AND THE ECONOMETRIC SIMULATION MODELS

Because we lack adequate terms for the simulation frameworks described in the previous two sections, we just call the former, *industrial simulation models* and the latter *econometric simulation models.* In the former we emphasize the finding of causal relations between various components of the system and making sensitivity-analysis experiments which may lead to rational business policy recommendations. In the latter, we more or less make extrapolations into the future based on known data. By their very nature, econometric simulation models may be only useful as a guidance for short-range economic forecasting.

SUMMARY

The computer is one of the greatest inventions of this century. Since its advent, its impact is felt in almost every area of research. Its major characteristics are its fast computing speed free of human drudgery and errors, and its vast storage space called *memory.* Its major applications are in the areas of data processing, numerical analysis, and computer simulation. In data processing, the computer with its accessories can store vast amounts of information, arrange and categorize them in proper order, and then permit the stored information to be retrieved instantaneously. The computer also can sort, collate, and tabulate numerical and alphabetical information with incredible speed. In numerical analysis the computer can make millions of computations in an unbelievably short period of time, thus yielding approximate numerical answers to problems for which analytical solutions cannot be found. In computer simulation, the computer can be programmed to simulate a real situation and perform simulated experiments in compressed time so that researchers can observe the causes and effects of related events without actually experimenting on the real system. This feature has found many applications in the analysis and design of systems. In cases where we do not know clearly the relationships among the components in a system, we cannot formulate mathematical models, which are the prerequisites for obtaining analytical solutions. However, we can use computer-simulation models to describe the complexities of the system. By experimenting with the model, we may learn more about the relationships so that eventually mathematical models can be constructed and analytical solutions can be sought. Thus computer simulation and analytical methods can be used in complementary fashion while studying an economic system. Computer simulation also applies to business games which simulate the oligopolistic competition in business, and to military games where they can evaluate the effectiveness of alternative strategies.

Computers are also used in real-time applications, which follows the direction of automating all routine operations in a system or organization.

PROBLEMS

1. What is a computerized information system? What are the important concepts involved in designing a computerized information system? Suggest ways to improve the current status of hardware (machinery), software (programs), and personnel in operating a computerized information system.

2. Draw a block diagram showing the computer logic of arranging the information on a deck of cards in descending order according to the identification number on each card.

3. Given a function $y = x^2 + 2x + 4$ find the approximate area under the curve from $x = 1$ to $x = 5$ by summing the rectangular areas from $x = 1$ to $x = 5$ by the increment of .01. Draw a block diagram showing the computer logic.

4. Draw a block diagram showing the computer logic of simulating the moves of three players according to given number of alternatives and given strategies (probabilities of making the choices), computing the average gain or loss of each player associated with a particular set of strategies and given payoffs after n moves.

5. Describe the major steps in a computer-simulation process and indicate what statistical methods are required in each step. Give simple explanation of these statistical methods.

6. Draw a block diagram showing how a firm can experiment with different inventory policies by using a computer-simulation model with known demand distribution, storage capacity, and cost structure.

7. Draw a block diagram showing how a factory can experiment with different maintenance policies by using a computer simulation model with known time distributions of machine-breakdown intervals, service-time intervals, and cost of production delay versus cost of additional mechanics or early replacement of machines.

8. Design a simulation model consisting of a purchasing department, a production department, and a marketing department. Simulate both the physical flows of raw materials, intermediate products, final products through the system, and the information flow among the three departments. Use a block diagram to describe the model.

9. Design a business game consisting of n players, wherein each makes periodic decisions on price, output, marketing expenditure, and capital investment. The measurement of success is the cumulated net profit. Use a block diagram to describe the logic of the game.

10. Design a model simulating a national economy. Show how fiscal and monetary policies will affect the gross national product, per capita income, employment, and distribution of wealth and income among the population. Use a block diagram to describe the model, discuss the feasibility of making the model operational and provide validation of the simulation results.

SELECTED REFERENCES

Bonin, C. P., *Simulation of Information and Decision Systems in the Firm.* Englewood Cliffs, N.J.: Prentice-Hall, Inc., 1963.

Borko, H., *Computer Applications in the Behavioral Science.* Englewood Cliffs, N.J.: Prentice-Hall, Inc., 1962

Bourne, C. P., *Methods of Information Handling.* New York: John Wiley & Sons, Inc., 1963.

Chorafas, D. N., *Systems and Simulation.* New York: Academic Press, Inc., 1965.

Forrester, J., *Industrial Dynamics.* Cambridge, Mass.: M.I.T. Press, 1961.

Gordon, G., *A General Purpose System Simulator.* IBM Advanced Systems Development Division, October 1961.

Head, R. V., *Real-Time Business Systems.* New York: Holt, Rinehart and Winston, Inc., 1964.

IBM Application Program: General Purpose Systems Simulator III (#B20-0001-0). White Plains, N.Y.: IBM Data Processing Division.

Ledley, R. S., *Programming and Utilizing Digital Computers.* New York: McGraw-Hill Book Company, 1962.

Markowitz, H. M., B. Hausner, and H. W. Karr, *SIMSCRIPT: A Simulation Programming Language.* Memorandum RM-3310-PR. The RAND Corporation, Santa Monica, Calif., November 1962.

Martin, J., *Programming Real-Time Computing Systems.* Englewood Cliffs, N.J.: Prentice-Hall, Inc., 1965.

McMillan, C., and R. F. Gonzales, *Systems Analysis.* Homewood, Ill.: Richard D. Irwin, Inc., 1965.

Naylor, T. H., J. L. Balintfy, D. S. Burdick, and K. Chu, *Computer Simulation Techniques.* New York: John Wiley & Sons, Inc., 1966.

Orcutt, G. H., M. Greenberger, J. Korbel, and A. H. Rivlin, *Micro-analysis of Socio-Economic Systems.* New York: Harper & Row Publishers, 1961.

Prager, W., and W. Freiberger (eds.), *Applications of Digital Computers.* Boston: Blaisdell Publishing Company, 1963.

Simulation. Technology Series, Corporate Communication BRT-12. System Development Corporation, Santa Monica, Calif., 1965.

Wilde, D. J., *Optimum Seeking Methods.* Englewood Cliffs, N.J.: Prentice-Hall, Inc., 1963.

Williams, W. F., *Principles of Automoted Information Retrieval.* Elmhurst, Ill.: Business Press, 1965.

chapter 10

Critical Path Method; Programming Evaluation and Review Techniques (PERT)

In a large system, there are many jobs which are inter-related. A complicated job usually consists of many components. A job is completely done only when all its components are completed. Some of the components, however, cannot be worked on simultaneously. They usually have to follow a given sequence. For example, to build a house you have to lay the foundation, erect the frame, put on a roof, and finish the walls before you can start working on the interior. To develop an area, you first have to clear the ground, built roads, put in sewerage lines, and connect electric power and gas before you can expect factories and houses to be built in the area. Thus, in order to be efficient with respect to time and cost, an overall plan has to be drawn in order to complete the job in the shortest possible time or in a specified time span and at minimum cost.

CRITICAL PATH METHOD

One of the methods used in this kind of analysis is the critical path method. We first list all the component jobs according to their proper sequence. The completion of a component job is called an *event*, which is related to a point in time. From the completion of one component job to the completion of the subsequent component job is called an activity, which is related to a time interval, being the time required to carry out the activity. Thus we have an overall network and events joined by activities. Then we estimate the required time for each activity and review the whole network to find the longest time path from the first event to the last event. The path is called the *critical path*. It also indicates the time required to complete the whole job. If we can find some way to shorten any part of the critical path until the original path is no longer the shortest path in the network we will in fact be cutting down the required time to complete the job.

PROGRAMMING EVALUATION AND REVIEW TECHNIQUE

PERT (Programming Evaluation and Review Technique) is very similar to the critical path method. The only difference is that in the critical path method there is only one time estimate for each activity. But PERT offers three estimates for each activity, an optimistic time estimate A, a pessimistic time estimate B, and the most likely time estimate M. The distribution of the time interval is assumed to be a beta distribution with mean

$$t_e = \frac{A + 4M + B}{6}$$

and variance

$$v = \left(\frac{B - A}{6}\right)^2$$

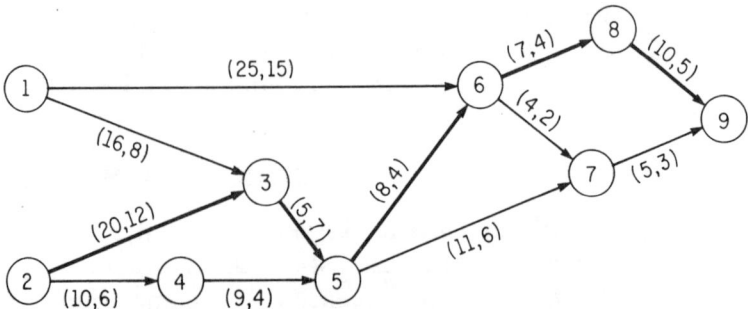

Fig. 10-1

Example 1

Suppose there is a job which consists of 9 events, the activities between the events, their time estimates and variances are as the following. We need to analyze the job, estimate the required time to complete the job, and find ways to shorten the time requirement so that the total cost may be reduced.

Events	Immediate Prerequisites	Activities	t_e	v_e
1	—	—	—	—
2	—	—	—	—
3	1,2	1–3	16	8
		2–3	20	12
4	2	2–4	10	6
5	3,4	3–5	15	7
		4–5	9	4
6	1,5	1–6	25	15
		5–6	8	4
7	5,6	5–7	11	6
		6–7	4	2
8	6	6–8	7	4
9	7,8	7–9	5	3
		8–9	10	5

The network of the job may be expressed as shown in Fig. 10-1.

Next we compute the time required from the inception of the job (events 1 and 2) to the completion of each event in the network. Using T_e to denote the require time (the longest time path from the inception to each event) and V_e to denote the total variance, we obtain the following:

Event	Longest Time Path	T_e	V_e	T_1	Slack
1	—	0	0	$20 - 16 = 4$	$4 - 0 = 4$
2	—	0	0	0	0
3	2–3	20	12	20	0
4	2–4	10	6	$35 - 9 = 26$	$26 - 10 = 16$
5	2–3–5	35	19	35	0
6	2–3–5–6	43	23	43	0
7	2–3–5–6–7	47	25	$60 - 5 = 55$	$55 - 47 = 8$
8	2–3–5–6–8	50	27	50	0
9	2–3–5–6–8–9	60	32	60	0

Thus the critical path is (2–3–5–6–8–9), the estimated total time required to complete the job is 60 and the estimated variance 32. Those events lie on the critical path have no slack time, but those not on the critical path have slack time. The slack time for those events are computed by first computing the latest expected time that each event can be allowed to occur without disturbing the completion time of the final event of the network. (In this case, event 9 is the final event.) Use T_l to denote the time span, the computation is made in the table. (Note that for those events lying on the critical path, $T_l = T_e$.) From the analysis we may make the following recommendations.

1. We may move some of the personnel or facilities from those activities which have slacks, namely (1–3, slack = 4), (1–6, slack = 43 − 25 = 18), (2–4–5, slack = 35 − 10 − 9 = 16), (5–7–9, slack = 60 − 5 − 11 − 35 = 9) and (6–7–9, slack = 60 − 5 − 4 − 43 = 8), to those activities lie on the critical path in order to shorten the critical time path so as to complete the entire job at an earlier date.

2. We may remove some of the personnel or facilities from those activities which have slacks, the job will still be completed in the same time span 60, but the total cost will be reduced.

TIME-COST TRADE-OFF

Sometimes when the expected project completion date is too late to satisfy our demand it may be possible to increase personnel and facilities along the critical path in order to shorten the project duration. However, the normal cost might be increased in a nonlinear fashion. This new cost, called *crash cost*, may represent overtime or holiday pay, a higher rental for manufacturing equipment, or the like. Subjective evaluation has to be imposed upon the time-cost trade-off to find a combination of project duration and total cost which is considered as optimum. The information which is required to make such a decision comprises the following.

1. *Data on Feasible Time Cost Trade-off Points.* The activity duration and its respective cost should be plotted for each activity as shown in Fig. 10-2. Because of the indivisibility of factors of production, the feasible points are generally only a finite num-

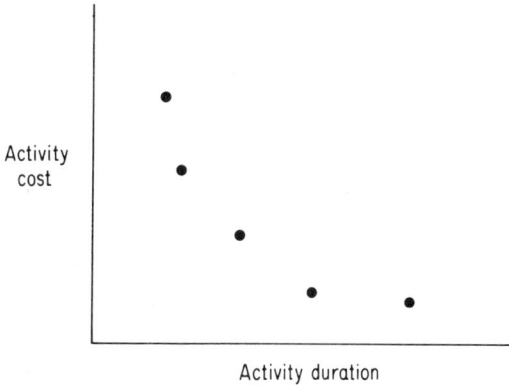

Activity cost

Activity duration

Fig. 10-2

ber, not in continuous form. If overtime or additional equipment and personnel are required to speed up the activities, then shorter activity duration usually corresponds with higher cost.

2. *Cost Rate of Buying Time.* When we join the feasible time-cost trade-off points by straight-line segments, the slope of the segments represents the cost rate of buying time between two points (see Fig. 10-3).

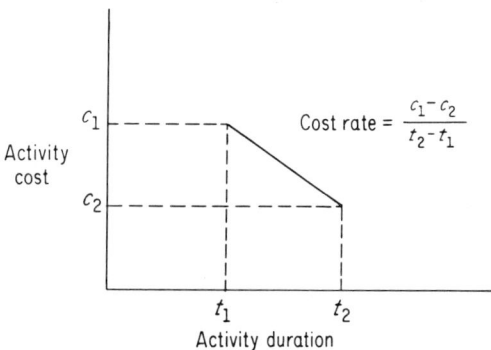

Activity cost

$$\text{Cost rate} = \frac{c_1 - c_2}{t_2 - t_1}$$

Activity duration

Fig. 10-3

Example 1

$c_1 = \$1,000, c_2 = \$600 \qquad t_1 = 2 \text{ weeks}, t_2 = 6 \text{ weeks}$

The cost rate is

$$\frac{1000 - 600}{6 - 2} = \$100 \text{ per week}$$

When the information is gathered, then the rule is
1. If the network has a single critical path, consider all activities on the path, select the activity that has the minimum cost rate and do the cost-time trade-off first. Follow the procedure until the time length of the original critical path has been shortened to equal the next critical path.
2. If the network has two or more critical paths, separate those activities on the critical paths into two groups. The first group contains those activities common to all critical paths, and the second group contains those activities not common to the critical paths. We then find the lowest cost rate among the activities in the first group and compare it with the cost rate of likely combination of feasible activities on different critical paths in the second group (based on the heuristic or "discovery" approach) to find the minimum cost-time trade-off accordingly.

Example 2
Suppose the expected time to complete the activities in a project network under normal conditions is as shown in Fig. 10-4 and also that the feasible cost rates are as given for

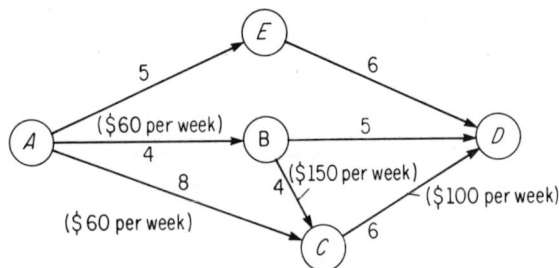

Fig. 10-4

the activities on the two critical paths. The two critical paths are

$$A \rightarrow B - C \rightarrow D \quad E(t) = 4 + 4 + 6 = 14$$
$$A \rightarrow C \rightarrow D \quad\quad E(t) = 8 + 6 = 14$$

The common activity for the two critical paths is $C \to D$, and its cost rate is $100 per week.

Now among the not-common activities, $B \to C$ is out of the question. (Time-cost trade-off rate is $150 per week.) Consider the combination of $A \to B$ and $A \to C$. In order to reduce the total project completion date for a week, we need to reduce both $A \to B$ and $A \to C$ a week which will cost $2 \times 60 = 120. Since it is greater than $100, we should choose to reduce the common activity $C \to D$, if we are willing to trade $100 for a week's time. (*Note:* We may reduce $C \to D$ only by 3 weeks at the maximum in this example, because if the reduction time exceeds 3 weeks, $A \to E \to D$ will become critical.)

SUMMARY

The critical Path Method and Program Evaluation and Review Technique are both designed to control the progress of a project by describing the project as a network of events and activities. They are most useful in supervising Federal government military projects that are contracted to civilian firms. They help to pinpoint the bottlenecks and slacks in the entire operation from the inception to the completion of a program. PERT is different from the Critical Path Method in that it not only gives three time estimates (pessimistic estimate, most likely estimate, optimistic estimate) but also provides a variance for each activity, the estimate used in the analysis being computed from these values by assuming that the distribution of the estimates is a beta distribution. PERT/cost gives time and cost trade-off ratios. If we need to speed up some activities so that the entire project can be completed at an earlier date, we know how much additional cost is involved. In view of PERT's ability to review, at all time during the progress of the job, the expected completion date and the expected program cost so that early adjustment or corrective action can be made, the Federal government now requires all contracting firms to submit PERT control programs along with the job specifications.

PROBLEMS

1. Given the events and activity time estimates of a project as shown in the accompanying figure, find the critical path and slacks between all the paths.

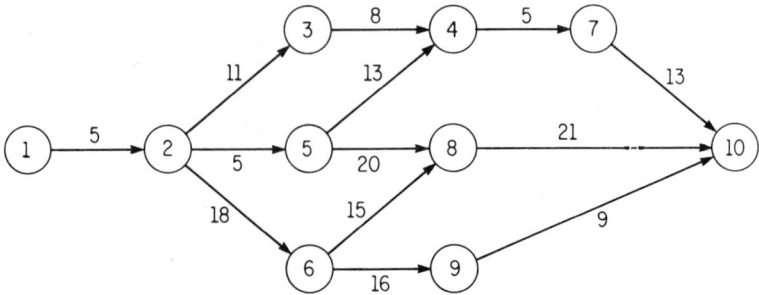

Prob. 10-1

2. Given the events and the three time estimates of the project shown in the accompanying figure, find (1) the expected time for each activity and the variance, (2) the critical path and the expected project completion date, and (3) the latest expected time which a completion event can be allowed to occur without disturbing the expected project completion date.

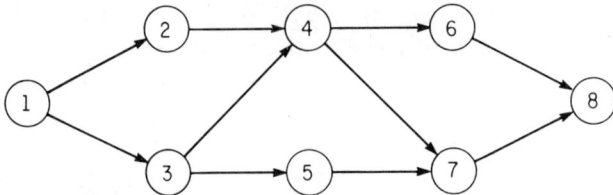

Activity	1-2	1-3	2-4	3-4	3-5	4-6	4-7	5-7	6-8	7-8
Optimistic estimate ----	5	6	8	9	7	3	4	10	5	2
Most likely estimate -----	7	7	10	11	10	4	5	12	6	3
Pessimistic estimate ---	10	11	12	15	13	7	8	15	8	5

Prob. 10-2

3. A contractor planning to build a house listed all the activities and the estimated time and cost required to complete these activities as follows:

Activity		Time Estimate	Cost Estimate	Prerequisite activities
Level the ground...............	(A)	7 days	$1,000	—
Transport bricks and cement to the site	(B)	5	500	—
Lay foundation	(C)	10	2,000	A,B
Erect frame.....................	(D)	15	3,000	C
Put up roof.....................	(E)	8	1,000	D
Plumbing.......................	(F)	20	1,500	C
Electric wiring..................	(G)	15	1,000	E
Gasline installation.............	(H)	16	1,000	E
Interior carpentry..............	(I)	30	3,000	F,G,H
Painting	(J)	15	2,000	I

Find the critical path and slacks between all the paths.

4. In Prob. 3 the contractor will be awarded a bonus of 20 percent of the total cost if he can complete the project in 90 days and $300 per day less if the completion date is later than the 90th day. What can the contractor do to shorten the completion date of the following activities at the extra cost specified?

Activities	Minimum Time	Extra Cost (% of original cost) per Day Shortened
A	5 days	.1
D	10 days	.1
F	15 days	.2
G	10 days	.2
H	12 days	.2
I	20 days	.2

What is the expected time and cost for the project?

SELECTED REFERENCES

Archibald, R. D., and R. L. Villoria, *Network-Based Management Systems (PERT/CPM)*. New York: John Wiley & Sons, Inc., 1967.

DOD and NASA Guide: PERT Cost Systems Design. Washington, D.C.: Office of the Secretary of Defense and National Aeronautics and Space Administration, 1962.

Federal Electric Corp., *A Programmed Introduction to PERT.* New York: John Wiley & Sons, Inc., 1963.

Johnson, R. A., F. E. Kast, and J. E. Rosenzweig, *The Theory and Management of Systems.* 2d ed. New York: McGraw-Hill Book Company, 1967.

Moder, J. J., and C. R. Philips, *Project Management with CPM and PERT.* New York: Reinhold Publishing Corporation, 1964.

Shaffer, L. R., J. B. Kitter, and W. L. Meyer, *Critical Path Method.* New York: McGraw-Hill Book Company, 1965.

chapter 11

Cost-Benefit Analysis and PPBS

COST-BENEFIT ANALYSIS

As we have frequently noted, economists and businessmen are interested in the maximization of profit and minimization of cost. If the cost of producing a product or providing a service can be reduced and the benefit can be extended to the consumers through pricing, everyone will be better off. Also, if the government can provide public services with less expenditures which results in tax reduction, the entire community will be benefited. Here we attempt a systematic analysis of the cost and benefit structures in an economic or business system. To do a cost-benefit analysis we may approach the problem in three different ways: (1) benefit is held constant, and we attempt to minimize the cost required to achieve the benefit; (2) cost is held constant, and we attempt to maximize the benefit achievable; or (3) we attempt to minimize cost and maximize benefit at the same time. In public finance, we usually estimate the available revenue for the next year and then try to allocate the sum to various projects so that the maximum benefit may be achieved. In operating a private business we usually try to minimize cost and maximize sales revenue at the same time. Economists generally use isoquant or equal output curves and isocost or equal cost curves to analyze the cost-benefit relationships. For example, a producer uses two factors of production—labor and capital—to produce a product. If the factors of production are mutually substitutable and if the marginal productivity of one factor diminishes when the other is held constant, then the isoquant and isocost curves will assume the shapes indicated in Fig. 11-1.

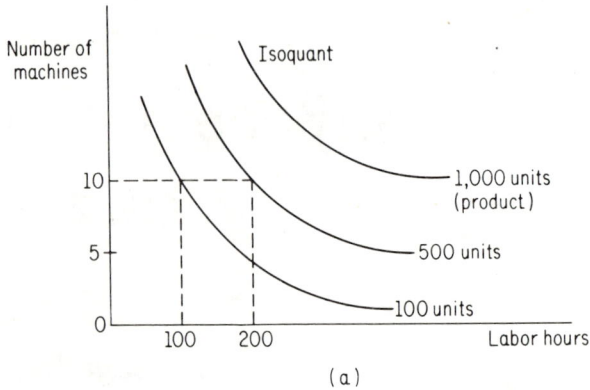

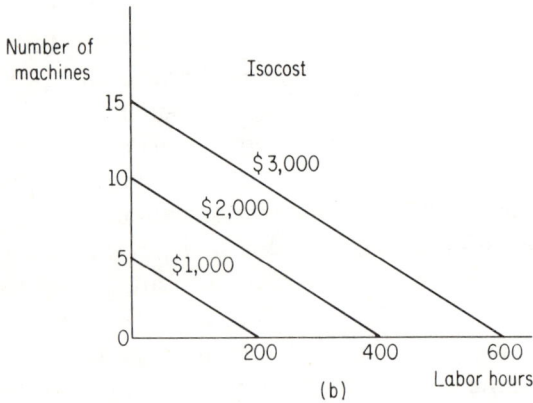

Fig. 11-1

The least-cost factors or resources mix to produce a given amount of output therefore will occur at the point where one of the isocost curves tangents to the isoquant which represents the given output (see Fig. 11-2a.) and the maximum output that a given amount of fund can produce will be at the point where the isocost curve, which represents the given amount of fund, tangents to one of the isoquant curves (the highest one that can be reached) (see Fig. 11-2b).

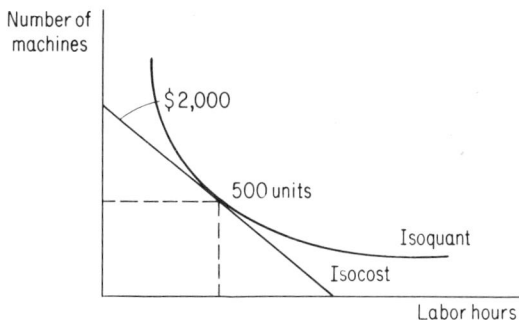

(a)

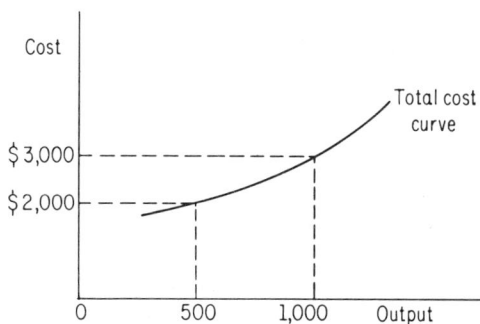

(b)

Fig. 11-2

This, however, is a static analysis in that time has not been taken into consideration. To be more accurate in measuring the size of the benefit, economists would recommend using a discount rate to compute the present value of the benefit if the benefit is obtained in installments over an extended period of time. (If cost is incurred in different time periods in the future, the cost also has to be discounted and transformed into present value for evaluation.) The reasons for discounting anticipated future benefit are (1) the limited life span of a human being, (2) the uncertainty about future income and future wants, and (3) the technical superiority of present goods, which implies that the present goods may be used as capital goods to produce more goods in the future. The choice of the proper discount rate to use is open to argument; some use the market interest rate as a reference and others make estimates about the rate of marginal efficiency of capital. Once the discount rate is selected, the present value of the expected benefit can be computed.

The formula for computing the present value is as follows: Suppose the benefit will last for n periods and in each period the estimated benefit is $b_i (i = 1,2,\ldots,n)$, and that the discount rate is r. Then the present values ($P_i, i = 1,2,\ldots,n$) for the benefit received in the n periods are

$$p_1 = b_1$$

$$p_2 = \frac{b_2}{1 + r}, \text{ since } p_2 + p_2 r = b_2 \quad \text{or} \quad p_2(1 + r) = b_2$$

$$p_3 = \frac{b_3}{(1 + r)^2}, \text{ since } (p_3 + p_3 r) + (p_3 + p_3 r)r$$
$$= b_3 \quad \text{or} \quad p_3(1 + r)^2 = b_3$$

$$\vdots$$

$$p_n = \frac{b_n}{(1 + r)^{n-1}}, \text{ since } p_n(1 + r)^{n-1} = b_n$$

The present value of the total benefit, therefore, is

$$P = p_1 + p_2 + \cdots + p_n$$
$$= b_1 + \frac{b_2}{1 + r} + \frac{b_3}{(1 + r)^2} + \cdots + \frac{b_n}{(1 + r)_{n-1}}$$

This is a geometric series if

$$b_1 = b_2 = b_3 \cdots = b_n = b$$

and we let

$$\frac{1}{1 + r} = u$$

Then

$$P = b + bu + bu^2 + bu^3 + \cdots + bu^{n-1}$$

and

$$uP = bu + bu^2 + bu^3 + bu^4 + \cdots + bu^n$$
$$P - uP = b - bu^n$$
$$P = \frac{b(1 - u^n)}{1 - u}$$

If the number of periods (n) approaches infinity, u^n approaches zero:

$$P = \frac{b}{1 - u}$$

$$= \frac{b}{1 - \dfrac{1}{1 + r}}$$

$$= \frac{b(1 + r)}{r}$$

As a numerical example, let $b = 100$ and $r = .1$. Then

$$P = \frac{100(1 + .1)}{.1} = 1,100$$

which indicates that with a significantly large discount rate such as 10 percent, the incomes in the distant future, say beyond the 64th period, have very small present values. In the following, we give two numerical examples to illustrate the procedure of cost and benefit analysis.

Example 1

The Vanline Company owns a fleet of trucks. The purchase price of each truck is $10,000, and the estimated operating cost and resale price of the truck by years is as follows:

	1	2	3	4	5	6	7	8
Operating cost ...	$1,200	1,400	1,500	1,800	1,850	1,950	2,250	3,000
Resale price......	$8,000	7,000	6,000	5,500	4,500	3,500	2,000	1,500

Assume that to the Vanline Company the use value of a truck is the same through the years (equal benefit). When should the truck be replaced to minimize the total cost?

We first compile a table like the following to indicate the average cost per year of owning and operating a truck.

Year	Total Capital Cost (purchase price − resale price)	Total Operating Cost	Total Cost	Average Cost per Year
1	$2,000	$1,200	$3,200	$3,200
2	3,000	2,600	5,600	2,800
3	4,000	4,100	8,100	2,700
4	4,500	5,900	10,400	2,600
5	5,500	7,750	13,250	2,650
6	6,500	9,700	16,200	2,700
7	8,000	11,950	19,950	2,850
8	8,500	14,950	23,450	2,931

From the table we conclude the company should replace the truck at the end of the fourth year, so that the average cost per year will be at the minimum ($2,600 per truck per year).

Example 2

A government training program was implemented to retrain a thousand civil service workers. They were taught to process all the documents and accounting records through a computerized system. The following information was gathered in order to do a cost benefit analysis of the training program.

1. Total cost = Capital cost + Cost of supervision and instruction + Cost of material and supplies + Cost of subsidies to the trainees during the training period

   Capital cost (purchase price − resale price) $1,000,000
   Cost of supervision and instruction $500,000
   Cost of material and supplies.......................... $300,000
   Cost of subsidies to the trainees during
      training period....................................... $200,000

2. Trainee's income
   Average annual income with retraining............... $8,000
   Average annual income without retraining........... $5,000

3. Transfer payment (unemployment subsidies, etc.) paid to the trainees annually
   Before retraining $30,000
   After retraining....................................... $5,000

4. Estimated period during which the trainees will be benefited by the training............................. 10 years

   Discount rate to convert future income to present value... 10%

From the above information, we may compute the following data.

1. Total cost = 1,000,000 + 500,000 + 300,000 + 200,000
              = $2,000,000
   Average cost per trainee = 2,000,000/1000 = $2,000
2. Increase in annual income for average trainee
       = $8,000 − $5,000 = $3,000
3. Saving in annual transfer payment to the trainees
       = $30,000 − $5,000 = $25,000
4. Total benefit per year for the total system (i.e., government and labor) = $3,000 × 1,000 + $25,000 = $3,025,000

5. Time period for present value factor = 10
   Present value for the 10-year benefit for the total system:

$$P = \frac{b\left[1 - \left(\frac{1}{1+r}\right)^n\right]}{1 - \frac{1}{1+r}}$$

$$= \frac{3,025,000\left[1 - \left(\frac{1}{1\cdot1}\right)^{10}\right]}{1 - \frac{1}{1\cdot1}}$$

$$\approx \$20,460,000$$

6. Benefit and cost ratio of the program:

$$\frac{\text{Total benefit}}{\text{Total cost}} = \frac{20,460,000}{2,000,000} \approx 10.2 \text{ times}$$

PLANNING-PROGRAMMING-BUDGETING SYSTEM

The economists state that government participation or intervention in economic activities is sometimes required for several reasons.

1. Economic externalities of households and business establishments, sometimes referred to as *social benefits* and *social costs*. For example, the smoke coming out of factory chimneys or automobile exhaust pipes may not be the cost to a particular factory or vehicle owner but the cost to the community as a whole—a social cost. Or water-resource projects such as dams or irrigation systems, may benefit not a single household or factory only but an entire region—and thereby produce social benefits. However, the job of trying to eliminate the smoke or of building a dam cannot be expected to be undertaken by private persons; the government has to be responsible for the job.

2. Natural monopoly industries—such as public utilities, light and power companies, or railroads, require a large amount of initial fixed cost but the marginal cost of their products or services decreases rapidly thereafter. This fact destroys the market-free competition, since the exist-

ing firm can block new entries by decreasing its price. When the firm creates the monopoly situation, it can set prices above normal level. Here again government intervention is necessary to protect the interest of the consumer.

3. The Federal government is required to protect the nation from possible outside aggression and to improve the domestic welfare. Thus the government needs to produce military weapons, make necessary purchases, and design fiscal and monetary policies to accomplish these objectives.

Since large amounts of money go through the different levels of governments every year because of these expenditures, programs of collecting and spending the money have to be carefully constructed and decisions have to be made as to which package of programs is to be implemented when, where and by whom.

In order to improve the basis for major program decisions and to assure efficiency in public spending, on August 25, 1965, the U.S. Government issued a directive ordering all Federal agencies to apply the Planning-Programming-Budgeting System (PPBS). The procedure that Federal agencies are directed to follow is:

1. Identify the national goals with precision and on a continuing basis.
2. Choose among these goals the ones that are most urgent.
3. Search for alternative means of reaching those goals most effectively and at the least cost.
4. Inform themselves not merely on next year's costs but on the second, third, and subsequent years cost of the program.
5. Measure the performance of the programs to insure a dollar's worth of service for each dollar spent.

Apparently this kind of planning means an overall review of the national goals and the design of programs to reach these goals. The national goals in broader terms are to provide common defense for the nation and to promote the general welfare of society. Broken down in details, they include health, education, economic development, employment and income distribution, safety, and related programs. Since every government is constrained by the scarcity of resources, planning therefore is to find a proper balance or mixture of objectives to be accomplished and to determine the proper sequence in time to reach them. It is of utmost importance to ascertain the true demand of the people and let the people have proper representation or voices at the planning stage.

Programs are closely related to the objectives. They are defined in terms of what we want to achieve, and they spell out the details of actions or processes in mobilizing resources to accomplish these objectives. Their structure should permit comparison of alternative methods of achieving the objectives. The Bureau of the Budget uses the following classification terms to guide the development of programs.

1. *Program categories*, which are the groupings of agency programs which serve the same broad objectives, such as health, education, economic development, and the like.

2. *Program subcategories*, which are within program categories with narrower objectives, such as air- and water-pollution control, improvement of science education, or the training of nonskilled labor.

3. *Program elements*, which are subdivisions of program subcategories. They usually aim at some specific achievement that contributes to the broader objectives. Each program element is an integrated activity which combines personnel, equipment, and other facilities. Examples of various program elements are found in the control of air pollution in the New York City area, which will require a number of trained personnel, a supply of anti-air-pollution chemicals, specialized equipment, and legislation or regulations that will lead to the decrease of air-pollution problems.

Program budget is the financial expression of a program. It gives explicit consideration of the pursuit of objectives in terms of their economic costs both at present and in the future.

The major difference between the PPBS and the traditional budgeting approaches is that the former focuses on the output or objective achievement of the programs, whereas the latter tends to emphasize expenditure inputs.

Even though PPBS is conceptually superior to the traditional budgetary approach on account of its broader viewpoint and wider involvement, it encounters difficulties in implementation. First of all, it requires a broad and integrated information system which will provide all the necessary information at the time when they are needed. Secondly, it requires a model which can accurately describe the causes-and-effect relationship among the various activities and adequately predict future events. Thirdly, after we have reviewed our national goals and mapped out alternative programs of actions to reach the goals, we will have to decide which alternative is best and which program should be initiated first. Because of their different situations and different preferences, people have different viewpoints regarding benefit. For example, in using the cost-and-benefit analysis discussed above to evaluate different programs the discount rate is a topic for argument. People who are more concerned with their immediate benefit tend to accept a high discount rate. People who look ahead to the future tend to accept a low discount rate. A project that appears to be a good choice when a low discount rate is chosen may be economically unwise at a higher rate.

Besides discount rate there are other problems such as the quantification of the social utility or disutility of certain events, and the prediction of the events that are to occur following a collection of actions and interactions due to the implementation of certain programs. These can confuse the picture for the decision maker. Thus PPBS is a good approach, but the full realization of its advantages depends on the development of other things such as the improvement of information-system and prediction techniques and the ability to obtain an accurate consensus of the peoples' preferences.

The major justification for this kind of overall planning programs may arise from the defects spotted in the free-market competitive economy. The command economy, similar to that of Soviet Russia, has its gross shortcomings, such as the destruction of private incentives and the creation of a bureaucracy or even a dictatorship. However, it also has its advantages—mainly in the coordination of economic targets in a consistent manner. If well designed and properly administered, PPBS may enable us to enjoy the advantages of both economic systems while at the same time avoiding their shortcomings.

SUMMARY

In recent years, more seems to be expected from the Federal government to perform its duties of providing for the common defense and promoting the general welfare. The result is that the Federal budget is getting larger and larger. If there is no proper planning and control for such large sums of money, waste and misuse of government funds cannot be avoided. In view of the fact that when waste and misuse are discovered it is usually too late to take any corrective measures, the U.S. Government issued the administrative order calling for the adoption of the Planning Program Budgeting System (PPBS). The procedure requires that agencies first list all their major objectives, then search for alternative ways to accomplish these objectives, and by using cost-and-benefit analysis to evaluate these alternatives on a continuous and long-range basis. After the optimum programs are selected, the agency must find the means to implement them.

It is not an easy job, since the cost involved includes social cost and the benefit includes social benefit. It is difficult to ascertain what people consider social cost and social benefit and to try to quantify them. Also, people place different values on future cost and future benefit. As we all recognize, democracy is not a perfect system but it is the only system that may yield maximum welfare to the general public.

PROBLEMS

1. A salesman tries to decide when he should trade in his automobile. The puchase price of a new car of the same specifica-

tions is $4,000. The operating costs per year and resale prices of a used car are estimated as follows.

	Year				
	1	2	3	4	5
Operating cost	$500	$600	$700	$900	$1,000
Resale price	$2,000	$1,500	$1,000	$750	$600

When should the salesman trade in his car if he wants to minimize the average cost?

2. A production manager needs to purchase a particular kind of machine. There are two different makes of the machine available in the market, A and B. The price of A is $10,000 and its running costs are estimated at $1,000 each for the first five years, increasing by $300 per year in the subsequent years. The price of B is $8,000 and its running costs are estimated at $1,200 each for the first four years, increasing by $400 per year in the subsequent years. The capacity and resale values A and B are similar. If the expenses of borrowing money is 10 percent per annum, which machine should the production manager buy?

3. A city government has only enough funds to finance one of the following two programs.

   (a) Low-cost housing program, which will house 100 families. The rental will be $50 per family per month, the equivalent will cost $100 more in the market. The land and construction cost will be $1 million, the annual maintenance and supervision cost is estimated to be $3,000 in the first five years, increasing by $1,000 in the subsequent years. The benefit will last at least 20 years before the site will be replaced by other projects.

   (b) Retraining program, which will retrain 1,000 persons. The training period will be three months. During the training period each trainee will be given $200 in subsidies per month. The rentals for instruction rooms and equipment are estimated at $100,000. The costs of materials and supplies are estimated at $200,000. The salaries of the faculty and staff are estimated at $100,000. The annual income of the average trainee is expected to increase $2,000, and the skill learned will last at least ten years before becoming obsolete. In addition, the city is expected to save $25,000 per year for the next 10 years.

   Assume that the discount rate is 10 percent, which program should be implemented?

4. If the objective of a community is to maximize social utility and minimize social cost with the constraints of budget and income, how can this model be constructed as a mathematical programming model?

SELECTED REFERENCES

Grosse, R. N., and A. Proschan, "The Annual Cycle: Planning-Programming-Budgeting," in Stephen Enke (ed.), *Defense Management*. Englewood Cliffs, N.J.: Prentice-Hall, Inc., 1967, chap. 2.

Hitch, C. J., "A Planning-Programming-Budgeting System," in F. E. Kast and J. E. Rosenzweig (eds.), *Science, Technology, and Management*. New York: McGraw-Hill Book Company, 1963, chap. 6.

McKean, R. N., *Efficiency in Government through Systems Analysis*. New York: John Wiley & Sons, Inc., 1958.

Quade, E. S., *Systems Analysis Techniques for Planning-Programming-Budgeting*. P-3322. Santa Monica, Calif.: RAND Corporation, 1966.

Calculus for Optimization

A. TWO VARIABLES: $Y = f(X)$

The necessary condition is $dY/dX = 0$. When the first derivative is zero, the tangent of the curve at the point is parallel to the X-axis, thus the point is either a maximum point, a minimum point or a point of inflection.

The sufficient condition should include either (1) or (2) as follows:

(1) $\dfrac{d^2 Y}{dX^2} < 0$

When the second derivative is negative, the slope of the tangent is changing from positive to negative at the point; thus the point is a maximum point:

(2) $\dfrac{d^2 Y}{dX^2} > 0$

When the second derivative is positive, the slope of the tangent is changing from negative to positive at the point; thus the point is a minimum point:

(3) $\dfrac{d^2 Y}{dX^2} = 0$

When the second derivative equals zero, the sign of the slope of the tangent does not change at the point; thus the point is neither a maximum nor a minimum but a point of inflection.

If the function $f(X)$ is of first order, no maximum or minimum point exists unless the range of the function X is bounded. Then the points on the boundary are to be checked to find the maximum or minimum value of Y. If the function $f(X)$ is of second order, a unique maximum or minimum point exists. The relations $dY/dX = 0$ and $d^2Y/dX^2 < 0$ indicate a maximum point. The relations $dY/dX = 0$ and $d^2Y/dX^2 > 0$ indicate a minimum point. When the range of the function X is bounded, the maximum or minimum point may not fall in the range, if that is the case, the points on the boundary are to be examined to find the maximum or minimum value of Y.

If the function $f(X)$ is higher than second order, there may exist more than one local maximum point and/or minimum point. These points then have to be compared to each other to find the global maximum or minimum point. When the range of the function X is bounded, the points on the boundary also have to be taken into consideration.

B. THREE VARIABLES: $Y = f(X, Z)$

Partial Derivatives

When holding the other independent variables constant and taking derivative of the dependent variable with respect to only one independent variable, we have partial derivative with respect to that independent variable.

Total Derivative

When all the variables in the function are allowed to vary simultaneously, we have the total derivative. Thus the function $Y = f(X, Z)$ has a total derivative with respect to X as follows:

$$\frac{dY}{dX} = \frac{\partial Y}{\partial X}\frac{dX}{dX} + \frac{\partial Y}{\partial Z}\frac{dZ}{dX} = \frac{\partial Y}{\partial X} + \frac{\partial Y}{\partial Z}\frac{dZ}{dX}$$

where $\dfrac{\partial Y}{\partial X}$ and $\dfrac{\partial Y}{\partial Z}$ are the partial derivatives. The conditions for maximum point are

(1) $\dfrac{\partial Y}{\partial X} = 0$ and $\dfrac{\partial Y}{\partial Z} = 0$

(2) $\dfrac{\partial^2 Y}{\partial X^2} < 0$ and $\dfrac{\partial^2 Y}{\partial Z^2} < 0$

(3) $\left(\dfrac{\partial^2 Y}{\partial X^2}\right)\left(\dfrac{\partial^2 Y}{\partial Z^2}\right) - \left(\dfrac{\partial^2 Y}{\partial X \partial Z}\right)^2 > 0$

The conditions for minimum point are

(1) $\dfrac{\partial Y}{\partial X} = 0$ and $\dfrac{\partial Y}{\partial Z} = 0$

(2) $\dfrac{\partial^2 Y}{\partial X^2} > 0$ and $\dfrac{\partial^2 Y}{\partial Z^2} > 0$

(3) $\left(\dfrac{\partial^2 Y}{\partial X^2}\right)\left(\dfrac{\partial^2 Y}{\partial Z^2}\right) - \left(\dfrac{\partial^2 Y}{\partial X \partial Z}\right)^2 > 0$

where $\dfrac{\partial^2 Y}{\partial X^2}$, $\dfrac{\partial^2 Y}{\partial Z^2}$, and $\dfrac{\partial^2 Y}{\partial X \partial Z}$ are second-order partial derivative.

C. SERVAL VARIABLES IN GENERAL TERMS: $Y = f(X_1, X_2, \ldots, X_n)$

The Hessian determinant is a determinant with partial derivatives as its elements, as follows:

$$|H| = \begin{vmatrix} \dfrac{\partial^2 Y}{\partial X_1^2} & \dfrac{\partial^2 Y}{\partial X_1 \partial X_2} & \cdots & \dfrac{\partial^2 Y}{\partial X_1 \partial X_n} \\[2ex] \dfrac{\partial^2 Y}{\partial X_2 \partial X_1} & \dfrac{\partial^2 Y}{\partial X_2^2} & & \dfrac{\partial^2 Y}{\partial X_2 \partial X_n} \\ \vdots & & & \\ \dfrac{\partial^2 Y}{\partial X_n \partial X_1} & \dfrac{\partial^2 Y}{\partial X_n \partial X_2} & \cdots & \dfrac{\partial^2 Y}{\partial X_n^2} \end{vmatrix}$$

The principal minors of the determinants are

$$| H_1 | = \frac{\partial^2 Y}{\partial X_1^2}$$

$$| H_2 | = \begin{vmatrix} \dfrac{\partial^2 Y}{\partial X_1^2} & \dfrac{\partial^2 Y}{\partial X_1 \partial X_2} \\[2ex] \dfrac{\partial^2 Y}{\partial X_2 \partial X_1} & \dfrac{\partial^2 Y}{\partial X_2^2} \end{vmatrix}$$

The necessary condition is

$$\frac{\partial Y}{\partial X_1} = \frac{\partial Y}{\partial X_2} = \cdots \frac{\partial Y}{\partial X_n} = 0$$

The sufficient condition should include either (1) or (2) of the following:

  (1)   Maximum point

$$| H_1 | < 0, \; | H_2 | > 0, \; | H_3 | < 0 \cdots$$

(The sign of the minors alternates from negative to positive.)

  (2)   Minimum point

$$| H_1 | > 0, \; | H_2 | > 0, \; | H_3 | > 0 \cdots$$

(The sign of the minors are all positive.)

D. OPTIMIZATION SUBJECT TO CONSTRAINTS

We use Lagrange multipliers when we want to maximize or minimize a function $f(X)$ subject to a side condition or constraint;

$$Q(X) = 0$$

where X is a vector $[X_1, X_2, \ldots, X_n]$. We may modify the original objection function by attaching the side condition (add or substract) to it with a multiplier called the *Lagrange multiplier.*

$$L = f(X) + \lambda Q(X)$$

where λ is the Lagrange multiplier and L is called the Lagrangian function. Then we can apply calculus methods to find the optimality condition which at the same time satisfies the constraint.

$$\frac{\partial L}{\partial X_i} = \frac{\partial f(X)}{\partial X_i} = 0 \qquad i = 1, 2, \ldots, n$$

and

$$\frac{\partial L}{\partial \lambda} = Q(X) = 0$$

E. DERIVATIVE OF AN INTEGRAL

Given the integral function

$$F(Y) = \int_{g(Y)}^{h(Y)} f(X, Y) \, dX$$

When the limits of integration are constants, $g(Y) = a$, $h(Y) = b$, and the derivative is simply

$$\frac{d}{dY} F(Y) = \int_{a}^{b} \frac{f(X, Y)}{Y} \, dX$$

Setting the derivative equal to zero will obtain the optimality condition. When the limits of integration are functions, the derivative becomes

$$\frac{d}{dY} F(Y) = \int_{g(Y)}^{h(Y)} \frac{\partial f(X, Y)}{\partial Y} \, dX + f(h(Y), Y) \frac{dh(Y)}{dY}$$
$$- f(g(Y), Y) \frac{dg(Y)}{dY}$$

Probability*

Probability may be defined as the ratio of the number of outcomes that correspond to the occurrence of a predefined experience to the total number of possible outcomes. The concept of probability distribution may be evolved through the following step-by-step derivation.

1. *Sample space.* A sample space consists of all the possible outcomes of an experiment.

2. *Sample-space probabilities.* The probabilities assigned to each of the outcomes of a sample space are the sample-space probabilities. They must be all nonnegative and their sum is equal to one.

3. *Events.* An event may include one or more outcomes of a sample space. For example, an event may be defined as getting a head in tossing a coin or getting an odd number in rolling a die. In the latter case, 1, 3, and 5 are considered odd numbers.

4. *Probability of the occurrence of an event.* The probability that an event will occur is the sum of the probability of all the outcomes associated with the event. In the above example the probability of getting a head in tossing a perfect coin is 1/2, and the probability of getting an odd number in rolling an honest die is

$$\frac{1}{6} + \frac{1}{6} + \frac{1}{6} = \frac{3}{6} = \frac{1}{2}$$

*This portion is taken from K. Chu, *Principles of Econometrics* (Scranton, Pa.: International Textbook Company, 1968).

5. *Joint events.* In conducting an experiment, sometimes two events will occur together. In other words, they both contain the same outcome. For example, in drawing one card from a deck of 52, we define the event of getting a spade as *A* and the event of getting an ace as *B*. Now if we draw an ace of spaces from the deck, we have a *joint event.*

6. *Joint probability.* The probability of the occurrence of this joint event will be written as $P(AB)$, which is called the *joint probability.*

7. *Mutually exclusive events.* If when one of the events occurs during an experiment the other cannot occur, they are *mutually exclusive events.* For example, if we draw a spade from a deck of cards, the card we have drawn cannot be a diamond. Thus getting a spade and getting a diamond are mutually exclusive events.

8. *Addition theorem.*

$$P(A + B) = P(A) + P(B) - P(AB)$$

The theorem states that the probability that either event *A* occurs or event *B* occurs is equal to the sum of the probability of event *A* and *B* minus their joint probability. For example, the probability of getting either a spade or an ace in drawing one card from a deck of 52 is

$$\frac{13}{52} + \frac{4}{52} - \frac{1}{52} = \frac{16}{52} = \frac{4}{13}$$

If *A* and *B* are mutually exclusive events, then $P(AB) = 0$ and the addition theorem becomes

$$P(A + B) = P(A) + P(B)$$

For example, the probability of getting either a spade or a diamond is

$$\frac{13}{52} + \frac{13}{52} = \frac{26}{52} = \frac{1}{2}$$

9. *Independent event.* Two events, *A* and *B*, are said to be independent if $P(AB) = P(A) \cdot P(B)$. For example, in tossing two coins, the event of getting a head of one coin (event *A*) is independent of getting a head of the other coin (event *B*), so they are independent events. If

$P(A) = \frac{1}{2}$ and $P(B) = \frac{1}{2}$, then $P(AB) = \frac{1}{2} \times \frac{1}{2} = \frac{1}{4}$, which we may verify intuitively from the sample space (HH, HT, TH, TT).

10. *Conditional probability.* When the occurrence of one event is dependent on the occurrence of another event, then the probability of the occurrence of this event is a conditional probability. For example, two cards are drawn from a deck of 52 cards. What is the probability that both cards will be spades? The probability of the first card being a spade, Event A, is of course 13/52. However, once a spade is drawn from the deck and is not replaced, there will be only 12 spades left in the remaining deck of 51 cards. Therefore, the probability of the second card drawn also being a spade, Event B, is 12/51. 12/51 is the conditional probability of Event B which is dependent on Event A, and is denoted by $P(B/A)$.

11. *Multiplication theorem.*

$$P(AB) = P(A) \times P(B/A)$$

In the previous example the probability of both cards being spades is

$$\frac{13}{52} \times \frac{12}{51} = \frac{1}{17}$$

When A and B are independent events $P(B/A) = P(B)$, the theorem therefore becomes

$$P(AB) = P(A) \cdot P(B)$$

The multiplication theorem can also be written as

$$P(B/A) = \frac{P(AB)}{P(A)}$$

or extended to become Bayes' formula,

$$P(H_i/A) = \frac{P(H_i)\, P(A/H_i)}{\sum\limits_{i=1}^{k} P(H_i)\, P(A/H_i)}$$

In drawing one card from a deck and knowing the card is an ace, the probability of its being also a spade, according to Bayes' formula, is

$$P(\text{spade}/\text{ace}) = \frac{P(\text{spade})\, P(\text{ace}/\text{spade})}{\substack{P(\text{spade}\, P(\text{ace}/\text{spade}) \\ + P(\text{diamond})\, P(\text{ace}/\text{diamond}) \\ + P(\text{heart})\, P(\text{ace}/\text{heart}) \\ + P(\text{club})\, P(\text{ace}/\text{club})}}$$

$$= \frac{(^{13}/_{52}) \times (^{1}/_{13})}{4 \times (^{13}/_{52}) \times (^{1}/_{13})}$$

$$= {}^{1}/_{4}$$

We can verify immediately that the probability of getting a spade from four aces of different suit is $^{1}/_{4}$.

We next illustrate the application of Bayes' formula in a sampling problem that is not immediately obvious.

Suppose the purchasing manager of a company buys machine parts from a manufacturer and knows that half the time the manufacturer sends him shipments with 40 percent defective parts, and the other half of the time sends him shipments with 10 percent defective parts. The company may use sampling techniques to assist him in determining whether a particular shipment is of better quality. The following table shows his assessment after taking one or two samples from each shipment.

ONE-SAMPLE CASE

Original Probability	Conditional Probability of One Sample	Joint Probability	Revised Probability
.50	.40	.20	.80
.50	.10	.05	.20
		.25	1.00

TWO-SAMPLE CASE

Original Probability	Conditional Probability of Two Samples	Joint Probability	Revised Probability
.50	.16	.080	.94
.50	.01	.005	.06
		.085	1.00

The above information indicates that if one sample is taken and it happens to be a defective part, then the proba-

bility of the shipment's being a better-quality shipment is
only 20 percent. If two samples are taken and both are defective, then the probability of the shipment being a better
quality shipment is only 6 percent.

12. *Random variables.* A random variable is a numerical-
    valued variable defined on a sample space. The sample
    space can be either finite or infinite. For example, in
    rolling a die let X be a random variable whose numer-
    ical value is specified by the outcome. Thus X can take
    on values 1, 2, 3, 4, 5, or 6.

Matrices and Matrix Operations*

A rectangular array of elements arranged in rows or columns is called a *matrix* (plural *matrices*).

Example 1

$$A = \begin{bmatrix} a_{11} & a_{12} & \cdots & a_{1n} \\ a_{21} & a_{22} & \cdots & a_{2n} \\ \vdots & & & \\ a_{m1} & a_{m2} & \cdots & a_{mn} \end{bmatrix}$$

1. Square Matrix

A matrix with equal number of rows and columns.

2. Unit Matrix

A square matrix with units in the principal diagonal and zeros everywhere else.

*This portion is taken from K. Chu, *Principle of Econometrics* (Scranton, Pa.: International Textbook Company, 1968).

Example 2

$$
I = \begin{bmatrix}
1 & 0 & \cdots & 0 \\
0 & 1 & \cdots & 0 \\
\vdots & & & \\
0 & 0 & \cdots & 1
\end{bmatrix}
$$

3. Diagonal Matrix

A square matrix has scalar elements, not necessarily equal, in the principal diagonal, and zeros everywhere else.

4. Symmetric Matrix

A square matrix whose symmetric off-diagonal elements are all equal—that is,

$$a_{ij} = a_{ji} \quad \text{for} \quad i, j = 1, 2, \ldots, n$$

5. Triangular Matrix

A triangular matrix is a square matrix with scalar elements in the principal diagonal and one side of the principal diagonal. The elements on the other side of the principal diagonal are all zeros.

$$
A = \begin{bmatrix}
a_{11} & a_{12} & \cdots & a_{1n} \\
0 & a_{22} & \cdots & a_{2n} \\
\vdots & & & \\
0 & 0 & \cdots & a_{nn}
\end{bmatrix}
$$

6. Transpose of a Matrix

The transpose of a matrix is the interchange of rows and columns of a matrix.

Example 3

$$
A = \begin{bmatrix}
a_{11} & a_{12} \\
a_{21} & a_{22} \\
a_{31} & a_{32}
\end{bmatrix}
\qquad
A^T = \begin{bmatrix}
a_{11} & a_{21} & a_{31} \\
a_{12} & a_{22} & a_{32}
\end{bmatrix}
$$

Rules of transposing matrices:

$$(A^T)^T = A$$
$$(A + B)^T = A^T + B^T$$
$$(AB)^T = B^T A^T$$

7. Addition and Subtraction of Matrices

If two or more matrices of the same order—that is, have equal number of rows and columns—we may add or subtract their corresponding elements.

Example 4

$$A = \begin{bmatrix} a_{11} & a_{12} \\ a_{21} & a_{22} \\ a_{31} & a_{32} \end{bmatrix} \qquad B = \begin{bmatrix} b_{11} & b_{12} \\ b_{21} & b_{22} \\ b_{31} & b_{32} \end{bmatrix}$$

$$D = A + B = \begin{bmatrix} a_{11} + b_{11} & a_{12} + b_{12} \\ a_{21} + b_{21} & a_{22} + b_{22} \\ a_{31} + b_{31} & a_{32} + b_{32} \end{bmatrix}$$

8. Scalar Multiplication

When a matrix is multiplied by a scalar, each element of the matrix is multiplied by the scalar.

Example 5

$$kA = k \begin{bmatrix} a_{11} & a_{12} \\ a_{21} & a_{22} \end{bmatrix} = \begin{bmatrix} ka_{11} & ka_{12} \\ ka_{21} & ka_{22} \end{bmatrix}$$

9. Matrix Multiplication

A first matrix of order $(m \times n)$ and a second matrix of order $(n \times k)$ may be multiplied to produce a third matrix of order of $(m \times k)$ by the following rule:

$$D = AB$$

where A is the first matrix, B is the second matrix and D is the product;

$$d_{ij} = \sum_{t=1}^{n} a_{it} b_{tj} \qquad (i = 1, 2, \ldots, m; j = 1, 2, \ldots, k)$$

Since the number of columns of the first matrix must be equal to the number of rows of the second matrix, the product BA may not exist. And $AB \neq BA$ except for symmetric matrices.

Example 6

$$A = \begin{bmatrix} a_{11} & a_{12} \\ a_{21} & a_{22} \\ a_{31} & a_{32} \end{bmatrix} \qquad B = \begin{bmatrix} b_{11} & b_{12} & b_{13} \\ b_{21} & b_{22} & b_{23} \end{bmatrix}$$

$$AB = \begin{bmatrix} a_{11}b_{11} + a_{12}b_{21} & a_{11}b_{12} + a_{12}b_{22} & a_{11}b_{13} + a_{12}b_{23} \\ a_{21}b_{11} + a_{22}b_{21} & a_{21}b_{12} + a_{22}b_{22} & a_{21}b_{13} + a_{22}b_{23} \\ a_{31}b_{11} + a_{32}b_{21} & a_{31}b_{12} + a_{32}b_{22} & a_{31}b_{13} + a_{32}b_{23} \end{bmatrix}$$

$$BA = \begin{bmatrix} b_{11}a_{11} + b_{12}a_{21} + b_{13}a_{31} & b_{11}a_{12} + b_{12}a_{22} + b_{13}a_{32} \\ b_{21}a_{11} + b_{22}a_{21} + b_{23}a_{31} & b_{21}a_{12} + b_{22}a_{22} + b_{23}a_{32} \end{bmatrix}$$

Thus

$$AB \neq BA$$

10. Determinant of a Matrix

Associated with any square matrix is a scalar quantity called the *determinant* of the matrix.

The determinant of a 2×2 matrix is defined as

$$\begin{vmatrix} a_{11} & a_{12} \\ a_{21} & a_{22} \end{vmatrix} = a_{11}a_{22} - a_{12}a_{21}$$

The determinant of a higher-order $n \times n$ square matrix is computed by the formula

$$|A| = \sum_{j=1}^{n} a_{ij}c_{ij}$$

where c_{ij} are the cofactors of the minors in A, $c_{ij} = (-1)^{i+j} |M_{ij}|$ and $|M_{ij}|$ is the determinant of the minor.

Example 7

$$\begin{vmatrix} a_{11} & a_{12} & a_{13} \\ a_{21} & a_{22} & a_{23} \\ a_{31} & a_{32} & a_{33} \end{vmatrix} = a_{11}(-1)^{1+1}\begin{vmatrix} a_{22} & a_{23} \\ a_{32} & a_{33} \end{vmatrix} + a_{12}(-1)^{1+2}\begin{vmatrix} a_{21} & a_{23} \\ a_{31} & a_{33} \end{vmatrix}$$
$$+ a_{13}(-1)^{1+3}\begin{vmatrix} a_{21} & a_{22} \\ a_{31} & a_{32} \end{vmatrix}$$

$$= a_{11}a_{22}a_{33} - a_{11}a_{23}a_{32} - a_{12}a_{21}a_{33}$$
$$+ a_{12}a_{23}a_{31} + a_{13}a_{21}a_{32} - a_{13}a_{22}a_{31}$$

11. Adjoint of a Matrix

The adjoint of a matrix is equal to the transpose of a matrix whose elements are replaced by its cofactors.

Example 8

Let $c_{ij}(i, j = 1, 2, \ldots, n)$ be the cofactors of matrix A. The adjoint of matrix A is

$$\text{adj } A = \begin{bmatrix} c_{11} & c_{21} & \cdots & c_{n1} \\ c_{12} & c_{22} & \cdots & c_{n2} \\ \vdots & & & \\ c_{1n} & c_{2n} & \cdots & c_{nn} \end{bmatrix}$$

12. The Inverse Matrix

Matrix inversion is similar to the operation of division. However, we write $1/A$ as A^{-1} and it applies only to square matrices. Let A^{-1} be the inverse matrix of A, the following property exists:

$$A^{-1}A = I$$
$$AA^{-1} = I$$

where I is the unit matrix of equal order as A.

Two methods are commonly employed to find the inverse matrix.

(a) The first method is computed from the adjoint and determinant of the matrix. Since

$$|A| = \sum_{j-1}^{n} a_{ij}c_{ij}$$

and

$$(\text{adj } A) = [c_{ij}]^T$$

$A \cdot \dfrac{1}{|A|} (\text{adj } A)$

$$= \frac{1}{|A|} \begin{bmatrix} a_{11} & a_{12} & \cdots & a_{1n} \\ a_{21} & a_{22} & \cdots & a_{2n} \\ \vdots & & & \\ a_{n1} & a_{n2} & \cdots & a_{nn} \end{bmatrix} \begin{bmatrix} c_{11} & c_{21} & \cdots & c_{n1} \\ c_{12} & c_{22} & \cdots & c_{n2} \\ \vdots & & & \\ c_{1n} & c_{2n} & \cdots & c_{nn} \end{bmatrix} *$$

$$= \frac{1}{|A|} \begin{bmatrix} |A| & 0 & \cdots & 0 \\ 0 & |A| & \cdots & 0 \\ \vdots & & & \\ 0 & 0 & \cdots & |A| \end{bmatrix} = I$$

Therefore

$$A^{-1} = \frac{1}{|A|} (\text{adj } A)$$

Thus only a nonsingular square matrix—that is, a matrix with nonzero determinant—can have inverse matrix.

Example 9

$$A = \begin{bmatrix} 1 & 3 \\ 2 & 4 \end{bmatrix}, \qquad |A| = 4 \times 1 - 3 \times 2 = -2$$

Cofactors matrix:

$$\begin{bmatrix} 4 & -2 \\ -3 & 1 \end{bmatrix}, \qquad \text{adj } A = \begin{bmatrix} 4 & -3 \\ -2 & 1 \end{bmatrix}$$

$$A^{-1} = -\frac{1}{2} \begin{bmatrix} 4 & -3 \\ -2 & 1 \end{bmatrix} = \begin{bmatrix} -2 & \dfrac{3}{2} \\ 1 & -\dfrac{1}{2} \end{bmatrix}$$

*Note that

$$\sum_{j=1}^{n} a_{ij} c_{kj} = 0 \qquad \text{when } i \neq k$$
$$= |A| \qquad \text{when } i = k$$

Check:

$$A^{-1}A = \begin{bmatrix} -2 & \frac{3}{2} \\ 1 & -\frac{1}{2} \end{bmatrix} \begin{bmatrix} 1 & 3 \\ 2 & 4 \end{bmatrix} = \begin{bmatrix} (-2+3) & (-6+6) \\ (1-1) & (3-2) \end{bmatrix}$$

$$= \begin{bmatrix} 1 & 0 \\ 0 & 1 \end{bmatrix} = I$$

(b) The second method is to find the row-operations matrix which will reduce the matrix to be inverted into a unit matrix of the same order. The row-operations matrix is then the inverse matrix.

Example 10

$$A = \begin{bmatrix} 2 & 3 \\ 5 & 6 \end{bmatrix} \quad [A \vdots I] = \begin{bmatrix} 2 & 3 & \vdots & 1 & 0 \\ 5 & 6 & \vdots & 0 & 1 \end{bmatrix}$$

Step 1. Divide the first row of $[A \vdots I]$ by a_{11}, which is 2.

$$\begin{bmatrix} 1 & \frac{3}{2} & \vdots & \frac{1}{2} & 0 \\ 5 & 6 & \vdots & 0 & 1 \end{bmatrix}$$

Step 2. Subtract from the second row, a_{21} multiples which is 5 times of the transformed first row.

$$\begin{bmatrix} 1 & \frac{3}{2} & \vdots & \frac{1}{2} & 0 \\ 0 & -\frac{3}{2} & \vdots & -\frac{5}{2} & 1 \end{bmatrix}$$

Step 3. Divide the transformed second row by its a_{22}, which is $-\frac{3}{2}$.

$$\begin{bmatrix} 1 & \frac{3}{2} & \vdots & \frac{1}{2} & 0 \\ 0 & 1 & \vdots & \frac{5}{3} & -\frac{2}{3} \end{bmatrix}$$

Step 4. Subtract from the transformed first row by a_{12} multiples $\left(\text{which is } \dfrac{3}{2} \text{ times}\right)$ of the transformed second row.

$$\begin{bmatrix} 1 & 0 & \vdots & -2 & 1 \\ 0 & 1 & \vdots & \dfrac{5}{3} & -\dfrac{2}{3} \end{bmatrix}$$

Since we have performed the same row operations on both A and I, the result must be $[I : A^{-1}]$.

Check:

$$AA^{-1} = \begin{bmatrix} 2 & 3 \\ 5 & 6 \end{bmatrix} \begin{bmatrix} -2 & 1 \\ \dfrac{5}{3} & -\dfrac{2}{3} \end{bmatrix}$$

$$= \begin{bmatrix} (-4+5) & (2-2) \\ (-10+10) & (5-4) \end{bmatrix} = \begin{bmatrix} 1 & 0 \\ 0 & 1 \end{bmatrix} = I$$

Properties of inverse matrices:

$$(A^{-1})^{-1} = A$$
$$(AB)^{-1} = B^{-1}A^{-1}$$
$$(A^T)^{-1} = (A^{-1})^T$$

Computer System and Programming

A computer system usually consists of five major functional parts.

1. *Input Unit*

   This is the unit through which the information of an input media, such as cards or tapes, is transmitted into the memory of the computer. If cards are used, information is transmitted from a card reader into the memory of the computer. If magnetic tapes are used, then information is transmitted from magnetic tape units into the memory of the computer. The latest development in computer input devices allows visual or voice inputs to be transmitted into the memory.

2. *Memory*

   The memory of a computer consists of many locations, each location being referred to by an individual and nonduplicated address. When information either in numerical, alphabetical, or special characters is transmitted into a specific location it becomes the content of that location. Information can be transmitted out a particular location as many times as required with changing the content. The content can be changed only by transmitting new information into the location. This feature sometimes is called *destructive read-in* and *nondestructive readout*.

3. *Arithematic and Logic Unit*

The arithematic and logic unit consists of many registers and computing circuits. Information can be transmitted from the memory to the arithematic and logic unit and back to the memory. The registers may may be viewed as temporary storing locations. The computing circuits can add, subtract, multiply, and divide numerical numbers. They also can compare two numbers, alphabetical or numerical, to test whether the numbers are same or different.

4. *Control Unit*

The electronic digital computer is sometimes associated with the term *Automata*. People not in the field may intuitively think that the machine can do things automatically, but this is not completely true. A human being has to program what he wants the machine to do exactly and to every detail. The term *program* is used here to represent the step-by-step procedure of solving a problem or performing a task. The program, which usually consists of many instructions, is stored in the memory of the computer. A human machine operator by means of a hand-manipulated control console directs the computer to pick up the first instruction from an initial location in which the instruction is stored. After that, the control unit takes over and follows the sequence of the location addresses to carry out all the instructions included in the program. While the control unit is in charge of the execution of the program, the sequence may be changed only by an instruction in the program.

5. *Output Unit*

After the execution of a program, the result of the performance or the solution of the problem is stored in some location in the memory of the computer. The information then is transmitted through an output unit onto an output media, such as cards, printed sheets, or visuoscopes, or the result may be stored on magnetic disks or tapes for future analysis or readout. The output unit may be a card puncher, a printer, or a tape unit, etc. A typical computer system is illustrated in the accompanying diagram.

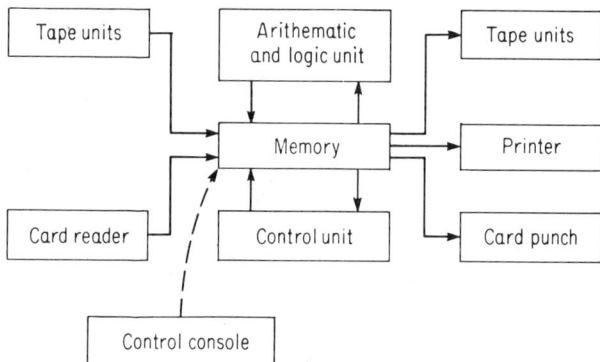

To fully explore the use of an electronic digital computer, it is necessary to have a general knowledge of (1) how electronic devices transmit and record information, (2) how the arithmetic operations are carried out by the machine, and (3) the elements of programming. Only then we will be prepared to discuss the applications of computer.

1. *Transmission and Recording of Information*

Most of the digital computers are electronic equipment. Numerical and alphabetical information punched on cards can be recognized by an input device (card reader) and transmitted into the memory of the computer. Inside the computer, however, the numbers may be represented by a binary number system, binary-coded decimal system, or other systems. For binary coding, the information is represented by electrical pulses passing along wires. The presence of a signal at a particular time and place represents 1 bit, and the absence of a signal indicates 0 bit. The following are examples of comparing decimal system, binary system, and binary-coded decimal system.

Decimal System	Binary System	Binary-coded Decimal System	
		2nd digit	*1st digit*
0	0000	0000	0000
1	0001	0000	0001
2	0010	0000	0010
3	0011	0000	0011
4	0100	0000	0100
9	1001	0000	1001
12	1100	0001	0010

Nonnumeric characters such as alphabetic letters and special characters are usually represented by six binary digits plus a error check bit. The first two of the bit positions are called B zone and A zone. When both B zone and A zone are zeros, the subsequent four bits represent a numerical character in binary-coded decimal. When B zone and/or A zone are ones, it represents either an alphabetic letter or a special character. The following are some illustrative examples.

Character	B Zone	A Zone	Numeric Portion
1	0	0	0001
2	0	0	0010
A	1	1	0001
S	0	1	0010

2. *The Arithmetic Operations*

In a binary system, additions are performed in four different situations:

$$(1) \quad \begin{array}{c} 0 \\ +0 \\ \hline 0 \end{array} \quad \begin{array}{c} 0 \\ +1 \\ \hline 1 \end{array} \quad \begin{array}{c} 1 \\ +0 \\ \hline 1 \end{array} \quad \begin{array}{c} 1 \\ +1 \\ \hline (1)0 \\ \uparrow \\ \text{carry} \end{array}$$

These operations are preformed by a set of AND and OR circuits. AND circuits have gates series-connected, while OR circuits have gates parallel-connected.

AND circuit:

OR circuit: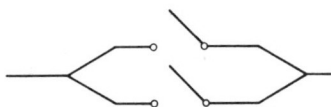

There are also *Inverter, carrier,* and *delay* mechanisms.

Subtraction is performed by adding the complement of the subtrahend to the minuend and dropping 1 from the highest position of the sum. For example,

$$51 \quad \text{(minuend)}$$
$$\underline{-23} \quad \text{(substrahend)}$$
$$28$$

In computer logic,

(1) complement of 23 is: $100 - 23 = 77$

(2) Add 77 to 51 $= \quad 51$
$$\underline{+77}$$
$$128$$

(3) Drop 1 from the highest position of 128, the result is 28.

Multiplication is performed by repeated operation of additions in accordance with the number of the multiplier minus one. For example,

$$18$$
$$\underline{\times 4} \quad \text{(multiplier)}$$
$$72$$

In computer logic,

$$18$$
$$\underline{+18} \quad (1)$$
$$36$$
$$\underline{+18} \quad (2)$$
$$54$$
$$\underline{+18} \quad (3)$$
$$72$$

When the multiplier consists of more than one digit, the procedure becomes one of successively forming partial products with each consecutive digit in the multiplier. For example,

$$35$$
$$\underline{\times 24} \quad \text{(multiplier)}$$
$$140$$
$$\underline{70}$$
$$840$$

In computer logic,

$$
\begin{array}{ll}
35 & 35 \\
\underline{+35} \quad (1) & \underline{+35} \ (1) \\
70 & 70 \\
& \underline{+35} \ (2) \\
& 105 \qquad\qquad 700 \\
\text{Shift one place} & \underline{+35} \qquad \underline{+140} \\
\text{to the left } = 700 & 140 \qquad\qquad 840
\end{array}
$$

Division is performed by substracting the divisor from the dividend repeatedly until zero or the first time a negative remainder is appeared. In the case of a negative remainder the divisor is added back once to obtain the proper quotient digit and remainder. For example,

$$
\begin{array}{r}
3 \quad \text{(quotient)} \\
\text{(divisor) } 7 \ \overline{)23} \quad \text{(dividend)} \\
\underline{21} \\
2 \quad \text{(remainder)}
\end{array}
$$

In computer logic,

$$
\begin{array}{ll}
23 & \\
\underline{-7} & (1) \\
16 & \\
\underline{-7} & (2) \\
9 & \\
\underline{-7} & (3) \\
2 & \\
\underline{-7} & (4) \\
-5 & \\
\underline{+7} & (5) \quad \text{(quotient)} \\
2 & \qquad\ \ \text{(remainder)}
\end{array}
$$

ELEMENTS OF PROGRAMMING

As mentioned in the previous section, the memory of the computer is divided into many locations. Each location has its unique address. Both data and instructions can be transmitted into these locations and become the content of these locations. *Program* is a term used to describe a sequence of steps or instructions to do some computations or to solve a problem. Using a particular computer language with its specific rules or grammar to write a program is called *computer programming*. Programming languages, in terms of their relation to ordinary English, may be classified on three different levels—machine language, symbolic language, and common language. The programs written in higher-level languages have to be translated into machine language before they can be used. The translation is done on the computer through a program, called a compiler, written in machine language.

Machine Language

Machine language generally uses symbols to represent instruction or operation codes and numbers to specify locations in the memory where the instructions or data are stored. Before a program can be written, four steps of planning have to be taken:

1. Analysis of the job
2. Sequence the required steps to perform the job
3. Writing the instructions
4. Determining areas of storage

Example

Assume a stack of IBM cards. On each of the cards two numbers are punched, the last month's balance and this month's transaction (which may either be positive or negative) of a customer's account. The job is to add the transaction amount of each customer to last month's balance which will yield this month's balance, and punch out the new balance of the customer on another card.

The sequence of steps may be represented by the accompanying flow chart.

In a hypothetical machine language this may be written as follows. Suppose the computer memory has fixed word length of locations. Each word contains ten digits. On each IBM card the balance of last month's account is punched in the first ten columns and the amount of the current month's transaction is punched in the second ten columns, with posi-

```
        ┌─────────────────────────────┐
        │        READ A CARD          │     Card to memory
   ┌───▶│  S - last month balance     │
   │    │  T - current month transaction │
   │    └─────────────────────────────┘
   │                  │
   │                  ▼
   │    ┌─────────────────────────────┐
   │    │  LOAD Accumulator * with    │     Memory to accumulator through
   │    │           S                 │     the arithmetic unit
   │    └─────────────────────────────┘
   │                  │
   │                  ▼
   │    ┌─────────────────────────────┐
   │    │  ADD to the accumulator with │    Memory to accumulator through
   │    │           T                 │     the arithmetic unit
   │    └─────────────────────────────┘
   │                  │
   │                  ▼
   │    ┌─────────────────────────────┐
   │    │  Store the content of the   │     Accumulator to memory through
   │    │       accumulator to        │     the arithmetic unit
   │    │           S                 │
   │    └─────────────────────────────┘
   │                  │
   │                  ▼
   │    ┌─────────────────────────────┐
   │    │        PUNCH A CARD         │     Memory to card
   └────│  S - current month's balance │
        └─────────────────────────────┘
```

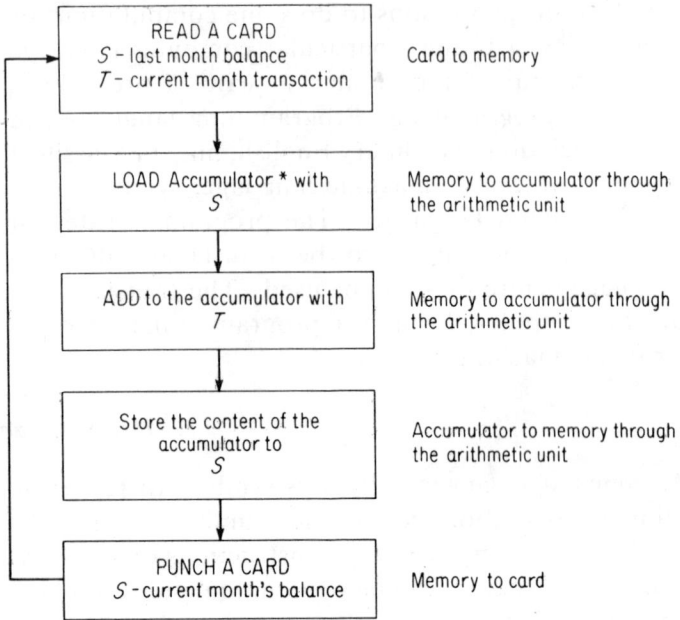

*Accumulators are similar to additional memory locations for storing data.

tive or negative signs attached. Also, we expect the new computed balance of current month's account will be punched in the first ten columns of a new deck of cards.

Instruction Location	Operation Code		Data Location	Next Instruction Location
0001	10	(read card)	0100	0002
0002	20	(load accumulator)	0100	0003
0003	21	(add to accumulator)	0101	0004
0004	40	(store)	0100	0005
0005	50	(punch card)	0100	0001

Memory Location	Content	Location	Content	
0001	1001000002	0100	0000001382	Last month's balance (After computation, location 0100 will contain 0000001405)
0002	2001000003	0101	0000000023	Current month's transaction
0003	2101010004	0102		
0004	4001000005	⋮		
0005	5001000001	⋮		

Symbolic Language

Using basic machine language, the areas of storage for instructions and data have to be carefully planned to avoid erasure or misidentification of data. Using symbolic language, the actual location address may be represented by an alphabetical symbol. As long as the symbol is unique, the programmer does not have to worry about assigning the actual locations in the memory.

I Address	Operation code	A Address	B Address
C	R (read card)	S, T	
	L (load accumulator)	S	
	A (add to accumulator)	T	
	ST (store)	S	
	P (punch)	S	C
			(Go to I address C for next instruction)

Common Language

The most simplified language for programmer to use, of course, will be a simplified form of English language combined with certain arithmetic statements. There are several such languages—FORTRAN, ALGOL, and CO-BOL among others. In the following, we use one version of FORTRAN (Formula Translation Language) to rewrite the previous problem.

```
1   READ, S, T
    S = S + T
    PUNCH, S
    GO TO 1
```

The FORTRAN language consists of constants (algebraic numbers, either integers or with decimals), variables (words, with a single letter as the first character, which may be subscripted) and expressions (constants and/or variables joined together by mathematical operators). And the statements are classified according to their usage to input statement (such as, READ, S, T), output statement (such as

PUNCH, S), arithmetic statement (such as, $S = S + T$) transfer of control statement (such as GO TO 1), conditional transfer statement (such as IF statement) and repeated operation or looping statement (such as DO statement). All the common languages for digital computers are basically similar but the rules or the construction of the statements are different. Details can be learned by reading the manual for a specific computer language. There are other languages designed to facilitate computer programming for some special purpose, such as GPSS and SIM-SCRIPT for simulating the operation of business systems. They may be learned only by carefully studying the manuals and by practice in writing programs in the language.

Index